LAGOS NEVER SPOILS

AFRICAN PERSPECTIVES
Kelly Askew, Laura Fair, and Pamila Gupta
Series Editors

Lagos Never Spoils: Nollywood and Nigerian City Life
Connor Ryan

Continuous Pasts: Frictions of Memory in Postcolonial Africa
Sakiru Adebayo

*Writing on the Soil: Land and Landscape in Literature
from Eastern and Southern Africa*
Ng'ang'a Wahu-Muchiri

*Power / Knowledge / Land: Contested Ontologies of Land
and Its Governance in Africa*
Laura A. German

*In Search of Tunga: Prosperity, Almighty God,
and Lives in Motion in a Malian Provincial Town*
André Chappatte

*The Infrastructures of Security:
Technologies of Risk Management in Johannesburg*
Martin J. Murray

*There Used to Be Order:
Life on the Copperbelt after the Privatisation of the
Zambia Consolidated Copper Mines*
Patience Mususa

*Animated by Uncertainty: Rugby and the
Performance of History in South Africa*
Joshua D. Rubin

African Performance Arts and Political Acts
Naomi André, Yolanda Covington-Ward, and Jendele Hungbo, Editors

A complete list of titles in the series can be found at www.press.umich.edu

Lagos Never Spoils

Nollywood and Nigerian City Life

Connor Ryan

University of Michigan Press
Ann Arbor

Copyright © 2023 by Connor Ryan
All rights reserved

For questions or permissions, please contact um.press.perms@umich.edu

Published in the United States of America by the
University of Michigan Press
Manufactured in the United States of America
Printed on acid-free paper
First published July 2023

A CIP catalog record for this book is available from the British Library.

Library of Congress Cataloging-in-Publication data has been applied for.

ISBN 978-0-472-07579-9 (hardcover : alk. paper)
ISBN 978-0-472-05579-1 (paper : alk. paper)
ISBN 978-0-472-22098-4 (e-book)

Publication of this volume has been partially funded by the African Studies Center, University of Michigan.

Library of Congress Control Number: 2023935025

For Rita, Terry, and Beth and for the love that we share . . .

CONTENTS

Acknowledgments	ix
INTRODUCTION Lagos Never Spoils	1
CHAPTER 1 Urban Ambivalence in Early Nigerian Films	28
CHAPTER 2 Television's City Situations	61
CHAPTER 3 Narratives of Entanglement	88
CHAPTER 4 New Nollywood and the New Image	123
CHAPTER 5 Love and Work in Lagos	147
CHAPTER 6 Dark and Gritty / Slick and Glossy	182
Conclusion	204
Notes	213
Filmography	247
Bibliography	251
Index	263

Digital materials related to this title can be found on the Fulcrum platform via the following citable URL: https://doi.org/10.3998/mpub.12472247

ACKNOWLEDGMENTS

Portions of this research have been previously published, and I appreciate the permission to reuse these works here. An earlier version of chapter 4 was published as "New Nollywood: A Sketch of Nollywood's Metropolitan New Style," *African Studies Review* 58, no. 3 (2015): 55–76. A portion of chapter 6 was initially published in "Dark and Gritty/Slick and Glossy: Genre, Nollywood and Lagos," *Journal of African Cinemas* 11, no. 3 (2019): 295–313. I thank all who were involved in the editorial process and those whose feedback helped polish these pieces.

My debts are numerous, and I am richer for them. This book represents my effort to honor these debts and the many people whose brilliance and kindness made this work possible. This book began with my doctoral research at Michigan State University under the guidance of Kenneth Harrow and a committee of dedicated and thoughtful advisers, Nwando Achebe, Carmela Garritano, Salah Hassan, and Karl Schoonover, whom I thank from the bottom of my heart. The initial fieldwork was conducted in 2013–14 with the generous support of the Fulbright program, an opportunity that first opened the door and, hopefully, will continue to do so for other scholars for years to come. Early draft chapters were shaped by experiences and conversations with other participants of the "Arts of Survival: Recasting Lives in African Cities" program in 2016 hosted by the Institute for Advanced Study at Indiana University. I extend my gratitude to the organizers, Eileen Julien, Akin Adesokan, Grace Musila, James Ogude, and Oana Panaïté, for creating the space and imbuing it with their energy and ideas. A West African Research Association Postdoctoral Fellowship in 2018 permitted me to complete additional work in Lagos that informs the final chapters. The bulk of this book was written in Kingston, Jamaica, where I took inspiration from the brilliance, integrity, and friendship of my colleagues, who deserve special thanks: Jennifer Brittan, Lisa Brown, Michael Bucknor, Nadi Edwards, Anthea Morrison, Rachel Moseley-Wood, and Isis Semaj-Hall. Thanks also to Carolyn Cooper for the reminders that Jah bless me with time in Jamaica.

Much of what I know about Nollywood I owe to conversations with Nigerian filmmakers, whose generosity continues to astonish and humble me and for which I will be forever grateful. In this book, I strive to offer my most sincere, thorough engagement with their works, history, and accomplishments, because these filmmakers deserve nothing less. No one deserves mention more than Tunde Kelani, who was the first to open his door to me and remains the first I turn to when in need. While conducting dissertation research, TK's offices in Oshodi became my haven in Lagos, where my spirits were lifted by the entire Mainframe family: Aunty Fali, MK, and Bisola Ojo, whose clarity of mind and kind heart will not be forgotten. TK has taught me a great deal about integrity and perseverance and has my lasting gratitude and deepest respect. I also offer warm thanks to Bond Emeruwa, Kunle Afolayan, and Emem Isong, who indulged me with their patience and knowledge. I would like to acknowledge Chico Ejiro, whose passing was a tremendous loss for many and whom I will remember fondly and with respect. I thank others in the industry who shared their time and insights: Afolabi Adesanya, Mahmood Ali-Balogun, Fred Amata, Andy Amenechi, Chineze Anyaene, Judith Audu, Ola Balogun, Olatunji Balogun, Bayo Bankole, Chike Bryan, Fidelis Duker, Ema Edosio, Yinka Edward, Keppy Ekpeyong-Bassey, Kenneth Gyan, Abba Makama, Emeka Mba, Kene Mkparu, Charles Novia, Femi Odugbemi, Yinka Oduniyi, Uduak Isong Oguamanam, Dare Olaitan, Daniel Oriahi, Tope Oshin, Nkem Owoh, Uduak Obong Patrick, Eddie Ugboma, and Eke Ume. My research would not have been possible without these generous individuals, and while I have learned much from them, any errors in this book are, of course, my own.

The other immense challenge I faced during my research was learning Lagos itself, however incompletely, which I could not have done without a host of friends. I must thank those who have shared their homes with me, including Yemi Oni, Adeola Olagunju, and Andrew Esiebo. I extend my sincere gratitude to Toyin Akinosho, David Aradeon, Michael Obochi, Kunle Tejuosho, and Tundun Tejuosho for speaking with me about their memories of a Lagos before my time and to Jahman Anikulapo for his assistance, reassurances, and friendship. I reserve special thanks to Abiola Lawal and Dami Oguntimehin, *àwon olùkó mi*, who gave countless hours to teach this hapless pupil Yoruba language. I apologize for my flawed ability with the language, as it does not reflect the personal commitment you both made to me and the language.

This book was made possible by colleagues whose prior work opened a space with rich potential and broad horizons for young scholars like me to explore. I thank Moradewun Adejunmobi, Akin Adesokan, Jane Bryce, Carmela Garritano, Jonathan Haynes, Brian Larkin, and Onookome Okome. I thank my friend Cajetan Iheka, who supported me throughout the writing of this book with his encouragement, careful eye, and keen feedback: *mo dúpé*. Finally, there is Ken Harrow, whose dedication to his students, colleagues, friends, and the field of African cinema represents an inspiration hard to express in words. Ken was my teacher and adviser, but he remains much more. He is my friend. And with great admiration and heartfelt respect, I thank him.

Across the years and hemispheres, the support of friends is what has kept me going. Their presence in my life makes all the difference. I thank Jonathan Grzywa, Nzingha Kendall, Delali Kumavie, Cori McKenzie, Joel Mulder, Wura Ogunji, Alanna Stuart, and Suj Truscott. These are the debts that fill me with joy. Finally, I thank my family, to whom I owe everything, lovingly.

Introduction
Lagos Never Spoils

In 2013, I lived for a time in Ikeja near the roundabout junction of Allen Avenue and Obafemi Awolowo Way. Most mornings I would join the queue of other commuters at the bus stop near the roundabout, where there stood, stacked behind us along the roadside, rows of paintings of famous individuals, such as Nelson Mandela, Wole Soyinka, Barack Obama, Oprah Winfrey, and, importantly, a number of Nollywood movie stars, including Funke Akindele, Peter Edochie, and Odunlade Adekola, among others.

I had seen similar stands of paintings with a similar cast of famous individuals at other intersections in Lagos. Their purpose was not immediately apparent to me, but I presumed that the works on display were for sale. To my mind it seemed unexpected, though not impossible, that Nollywood fans would go so far as to buy portraits of their favorite actors. I stopped one morning to inquire with the artist, who explained that the portraits were not for sale but rather served as a measure of his artistic ability, as the paintings demonstrated, even at a glance, how accurately he could capture the image of the actor. After all, these were the most recognizable faces in the city, a collection of shared reference points and a reminder that Nollywood remains one thing that the twenty million people in Lagos hold in common.

Throughout Lagos, Nollywood films flash from TV screens at fast food restaurants, waiting rooms, bus stops, and viewing parlors. They attract distracted glances rather than rapt attention, and as such viewers take in fleeting bits and pieces, fragments of a story, a generally familiar scenario that can be enjoyed without knowledge of the specific backstory.[1] Nollywood's imagery adorns film posters, billboards, public transportation, newspapers, and soft-sell magazines. No neighborhood is without a shop that sells Nollywood

Figure 1. Nollywood portraits at Allen Roundabout in Ikeja

movies. Production offices, postproduction facilities, and acting schools are scattered throughout the neighborhood of Surulere. Film crews in Lekki and Ajah shoot inside swank new houses that provide the backdrop to stories about the good life in the big city. Film premieres with televised red-carpet events take place at multiplex cinemas in the shopping malls of Ikeja and Victoria Island. In light of this, the Nollywood stars who smile at commuters near the Allen Avenue roundabout represent but a single trace of the wider embeddedness of the films and the industry within the city.

Lagos Never Spoils is a book about this relationship between Nollywood and Lagos. It approaches Lagos as a crossroads of cultural flows that provide the city's film industry with an array of commodities, tropes, sentiments, aesthetics, and concepts with which to apprehend historical shifts in city life. Beginning in the 1970s, filmmakers produced adaptations of the popular theater's stage performances as well as original works that screened in urban cinema halls across the Southwest. By the 1990s, video filmmakers combined video technology, small-scale financing, and distribution networks embedded within the informal economy to produce tremendously popular films for audiences across West Africa and the diaspora. Today, Lagos serves as the regional media capital, where local production companies shoot commissioned content for global distribution giants such as DStv, iROKOtv, and Netflix. In fact, after decades of screen representation, Lagos has become arguably the most influential image of West African city life for Nigeria, the region, and perhaps the world.

This book builds upon a long-standing interest in cities and cinema within film studies, where inquiry consistently centers on the notion of a special correspondence between the city and cinema. The two are typically compared on the grounds of the simultaneous historical emergence of cinema and urban modernity, for instance, or the aesthetic correspondences between the audiovisual sensations of cinema and those of the city, or the embeddedness of film industries within cities.[2] Charlotte Brunsdon calls this mode of criticism "city discourse" and suggests, elsewhere, that it construes city/cinema connections in ways that range from "geographical literalism" to more figurative notions of correlation.[3] Thus, the sense of a unique relationship between cinema and the city is generally taken for granted, even though the nature of the correspondence is understood in a variety of divergent ways.

Lagos Never Spoils challenges one vital assumption of this existing body of scholarship, namely, the Eurocentrism that presumes that *the* city invokes a place, an environment, a built form, or a set of experiences that all readers already know. Because studies of city cinema focus overwhelmingly on cinema in American and European cities, I argue that they have installed a normative notion of cinema and *the* city that excludes the particularity of cities in the Global South and the place of screen media within them. This false generalization from environments where, in reality, a minority of the world's urban population reside in turn sustains a myopic view of how cities *ought* to work and risks perpetuating damaging assumptions about the supposed dysfunctionality of cities beyond the Global North. In fact, following decades of urbanization, cities of the Global South are today "far more normative," as Dominique Malaquais argues, "if only because they are infinitely more numerous."[4] This casts serious doubt around whether the city debated in Western film studies resembles what the world's majority know and experience of urban life.

As such, this book is invested in unthinking normative notions of the city, reconsidering certain established assumptions about cinema, and redressing the glaring omission of African cities and screen media from film studies debates. To better understand the correlations between screen media and the city, *Lagos Never Spoils* introduces and develops three critical concepts:

ambivalence, *entanglement*, and *enclosure*. These terms provide the conceptual threads that bind the book and guide my interpretation of the films, video films, and television programs examined throughout. I place aside the recurrent tropes of Western urban theory, such as sensorial shock, fragmentation, and flânerie, and instead build inductively upon firsthand experiences in Lagos, interviews with Lagos-based producers and distributors, conversations during and after film screenings, and a growing body of innovative research on urbanism in Africa. Stated succinctly, this book pursues a politics of dissensus.[5] As urbanist AbdouMaliq Simone writes, today "many of the sounds emerging from African cities are rendered inaudible or inexplicable.... Urban politics must thus concern the invention of a platform or a scene on which the cacophony of urban voices are audible and become understood, and on which speakers are made visible."[6] *Lagos Never Spoils* contends that popular screen media is one such platform, particularly in the sense that Nollywood supports a continuous and cacophonous discourse about Lagos and everything the city embodies for Nigerian audiences. My approach aims to upend dominant scholarly assessments of Nollywood movies as too "noisy" for serious study and insists, on the contrary, that popular screen media like Nollywood represent a crucial scene of dissensus, one that reframes what can and must be said about urban life in West Africa today.

Although my focus centers on Nollywood, which I approach as both an industry and a body of texts, this investigation also encompasses celluloid films and television programs that predate the video film industry, as well as contemporary streaming content that suggests one possible future of Nigerian screen media. I will use the term "screen media" as Lindiwe Dovey does, to refer to film, video, television, and small-screen materials but also to unsettle expectations surrounding "the cinematic city."[7] Throughout, I pair textual analysis with industry analysis attuned to the ways in which Lagos shapes the production and circulation of screen media and in which the industry in turn shapes Lagos. Thematically speaking, the chapters in this book examine films about oil-boom wealth, television sitcoms about tricksters, video film dramas about urban social networks, glossy romantic comedies about love and labor, and video streaming content about the pleasure of moral transgression. This book contends, ultimately, that Lagos never spoils because residents work continually to ensure the city sustains something for them and that Nollywood—the industry and the body of films—both embodies and represents this continual urban transformation.

LAGOS

Lagos is exceptional in many ways. It is exceptionally large, with an estimated population upward of twenty million, a size that leaves urban geographers to question how it is even possible for the city to support so many people with a minimum of infrastructure and formal amenities.[8] It is exceptionally wealthy by comparison to Nigeria's other urban centers and also a place of exceptional inequality. The city is exceptional in terms of its ethnic diversity, rapid spatial expansion, economic connectivity, and regional cultural influence. The city's reputation during the 1990s was one of exceptional dysfunction, urban breakdown, and violence. Indeed, some wondered aloud how Lagos avoided a full descent into a permanent state of chaos.[9] But things improved with Nigeria's return to democracy and its gradual emergence from the deep desperation created by economic structural adjustment, and in more recent years, some of the exceptionalism has given way to normalcy. Once notorious for widespread armed robbery, Lagos has since seen a significant reduction in crime. Area boys still operate to some degree in every neighborhood, but residents and motorists no longer fear intimidation or extortion on main streets. An unpredictable "go-slow" or "no-go" can still make for a hellacious commute, but always eventually traffic moves. Whereas Oshodi once exemplified the intense friction created by the compression of a multitude of people and commercial activities, today, with the market and the bus stops contained along the shoulder of the highways, traffic and trade move more or less smoothly.[10] Thus, although it remains an outlier in most developmentalist measures of urban normativity, Lagos is nonetheless a city that works. It has become a place where many things are possible and where Nigeria's tremendous capacity for creativity, ingenuity, and cultural accommodation is on full display.

Simply put, what makes Lagos remarkable is what residents have made of it. On the campaign trail, former Lagos state governor Bola Tinubu introduced the Yoruba-language slogan Èkó ò ní bàjé (Lagos shall not spoil). The phrase has been widely adopted since and adapted occasionally to comment on the ironies of life in the city, as when a friend first explained this phrase to me and another immediately responded with a joke: Èkó bàjé o! (Lagos indeed spoiled!). On city streets, the motto appears scrawled in other irreverent variations, such as Èkó ò ní bàjé jù bàyìí lo (Lagos will not spoil more than this).[11] Such twists on the slogan readily convey the ambivalent mixture of hope and frustration that Lagos stirs up, but the slogan also captures the resilience and persistence with which residents of Lagos lead life despite it all. My adaptation of the phrase underscores the latter, namely, that Lagos never spoils: it endures. This book is concerned with change and endurance as two fundamental features of everyday life in West African cities. I am interested in the circumstances that make it possible both for residents to persist in pursuing their various projects and for the city to remain a platform that supports these projects and creates space for even more to emerge. I argue that Lagos never spoils because its residents continually and opportunistically work to combine contingency and endurance in ways that make the city work for them.

Originally a settlement of Yoruba farmers and fishermen called Èkó, the city became the epicenter of the regional slave trade in the nineteenth century and thereafter was known to Europeans by its Portuguese name, Lagos. In 1861, the British seized and established Lagos as a Crown Colony, an event that "marked the beginning of Lagos as the premier commercial, administrative, and political center of the country that would later in 1914 be known as 'Nigeria.'"[12] The British made minimal investment in developing the city but were forced into more direct oversight following an outbreak of plague in the mid-1920s. This event led to the first major slum clearance along the cordon sanitaire between colonial and indigenous districts.[13] The city port remained a colonial entrepôt, while residential neighborhoods on the mainland continued to expand and envelop nearby towns. The island witnessed a modernist construction boom in the fifteen years prior to Independence as tall office buildings shot up to house new governmental entities, local and foreign banks, communications companies, and the headquarters of British Petroleum, Shell Petroleum, and other oil companies.[14] At Independence, a million people lived in Lagos, the capital of the new nation. However, in subsequent years, that figure exploded as Lagos swelled with migrants seeking wage labor and refugees fleeing the violence of the civil war in the East.[15] The influx left newcomers with little choice but to settle in sprawling, underserviced working-class neighborhoods, and yet historically, Lagos owes its unique ethnic pluralism to similar waves of migration, such that, although Yoruba remains the most widely spoken indigenous language, in addition to English and Pidgin, the city does not belong to any one ethnic group.

In the 1970s, the oil boom increased government revenue twentyfold and helped to finance gigantic prestige projects and sweeping efforts to remake Lagos in the image of a modernist city of expressways, industrial parks, and large cultural monuments. However, the adoption of economic structural adjustments in 1986 marked the end of the oil boom and the beginning of the most desperate years in the city's history in which past improvements were largely wiped out. Austerity measures, currency devaluation, unemployment, crime, and commodity shortages were part of the hardship experienced during this period of urban crisis, but Lagos continued its rapid growth and soon became one of the most populous cities in the world.[16] In the early 2000s, international urban specialists took note and began to invoke Lagos as an illustration of either the supposed dysfunction or the laudable resourcefulness of African cities, a failure of urban governance or a success story of a certain notion of laissez-faire urbanism. Both narratives relied on generalizations about the city that have not held up with time.

Jankara Market is a telling example that demonstrates my point. The marketplace abuts one of the immense concrete interchanges off Third Mainland Bridge, where traffic from the mainland reaches Lagos Island. The location appears in Rem Koolhaas's account of Lagos, in which it serves as a symptomatic space in his diagnosis of the city. At the time of Koolhaas's visit in the 1990s, the vacant space inside the looping cloverleaf of the expressway was occupied by marketers who refurbished and resold metal wares. "The market has adapted the new highway infrastructure to its highest potential," Koolhaas writes, adding that "from scrap collection to sorting to design to assembly to re-sale, the entire chain of commodity production occurs within the highway interchange."[17] He concludes, having observed this "buildingless factory," that the urban spatialization of capital, paired with the self-organizing initiative of the labor market, demonstrates a more efficient logic than the concrete expressway prescribed by the norms of formal urban planning. The infrastructural and developmentalist vision of planners represents the old way, according to Koolhaas, while the minor practices of individuals making do represent the new urbanism to come, not only in Africa but around the world. And yet today, in Lagos, even that vision of the new is now old.

The Lagos state government cleared and converted the location into a park, and today the Lagos state flag flies over green grass, flower beds, and park benches. However, the most telling sign of the times is quite literally an enormous electric billboard in the middle of the small park emblazoned with vivid advertisements for global brands of beer, electronic devices, jewelry, and banking services. The flickering images are address to the millions of eyes that commute along Third Mainland Bridge each day. The billboard, which runs on an electric generator the size of a shipping container, also illuminates the adjacent neighborhood at night, where blighted houses across from the park would otherwise sit in complete darkness during the city's daily power outages. The collision of extremes, in which wealth and poverty sit cheek by jowl, illustrates the tight compression of inequalities within the city; but more to the point here, it underscores the fact that Lagos contains many lines of flight simultaneously and is not readily reduced to a single narrative.

As such, this book avoids grand historical narratives that flatten the complexity of Lagos and instead responds to Ato Quayson's call in *Oxford Street* for more nuanced attention to the interplay between the ephemeral details and structural underpinnings of everyday life in African cities. My account of Lagos will draw upon the scholarship of African urbanists, including AbdouMaliq Simone, Ato Quayson, Dominique Malaquais, and Sarah Nuttall, who approach African cities as opportunities to creatively reimagine the notion of urbanism itself.[18] This body of scholarship foregrounds improvisation, contingency, provisionality, and endurance as among the most important features of African urbanism. From this perspective, everyday life in Lagos is characterized by unpredictable change; both material abundance and precarity; the collision of cultures, languages, and ethnicities; and a locally situated worldliness.[19]

Perhaps above all else, everyday urbanism in the Global South is characterized by relentless change. In many African cities, in particular, change is so ubiquitous and intense it generates an entirely unique experience of city dwelling.[20] In numerous districts of Lagos, for instance, what defines everyday life is the dramatic extent to which daily life must be continually redefined. Some change unfolds subtly, almost as the background condition for everything else. The continual devaluation of local currency, for instance, necessitates the daily renegotiation between customers and shopkeepers of prices for all kinds of goods and services. Other changes are sudden, as with the demolition of a neighborhood marketplace—a common task of the KAI-KAI police in Lagos—or a sudden ban on motorcycle taxis that leaves countless young men without work and even more workers without a means of commuting. Various changes unfold at uneven paces, overlap, and pile up, and in response residents must syncopate the rhythm of their daily routine to reconcile several variables at once. In Elizabeth Povinelli's words, "Nothing is ready to hand," insofar as nothing "simply works" for entire districts of residents, and therefore "everything must *become* a 'theory' in the sense of a self-conscious encounter with the world" simply to make it work.[21] For this reason, it takes a great deal of endurance to live in Lagos, and yet, paradoxically, these experiments in flexibility, provisionality, and contingency are precisely what permits Lagos to endure. Even as authorities endeavor to curtail the resulting unruliness, they must surely know that without residents generating their own ad hoc arrangements, the city would grind to a halt. My point is not simply that Lagos defies normative expectations about the livability and functionality of cities but that Lagos could not hold out something for so many people if it was somehow brought into conformity with the plans and principles of normative urbanism, and this fact challenges us to surrender comfortable urban imaginaries in favor of a more complex set of questions.

In Lagos, tremendous contestation can exist around even simple questions, such as who can do what with whom and under what circumstances.[22] Of course, such a question cannot be answered once and for all and is instead meant to remain open-ended. However, to navigate life in a city like Lagos, one must settle upon an answer, even if only provisionally or as long as something lasts or, ideally, until some better arrangement comes along. Rather than succumb to the bewildering variability and contingency that Lagos throws up, its residents work to firm things up within their social networks, to fix arrangements in place. City residents alternate between striving to gain a reliable foothold from which to endure—come what may—and experimenting with urban contingency to discover new ways of affecting what may come, an alternation between the provisional and the durable that I refer to as open endurance.[23]

The urban convergence of diverse things, people, and ideas generates a certain cosmopolitanism—or Afropolitanism, as the case may be—composed of a social and cultural openness.[24] It enables residents to delink themselves from the norms of a familiar social order in favor of more extroverted forms of self-fashioning.[25] It permits residents to flirt with ways of being otherwise, and this sense of being open acknowledges the "promiscuity"—cultural, social, ideological, and emotional—that life in large cities encourages or even demands.[26] However, to be open also implies potential exposure to harm, manipulation, and deprivation, and, in this respect, vulnerability and contingency serve as cognates. There is, after all, a difference between an openness born of pragmatism and duress rather than of pleasure and desire. In contrast to the freedom that the city affords to become someone different, "in these situations, to be the same, to be durative, may be as emancipatory as to be transitive."[27] The desire to foreclose some of this excessive openness is only natural in cities where weak governance, insecurity, sparse economic opportunity, unmet material needs, and strained social relations combine to upend the sources of stability upon which individuals once relied, which brings us to endurance.[28]

Urban endurance has to do with what it takes to hold together a tenuous set of arrangements that are continually subject to change because, as Simone writes, "no matter how improvised, lives need to be held, supported."[29] Social bonds—between family, friends, ethnic relations, fellow worshipers, coworkers, or neighbors—are largely what hold life together in many African cities. Perhaps the most enduring support is the family and the moral economy of reciprocal obligations between family members. To protect against the hardships of the city, residents—especially newcomers—rely upon relatives, ethnic associations, and religious affiliations.[30] But the stability of such social bonds is always being tested, and stability itself becomes claustrophobic when its underlying conditions foreclose mobility and fix one in place. When an individual migrates to Lagos, for instance, pressure mounts to use this privileged new position to support family and friends back home. Intimate relationships become the source of acrimony on both sides, social bonds grow brittle, and some urban residents look to evade and defer what feel like overwhelming moral obligations.[31] What one can expect and demand of whom, and under what circumstances, is increasingly open to negotiation.[32] As such, I will consider the way that intimate relationships offer both attachments to ideas about stability and belonging and the desire for detachment from constraints on individual becoming. Many of the films I discuss throughout this book illustrate that social relations, whether supportive or stifling, are a central preoccupation of urban life and that we must hold in mind both thoughts at once to appreciate the affective posture I call open endurance.

Endurance is also a question of what lasts amid the ceaseless circulations of globalization, the breakdown of neglected habits and materials, or the transformations of cultural identity. The durability of various practices, subjectivities, and modes of signification is of interest here.[33] The concept points our attention to patterns that persist in spite of the tectonic shifts of urbanization and should also bring to mind the enduring values and beliefs that continue to guide individuals and to offer a ballast against the shifting currents of urban culture. Similarly, the opportunities that attract many migrants to the city can, in light of personal rationalizations, justify the tremendous amount of hustle it takes to succeed in Lagos. Aspirations can be powerful. A dream of the good life can drive individuals to stay the course, despite the obstacles they face on the path to its attainment.[34] In this regard, endurance can be predicated on greater engagement with, rather than retreat from, the forms of urban contingency discussed above, and as such, we need a nuanced understanding of endurance as a social practice as well as an affective experience.

Like Simone, my sense is that what matters is not simply what permits Lagosians to keep going but what allows *"for endurance to be something that is felt, where what was aspired to, what was sacrificed for, what was the compelling imagination of all the strivings and hard work of care is not lost."*[35] This concept describes a strategy for coming to grips with precarity and discovering how the individual can outlast conditions that may be outside his or her control, but it also implies the other end of the bargain, namely, the attachments that make enduring the daily difficulties of city life worth it. In this respect, it speaks to abundance as much as to scarcity, the uncertainty of living precariously as well as the stability embodied by fantasies of the good life. This book is concerned with the circumstances that enable transformation and endurance and what role popular culture plays in creating and shaping such circumstances.

Here, both the provisional and the durable have positive and negative connotations. For instance, precarity can produce an exhausting uncertainty within which the terms of daily life are reinvented each day. But when flexibility stems from the loosening of social or cultural order, it has the potential to open up new socialities and subjectivities. Similarly, having fixed in place the means of meeting one's basic needs frees one to pursue new opportunities beyond the incessant labor of firming up a crumbling toehold on the city. And yet, by contrast, stability can become claustrophobic when its underlying conditions leave one stuck in place. Open endurance describes this vertiginous relationship between flux and fixity, which is one not of juxtaposition but rather of countervailing alternation. All things considered, the political implications of conceptualizing urbanism in this way are not clear, which is the strength of thinking along these lines. The aim is not to arrive at ready prescriptions for smoothing the frictions of life in Lagos or to conjure visions of the modernization of the city.

My intention is not to identify some essential quality of Lagos. On the contrary, I argue that open endurance brings into focus dimensions of life that are increasingly common to cities around the world, especially given the intensification of the effects of globalization and neoliberal capitalism. As Sarah Nuttall and Achille Mbembe observe, "Fracture, colliding, and splintered orders of urban life can be seen to characterize, increasingly, many cities around the world, including Europe and the United States."[36] I propose that an ethos of open endurance is adopted where conditions of precarity and its associated forms of instability and uncertainty press individuals into a bargaining between flexibility and stability in life. In other words, where circumstances of precarity require individuals to hazard greater exposure to those same conditions of vulnerability, not as acquiescence but rather as agency, there one discovers the affective structure I am calling open endurance. At the same time, I do believe Lagos is unique in the sense that, all things considered, the remarkable lives that Lagosians have elaborated in the process of keeping the city working exemplify what open endurance entails. These are distinctions of intensity, not of kind.

Finally, if there is a structure of feeling undergirding everyday life in Lagos, an attitude or mindset, a hustle that characterizes the city, then exploring and understanding its presence within Nollywood—the industry and the films—gets at the heart of the entanglement between media and urbanism. This book aims, perhaps ambitiously, to demonstrate how aesthetic objects register and partake in an affective structure that indexes a spatial-historical situation, namely, urbanism in the largest city in West Africa over four decades of unprecedented economic, social, and cultural change. Whether this can be compellingly demonstrated is the question this study takes up. Thus, with transformation and endurance as fundamental features of everyday life in West African cities, it remains to discuss how screen media enregister their interplay over time.

URBAN AMBIVALENCE

A central argument of this book is that ambivalence affords an elasticity that opportunistically accommodates unpredictable change and thereby represents one of the unexpected ways in which the conditions of city life—especially its demand for improvisation—are inscribed into screen media texts. Ambivalence structures the representation of Lagos in Nigerian screen media in the sense that no single dominant attitude about Lagos emerges from its recurrent representation on screen. Instead, the city evokes a mixture of popular misgivings and aspirations. In her study of Yoruba popular theater, Karin Barber uses the phrase "radical conservatism" to describe the contradictory ideological outlook of the plays produced and performed by traveling theater troupes. She goes on to remark insightfully that ambiguous narrative construction "does not result in a judgment, it rather compels a suspension of judgment."[37] Along the same lines, I will approach textual ambivalence and outright contradiction not as shortcomings of popular screen media but rather as a strength derived from ideological, moral, and affective elasticity. The most enduring screen texts are often those in which the deferral of judgment allows audiences to continue to interrogate and respond to the uncertainties that arise within a context of rapid social and cultural transformation. As this book aims to illustrate, undecidability runs throughout the films, television programs, and videos produced in and about Lagos from the 1970s to the present. I contend that Nollywood does not resolve but rather absorbs this ambivalence toward Lagos because such affective elasticity enables viewers to accommodate the unpredictable shifts of urban life.

However, my point speaks to more than the spectatorial encounter with individual films or groups of titles. The ambivalence of the films stems from the industry that generates them, especially its conditions of production, distribution and consumption, and this becomes apparent through the dual approach this book adopts, one that interweaves textual and industrial analysis. What allows this body of screen texts to accommodate so much variation is precisely the fact that Nollywood produces so many titles so quickly. Nollywood's organization as a decentralized, self-sustaining commercial film industry closely attuned to the tastes of audiences enables, and even encourages, the uninhibited production of different images and stories of life in Lagos and thus hosts a cacophony of urban perspectives. In recent years, new concentrations of capital in parts of the industry protected by pockets of formal documentation and regulation have introduced new itineraries and temporalities of film production and circulation. This allows some filmmakers to employ a "slow and restricted release" of their film across distribution formats, from theatrical exhibition to online streaming services and television broadcast, such that the slow, scarce availability of a film garners it cultural capital and a level of distinction in an overcrowded field.[38] Importantly, although this book attends to Nollywood's multiple modes, with their corresponding production practices, distribution structures, spatial emplacements within Lagos, and formal aesthetic trends, I contend such distinctions reveal the most important insights when placed in a comparative relation rather than when held apart as unrelated phenomena. This does not flatten significant differences but rather underscores the crucial assertion that Nollywood generates an ongoing discourse about Lagos that stimulates wide-ranging, divergent perspectives that appear within the films as ideological and affective ambivalence toward the city and includes the simultaneous persistence of long-standing elements of film culture and industry practice alongside rapid transformation in other corners of the industry. Ultimately, this interaction between the industry, the films, and the audience drives the ongoing contemplation and reimagination of what urban life promises, for better or worse.

In this respect, Nollywood offers a counterpoint to canonical African cinema. The shift of scholarly attention toward the Nigerian film industry historically addressed a central irony of African cinema, as others duly note, namely, "that it refers to the films Africans produce and not those they watch."[39] I would add, furthermore, that earlier scholarship on African film understood cinema as an ideological but not an industrial system, and largely for historically valid reasons. From its inception in the 1960s, African cinema struggled with the prohibitive costs of celluloid film production and inadequate infrastructure for distribution across the continent, which left filmmakers dependent upon foreign funding and production assistance.[40] Thus, while Abidjan, Bamako, Dakar, and Kinshasa featured in African films, these films were not screened in cinema halls in those cities but instead circulated more commonly within the postproduction facilities, university classrooms, and art house cinemas of the Global North. Similarly, scholarship on African film demonstrated little interest in African cities as such. With Marxism and cultural nationalism as governing critical paradigms, film critics largely bypassed the city in search of ideological struggle or recognized its significance only in view of a series of structuring oppositions: European versus African space, alienation versus identity, individualism versus community, and modernity versus tradition.[41] As a result, the depiction of urban life in African film seemed inevitably subject to an "aesthetics of spatial dualism."[42] Nollywood, by contrast, articulates an array of perspectives on urban life.

Furthermore, Nollywood prompted a turn within African films and media studies toward popular culture as a window onto everyday life.[43] A central premise of this pivot was the notion that Nollywood movies shed light on the anxieties and aspirations of ordinary audiences. This was an important claim in the legitimation of the field, and considered from the present standpoint, it is notable how frequently Lagos was called upon to illustrate the point. Several early essays on video film argue that Nollywood both arose from and reflected the social milieu of the city. "The films are," as Jonathan Haynes writes, "a means for Nigerians to come to terms—visually, dramatically, emotionally, morally, socially, politically and spiritually—with the city and everything it embodies."[44] What makes this approach compelling and distinguishes it from previous work on African cinema is, again, the notion of a correlation between an emergent film industry, the films it produces, and the city of Lagos.

However, my notion of urban ambivalence denotes more than the mixed feelings of anxiety and desire calcified together into some knotted impasse. Nollywood films stir a continual discourse on Lagos that sustains multiple ways of thinking and feeling about the city, and the interpretation of an individual film is often the result of how this ambivalence is settled or left unsettled by the spectator. My selection of screen texts in each chapter is intended to plumb the fault lines of urban ambivalence. In chapter 1, for instance, I discuss how celluloid films produced by Yoruba popular theater troupes during the 1970s oil boom tended to incorporate spectacular *visuals* of the Lagos cityscape transformed by oil wealth into *narratives* about work that never pays, money that flows from evil deeds, and forms of pleasure so exuberant they kill. The accumulation of wealth was thus celebrated and censured in turns, producing an ambivalence about money and its morality that endlessly resurfaces in Nollywood's representation of the big city. In fact, the undecidability surrounding aspirations for urban affluence and the misgivings attached to the profound gap between material abundance and scarcity in Lagos represents, arguably, one of the most persistent sources of ambivalence in urban screen texts. Of course, undecidability attends more themes than this alone. A fuller list of urban themes will emerge in the chapters that follow, but an initial list would include the merit of hard work, the allure of fast money, the efficacy of religious faith, the power of occult forces, the relevance of deep cultural practices and knowledges, the appeal of global popular culture, the role of women in society, and the question of whether family bonds are enabling or constraining. These dimensions of city life have proven the most meaningful for audiences and filmmakers from the early film productions of Yoruba popular theater troupes and the first generation of video film producers to the latest New Nollywood releases and even some new corporate blockbusters.

Narratives about urban life often touch upon work, its unreliable availability, its arduousness, and its limited affordances. Such stories center as much on unlikely tales of extravagant fortunes made and lost as they do on modest dreams about earning enough to have a piece of the good life. Hence, work and wealth represent twin concerns, but the two themes also bleed into wider moral considerations. For instance, in films produced by Yoruba theater troupes during the oil boom, such as *Orun Mooru* (Heaven Is hot; Olaiya, 1982), *Owo L'Agba* (Money Power; Balogun, 1982), and *Taxi Driver* (Afolayan, 1983), the accumulation of wealth without work is accomplished with the assistance of occult powers. Characters who amass fortunes by magical means allow the films to discern between different kinds of wealth and to comment on the morality of hard work. In video films released during the economic structural adjustment and political instability of the 1990s, money troubles drive characters to desperate measures. Unemployed male characters turn to armed robbery, as in *Silent Night* (1996), while the female protagonists of *Glamour Girls* (1994) and *Domitilla* (1996) turn to prostitution. In both instances, the absence of honest work generates a moral dilemma for the characters to resolve and for the audience to reflect upon. Work is, in this sense, tethered to wider questions of the moral foundation of wealth, the value of an honest livelihood, and the temptation or necessity of finding other ways to earn money when hard work fails to pay.

Insecurity is another major thematic focus of urban narratives. Historically speaking, the rise of the video film format in the 1990s coincided with the breakdown of social order in Lagos, and as a result, the city figures in many Nollywood classics as a hostile force that overwhelms the good intentions of those who come to Lagos to get ahead. Other narratives, such as *Rattlesnake* (1995/1996) and *Owo Blow* (1996/1997), begin with an urban middle-class family whose slow decline into poverty is triggered by the sudden loss of the breadwinner, the father. In response to the disorder of the public sphere, these films often turn inward to the family for contentment, for safety, and as a means of living on amid insecurity. Aesthetically speaking, a compelling narrative was one that helped rationalize the rupture of the fabric of society, and many films accomplished this by drawing upon melodramatic codes that recast urban crisis in moral terms as a struggle between virtue and vice. In this sense, video films did more than simply reflect the breakdown of social order in Lagos; they also fostered a melodramatic urban imaginary that structured popular anxieties about violence, inequality, and the dissolution of social bonds.

Given that urbanization places pressure on families to adapt to uncertain circumstances, it should come as no surprise that the family is at the center of many Nollywood urban narratives. Families are unsettled by both the privileges and the hardships of city life, which disrupt household roles, undermine generational authority, and strain bonds with relatives back in the hometown or village. Numerous films, videos, and television programs dramatize different dimensions of these shifts in familial relations. I contend that Nigerian family dramas hinge on the same question, albeit as seen from opposing vantage points, namely, whether family bonds enable or constrain individual characters or whether a character's crass individualism undermines the important social obligations that one has to family.

The topic of culture itself is a recurrent subject of many urban screen narratives, as some films extol the importance of deep cultural knowledge and customs, while others aim to captivate audiences with displays of global popular culture. Nollywood is large enough to accommodate both. To arrive at a single conclusion on what Nollywood has to say about urban cultural change would be impossible. However, the representation of local and global culture—or village and urban customs, which often serve as their shorthand—has the tendency, broadly speaking, of generating spectatorial responses of either outrage or desire. Other scholars have written compellingly about these two particular affective responses. Brian Larkin discusses the aesthetics of outrage as one mode of spectatorship unique to video film, for instance, while Akin Adesokan argues that other films adopt an aesthetic of exhortation that calls explicitly for moral correctives within society.[45] Meanwhile, Carmela Garritano examines the ways in which the depiction of global culture in the Ghanaian video film industry is bound up with various forms of desire. As she brilliantly observes, films often fluctuate between outrage and desire, and the ambiguity between the stimulation and containment of desire typically situates itself in the gap between image and narrative.[46] Like Garritano, I will attend in particular to the fissures and contradictions that appear within and between the texts I examine, with the understanding that such fault lines express a great deal about the social and cultural unruliness of Lagos itself.

One could object that the themes I enumerate above pertain to all walks of life, not simply to life in Lagos or even Nigerian cities generally, and that, therefore, there is nothing particularly urban about my selection. On the contrary, following Doreen Massey, I argue that cities engender distinct modes of everyday life but "that particularity consists primarily in an intensification, a dramatic exaggeration" of characteristics also found elsewhere in the world.[47] In other words, what makes urban screen media distinctive is not a difference of kind but one of intensity. This book proposes new methods of reading these screen texts as inscribed by—rather than merely reflecting—conditions in Lagos and generates interpretations that push the formal analysis of Nollywood into new terrain. I show that screen texts enregister fundamental, but often overlooked, features of West African urbanism and therefore have much more to tell us about Lagos than previous approaches to Nollywood suggest.

NETWORKS OF ENTANGLEMENT

Let us abandon the notion of cities as bounded space and, instead, envision them as composed of networks of circulation and the capacity to combine. From this perspective, the movement of people, things, and ideas into assemblages according to specific configurations of material circuits creates the city as we experience it. Therefore, each city can be understood as a distinct place, as well as a unique event that unfolds continually and consists of the ceaseless encounters resulting from various networks coming into contact.[48] In short, the coming together *is* constitutive of urbanism, and thus, more than anything else, networks and relationality form the basis for all experiences of city life.

The network trope reveals an emergent parallel between urban studies and media studies, particularly where the latter has come increasingly to understand media industries as composed of some networks that draw together the creative and material resources of production and others that move media content along routes of distribution.[49] Where the networks of media production become embedded within those of major cities with the cultural, financial, and creative capital that film industries require, the result is the rise of what Michael Curtin calls a media capital.[50] Therefore, networks of circulation represent a constitutive quality of both cities and screen media industries, and this recognition provides a common basis upon which to examine their mutual embeddedness. It also helps to underscore the decentered and fragmented nature of Nollywood and by extension allows for more complicated narratives about the historical development and future trajectories of Nigerian screen media. As this book aims to underscore, some of Nollywood's networks of production and distribution are more embedded within Lagos than others configured around large cities in the East and the North, for instance. Elsewhere in Nollywood, production is organized around local networks of media professionals based in Lagos, while distribution of the films created is oriented toward transnational audiences on subscription-based television and online streaming services, which I discuss in chapter 5 as a respatialization of the industry. Attending to these different networks of production and distribution informs my grouping and analysis of films throughout this book. While charting networks is important in itself, I am ultimately more interested in thinking about how such configurations, combinations, and encounters create and sustain Nigerian media urbanism.

Consider Idumota marketplace in the heart of Lagos Island. Post-

Introduction • 19

Figure 2. Idumota Market on Lagos Island

Independence city planners intended this district to serve as the financial center of the city—and by extension the nation—but after companies migrated operations to Victoria Island, the district was occupied by smaller-scale marketers of electronics, media, home appliances, textiles, counterfeit clothing, and other general consumer goods.[51] Idumota also became—among many other things—the central hub of finance and distribution for the nation's burgeoning video film industry.

Today, the ground level of the marketplace is a maze of narrow corridors lined with racks of videos in flashy paper jackets. One is confronted everywhere by images competing to stand out in a blurring together of commodities. Film producers come from neighboring states to pitch projects to financiers whose offices are located on the top floors of crumbling concrete four-story buildings. Actors drop by to keep their faces fresh in the minds of those casting new roles. Meanwhile, video vendors from across the region arrive to buy video discs in bulk from wholesalers along the street. Virtually all distribution for the Yoruba-language industry—one of those virtually freestanding media networks existing apart from other networks in the East, in the North, and even in the English-language video market at Alaba elsewhere in Lagos—flows outward from this point.

All new videos are released on the same day of the week, and on these days, video sellers from across southern Nigeria descend upon the marketplace to purchase in bulk. The influx makes crowding along the street palpable. The space of the market becomes an intense flurry of commerce, movement, exchange, and mingling. On one such day, I arrived to visit a friend who worked with a major marketer, and while waiting I struck up a conversation with several video vendors about their journey into Lagos that morning from Ogun and Osun States. Another vendor nearby had traveled from Ekiti State, another from Ondo State, and so on. I remained seated on a concrete step, but the list in my notebook soon contained the name of every predominantly Yoruba state in Nigeria, the entire Southwest represented in one lane of the marketplace and the same activity unfolding in dozens of other lanes. Video vendors wake before dawn, travel by road into the heart of Lagos, purchase stacks of discs, and board yellow *danfo* buses for Oshodi motor park to connect with other buses destined for smaller cities. They must depart Lagos before midday traffic in order to reach home that night, to avoid the risk of traveling after dark. The same process, we should imagine, was simultaneously taking place at Alaba market on a larger scale, with vendors journeying the Badagry Expressway to marketplaces in Benin, Ghana, and Cote D'Ivoire, and in the East the same mode of circulation flows outward from Onitsha.[52] This is, after all, what informal networks of circulation look like: cash sales of physical merchandise to innumerable small vendors by marketers operating with small capital bases. It is along these local and transnational itineraries that the Nigerian video film industry extends its distribution networks and comes to capture the eyes and imaginations of audiences across the country, region, and African diaspora at large.[53]

Manthia Diawara contends that West African marketplaces are inherently transnational spaces that orient merchants and customers toward other locales and regions and therefore serve as catalysts of vernacular modernity in the region.[54] But marketplaces are also trans-urban spaces that connect towns and cities across West Africa. Even marketplaces that serve rural communities are largely located within or nearby a town and are oriented, in Diawara's sense, toward major urban centers and the larger suppliers there. As my description of Idumota illustrates, Nollywood's distribution apparatus rides atop—or more likely is squeezed into the back hatch of—a preexisting popular economy of commercial networks. Jonathan Haynes points out that

Nollywood long lacked the large capital investments that other film industries enjoy—studio headquarters, production lots, cinema chains, and so on—and as a result, its footprint in Lagos is less visible.[55] In lieu of such structures, the industry relies on the marketplace, its human and financial resources, its business practices, and its particular culture of commerce.[56] The major video markets are embedded within the same marketplaces through which the vast majority of the region's consumer goods are imported and pumped outward to the smallest capillaries of these networks. However, as much as marketplaces establish connections, they also create strategic disjuncture, a fact that Nollywood's marketers have leveraged to their advantage for years. Under the cloak of the marketplace's informal economy, the film industry's finance and distribution networks have enjoyed refuge from government regulation, taxation, legal grievances, and other frictions faced by counterparts in the formal sector. The marketers wield power in Nollywood by maintaining control of national trading networks, knowledge of sales figures, and first-line access to profits, as Jade Miller thoroughly details, concluding that they found an asset in informality where others saw only liability.

> The marketers, both beneficiaries and architects of this system, are fully aware of the ways these business practices reserve power for themselves and limit opportunities for outsiders. In this way, informality in distribution is less a "challenge" for a burgeoning industry . . . but rather, a conscious and active strategy by networks of small-scale savvy entrepreneurs to discourage competition from better capitalized challengers.[57]

Along these lines, Miller argues compellingly for the value this "gap" affords minor cultural industries that thrive on neglect by dominant global media flows. Miller's work makes the important argument that outside dominant networks of media production and distribution lies a tremendous amount of cultural activity, and from this perspective, the periphery becomes the center of a tremendously creative milieu.

As an industry, therefore, Nollywood compensates for the absence of capital and built infrastructure by mobilizing "people as infrastructure," and in this sense video markets illustrate the role of screen media in the formation of everyday city life. AbdouMaliq Simone's notion of people as infrastructure refers to "the ability of residents to engage complex combinations of objects, spaces, people, and practices. These conjunctions become an infrastructure—a platform providing for and reproducing life in the city."[58] Ultimately, urbanism of this sort, which consists in assemblages of people, materials, and time, is what makes most things in Lagos possible, from the minutia of everyday routines to the creation of the largest and most productive film industry in the region. In fact, the collaborations of residents generate the collective force that holds the city together, even as the population explodes and the city continues to expand. There is always more going on between residents than anyone knows, including the residents themselves, and in this sense, the social lives of residents become the dark matter of the urban universe, the abundant element that fills the gaps.

I contend, furthermore, that the notion of people as infrastructure even casts Nollywood films in a new light. When everyday life is—in both senses—held up by a web of interpersonal relationships, one must dedicate attention and effort to the maintenance of this infrastructure, and city life comes to entail continual concern for relations with family, friends, business partners, and even strangers. It means searching out a balance of obligations to one another, as well as upending balance in search of other possibilities, and includes the entanglements that result. In chapter 3, I discuss Nollywood narratives that present the city as composed of social entanglements, a concept less uniform and more flexible than a networked map of disinterested nodes and links, especially where entanglement entails performative enactments of social connection. Here, entanglement refers to the social bonds that hold urban residents together, or pull them apart, but more specifically designates a paradox of urban social relations wherein connections are necessary for social advancement, even as the same bonds, under different circumstances or seen from another vantage point, begin to appear like social bondage. This approach challenges the "mapmaker" perspective of urban networks and asserts that social connections between residents are not disinterested nodes and links but rather fluid relations imbued by cultural and moral values concerning the shared obligations of family, friends, and neighbors.

Interestingly, as chapter 2 demonstrates, in television programs that preceded Nollywood, like *Basi and Company* (1986–90), Lagos represents the intricate social fabric of the nation, as characters of diverse cultural, linguistic, ethnic, and class backgrounds collaborate on-screen together within the capital city. By contrast, as I discuss in chapter 3, *Living in Bondage* (1992), *Violated* (1996), *Owo Blow* (1997), *Died Wretched* (1998), and other early video films portray marriages, families, and friendships torn apart by the economic hardship, moral uncertainty, and general insecurity of Lagos during the 1990s. Both examples envision particular historical social entanglements that define Lagos—whether as tapestry of national culture or torn social fabric—and demonstrate that screen media imagines the city more as a latticework of characters and narrative relationships than a space of "cinematic" visuals. This is an important departure from the common viewpoint that urbanism pertains primarily to the city form—its built spaces, infrastructures, and commodities, for example—and only secondarily or tangentially to the social connections between residents, which become viewed almost as by-products of city structures. I contend that the reverse is equally true, and sometimes even truer, as when people and social connections substitute for a structural shortage of urban forms. In this respect, early Nollywood's vision of social entanglement supplants the dominant view of cinema and cities as principally spatial entities.

ENCLOSURE

In recent years, new distribution channels have emerged in Nollywood catering to upmarket audiences, and several media companies—backed by formal investors—have generally assumed the control of these new modes of distribution. This represents a welcome development for those within the industry who have long sought modes of distribution immune—or at least resistant—to piracy and the commercial risks associated with informality.[59] The advent of satellite television, theatrical exhibition, and video streaming services has created new venues for the circulation of Nollywood films that can keep a film cordoned off from video markets, unauthorized reproduction, and undocumented distribution if the producers and distributors so choose.[60] These channels of distribution also introduce new revenue streams in ticket sales, subscriber fees, advertisements, and sponsorships that can, for some producers, displace video disc sales, which piracy and oversaturation have rendered increasingly unreliable. However, one controversial by-product has been "the concentration of capital and resources around the activity of a small number of big media corporations."[61] The companies in question include Filmhouse/FilmOne, iROKOtv/ROK Studios, Multichoice, EbonyLifeTV, and the latecomer, Netflix. Some media scholars have come to characterize this shift as the corporatization of Nollywood.

The outgrowth of this corporate segment of the screen media industry should be viewed in light of other current developments in the city, including the notion that Lagos is poised to become a creative hub, a recurring refrain in recent years. In reality, as the city grows more stable and prosperous, the neighborhoods of Ikoyi, Victoria Island, and Lekki have attracted the majority of the human, creative, and financial capital. Companies have eagerly established offices in Lekki, the fastest growing district of the city. On Victoria Island, young entrepreneurs and "creatives" congregate at coworking spaces said to stimulate innovation and collaboration. Professional environments of this sort are in keeping with the wider global evolution of the nature of work, and the return migration of Nigerians from the diaspora has undoubtedly been an integral factor behind this recent urban change. Furthermore, the island now hosts many forms of leisure: shopping and fine dining, new venues for arts and culture, and multiplex cinemas. New art galleries and international exhibitions have expanded the urban ecosystem within which the public, artists, curators, and collectors converge.[62] However, while these developments unfold on the island, growth continues at the city's expanding edges.

To live in the peripheral districts of mainland Lagos can often be more affordable and comfortable, both for newcomers and lifetime residents who save enough to buy land and build a house. In the evenings as commuters idle in traffic, the twelve-kilometer Third Mainland Bridge is transformed into a winding red slice of taillights that snakes across the dark waters of the lagoon. Vehicle headlights illuminate the patchwork sails of fishermen's canoes that pass underneath the bridge on their way back to Makoko, an entire city district built atop the lagoon. Truly desperate conditions exist in such communities that dot the mainland, communities that Lagosian architect David Aradeon has called the "fringe within the center" (personal communication, September 18, 2013). Both the prosperity that concentrates on the island and the abandonment of entire districts elsewhere in the city bear witness to neoliberal and "late liberal distributions of life and death, of hope and harm, and of endurance and exhaustion across social difference."[63] Furthermore, these distributions are created and sustained through ideological, affective, and material processes of enclosure, which denotes the various ways urban residents wall off or remove themselves from the exhausting demands of life in Lagos. My use of the term "enclosure" should not be narrowly construed as a rebuke, although this study does offer a critique of the processes of enclosure underway within the industry itself, but rather viewed as an ambivalent recognition of the desire to detach from the constraints on individual freedom and the pervasive urge to control the messiness of city life, including its provisionality, contingency, and unpredictability.

Enclosure comes to the foreground in the second half of the book, which pivots to recent developments in Nollywood and Lagos, such as the rise of New Nollywood and the formation of new distribution channels. It charts the restructuring of media production and circulation around formal corporate media houses, such as iROKOtv and Netflix, and examines how this generates new screen representations of life in Lagos. In chapter 5, I interpret New Nollywood romantic comedies, including *Phone Swap* (2012), *The Meeting* (2012), *When Love Happens* (2014), and *Wedding Party* (2016), as visions of life getting better in Lagos and examine the familial, ethnic, and professional contours of this aspiration. These narratives pair professional and romantic plotlines—protagonists follow their heart as well as their professional calling—and in this way present career and courtship as spheres similarly governed by an ethic of self-reliance and self-fulfillment. These romantic comedies illustrate that work is not just about the production of commodities, services, and revenue but also about the production of particular forms of subjectivity and new ideas about love, marriage, and family. While love is central to the genre, more fundamentally, romantic comedies create permissive storyworlds and affectively heightened depictions of a better life and thus underscore by virtue of elision anxieties over common encumbrances. Within this representational enclosure, Lagos figures as a shining city free of chronic power outages, poor roads, congested traffic, and generalized scarcity, while individual characters are freed from the moral economy of social entanglement and familial obligations. Here enclosure figures as normative urban individualism, which I contend must be viewed in light of my argument above that Lagos offers a platform for so many people precisely because it defies normative modes of city life.[64]

Chapters 5 and 6 intend to shift focus from consumption to production and subsequently explore the ways in which New Nollywood films enregister changing production practices and how these changes connect to shifting modes of distribution. I contend that one force driving processes of enclosure within Nollywood has been the introduction of logistical management techniques found in creative industries elsewhere, what Stefano Harney calls "the commodification of the arts through the commodification of those who produce them."[65] This entails not only the commodification of the creative labor of media professionals but also that of audiences whose strong engagement with Nollywood engenders its value. Whether we term this "collective life" or the "general intellect," it represents "a generativity without reserve."[66] This value derives from the creation of "cultural and artistic standards, fashions, tastes, consumer norms and . . . public opinion,"[67] and its "commodification" is accomplished in part with an expanding range of logistical instruments and practices employed in creative industries.[68] In other words, the aim of corporate distributors is to position themselves to harvest the fruits of Nollywood's cultural creativity. One method is to purchase countless films pre-bundled for television broadcast across Africa, while another is to contract individual Nollywood producers to create content for subscription television and streaming services. In both cases, corporate distributors are not creators as much as managers of screen media culture. In fact, Harney goes so far as to claim that management techniques in creative industries resemble other forms of neoliberal governmentality within which the state is said to "govern from a distance."[69] And, indeed, Nollywood's new corporate distributors remain largely removed from the messy business of filmmaking within an informal industry. Producers, by contrast, are left to ply their creative trades under conditions of precariousness. Here enclosure pertains to barriers within Nollywood itself, particularly the enclaves of formality meant to safeguard the business of distribution from the risk and unpredictability of film production, which still takes place in the informal economy. In this sense, global media distribution networks depend upon local media production conditions, which grow from the material and human infrastructure of the preexisting straight-to-video industry, and based on interviews with media professionals who produce commissioned works for iROKOtv and Netflix, I argue that this represents a significant reconfiguration of Lagos as a media capital.

In chapter 6, I illustrate some implications of these trends with reference to several dark and gritty films that complicate the norms of New Nollywood, thus far, including *Taxi Driver* (2015), *Gbomo Gbomo Express* (2015), and *Juju Stories* (2021), among others. At a time when Lagos has grown relatively safe, these films feature bleak depictions of the city organized within transgressive narratives that adopt global genre conventions in a repudiation of glossier portrayals of Lagos and urban affluence. In such films, Lagos does not simply reprise its historical role as the embodiment of popular anxieties concerning insecurity, material inequality, and social breakdown. On the contrary, the dangers of urban life are adapted so as to afford audiences pleasure in transgression itself, such that Lagos becomes, representationally, an object of attraction rather than abjection. The specific example of *Juju Stories*, the Surreal16 Collective's most recent anthology film, illustrates what I term "cinephilic intertextuality," with which some young filmmakers situate their works in dialogue with unexpected interlocutors in arthouse and world cinema. My inquiry challenges the notion that genre arises in response to social and cultural events and proposes instead that New Nollywood genres respond to new production practices among Lagos-based filmmakers, evolving audience tastes, and unlikely affinities with the Lagos art scene.

Finally, this book aims to disrupt the tendency to conceive of urban change and cultural shifts within the predetermined framework of a developmentalist narrative. Discussion of structural shifts in Nollywood and my argument that formal corporate global distribution remains dependent upon informal, precarious local media labor based in Lagos speak to current debates on media globalization. However, the arc of those debates must also acknowledge the enduring persistence of the video film industry, which remains a formidable cultural force. Upmarket and mainstream Nollywood coexist, and, when viewed side by side, they reveal once more the ambivalence and contradiction of Nollywood's urban imaginary. It bears emphasizing that the majority of the industry's producers and marketers continue to operate in the informal sphere, and it is their example that inspires the spinoff industries in Senegal, Côte d'Ivoire, the Democratic Republic of Congo, Kenya, Tanzania, and the global African diaspora. Therefore, as Nollywood begins to selectively integrate with global media networks, it also inspires the growth of other minor screen media networks in other minor media capitals, and in this sense, Nollywood also suggests the future of media urbanism elsewhere in Africa. After all, cities of the Global South like Lagos and popular screen media like Nollywood will remain, in the years to come, the basis upon which the majority of the world experiences media urbanism.

CHAPTER 1

Urban Ambivalence in Early Nigerian Films

The oil boom of the 1970s and 1980s brought immense concentrations of money to Lagos, which was at the time the political and financial capital of Nigeria. The signs of this newfound wealth were visible throughout the city, notably in the modernist freeways, skyscrapers, and airport, as well as in the changing fashions, consumer goods, and forms of leisure. The production by local filmmakers of films for local cinemas, where before only imported films were screened, also represents one such shift in cultural production and consumption during this period. Alongside these economic and social shifts was a parallel current of cultural and artistic change, including the rise of professional Yoruba traveling theater companies and the decision by some of these troupes to adapt their works to film.[1] Hubert Ogunde's Ogunde Pictures Company, Ade Afolayan's Friendship Motion Pictures, and Moses Olaiya Adejumo's Alawada Film Company, for example, created film adaptations from their most popular stage plays, sometimes conscripting the help of a director or producer with formal training in filmmaking, like Ola Balogun. The subsequent films came to center on two broad genres: epic films based in Yoruba metaphysics and contemporary dramas in urban settings.[2] In the transition from stage to screen, the popular theater preserved its attention to the immediate social circumstances impacting the lives of audiences, as well as its cast of characters, repertoire of scenarios, and mode of address. In spite of critics who found the films too stagey, the Yoruba theater companies dominated Nigerian film production in the 1980s and even survived the transition from celluloid film to video technology into the 1990s.

The release of *Kongi's Harvest* in 1970 marked the first feature film produced by Nigerians for commercial distribution within the country. The following decade saw a precipitous increase in the number of films and film producers on the scene.[3] By 1980, a small cohort of local filmmakers had released twenty-one films, and by the end of that decade the number had climbed to fifty-one films.[4] Nevertheless, Nigerian cinema remained an "artisanal, informal, and sporadic" endeavor held together by personal relationships between producers, crew, performers, private financiers, and cinema operators.[5] The local cinema that subsequently emerged was grounded in film as a popular commodity at a time when African cinema elsewhere sought grounding in the politics of decolonization or the aesthetics of cultural authenticity. As a consequence, early Nigerian filmmakers depicted Lagos not as a site of struggle for decolonization, modernization, or Africanization, as the city was typically represented in Francophone African cinema, but as a place of work, wealth, leisure, and moral dilemmas.

Virtually all the films produced during this period have disappeared amid the archives of foreign postproduction labs, decomposed due to lack of proper storage, or become subject to disputes over proprietary rights after the death of the filmmaker. However, a small number have survived or been recovered, among them Moses Olaiya Adejumo's *Orun Mooru* (Heaven is hot, 1982) and Adeyemi Afolayan's *Taxi Driver* (1983), the films at the center of this chapter. While other scholars have offered indispensable surveys of films from this era, my focus will center on these two films to the exclusion of other surviving films by Ola Balogun and Eddie Ugbomah, given that neither filmmaker was a member of the traveling theater. The stories and images of Lagos in *Orun Mooru* and *Taxi Driver* touch upon popular preoccupations about the moral foundations of wealth, the value of labor, and the pursuit of the good life in the city. Moreover, they illustrate an ambivalent ideological and aesthetic tendency of the popular theater to oscillation between entertainment and edification, a tendency expressed in representations of Lagos as a space of pleasurable attractions and powerful moral challenges. To elaborate this point, I intend to interlace my interpretation of the films with a discussion of exhibition in Lagos and the spaces where Nigerian audiences would have attended screenings of the Yoruba theater's films. I focus, in particular, on the largest venue for cinematic exhibition in Lagos, the National Arts Theatre in Iganmu, which was constructed during the oil-boom years as part of Nigeria's bid to convene the Second World Festival of Black and African Arts and Culture in 1977—or Festac '77. I examine the NAT from several angles, as one of several major public works projects in Lagos that arose from the oil boom and came to establish the most enduring features of the city's built environment, as an architectural spectacle akin to the visual attractions of urban modernity that appear in the films themselves, as an assemblage of infrastructures designed to produce an ambient experience of "modern" moviegoing, and as the literal intersection between Nigerian cinema and the city.

Nigeria's post–Civil War oil boom was unprecedented by nearly every quantification of its economic dimensions.[6] As if overnight, Nigeria became the wealthiest African nation and the one perhaps most dependent upon a single commodity for its rising fortunes. Its integration into the global economy as a major oil producer occurred at a dizzying speed, although the effects were unevenly felt, owing in part to the fact that government distribution of new resources was designed to produce political loyalty as much as economic development.[7] In 1973, the then military head of state General Yakubu Gowon famously remarked that Nigeria's problem was not money but rather how to spend it. A large portion of subsequent spending was poured into the commission of enormous prestige projects across the nation, with a number of the largest in Lagos itself. The ruling elite favored spectacular architectural undertakings as a performance of political power and a testament to their vision of African modernity.[8] Thus, infrastructural plans outlined—but never financed—under the Second National Development Plan were revived, while additional measures toward infrastructural modernization were initiated under a Third National Development Plan (1975–80), which, among other things, reenvisioned Lagos as a modernist city of expressways, industrial parks, and large cultural monuments. In this fashion, the windfall of oil wealth triggered a corresponding construction boom during which a number of the city's most enduring physical structures were erected and spatial relations established.

This push for infrastructural development acquired mounting urgency as Nigeria prepared to host two high-profile cultural events, namely, the All Africa Games in 1973 and the Festac '77.[9] The largest of these projects included the National Stadium, the National Arts Theatre, and Festac Town. For its part, the National Sports Stadium near Surulere entailed a muscular structure with a hulking concrete bowl designed to seat sixty thousand spectators and four concrete masts of floodlights that tower over the surrounding cityscape. Preparations for Festac '77 entailed further investment in key urban spaces, including the construction of the National Arts Theatre complex at Iganmu; renovations at Tafawa Balewa Square, which was once the colonial race course in downtown Lagos Island; and the creation of an extensive housing complex dubbed Festac Town that pushed into the city's westward suburbs.[10] For several years after the All Africa Games and Festac '77, Lagos continued to undergo expansion and rebuilding while revenues permitted: the Lagos Trade Fair Complex, the New Secretariat in Ikoyi, government housing complexes in Victoria Island, and the new international terminal of Murtala Muhammad Airport were all completed by the end of the decade, after which a global recession staunched the flow of oil receipts.[11]

This chapter examines the conjuncture of the passage into a petro-capitalist economy and the emergence of local film production, beginning with the ambivalent representation of Lagos's new overlay of modernist architecture and infrastructure in films produced by popular theater companies. Such ambivalence turns on the fact that the freeways, bridges, office buildings, and airport offered an iconography of Nigerian modernity that attracted popular speculations about the social and moral implications of the newfound wealth that made these icons of urban modernity possible. The signs of petro-prosperity were visible, but the sources and flows of wealth were not, and, as a result, popular rumors of quick money and unearned fortunes connected conspicuous signs of wealth to unseen activities, sometimes imagined as unfolding within the realm of the occult. As my reading of *Orun Mooru* will demonstrate, the portrayal of money rituals and magical conceptions of money cannot be disregarded as fabulation or superstition but rather should be viewed as a fictionalized speculation about the cultural and moral implications of the rapid transformations of the oil boom. The surface exteriorized modernity but also concealed the abstract processes of its production; therefore, filmmakers envisioned not only the surface appearance of urban change but also what lay behind or beyond the surface, including the imagined sources of change and its consequences.

This line of argument challenges the common assumption that the key facets of "metropolitan life lie on the *surface*, in the ephemeral and the visible." Instead, it acknowledges, as Sarah Nuttall and Achille Mbembe do, that "beneath the visible landscape and the surface of the metropolis, its objects and social relations, are concealed or embedded other orders of visibility, other scripts that are not reducible to the built form."[12] Popular stories about the sudden amassing of wealth without work, the circulation of money within mysterious networks of patronage, or the violent consequences of this new speculative/spectral economy exemplify the alternative scripts with which Nigerian films represented the transformation of Lagos. I argue these films incorporate spectacular *visuals* of the Lagos cityscape transformed by oil wealth into *narratives* about work that never pays, money that flows from evil deeds, and forms of pleasure so exuberant they kill. The films denounce the seductive power of oil wealth and society's integration with global fast capitalism while, at the same time, partaking in this seduction. The accumulation of wealth is, thus, celebrated and censured in turns, producing an ambivalence about money and its morality that will continually resurface in future years in Nollywood's representation of Lagos.

ATTRACTIONS AND OBJECT LESSONS

As Biodun Jeyifo quips, the Yoruba traveling theater was a tremendously hazardous line of work. He points as explanation to one crucial figure: "The country had fifty-five thousand miles of roadways but only nine-thousand and five hundred were paved."[13] The fact that all Nigerians faced the same risk of mechanical breakdown, car accident, or any number of other dangers does not deflate the flourish of Jeyifo's point, since both theater performers and their audiences would have appreciated the hazardousness of the transportation infrastructure of Nigeria. Nevertheless, the roads enabled the long-distance tours that were integral to the "economic survival and artistic impact" of the popular theater itself.[14] To sustain themselves, some theater companies journeyed as far west as Ghana, as far north as Kano, and as far east as Rivers State to reach their audiences, and then they got back on the road to return home to Lagos, Ibadan, or Oshogbo, where many troupes were based. Therefore, when transportation infrastructure appears in the films produced by theater companies, such as *Taxi Driver* and *Orun Mooru*, its figural presence lends insight into what Patricia Yaeger calls "stories of people's massed relations to infrastructure."[15]

The oil boom allowed the federal government to make significant investments in the nation's infrastructure. In Lagos, this included an extensive network of expressways centered around Lagos Island—then the seat of the federal government—and extending toward the mainland where the majority of the city's rapidly growing population resided. The creation of Eko Bridge provided a crucial second access point between the central business district of Lagos Island and the mainland, while the existing Carter Bridge received badly needed renovations.[16] A ring road expressway was built to encircle the downtown, linking the marina and central business district to the government secretariat offices in the old colonial district of Ikoyi. The Lagos-Badagry Expressway stretched westward to the border with Benin, while Western Avenue provided access northward to Surulere and onward to the suburbs of

Mushin, Ikeja, and Agege. These roadways and bridges conformed to a vision of Lagos that, as urban geographer Giles Omezi remarks, was imagined by the state, in collaboration with its cadre of British, German, Greek, and Italian architects and contractors. The aim was to create built spaces "inscribed and reinforced by an iconography of modernity," which ultimately would "fuse concepts of modernization into the consciousness of the people" and project the appearance of a powerful new nation to the rest of the region and world.[17]

The new expressways consisted of an elaborate series of concrete flyovers and bridges that Omezi calls the "modernist overlay" of Lagos, suggesting its design took little account of the actual nature of traffic in Lagos and instead worked from abstract principles oriented around the infrastructural ideal of free-flowing urban mobility. "Flows of production were articulated," Omezi writes, "in an infrastructure overlay that recalled the modernist city vision of the early twentieth century and were literally constituted as a metaphor to an aspired modernity buttressed further by the inclusion of sites of cultural production within its framework."[18] However, the swelling population of Lagos meant that demands of traffic continued to outstrip the expansion of transportation infrastructure, and as historian Ayodeji Olukoju's study of Lagos infrastructure indicates, residents inhabited and used the city in ways that were unimaginable to its designers.[19] Thus, in spite of the vision of Lagos's foreign planners and contractors, these roads became the sites of "go-slow" and "no-go" traffic, where marketplaces spilled onto the asphalt, street hawkers pressed goods into the windows of busloads of tired commuters, and the anticipated flow often ground to a halt.

When Yoruba theater companies began to produce films set in Lagos, the films gravitated toward these same built spaces, infrastructures, and modern amenities, which the dramatists-cum-filmmakers utilized as both attractions and object lessons, as I explain below.[20] In this way, the city's skyscrapers, bridges, and expressways offered themselves as "entextualized forms," whose sway over the imagination stemmed from the fantasies and desires generated by architecture and infrastructure rather than the mere technical function they performed.[21] Moreover, the on-screen "entextualization" of Lagos's built forms was inflected by the medium of its representation, which combined cinematic and theatrical aesthetics. Film lent itself to visual spectacle, but the strength of the Yoruba theater's existing repertoire of dramatic scenarios, characters, acting styles, and spaces of performance stemmed from the imagination and creativity of the performers, the plays' moral lessons pertaining to recent social transformations, and Yoruba language itself, which was the deep cultural reservoir that gave the theater life. As a result, the popular theater's films, including *Orun Mooru* and *Taxi Driver*, adopted several different modes of address: pedagogical, moralistic, exhibitionistic, theatrical, and cinematic, for instance. The novelty of the medium and the resilience of the theatrical tradition combine in these films to generate a productive disjuncture between the visual and narrative tracks, in which each "speak" about the city in distinct voices. As such, the polyphony of these films represents both a byproduct of the aesthetic transition from stage to screen and an expression of ideological ambivalence concerning the social transformations that reshaped Lagos in the 1970s and 1980s.

Ade Afolayan's *Taxi Driver* opens at a crossroad, literally. The frame captures a wide intersection in Lagos with high-rise apartments along one corner, construction materials along another, and the sands of Victoria Island blowing across the asphalt, at which point an iconic yellow taxi cab crosses the intersection and the film gives chase. The camera takes up the passenger seat and rides along with Tunde (Ade Afolayan), the eponymous taxi driver, as he seeks passengers in downtown Lagos. The central musical theme fades in, a song featuring electric synthesizer, guitar, horns, and the cheerful tenor of pop music. From its mount above the taxi's wheel well, the camera scans the line of parked automobiles along the entranceway to the Eko Hotel. As Tunde arrives, the polished surface of the taxi's chasse reflects the rows and columns of balconies of the building's facade, and after catching a glimpse of the elegant guests congregating outside the lobby, the taximan circles back onto the city's streets. The film is not yet ready to take a fare, which would plunge the film into dialogue, reveal its characters, and introduce narrative motivation. Instead, with fuel in the tank and much more of Lagos to see, the ride continues. The sequence cuts to a remarkable view of downtown as observed from the window of the taxi as it cruises gracefully along the elevated ring road expressway along the waterfront. The frame tracks past the headquarters of NITEL, the Nigerian telecommunications parastatal, flanked by several other towers, cuts next to a shot of the Independence Building and the concrete sound system masts of Tafawa Balewa Square, and cuts back to its original vantage point, peering over the expressway guardrails as skyscrapers, office buildings, bank headquarters, the Nigerian Ports Authority, and the unmistakable facade of the Church Missionary Society chapel glide across the frame.

The sequence brings to life the architectural performance of progress and development, as well as the infrastructural ideal of unfettered urban mobil-

Urban Ambivalence in Early Nigerian Films

Figure 3. Lagos cityscape envisioned from the expressway in *Taxi Driver*

ity. It *envisions* Lagos, particularly in Birgit Meyer's sense that it engenders a visual imaginary crystalized around a dream image, rather than a mirrored reflection, of the city.[22] All visual mediation, of course, entails selection and exclusion inherently, and the visual construction of Lagos here is no different. The sequence cuts away before Tunde reaches the crowded marketplace and traffic bottleneck at Eko Bridge, which lie just ahead, beyond the marina, and thereby selectively foregrounds the high-rise commercial architecture visible from the expressway while bypassing the older, denser residential districts of Lagos Island. The film appropriates these built spaces in order to construct its own urban imaginary, one imbued with positive sentiment: optimism, confidence, and pride. As Brian Larkin argues, infrastructure is often mobilized in projects of political address "to represent the possibility of being modern, of having a future, or the foreclosing of that possibility and a resulting experience of abjection," adding that this "happens on the individual as well as on the societal level."[23] If the towering government offices and financial headquarters address themselves to the public as embodiments of Nigerian modernity, the film becomes an interlocutor and draws these structures into a dialogue between architectural speech act and cinematic mode of address.

The modernist vision that guided the construction of these buildings—as described by Omezi above—is what the film wishes to tap and syphon for its own narrative purposes, but the story that would embed—and thereby re*envision*, in Meyer's sense—these images into its own ideological framework has yet to commence. So, the drive continues.

The brief visual pleasure of this view of Lagos is accentuated by the subtle kinetic energy of gazing at the skyline from an automobile speeding down the expressway, and in this fashion, the cinematography captures the aesthetics of urban infrastructure. The level surface of the smooth new expressway produces what Larkin terms "a sensing of modernity, a process by which the body, as much as the mind, apprehends what it is to be modern, mutable, and progressive."[24] As a kinesthetic index of the expressway asphalt, the film image illustrates Larkin's point that the significance of infrastructure does not derive strictly—or even primarily—from the function it performs but arises from the form it presents to one's senses. After all, the elevated expressway encircling the Lagos marina is used to generate this panoramic gaze, such that the road's even pavement literally undergirds the visual pleasure with which the viewer beholds the modernist skyline of Lagos. However, even as the roadway generates the pleasure of speed and fluidity, it also holds the potential to produce the negative affect attached to inadequate provision, material degradation, and the inevitability of mechanical failure, as Lindsey Green-Simms so astutely explains,[25] and thereby serves, in the works of early Nigerian filmmakers, as an object that ambivalently contains both positive and negative registers of everyday urban experience.

As *Taxi Driver*'s opening sequence continues, it exits the expressway onto the mainland's rough roads, which offer a stronger sense of the challenges of the city's built environment. Tunde is soon navigating dusty streets where *danfo* buses disembark passengers in the middle of traffic, low-slung zinc roofs line the street, and open gutters divide the roadway from residential compounds. The ride comes to an end when the taxi breaks down and Tunde must pull onto the sandy shoulder. While he attempts in vain to push his taxi off the street, his passenger—a wealthy young woman named Moji—leaps from the vehicle and impatiently declares that she must now find another car and will not pay Tunde any fare. In the subsequent squabble over payment, they exchange insults and young working-class men gather to heap scorn on the arrogant woman. A wealthy man in a Volvo intervenes, pays Tunde his fare, and offers to drive Moji to her destination—a well-to-do neighborhood in Ikeja—while the growing crowd gawks at the pretensions of the elite. After the two depart, Tunde discovers the woman's forgotten bag of money and jewelry under the passenger seat and must decide whether to keep or return it. The exchange has the qualities of a narrative set piece, one staged to clarify a moral perspective and distill a specific moral lesson. Thus, in place of visual spectacle, the narrative picks up with a social and moral dilemma. The mode of address has suddenly switched and momentarily elevates the squabble between characters into a struggle of larger ethical principles. It prompts audiences to contemplate the conduct of the various parties, given the circumstances, and to ask what about this scenario they could apply to their own lives. In other words, *Taxi Driver* takes a sharp turn toward the dramatic terrain most familiar to the popular theater professionals behind the film's production and that of many other celluloid films of the period.

Karin Barber has discussed the resilience—cultural, material, individual, and moral—undergirding the Yoruba theater's activities and reminds us that such resilience existed in the face of tectonic social transformations.[26] Among the enduring values subtending the popular theater was the individual and collective will to self-betterment, which Barber describes as stronger than simply an aspiration for better living. In her words, the Yoruba traveling theater "had an affinity with the vigorous activities of local communities which founded town improvement unions, opened schools, and built roads and bridges without the support (let alone the instigation) of central government."[27] Interestingly, however, from the moment the Yoruba theater companies transitioned from a voluntary company of civic-minded Christian elites to professional salaried performers, the public perceived them in an entirely new light and no longer held much esteem for their efforts, according to Barber. The theater companies became viewed as groups of reprobates: drinkers, pot smokers, and womanizers. The actors were scorned for drumming, dancing, and playing around while others were hard at work supporting themselves, and in response, the actors tried adamantly to combat this disreputable image of their profession. One strategy was the production of plays that "adopted the speaking position of a preacher or teacher from which to edify the audience," a mode of address that soon evolved into a defining feature of the traveling theater's formal aesthetic.[28] Although no social mandate endowed the traveling theater performers with this special authority to speak on the correct path to "enlightenment/*ilàjú*," the plays were nonetheless received by audiences in this spirit. Audiences actively engaged the plays and remained especially attentive to "extract from the dramas the lessons which they could then apply to their own lives."[29] As the plot, characterization, and mode of address of Afolayan's *Taxi Driver* make evident, this benevolently pedagogical function of the popular theater survived when the plays migrated to screen and ensured that early Nigerian films served both as entertainment and edification.

The hostile exchange between Tunde and his passenger exemplifies a pedagogical mode of address. When Tunde's taxi breaks down and his passenger quarrels with him, refuses to pay, departs with a different motorist, and forgetfully leaves behind a large sum of money, it narrativizes the moral conundrum as an opportunity to debate and discern the correct conduct given the circumstances. Indeed, the narrative draws out the matter, allowing Tunde to take the money home temporarily, where his young son awaits him. The boy's mother, we learn, abandoned the home when the family's immiseration became unbearable and took up with a wealthier man named Chief Anjuwon, who paid the outstanding debts at her beer parlor. As Tunde and his son contemplate whether to keep or return the passenger's 2,000 naira, the neighbor drops by to announce that the electricity bill is overdue, despite the power outage, punctuating Tunde's dilemma. The film crosscuts Tunde's decision with Moji's reflections on the foolishness of her behavior, having now realized her mistake. As her friend pointedly states, the taxi driver has no reason to return the money, and thus Moji's squabble over the 15-naira taxi fare has cost her the 2,000 naira she left in the cab. (The working-class—and misogynistic—outlook of the popular theater is palpable throughout the staging of this social conflict and its ultimate resolution.) Tunde is tempted to use the money to pay his mounting bills, spoil his son, or buy back the loyalty of his wayward wife, but inevitably he does the honest thing and restores the money to its owner without expecting a reward. The ordeal shames Moji, prompts her to rethink her initial estimation of this man, and even sparks her romantic admiration for his simple way of life and honest values. From this point onward, the film centers around Tunde and Moji's unlikely love story, which along the way confronts several challenges that arise and subside episodically. Moji's friend strongly advises her not to become involved with an ordinary taximan, especially when she already has a respectable, wealthy suitor who enjoys the approval of her parents. Inevitably, her mother does discover the relationship and, feeling deeply scandalized, insists that as the daughter of the police commissioner and a successful businesswoman Moji must marry someone of equal or better status. Moji views this as marrying for money and refuses to do it, declaring instead her intention to marry an honest man. In fact, the choice between wealth and honesty is repeated several times. Although the mother remains adamantly opposed, the father reminds her that he was a mere constable when they married and has since risen to the rank of commissioner. The young taxi driver should enjoy the same benefit of the doubt, he reasons, and if the man's character has captured his daughter's heart, then he sees no reason to bar them from marriage.

Meanwhile, Tunde confronts his own tribulations. First his taxi becomes embroiled in a bizarre accident when a passenger, eager to get his pregnant wife to the hospital, takes the wheel and charges the vehicle into a crowded party that has spilled into the street. The subsequent police investigation presents another moral dilemma ultimately designed to reiterate Tunde's honesty, dignity, and innocence. Although cleared of wrongdoing in that incident, Tunde next becomes entangled in an occult murder, as the sole witness to an innocent woman's death by the powerful cultist Chief Anjuwon, the same wealthy man who seduced Tunde's wife. The chief uses his powerful reputation to evade the charges and even manages to have Tunde arrested for leveling slanderous accusations, but the protagonist is, in another patently pedagogical set piece, absolved of any wrongdoing. The humble taximan stands before the police commissioner—Moji's father, his future father-in-law—accused of fabricating the entire account of the murder, when the commissioner gets a phone call announcing that the car belonging to Chief Anjuwon has been discovered with the body of the woman in its trunk, and the police immediately set to rooting out the cultists. These episodes repeatedly underscore that, as long as his moral character is strong, Tunde's poverty cannot be viewed as a mark of shame. His modest composure is unshaken even as his wife abandons him, his social superiors deride him, and the police falsely accuse him, because strong character outstrips money, status, and power.

The taxi driver thus functions as an everyman figure whose line of work is uniquely intertwined with the city's social and spatial environment. By centering the film on this figure, Afolayan draws the city into the popular theater's ideological framework, one that generates pleasure through exhibitionistic displays of novelty as much as reflection on the individual's character, conduct, and moral outlook. To illustrate this point, I return to the bizarre car accident at the heart of *Taxi Driver*, a sequence that unfolds in the city streets and combines a spectacular disaster with a pedagogical set piece. A naming ceremony is underway to celebrate the birth of a wealthy man's child. The street has been occupied by the guests, who have set out tables and benches to feast and drink beer. Electric lights strung above the roadway illuminate the festivities while the sounds of an *apala* band blare from the sound system.

From its perch above the revelers, the camera pans over the dancers, who press naira notes onto one another's sweaty foreheads. It then cuts into close-ups of heads bobbing and hips gyrating to ensure that the pleasures of the party do not go unnoticed.

As Tunde arrives, his headlights illuminate the words "road closed" scrolled across the celebration's impromptu roadblock. He and his passenger spill from the vehicle and frantically begin clearing the street, explaining that the passenger's wife is in labor and must arrive at the hospital urgently. The wealthy man callously replies that he will not halt the naming ceremony just because someone needs passage to the hospital. The argument persists, the pregnant passenger dies, her husband discovers the lifeless body, and, overcome by emotion, he commandeers the taxi and plows the vehicle through the roadblock into the thick crowd of dancers. The casualties are numerous and gruesome, and when the police arrive, they arrest all parties involved: the bereft passenger, the wealthy man, and Tunde. With much head shaking and hand-wringing, the victims of the car accident are announced: nine dead, including the pregnant woman. The police commissioner, Moji's father, is called upon to settle such a grave matter. The three men are marched into the commissioner's office as the lieutenant explains each man's role: the taxi driver whose vehicle killed the people, the man who drove the taxi into the people, and the rich man whose naming ceremony obstructed the road to the hospital.

In this manner, the film sets forth a moral puzzle and invites viewers to discern for themselves the culpability of each involved. Who is at fault? How could each have acted differently? Other implied questions have clearer answers: does a person's wealth grant them special privileges over the city? Is the naming ceremony of the rich man's child more important than the birth of another man's child? The police commissioner, a natural figure of didactic authority, delivers the verdict: everyone knows that it is illegal to block the city's streets, and no one is above the law, so the rich man's selfish behavior is therefore responsible for the deaths of his party guests, the wife, and the unborn child. In effect, the enjoyments of the wealthy man (who the performers continually refer to as *olówó*, or rich man) bear a human cost for the bereft husband, a cost further compounded by his delirious decision to speed the taxi into the crowded street party. While the loss of human life represents a tremendously grave moral consequence, perhaps the ultimate price for wickedness, these are the dramatic terms with which the popular theater prompted and underscored the moral lesson. What is more, here urban infrastructure provides the space in which to stage the film's commentary, and the specific occasions for the characters, social forces, and larger ethical principles jostle with one another. The film draws the city street into the center of the narrative frame, integrates the public and private use of the roadways into the film's moral, and thereby attends to those questions surrounding Lagosians' "massed relations to infrastructure—where it takes you, who uses it, and who is forced to live under or do without it."[30]

In a city of turbulent social relations—not to mention occult agents—what remains constant is Tunde's honest character, his will to self-betterment, and his taxi, which becomes symbolic of the former two. The marriage of Tunde and Moji, marked by an elegant wedding ceremony sponsored by the taxi drivers' union, underscores the point that an honest livelihood, a family, and happiness are possible for the ordinary man willing to work and maintain his moral convictions. The newlyweds depart the Lagos City Hall within a magisterial Rolls Royce, flanked by dozens of yellow taxi cabs that escort them through the streets of Lagos Island toward the happy future that surely awaits them. Thus, visually speaking, the film returns to the same iconography and optimism with which we are introduced to Lagos in the opening sequence: automobiles, paved city streets, and the architecture of downtown Lagos. Ultimately, the film suggests, great things are possible in Lagos, if one can just keep one's moral bearings.

THE NATIONAL ARTS THEATRE

In the summer of 2018, I took a taxi to meet a filmmaker near Oshodi, and as we lurched through traffic, the driver and I began to discuss film in Nigeria before Nollywood. Mr. Wasiu was an elderly Yoruba man, as taxi drivers in Lagos often are, and I supposed he belonged to the generation who witnessed the rise of the professional popular theater troupes and their transition to film. I was eager to learn what he recalled, if anything, about the films released by the theater companies, especially Ade Afolayan's *Taxi Driver*, so I inquired. Had he seen Ade Love's movie about a taxi man? He had. I was, of course, fascinated to know what Mr. Wasiu, today a taxi driver, would remember about the film *Taxi Driver* and whether he would share his insights into aspects of the film that I had perhaps neglected or failed to understand. When I asked him what he remembered about seeing *Taxi Driver*, he responded, "There was AC." I paused, puzzled. As it turned out, Mr. Wasiu saw *Taxi Driver* screen at the

National Arts Theatre, the city's preeminent exhibition space with amenities like air-conditioned halls, cushioned seats, and a large sound system, thus the best venue to witness local cinema. Intriguingly, more than any detail of the story, what Mr. Wasiu remembered of viewing the film was the ambience of the theater in which it screened, which serves as a reminder that what made these films memorable—and meaningful—was not only the language, culture, and messages embedded in the story, or the attractions contained within the frame, but also the spaces in which audiences viewed them.

What Mr. Wasiu remembered of the National Arts Theatre, the feel of the air-conditioned exhibition hall, is what Brian Larkin terms infrastructure's "production of ambient experience."[31] We often understand a movie theater as oriented around the screen, the visual representations that appear on its surface, and the world the film thereby constructs, to which the viewer becomes sutured by the surrounding cinematic "apparatus." However, this conceptualization of cinema and its aesthetics contains a representational bias—for lack of a better term—that privileges the interpretation and critique of the meaning of a film, which is presumed to unfold in the spectator's engagement with the film's images and sounds, and *not* the exhibition space itself. Such an approach erases the ambient environment of the theater and what is commonly called the cinema experience, which also holds sway over the spectator's bodily engagement with a film and even exists prior to the psychic or cognitive process where "meaning" in the representational sense is forged. From a nonrepresentational perspective, the architectural design, infrastructure, technologies, and amenities of an exhibition hall produce experiences that spectators find memorable and meaningful. Larkin's argument, for example, draws upon the notion of aesthetics as the experience of embodied presence itself rather than a mental apprehension of representations. Moreover, embodied experience is "governed by the ways infrastructures produce the ambient conditions of everyday life: our sense of temperature, speed, florescence, and the ideas we have associated with these conditions."[32] Therefore, infrastructures and technologies such as a steady power supply and an air conditioner are not primarily symbols or signs of modernity but rather the systems that generate the "sensing of modernity" to which Larkin refers.[33] From this vantage point, the memory of the chilled air that circulated throughout the National Arts Theatre during local film premieres attended by literally thousands of viewers represents an aesthetic recollection of Nigerian cinema. Furthermore, it underscores that, despite the important formal and cultural features shared by the plays and films of the popular theater companies, what made these films distinct from theater is not simply the film medium but also its mode of exhibition, which can take place in small settings with a white cloth and a 16-mm projector or the main hall of the theater amid a crowd of five thousand. Although Nigerian filmmakers screened their films in a variety of venues around the Southwest, some makeshift and others formal, every filmmaker hoped to premiere at the National Arts Theatre, the supreme benchmark of local cinematic experience (Afolabi Adesanya, personal communication, August 11, 2018).

The National Arts Theatre was originally commissioned to serve as the central staging point for Festac '77. The enormous international exhibition, held in Lagos from January 15 to February 12, represented a profound historic convergence of people and ideas from every corner of Africa and its diaspora and, according to organizers, staged Africa's passage into a modern, progressive future. As the organizers proclaimed, the festival aimed to "restore the link between culture, creativity, and mastery of modern technology and industrialism . . . to endow the Black Peoples all over the world with a new society, deeply rooted in our cultural identity, and ready for the great scientific and technological task of conquering the future."[34] The event sought to recount the past so as to better face the future. Recent histories of the festival from the perspective of attendees contain moving personal memories of the connection that was inspired by the cultural and artistic performances celebrating the heritage and identity of people of African descent hailing from countries across the continent and the diaspora.[35]

The festival also left a significant material and symbolic imprint on Lagos, through the production of new spaces and spatial relations within the city. The Tafawa Balewa Square parade grounds were renovated to accommodate a portion of the opening ceremonies, while an entire neighborhood dubbed Festac Town was erected to host the festival's foreign participants. Once the foreign delegates departed, the fifteen-thousand-unit neighborhood was meant to alleviate Lagos's chronic housing shortage and become a permanent, fully integrated district of the city, which is why its planners included detailed schemes for light industry and social use beyond festival activities.[36] Finally, there was the National Arts Theatre itself, erected atop the swampy terrain of Iganmu and amid the flyovers and interchanges that connect several branches of the city's network of expressways. In this sense, the National Arts Theater exists at the literal intersection of cinema and the city. The structure rises precipitously above the mainland skyline, dominated as it is by low-rise construction, and offers a landmark visible from surroundings neighborhoods.

Symbolically inscribed across the surface of the National Arts Theatre is a modernist architectural vision of this restorative link between the nation's cultural roots and its desired status within the world. Its circular structure resembles "a cosmographic wheel radiating out through architectural 'spokes' and superhighways to embrace the modern world," as Andrew Apter observes in his gloss of the structure's discursive signs. "Viewed from the outside, the Theatre's facade looked like a giant crown rising out of the earth, as if linking the wealth of the land—its chthonic traditions and subterranean oil—with national territory and sovereignty."[37] The national coat of arms that perches fixed above the theater's main entrance combines with the roof's saddle curve and the circular base of the structure to create an architectural design resembling the military cap of Nigeria's head of state, General Obasanjo.[38] Below the coat of arms, sculpted black figures populate the ring that encircles the theater's vertical concrete spokes. Above one entrance, this crown-like ring features the carved image of the globe cleaved in two, split along the Atlantic Ocean with North America and South America and the Caribbean on one side and Africa on the other. Situated between this doubled image of the world rests the trademark Benin ivory mask, the historic icon of the event.

The ambitious size of Festac '77 called for an exhibition hall of equal proportion, one that would also embody the celebration of a Black cultural renaissance grounded in tradition and oriented toward an African modernity.[39] The enormous structure housed two cinema halls with the capacity to seat nearly seven hundred viewers each and a main exhibition hall that could host as many as five thousand visitors. Each hall was outfitted with 16-mm, 35-mm, and even 70-mm projectors, as well as an array of specialized lights, plush seating, and indeed central air-conditioning. Outside the hall were lounges, a large foyer, snack bars, and VIP rooms, of course, all powered by a high-capacity electric generator on-site.[40] During the festival, the theater bustled with performances and displays of so-called traditional art forms—dance, sculpture, and folk art—as well as modern works—photography, contemporary dance, and film—under one roof. Films screened every day of the festival in Cinema Hall I and II from four o'clock in the afternoon until midnight, with titles like Sembene Ousmane's *Xala* (1974) and Daniel Kamwa's *Pousse-Pousse* (1976) appearing on the program. However, Nigerian filmmakers like Ola Balogun and Eddie Ugbomah were excluded from the festival, on the basis that, as *independent* filmmakers, they lacked official standing to represent the nation's accomplishments in cinema. Sanya Dosunmu, spokesman of the Nigerian Film Producers Association, publicly objected, but to no avail.[41] The honor of representing Nigeria's cinema at the festival went to the state-sponsored Federal Film Unit, which at the time had produced and therefore screened only one feature film and a collection of public health documentaries.[42] One can only speculate whether international delegates flocked to attend a documentary on tuberculosis mitigation rather than enjoy the many other festival activities.

There were other more glaring contradictions surrounding the National Arts Theatre, as well, including the oft-cited fact that, intriguingly, the building is a reproduction of the National Palace of Culture and Sports in Verna, Bulgaria. In fact, the state had a pattern of commissioning public works whose architectural design was borrowed directly from Europe, especially the Eastern Bloc.[43] The builders incorporated indigenous friezes and sculptures into the design of the theater in an effort to stamp an imprint of national culture upon the building, a literal facade of Nigerianness, despite the inconsistency that this implied. However, no one I spoke with about their recollections of the theater during Festac '77 and subsequent years expressed a fundamental rejection of the building, or even outrage, over this fact, a reminder that the politics of these built spaces are not simply encoded into their surfaces in discursive signs, once and for all. Instead, architecture and infrastructures "generate complicated emotional investments that induce a range of sometimes counterintuitive responses and distinct, if ephemeral sensibilities,"[44] and this can include the ambivalent, concurrent feelings of promise and failure.

In the years after Festac '77, the National Arts Theatre served as the distributor-cum-exhibitor of the federal government but also proved to be an ideal exhibition space for independent local films. Given the building's modern amenities and unmatched seating capacity, filmmakers like Hubert Ogunde, Ola Balogun, Ade Afolayan, and Eddie Ugbomah took pains to ensure their films premiered at the theater. The 1979 debut of Ogunde's first film, *Aiye* (dir. Ola Balogun), is one legendary example. The film screened at the theater three times a day from December 17 until December 26, as was customary during public holidays, and attracted audiences of unprecedented size and enthusiasm by some reports. As one film reviewer with the *Daily Times* wrote, "A crowd of mammoth proportion besieged the National Theatre during the recent screening of 'Aiye.' In fact, damages done to the Theatre by the last day's crowd will take quite some time to repair" (Agiobu-Kemmer, *Daily Times*, January 10, 1980, 12). It was evident to Ministry of Culture officials, the custodians of the theater, that indigenous cinema attracted an immense popular presence and large box office revenues because the events are highlighted in the theater's quarterly report to the public. One such report documents in great detail and with a tone of pride the number of screenings, the size of audiences, and a brief review of the films. In 1982, the theater hosted three "indigenous" screenings, Baba Sala's *Orun Mooru* (dir. Ola Balogun), Ola Balogun's *Money Power*, and Ghanaian director Kwaw Ansah's *Love Brewed in the African Pot* (1981). Under the auspices of the Nigerian Film Distribution Company (NFDC), the National Arts Theatre screened sixty-two films that year, but fully one-third of their box office revenue came from these three local films alone. Revenue from these films totaled almost 125,000 naira as compared to the 172,000 naira that the NFDC generated screening forty-two films from its own holdings, which included foreign films acquired after the nationalization of the American-based distributor American Motion Picture Export Company, Africa (AMPECA), as I discuss below. By contrast, for two weeks, more than eight hundred viewers entered the cinema halls of the theater each day to see *Money Power*, while *Orun Mooru* turned out some fifteen hundred viewers a day for seven straight days. The report concludes by gently exhorting Nigerian audiences to continue to patronize local cinema and thus demonstrate their favor for "any good African film" over "its foreign counterpart."[45] As these figures indicate, audiences gravitated to local films in larger numbers and with greater enthusiasm than imported films.

However, the theater's prestige began to fade as government mismanagement slowly eroded the institution's symbolic value as the edifice of national culture. Before the enactment of the 1972 Indigenization Decree, AMPECA distributed the usual Hollywood fare on behalf of major studios like MGM, Columbia, United Artists, and 20th Century Fox, as well as Hong Kong, Italian, and Indian films.[46] The relationship between the distributor and the exhibitor was so successful that when the Indigenization Decree came to pass, the Ministry of Culture saw fit to purchase AMPECA and nationalize it. The distributor was renamed the Nigerian Film Distribution Company even though, as Afolabi Adesanya pointed out to me, the NFDC inherited the imported film stock from AMPECA and had little choice but to screen the films on hand. The resulting arrangement, in which the nation's finest cinema halls would every week publicize and screen American B films like *Jaguar Lives*, was an embarrassment to proud Nigerians (*Daily Times,* January 11, 1980, 19) and even "injurious to Nigerians" generally (Mgbejume, *Daily Times,* December 8, 1979, 21). One particularly egregious example involved the screening of *Mandingo* (1975), an American film that romanticizes plan-tation slavery and presents semipornographic depictions of sex between slave and master, which prompted one anonymous Lagosian to submit an editorial to the *Daily Times* titled "Theatre of Insults" that declares "something strange is going on these days at the National Theatre."

> Right now there is an offensive film called "Mandingo" being shown at the Theatre. If there was ever any film that deliberately set out to denigrate and malign black culture, this film is it. And yet it is being shown, apparently with the blessing of government functionaries. . . . A serpent's colours may be "beautiful," but you do not therefore know why the National Theatre, which is supposed to be the bastion of black pride, should be converted into a place where black people may be insulted with the blessing of government officials. ("Theatre of Insults," *Daily Times,* January 20, 1980, 5)

That the nation's greatest cinema hall should screen imported films outraged local filmmakers, as well, and bolstered complaints that the theater and NFDC were uninterested in fostering local productions.[47] However, suspicions of bad faith failed to acknowledge the distinction between the theater's role as an exhibitor and the NFDC's purview as distributor (Afolabi Adesanya, personal communication, August 11, 2018). Nonetheless, neither institution took it upon itself to buy the rights to Nigerian films, which severely limited the role of the theater and the distributor in the marketing of Nigerian film. Local distributors simply did not wish to buy outright Nigerian films from the producers.[48]

Throughout the 1980s the fortunes of the theater continued to decline, due in large part to an impasse between various branches of the government with competing claims to the authority to manage operations (and thereby revenue), as well as neglect for the general maintenance of such a large facility. The venue remains open to public and private events today, although of dramatically pared-down scale by comparison to the past. For decades, the five-thousand-seat main exhibition hall has sat shuttered following the death of two moviegoers and the maiming of seven others in a stampede in May 1992. As the story goes, the box office oversold tickets to a screening of Hubert Ogunde's much-loved film *Ayanmo* (Destiny, 1988), which left the main hall at overcapacity and terribly overheated, at which point "the poorly-maintained and overworked chillers in the hall gave way."[49] The explosion caused by the short-circuited central air conditioner startled spectators, but it was the fear of fire that sparked the stampede. The journalist, activist, and culture critic Jahman Anikulapo recounts the event in detail in his evocative piece "The Death Metaphor."

> A sudden burst of confusion overwhelmed the belly of the vast hall, yielding a cacophony of cries and shrieks of agony, furiously stampeding feet and then . . . blackout! In no time, the ambience of the hall which moments ago had been a spot for fun had become a site of anguish. In the aftermath of the pandemonium, nine tiny bodies lay on the ground, while the fumes of sweat and blood ruled the atmosphere.[50]

If the built environment of the cinema hall produces the ambient experience of modernity, with its associated sentiments of pleasure and pride, the violent breakdown of those same infrastructures can generate strong fears, anxieties, and pain. Importantly, it also produces a sense of injustice and the view that the responsibility for such failures lies with those who rule. As Anikulapo eloquently states in his assessment of the tragedy as a metaphor for the nation, "Rulership is occult, government is secrecy and the people are stranded at the borders of national wellbeing."[51]

Periodically, in recent years, rumblings in the press about incipient plans to privatize the cultural monument have drawn impassioned protest from advocates of local arts and culture, as well as from the community of artists who continue to produce and market works on the grounds. In this sense, the theater remains a point of condensation where frustrations over official waste, corruption, and neglect have accumulated. However, others have called for restoration efforts to be arranged so that the theater can again become a crossroads of arts and culture, especially in light of its historical significance. That history includes the government's effort to give concrete form to an idea of African modernity, as well as national development, by erecting such massive public works projects. However, far more importantly, the building's history includes the personal memories of ordinary Nigerians, for whom the National Arts Theatre fulfilled more immanent and modest expectations: to take in a film—a Nigerian film if one was fortunate, to sing along with the popular musicians moonlighting as movie stars, to see new styles of dress and ways of speaking, to hear a familiar moral articulated in a new way, to share a social space with other moviegoers, to sink into the softness of a cushioned seat and feel the crisp, cool air circulating. To enjoy what Nigerian cinema and the city had to offer.

OIL WEALTH AND OCCULT POWER

One of the films that screened at the National Arts Theatre to great success was *Orun Mooru*, a collaborative production of comedian Moses Olaiya Adejunmo, most widely known by his stage name "Baba Sala," and director Ola Balogun. The film narrates the fortunes and misfortunes of Baba Sala, an electronics dealer who made good money selling imported television sets, radios, and electric fans but loses everything in a fraudulent get-rich-quick scheme and struggles through several hapless attempts to regain his footing in the new petro-economy. The narrative unfolds between the village, where life is slow but relatively stable, and the city, where money is earned and lost. The transition between spaces is triggered by the protagonist's chance encounter with an old acquaintance, Adisa, who has since become a jet-set businessman. When Adisa's Volkswagen breaks down on a rural dirt road, it is Baba Sala who discovers and assists him to start the car. At first, neither recognizes the other, and Adisa remarks on how far Baba Sala has sunk since his days as a successful marketer making a good living from his trade. Baba Sala explains that he lost all his property when he allowed himself to be swindled by a fraudster claiming to know a money ritual involving oil barrels (which I discuss below). Adisa takes pity and loans him a thousand naira to rebuild his life.

With this gift in his pocket and a determination in his heart, Baba Sala sets out for the marketplace in Lagos to reestablish his trade in electronics, but soon after arriving in the city, a band of pickpockets relieve the foolish man of his cash. Crushed by the loss, Baba Sala turns to suicide, comically failing several attempts before flinging himself off a bridge. As he plunges into the water below, the character passes a threshold into another metaphysical realm of magically endowed spirits, and the film itself takes a metaphysical turn characteristic of Yoruba theater and cinema. A female spirit in the *ilé ayò* (house of joy) offers Baba Sala two magic eggs and the instructions that he should break the first egg to release an unearthly amount of wealth and break the second egg when he finishes spending that money. The protagonist returns miraculously to the world of ordinary humans and discovers a mansion, a fleet of automobiles, and two young wives waiting for him. When he breaks the first egg, it releases heaps of naira. Baba Sala immediately puts his extravagant riches to work, hosting a lavish party with music and food. Adisa attends to celebrate his friend but also to caution moderation and thrift. Despite his friend's warnings, Baba Sala greedily breaks the second egg to redouble his wealth, but the egg instead unleashes a monstrous ogre, who viciously seizes the protagonist. The film cuts away from the struggle as Baba Sala wakes from this nightmare and learns that his suicide attempt failed when fishermen pulled him unconscious from the water and carried him home to recover. At the narrative's close, we leave Baba Sala where we first found him, down and out in a small village outside Lagos.

Moses Olaiya Adejumo released *Orun Mooru* through his Moses Olaiya Alawada International Group, the company that also produced and distributed photo-magazines and audio recordings of his theater performances.[52] He recruited Ola Balogun as director, coproducer, and cowriter and presumably drew upon the crew and technicians at the television facilities in Ibadan, where some of the production took place. Although *Orun Mooru* was Adejunmo's first feature-length film, his Alawada Theatre troupe had previously utilized film in live performances to portray spectacular episodes that could not be reproduced on stage. In fact, Adejumo revealed in one interview that his first experiment with film projection during performances utilized the footage that became the suicide scene in *Orun Mooru*.[53] The bulk of Alawada Theatre's plays revolved around Adejumo's comic persona, Baba Sala, a man notoriously tight-fisted, lecherous, and lazy but still able at times to play the trickster. As Tunde Lakoju writes in his thorough review of the actor's career, "He was always the poor applicant, houseboy, messenger, laborer, always exploited and cannibalized by horrible social, political and economic systems."[54] The same describes his character in *Orun Mooru,* who, for instance, sings absurd love ballads to a woman who, unbeknownst to him, is deaf, and, later in their amusing living arrangement, he suffers both her dull wits and fistfuls of her thumps and jabs to comedic effect. While the performance that Baba Sala delivers may seem foolish, the wisdom his story imparts is not, and although the narrative is not a morality tale per se, like any good Yoruba story, it does have a moral.

Important narrative conventions in *Orun Mooru* also suggest substantial continuity with the theater troupe's materials and mode of narration. Especially after the film departs the village it turns concertedly to a treatment of work and wealth in ways that correspond closely with characters and narrative tropes in popular theater that, as Barber argues, capture the social and cultural implications of the new petro-capitalist economy. The figure of the good rich man, for instance, became integral to Yoruba plays that dealt with oil wealth. According to Barber, this stock character stood for well-founded prosperity and thus established the distinction between honest and false riches, the latter achieved by spurious or ill-founded means, often money magic or robbery.[55] In *Orun Mooru*, Adisa's character embodies the figure of the good rich man, the nouveau riche whose hard work, signaled by his business connections to Ghana and, indirectly, by his wife's resourcefulness managing her own tailor shop, legitimates the couple's accumulation of wealth and thus his individual self-aggrandizement. He dresses fashionably and travels freely, both by airplane and by automobile. A man of some means, he married and fathered two children, but he had no more children or wives than this because he values thrift and lives within his means. His character stands for the fulfillment of the dream that during this period drew many to Lagos—to build one's fortune on honest work in an economy full of opportunities and to enjoy the comforts and enjoyments that prosperity made possible. Barber suggests that the figure of the good rich man offers an important release of ideological pressure in the sense that his presence holds open space for the long-standing value within Yoruba culture placed on enrichment through work, self-reliance, and moderate accumulation. More than the mere embodiment of these principles, Adisa is the voice of good sense who benevolently counsels Baba Sala and offers him a second chance at his trade in electronics. This relationship was the stock scenario of the Alawada Theatre's stage productions, according to Lakoju, who writes that "Adisa, his friend, is always the top executive who comes to his aid or to his ransom whenever he is in trouble."[56] Intriguingly, in our conversation about the film, Kunle Afolayan remarked to me that in staged performance his father, Ade Afolayan, played Adisa's role albeit under the character name Amoda, an *oriki* praise name that roughly means "the creator knew well when he made this child." Thus, the good rich man is also charitable, willing to bail out a friend whose ambitions for wealth outstripped his willingness to work for them. It was, after all, Baba Sala's drive to acquire that led him to lose everything, a fact that underscores the film's injunction against overreaching appetite.

In a remarkable scene, Baba Sala falls for a scam involving oil, money, and ritualistic magic, a combination and scenario that seems to spring directly from the imaginary of popular rumor and merits close attention. Baba Sala owned an electronics shop; made a stable business of selling electric fans, televisions, and radios; and could even afford to hire a clerk to assist. After working a stint, the young clerk disappears without notice, only to return a month later driving a new automobile, wearing finely tailored lace, and bearing gifts for his former employer. Baba Sala must know the young man's secret and, after ruling out stealing and smuggling, demands to know how one could amass such riches in such a short time. The young friend alludes to a man who taught him a new kind of work and offers to introduce Baba Sala. Although the audience easily recognizes the swindle afoot, our greedy protagonist eagerly assents, and the film cuts to a den of scammers where the young man returns to inform his "boss" Adigun, an herbalist performed by visual artist Twin Seven Seven, that he has "hooked" a "good catch." Later, the herbalist offers Baba Sala a token demonstration of his power to multiply money and commands his victim to bring 100,000 naira so he might magically increase it one hundredfold. The old man sets straight to selling his shop, his wife's shop, and all his worldly possessions to come up with the required sum and, following the herbalist's instructions, places the money inside six empty oil drums set apart in an empty room. His wife, Iya Sala, recognizes the speciousness of the ritual and admonishes him against it, but the greedy man cannot be dissuaded. Adigun calls for a hen, a snail, a bolt of cloth, and a duck, a request that Baba Sala happily fulfills. Adigun explains that he will stay in the room for seven days—as Baba Sala feeds him lavish meals, of course—to work the magic ritual that will multiply the money. When Baba Sala returns, the barrels are covered in a white cloth, and the trickster warns that they must not be unveiled before the hen is killed and its blood sprinkled over the oil drums to ready the money for spending. Adigun departs, and the old man performs the prescribed ritual. When Baba Sala lifts the cloth from the oil drums he finds them filled to the brim with cash, each drum containing larger denominations, from five- to twenty-naira notes. But when he plunges his hands into the barrels of money, he immediately discovers the ruse. The barrels have been overturned and a small smattering of cash notes have been spread over bottom, creating the illusion of a barrel full of money. Realizing his disastrous misstep, Baba Sala collapses over the empty barrels in a slapstick gag that punctuates the tale of "magic" money.

The scene introduces the first mention of the occult economy that makes up an important dimension of the film's storyworld. Discussion of the occult by screen media scholars typically draws upon the work of cultural anthropologists like Jean Comaroff and John Comaroff, who contend that "the work of ritual—of building and contesting social realities by way of formally stylized, communicative active—is unceasing" rather than an isolated, exceptional event.[57] That is to say, the argument for the modernity of the occult rests, in part, upon the recognition of the ordinariness of such rituals in everyday life. The film's mobilization of the occult illustrates the drive to seek alternative rationalizations for the growing disparities between those who appeared to

Figure 4. Baba Sala discovers the magic money ruse in *Orun Mooru*

amass, suddenly, colossal sums of money without work and those for whom honest toil continued to produced little or no prosperity. Greed leads Baba Sala to gamble away a comfortable existence earned honestly, all on the spurious assurances of a ritualist who promises to produce money from magic, but the imaginative surplus the film invests in the portrayal of the occult activities suggests as much concern for the mechanisms as the morality of the money ritual. Jean Comaroff and John Comaroff write in their discussion of the modernity of occult rituals that "rites deploy such things as poetic tropes, juxtaposition, and redundancy to implode and (re)order experience. But precisely *how* they are mobilized to work their magic typically goes unexplored."[58] Thus, more than merely a system of signification, or an "idiom," rituals like witchcraft and sorcery consist of objects, bodies, and an ever-evolving collection of materials: the materiality of magic, so to speak. Nigerian screen media can only ever offer representations of the occult, meaning that what we see of its materiality remains subject to mediation. At the same time, close attention to the materials brought together in depictions of ritual can reveal the ways in which screen media appropriates—or absorbs—aspects of ritual signification in order to survive and grow with the world it represents.

In *Orun Mooru*, the sequence only proposes a ritual, albeit in elaborate detail, but that is enough for Baba Sala. That the proposed rites impoverish rather than enrich the protagonist does little to diminish its power to attract the imagination, to lure the narrative into a detour where it openly hypothesizes about how such rituals should look. The incorporation of oil drums provides the surest link between the film's magical conception of money and the mineral resource fueling the frenzy. Other elements, such as the hen's blood that unlocks the money for spending, share a certain logic with signifying economy of the occult elsewhere, which can often be composed of visceral objects and vital properties, like blood.[59] In video melodramas of the 1990s, the blood spilled would invariably be human and often that of the ritualist's own relative, which drives home more forcefully than *Orun Mooru* the gravity of the moral bargaining around wealth and human value. Here, however, the other ritual objects Baba Sala must collect are cash and the empty oil drums to hold the magic money, and yet there is nothing especially magical about the notion of creating wealth from oil, which this combination implies. The missing magical element would seem to be work itself, that unknown variable in the formula for the creation of oil wealth. And yet, what made the oil boom such a delirious time for Nigeria was the prevailing sense that, as Barber remarks, "none of the wealth is *produced* by labor; all of it is *acquired* from the petro-naira boom."[60] As a formal convention, the trope of the occult ritual narrates the abstraction of value under petro-capitalism, its seeming power to conjure value from nothing in the alchemy of oil.[61] The sequence treats speculation with suspicion and casts doubt on the dissociation of the consumption from the production of wealth, since there is little to trust in a form of wealth that one cannot produce oneself through tangible means.

Finally, the notion of a magically endowed man who lends his services in secret to the rich and powerful resembles the networks of patronage widely believed to channel the selective flow of petro-naira through society. Adigun's departure is peppered with allusions to his imminent visit to the oba, who requests he perform the same ritual, and Baba Sala has already witnessed the man's power to transform a store clerk into one of the town's notable businessmen. To be connected to Adigun is to enter the secret clique of the rich and powerful, a scenario that returns in video films like *Living in Bondage* (1993), *Rituals* (1997), and *Blood Money* (1997), which all envision rituals as the activity of secret societies, networks of individuals willing to bargain in blood (see chapter 3). Historically speaking, as the ruling class rushed to enrich themselves and erect political alliances, the government contract became the premier technology for distributing money from the central source of wealth to the nation's margins. In a grotesque satire of this process, Balogun's *Money Power* sneaks into the back room with the corrupt chief B. C. Ade as he negotiates his take of just such a government contract. People came to speak euphemistically of this distribution of wealth as the "national cake" from which each sought their own slice. As Barber explains:

> The intense competitiveness of this economy—with foreign firms competing for contracts, government officials competing for the power to award them, and middlemen competing for access to both foreign firms and government officials—has led to the formation of cliques and cartels, squeezing out small operators and concentrating the really big money in a very few hands.[62]

While social connections lent one an advantage in the competition for lucrative contracts, here the herbalist Adigun serves that function, the embodiment of a mysterious source of money and a connection with whom brings one into a network of patronage and permits one to tap into the circulation of wealth that has already enriched others in the know. As Baba Sala remarks to himself, "Those who do not know the source of wealth of others will always run in circles," a significant but ambivalent observation given the ill-fated outcome of his logic.

In the oil drum episode, the magic is promised but never performed, since the film reserves genuine manifestations of supernatural powers for the metaphysical realm in which the narrative later enters when out of destitution Baba Sala attempts suicide. Plunging from the concrete bridge, he is transported to a world beyond the domain of mere humans, a forest stalked by skeletons, ogres, and spirits, a metaphysical realm with a more substantial cultural genealogy than urban folktales, something more akin to the literary imagination of D. O. Fagunwa or Amos Tutuola. According to Jonathan Haynes, the film production relied on the Osun-Oshogbo Sacred Grove, with its neo-traditional sculpture and architecture, to recreate space of the underworld.[63] It is there Baba Sala encounters the monstrous figure of Death and explains that the world has become filled with troubles and he is therefore fed up with life. He welcomes death. But you cannot seek Death; rather, he seeks you in good time, and as the creature exclaims, if it is immediate death Baba Sala wants, he will find it at *ilé áyò*, the house of joy. "Go to the house of joy," he commands. "That is where you find instant death." There Baba Sala discovers a beautiful grove of young, attractive sirens and a female spirit who provides two magic eggs with the instructions for Baba Sala to break the first egg to release an unearthly amount of wealth and to break the second egg when he finishes spending that money.

The benevolent spirit transports Baba Sala back to the world of humans, sending with him two spirit maidens who are to become his wives. Baba Sala discovers that the spirits have worked miracles for him, providing him a gigantic compound with a plaque reading "Baba Sala's Lodge" scrolled across its ornate front gate. Within he discovers a luxurious white villa with a spacious parlor, a bar and bartender, a small fleet of Mercedes-Benz automobiles and his own chauffeur, and other trappings of the nouveaux riches. The final scene of the film depicts the resplendent party that Baba Sala hosts with his magic money in what Haynes has called "a wild ego fantasy."[64] The forward inertia of the narrative slows, settles in, and seems happy to linger here a while. The scene drags on as the camera works its gaze deliberately over the array of pleasures. As it does so, the film subtly transitions from a narrative to a nonnarrative mode of address, not unlike the visual attractions of *Taxi Driver*, discussed above, or a certain exhibitionism that Carmela Garritano identifies in early Ghanaian popular film.[65] That a similar festive scenario features in Balogun's *Money Power* and Afolayan's *Taxi Driver* suggests that Nigerian filmmakers of this period decidedly favored such sequences, especially to showcase musical performances of popular genres. All three films include musical numbers, in which characters sing atop a semi-diegetic soundtrack, songs that became spin-offs to be sold as stand-alone recordings, but such interludes remain situated within the narrative and its storyworld. In the final scene of *Orun Mooru*, the mediating barrier of narrative is lifted momentarily so that the entertainment—for which the filmmaker surely dedicated a significant portion of the film's budget—may simply be exhibited directly to the audience. Thus, it offers up the feel of witnessing a scene of consumption firsthand, which in itself is a form of consumption of the astonishing material manifestations of living large. In his contemporaneous review of the film, Niyi Osundare comments that the closing sequence falls ambivalently between "chastising crass materialism and encouraging it" and that "the vulgar opulence of Baba Sala Lodge, his glossy Mercedes, lavish furnished rooms, etc. look at times like veritable advertisement of debauched appetites."[66] Thus, the film creates an ambivalence in the face of Baba Sala's wished-for wealth that situates us somewhere between seduction and skepticism.

There is a Yoruba proverb that states ìsé kìí pani, ayò ni pànìyàn, or "Poverty never killed anyone. It's joy that kills." The wisdom of such a statement turns on the unexpected juxtaposition of delight and death, the looping around of pleasure into pain, an irony the film exploits for amusement, as well as instruction. Recall that, in his moment of deepest desperation, without two kobo to rub together, Baba Sala attempts to throw his life away to ease the misery of living, and yet his poverty cannot kill him, even if he wished it would. He must instead, as Death ironically remarks in an oblique echo of the proverb, "go to the house of joy. That is where you find instant death." And, indeed, the film's elaboration of this ethos results in Baba Sala's brush with an ecstatic death by excessive enjoyment, wherein the second magical egg promises ultimate pleasure but delivers its ultimate penalty. In the ironic logic of the proverb, a continuum from the worst pains of impoverishment to the greatest pleasures of wealth is folded back on itself. In similar fashion, Baba Sala's journey from modest means to pauperism, to unimaginable wealth and back again, traces the ostensible easy-come-easy-go nature of money under the fast capitalism of the oil boom.

In the end, the protagonist wakes from his reverie having been returned to the village, in a narrative reversal that resembles Baba Sala's own jolting recognition of the illusion of the oil drum ritual. Like the protagonist himself, who plunges his hands into the oil drums brimming with money only to discover the ruse, the sequence abruptly extricates the audience from its participation in the film's exhibitionist display; it pulls us, too, from drowning in the final flood of riches. Osundare takes the social message of the film to be a warning against "the perils of sudden, unearned wealth (*owó ojíji*) rampant in contemporary Nigeria, the menace of the pot-bellied, damasked (or laced) millionaires who 'spray' wads of naira like used tickets."[67] And yet, as Osundare himself observes, the idea and imagery of sudden wealth prove tenaciously seductive. In this sense, the lavish fantasy scenarios of the film stand in contradiction with the overt moral message about the distinction between hard-earned, legitimate wealth and the oil riches of fast capitalism. The naira notes on those barrels were merely surface, the appearance of a much larger quantity of money, which masked the emptiness of the oil drum. As this would suggest, one stands to lose a great deal—everything even— within this new petro-capitalist economic order. And yet, when work does not pay, other possibilities must be imagined.

VIDEO MARKET AS ARCHIVE

In 2013, I made regular visits to Idumota market, which at the time served as the wholesale distribution hub for Yoruba-language video films. In conversa-

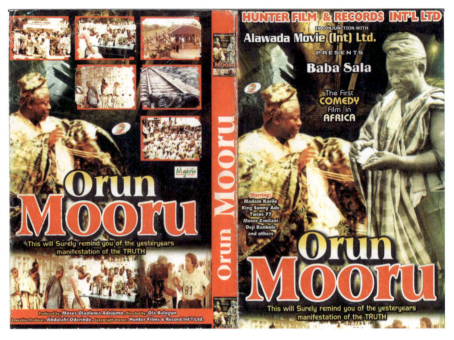

Figure 5. Pirated VCD of *Orun Mooru* circulating in video markets

tions with video vendors, I emphasized my interest in buying the oldest video films on hand but rarely discovered anything more than a decade old. During one visit, however, a vendor I regularly patronized approached me and mentioned he had found a very old film in the market, and when we reached his kiosk, he produced a copy of *Orun Mooru* on video CD.

Ironically, although virtually none of the celluloid films produced in the 1970s and 1980s are available in archives, university libraries, or distributors' holdings, a few have been preserved through piracy and the video market's incentive to supply a specific local public with movies that appeal.

It is widely known that Baba Sala's film was pirated while still completing its theatrical release, and that this nearly bankrupted the filmmaker. Details of the event are impossible to corroborate, but Baba Sala's son recounts a version that roughly matches the account I heard from a filmmaker involved in the film's production. Baba Sala's assistants brought a celluloid reel of *Orun Mooru* to screen at a cinema near Lagos, and afterward the cinema owner, speaking gushingly about the film, asked that his wife view it at their home (she observed *purdah* and did not visit cinemas). He promised to pay the assistants handsomely and to return the film promptly, but when the assistants came for the film the following day, the man and the film were gone. Sometime later, a videocassette of *Orun Mooru* emerged, confirmation that the film had been pirated. Although difficult to conclude decisively, the video CD that I purchased at Idumota does appear—and sound—like the video recording of a projected celluloid film. That the film continues to circulates among audiences today because it has been preserved by the impulses of the video market contains a telling irony. The film survives because a celluloid production was video recorded, pirated, and sold in the marketplace, which bankrupted the producer but also preserved *Orun Mooru* to be digitized and resold in Idumota three decades later buried among the piles of video films created by a Yoruba-language film industry that owes a cultural and aesthetic debt to the popular theater and figures like Baba Sala. In this sense, the marketplace represents an archive, piracy a means of preservation, and the video film industry a living legacy of the popular theater, which should underscore the *openness* that enables this cultural object to *endure*. It illustrates that the film continues to resonate with a Yoruba-speaking public for whom it is possibly a nostalgic reminder of a moment in local media history, or a taste of the humor of a cherished recurrent character, or perhaps an articulation of preserved cultural values.

The preexisting genres, modes of address, characters, and story lines of the Yoruba theater proved to be powerful creative resources for envisioning the transformation of work and wealth in Lagos and their implications. The explicit production of scenarios of moral instruction, as seen in *Taxi Driver* and *Orun Mooru*, represents both the viability of a cultural aesthetic and mode of address and the durability of these ethical principles and the appetite for such instructive insights. Of course, the effort to enlighten audiences pragmatically complemented the drive to entertain. However, it would be a mistake to view the visual attractions and sonic performances of these films as mere ephemera, something that fades in memory, as opposed to the meaningfulness of the moral lesson that resonates culturally and thereby endures. Ephemeral pleasures also generate meaningful experiences that etch themselves on individual and collective memory. The sequences of songs and visuals of Lagos in *Taxi Driver* and *Orun Mooru* offer pleasurable moments for the audience's vicarious consumption, but those enjoyments were not locked within the frame of the film. Spaces of exhibition, such as upscale cinema halls and the National Arts Theatre itself, unlocked these pleasures for the direct enjoyment of the enormous audiences that attended Yoruba film screenings in Lagos. But as much as it created embodied experiences of modernity's promise, the theater itself also embodied certain failures of Nigerian modernity and remains marked thus in public perception by an ambivalence surrounding what works and what falls apart. As with the films themselves, this ambivalence is not simply anxious or uncertain but, rather, productive, generating an elasticity able to maneuver and accommodate the unanticipated.

CHAPTER 2

Television's City Situations

Across much of the scholarship on cinematic cities, one preconception remains especially prevalent, namely, the notion that a city exists *out there*, amid its built spaces, infrastructures, and commodity flows, and that cityscapes are composed principally—if not exclusively—of exterior spaces. It is true that, in many West African cities, public space provides the staging ground for countless interactions, each marked by particular performative scripts that are themselves the stuff of urbanism, as Ato Quayson eloquently demonstrates with reference to Oxford Street, Accra.[1] And there is, indeed, an undeniable, singular energy in Lagos's streets and public spaces where innumerable activities pile up and jostle for room. This being so, it is surprising that video films produced in or about Lagos do not present more visually recognizable images of the city, especially those produced during the 1990s before production was dispersed eastward to Onitsha and Asaba. One might expect, for instance, that productions would venture into the streets to showcase the distinctive spaces of Lagos: the marketplaces, motor parks, bridges, waterways, skyline, and streets. And yet, as Wole Ogundele notes, early Nollywood rarely offers more than several similar aerial shots of the Lagos Island skyline, the freeway overpasses, the view across Five Cowries Creek, or the wide avenues of upscale neighborhoods.[2] This repertoire of establishing shots is so common that Jonathan Haynes wonders aloud whether it is the same stock footage recycled across films.[3] The city's public spaces quickly give way to the principal focus of attention, the action and dialogue that unfolds indoors, in private, typically between characters with some sort of established relationship, not among strangers on the street, as I discuss further in chapter 3. What movement through urban space there is generally involves editing from one setting to the next, a visual leap that more closely approximates the television viewer's change of channel than the flaneur's cinematic ramble through the arcade.[4] The result is a claustrophobic repetition of interior settings—an upper-middle-class parlor, the office, the occasional restaurant, and the gateway as it swings wide to permit an advancing Mercedes—while the urban space beyond the compound walls remains an enigma. In fact, given the disproportionate amount of time that mainstream video films spend in the sitting room or parlor, one should be forgiven for the lingering sense of having been there before—something like spatial déjà vu.

The representational aversion to public space stems in equal parts from the practical constraints on production and the tradition of representation that Nollywood inherited from television. Historically, the medium of television tends to render a city setting in bits and pieces before plunging into dialogue where the principal action of televisual narrative unfolds. "This mélange of elements—studio-shot interiors, limited location-shot exteriors, and place-identifying title sequence—are," as Charlotte Brunsdon asserts, "the characteristic components of the twentieth-century television city."[5] Along the same lines, establishing shots of Lagos from above, I would contend, serve an expositional role more as invocations of location than visual representations of a "cinematic city" and present—alongside other televisual techniques—an especially productive departure from the dominant focus of city/cinema scholarship on built form as the principal visual signifier of "citiness," disrupting the common fixation on a narrow set of cinematic tropes, especially the frequent analogizing of the flaneur's street-level movements. The particular history of representational and production practices in Nigerian screen media industries—film, television, and video film—liberates the representation of Lagos from what Esi Dogbe cleverly terms the "edifice complex" of modernist urban imaginaries elsewhere.[6] In the same vein, this chapter examines Lagos as a television city—and pointedly not a cinematic city—in the sense both of how video films represent the city and of where this mode of representation originated. This claim is grounded in the historical continuity between Nigerian television and Nollywood video films, as evident in the formal attributes of television programs whose production techniques appear to have been subsequently adopted by video film producers, which would account for Nollywood's particularly televisual rendition of Lagos on-screen.

Television played a fundamental role in shaping how, in later years, Nollywood would imagine and represent Lagos. In Jonathan Haynes's estimation, "the most important factor that enabled and shaped Nollywood was Nigerian television."[7] The decade preceding the advent of video film was an exceptionally fertile period for the Nigerian Television Authority (NTA), according to Haynes, who notes that the first generation of video film producers accrued experience in screenwriting and production at the NTA, training on television sets rather than film productions. Akin Adesokan has also discussed the continuity of personnel and expertise that carried over from Nigerian television to video film and notes the distinction between these producers and others who transitioned from Yoruba celluloid films into video film.[8] This all remains in keeping with the eminent television producer Segun Olusola's vital claim that, historically speaking, Nigeria reversed the supposed primacy of cinema over television.[9] In Nigeria, television came first, and, according to Olusola, it did not follow cinema in form, nor was it perceived as the imitative, mass-mediated cousin of cinema. It should, therefore, come as no surprise that, when Nollywood began training its camera on Lagos, its producers drew their technical proficiency and stylistic inspiration from this strong televisual tradition.

Although distinctions between the specificity of television, cinema, and popular theater should be noted, it was not unusual in Nigeria for crew and performers to work across media. Ogundele describes how Yoruba popular dramatists like Hubert Ogunde and Duro Ladipo initially turned to television to mitigate the uncertainties and risks of continuously taking a show on the road.[10] The security of a contract for a standard weekly thirty-minute slot, the comparatively large audiences that television delivered, and the prestige of the new technology itself made it an appealing platform to debut new plays or rework the old repertoire.[11] Naturally, actors outside the Yoruba tradition like Jab Adu and Sanya Dosunmu found their skills transferable between television and film. Similarly, the technical personnel called upon by filmmakers like Ola Balogun were on temporary leave from their steady job at the NTA. One of the most notable examples of this would be Tunde Kelani, who was selected as a Western Nigeria Television Service (WNTV) cameraman after a rigorous vetting and later used his own savings to put himself through a year of formal instruction at the London International Film School. When Vincent Maduka, the director general of the NTA, learned of this, he insisted that the television station fund the completion of his degree, training that later made Kelani a valued asset on film productions of Baba Sala's *Orun Mooru*, Hubert Ogunde's *Jaiyesimi*, and Afolabi Adesanya's *Vigilante*, among others. Of course, unlike film and theater, the regional and federal television stations could count upon the resources and privileges that came with state sponsorship.

Famously dubbed "First in Africa," WNTV was founded in Ibadan in 1959, a year before Independence. This was followed closely by the Eastern Region's unveiling of its own television station in Enugu, Eastern Nigeria Broadcast Corporation Television (ENTV), as part of the Independence celebrations on October 1, 1960. The Northern Region responded in March 1962 by launching Radio Television Kaduna (RTK), a sequence of events that suggests the "regional one-upmanship" with which the stations were erected as symbols of political prestige.[12] A month later, in April 1962, Lagos acquired its own first television station, the Nigerian Television Service (NTS), which was established by the federal government in cooperation with American NBC International, a partnership that endured for five years.[13] Despite discrepant accounts of the number of television viewers, there is no disagreement that the majority of the nation's viewers were located in or near cities. "Television stations were very few," Ogundele writes, painting a modest portrait, "and their reach did not extend far beyond the capitals in which they were located."[14] Along the same lines, Esan notes that "services required for television reception were largely limited to urban areas. The television sets were expensive, available only to those on higher income or public servants who had access to the government-supported television loan facility. Both groups were characteristically to be found in urban settlements."[15] Therefore, despite government officials' aspirations that television should generate sweeping changes regionally and nationally, the broadcast range of most television stations was limited to major urban centers and their immediate surroundings largely due to inadequate infrastructure.

Because television was initially an arm of the government intended to extend their message to audiences around their respective regions, news reports and educational content formed the bulk of initial television programing. In the East, for instance, the program *Tales by Moonlight* adapted folktales that conveyed moral values and practical lessons, while in the Southwest *Kaaro Oojire* and *Agborandun* sought to instill in audiences an awareness of rights, responsibilities, and cultural heritage.[16] The founding decree of the NTA tasked all stations with the promotion of citizenship and a shared sense of patrimony, stipulating that television must "operate in the national interest" and "give adequate expression to culture, characteristics and affairs of different parts of Nigeria."[17] Nonetheless, the programs that managed to both entertain and enlighten were the most popular and enjoyed favorable timeslots. On Sunday evenings, the highpoint of family viewing, the Lagos-based NTS aired *Village Headmaster*, the hugely successful drama series by

Segun Olusola that ran from 1968 until the mid-1980s. Set in a fictional village, "the show portrayed a range of domestic and social dilemmas stemming from the need for a re-alignment of old ways to new lifestyles endorsed by Western education, hence the headmaster's prominence and the superiority of his counsel despite the presence of traditional political structures."[18] The village setting clearly scans as an allegory of a nation undergoing deliberate efforts at modernization. The village consisted of a "cross-section of socially recognizable types,"[19] including the headmaster and his wife the schoolteacher, a shopkeeper who moonlighted as a traditional healer, and a bar owner who provided the community a steady flow of gossip, as well as the village ruler and his attendant chiefs. The cast and characters of the imagined village felicitously reflected the dominant ethnic groups of the nation with its federalist structure at a time when Lagos served as the federal capital and the principal market of NTS broadcasts.

A second wave of Nigerian television, which began with the return to normalcy following the civil war (1967–70), introduced programs more deliberately developed to appeal to audiences.[20] For instance, *The Masquerade* was inspired by the need for laughter to salve the traumas of the war, as others have noted.[21] The program was produced from Enugu, and later Aba, and featured topical humor about mundane difficulties and social commentary in Pidgin, including the comic neologisms of the program's lead character, Chief Zebrudaya (Chika Okpala).[22] The show returned to the air in the 1980s as *New Masquerade*, with Okpala as director and producer alongside cocreators Peter Igho and James Iroha at the NTA studio in Enugu. The cast of characters continued to center around Zebrudaya and his wife, Ovularia (Lizzy Evoeme), but included also Prince Dr. Jegede Shokoya (Claude Eke) and his wife, Ramota (Vero Njoku), a Yoruba-speaking family. In fact, the action in early episodes took place largely within the households of these two families, although the program was designed as a similar cross-section of social and ethnic identities. The episode "All and Sundry," for instance, opens with banter between Jegede and the laborer who works his farm concerning wages and promotion. Prince Dr. Jegede denies the promotion on the grounds of lack of "paper credentials," and when his wife objects, he questions if she has the proper qualifications for her marital role and threatens to send her back to her village if she does not obtain said credentials. After Ramota attempts to enroll in the open university, the cast gathers in Zebrudaya's sitting room to chide Jegede's callousness toward his wife and mock the emptiness of the "Dr." in his own title. Later episodes came to foreground the Pidginphone antics of the iconic comic duo Gringory (James Iroha) and Clarus (Davies Ofor). In "Exam Malpractice," the two instruct Ramota in a range of trickster's tactics for cheating on a placement exam, which sets up the episode's overt message that money cannot buy merit, no matter how widespread the practice of bribery, because weak character holds back a nation more than any lack of technology or development. The unnamed location of *New Masquerade* is clearly a modest-sized city even though the topical themes and familiar scenarios ensured the program remained broadly relatable.[23] The program's attempt to represent ethnic, linguistic, and class diversity was in keeping with the NTA's efforts to broadcast an image of Nigeria that encompassed many walks of life. Television thus promoted the idea of a shared national patrimony beyond the divisions between ethnicity and language, even as the production, transmission, and reception of such television programs anchored around cities with broadcast infrastructure.

ENUGU TO "LAGOS"

Why do video films produced in and about Lagos, from classics to mainstream current releases, so rarely depict urban public spaces beyond B-roll and establishing shots? How can the city be said to occupy such a central place in the popular imagination when recognizable images of Lagos in video film are so brief and peripheral? To understand this idiosyncracy of Nollywood's Lagos, we should pay close attention to the production practices and representational conventions of Nigerian television. I turn here to textual analysis of *Basi and Company*, a popular television program created by the writer and activist Ken Saro-Wiwa that ran approximately 150 episodes from October 1986 to October 1990. The series was produced privately by Ken Saro-Wiwa's company Saros International at the studios of the Anambra Broadcasting Service in Enugu and was broadcast nationally through the NTA transmitter at ENTV.[24] Although produced in the East, the program is set in Lagos, which distinguishes it from other series programs that avoided such a specific setting in favor of a fictional village (*Village Headmaster*) or a nondescript town (*New Masquerade*). Instead, the characters, scenarios, and dialogue of *Basi and Company* were explicitly enmeshed with the nominative setting of Lagos, even though an image of the city never appears on-screen, which resembles but precedes the representational and production practices of the video film industry. The Lagos of *Basi and Company* is a television city, and as Charlotte Brunsdon insists, "each television city must be considered both as a representation (of a particular city) and as an institutional production (of a broadcaster or production company)."[25] In the absence throughout the series of any visual representation of the cityscape, the screenwriters and actors of the Saros International production company created various "city situations," or stereotypical urban scenarios, which sufficed to fashion a plausible urban neighborhood out of dialogue, casting, and performance rather than cinematography. The televisual aesthetics that made this possible would later provide Nollywood producers the techniques to create innumerable urban narratives without being constrained by the pragmatic limits to how much Lagos could be visually depicted, and in this respect, the televisual Lagos of *Basi and Company* prefigures the conventional representation of the city on video film.

Set within the fictional neighborhood of Adetola Street, the program simultaneously celebrates and satirizes the hustle needed to get ahead—or keep one's head above water—in Lagos. It adheres closely to conventional sitcom format, including a cast of recurring characters, fixed in setting and confronted by a new comic situation in each episode. At its heart is Basi (played initially by Albert Egbe and later Zulu Adigwe), one of the city's multitude of unemployed who fancies himself a millionaire temporarily down on his luck. In his routine get-rich-quick schemes, Basi is accompanied by his roommate Alali (Tekena Harry-MacDonald). Living above them is Madame the Madame (Aso Douglas), the landlady and member in good standing of the American Dollar Club. The young and fashionable Segi (initially Timi Zuofa and later Mildred Iweka) occasionally drops by on her way to and from the Island. The owner of the neighborhood beer parlor, Dandy (Lasa Amorro), and his most loyal customer Josco (Emmanuel Okutuate) act as sometimes rivals to the program's eponymous protagonist. The program's premise deals ironically with widespread ideas about easy money in the big city, such that each episode witnesses the attempt—and inevitably failure—of one of the regular ensemble to hatch some dubious ruse. "To be a millionaire, think like a millionaire" is the program's oft-recited motto. Perhaps because Saro-Wiwa described it as a modern folktale, many have observed the program's parallels with trickster tales.

Each episode in the series takes place across three set designs. First, Basi and Alali's threadbare room, grandiosely nicknamed "the Palace," is furnished with a sagging cot, empty cupboard, and tattered chairs where the friends hatch the get-rich-quick schemes to help forget their grumbling bellies.

Figure 6. Basi and Alali's rented room in the episode "Dead Men Don't Bite"

The second set, the sitting room in Madame the Madame's second-story apartment, is fully furnished with plush decorations, including a framed certificate of membership from the American Dollar Club.

The third set, the bar that Dandy struggles to keep stocked, even though most customers drink on credit, is the most public and therefore the space in which, at the end of the episode, most comic situations are publicly resolved.

Shot on a television sound stage and edited between four camera set-ups, every episode presents a stationary view of the same two-thirds of each room throughout the duration of the series. There is no reliance on match on action cuts to suture space to space, nor following or tracking shots to move within space, lending the program a spatial flatness and a circumspect sense of continuity.

The program provides no establishing shot to visually situate the action in Lagos per se; instead, its themes rehash urban legends, its characters adopt city fashions, and its dialogue bursts at the seams with discussion of Lagos. In one exchange at the outset of the episode "Transistor Radio," Alali laments about trekking from Somolu to the Island every day for three months—"Don't I

Figure 7. Madame the Madame's apartment in the episode "The Courier"

Figure 8. Dandy's bar in the episode "The Courier"

know all the sign boards, all the bus numbers?"—but Basi sees nothing in this to complain about. "Have you slept under Eko Bridge, or the rubbish dump at Isolo?" he retorts, "Have you been thrown out by your landlady for nonpayment of rent? Have you slept in the back of a truck and woken up to find yourself in Ibadan, one hundred kilometers away?" He goes on, "Ten years I've roamed this city. I and the streets of Lagos are friends. I know all their names, and they recognize my footsteps." Later in the episode Basi recounts the news report of one unfortunate migrant to Lagos who made it big after tossing himself from Eko Bridge. When police dragged him from the lagoon, a Good Samaritan offered him a job, and he today has all the trappings of success: cars, wives, and work as a pastor. In the episode "The Proposal," Madame dresses to impress a new suitor, adopting a hairstyle she calls the "Eko Bridge" and wearing an enormous head tie "as tall as the NECOM skyscraper," in reference to what was the tallest building in West Africa when erected along the Lagos marina in 1979. In the episode "The Candidate," Josco convinces Dandy to run for the office of governor of Lagos, since he is a man of the people, after all. Josco, who describes himself not as homeless but rather as a "humble resident of Eko bridge," reports that "all the boys under the bridge, above the bridge, at the wharf, all the patrons of this bar support you." The program never cuts away to venture out into these spaces but instead remains fixed in one of its three interiors. And yet the producers, screenwriters, and characters succeed in engendering a fully formed storyworld, one even more expansive and complex than we might have thought possible given the sparse means available to the producers. This is not uncommon for "how place is signified in audiovisual fiction," as Brunsdon notes. "Although it may seem obvious to start with location filming, in fact the setting for audiovisual fiction is produced through a complex orchestration of elements. Accent, music, props, writing, costume—each of these can tell an audience where a scene is set, and often these methods are more important in confirming location than where something was actually filmed."[26] (The producers of *New Masquerade* use the same technique of peppering dialogue with spatial cues, which effectively displaces the privileged role often attributed to vision in the representation of space.) These programs produce an urban imaginary without relying on a visually spectacular cinematic mode of rendering urban space and thereby challenge the commonplace notion that the city is out there, in the streets where everyday life unfolds, not in here, in the parlors, sitting rooms, bedrooms, and barrooms where urbanism is experienced as a set of social relations and city "situations."

The episode "Dead Men Don't Bite" illustrates this type of humor and how it grew from the recurring framework, or comic situation, that provides the program its premise. When Basi's uncle passes away, the family publishes an obituary announcement listing the man's many children living in Germany, the UK, and the USSR and his nephew Basi in Lagos. The family believes that since arriving in the city, Basi would have surely found some success and would surely contribute something to the funeral. Without a kobo to his name or a cup of *garri* in his cupboard, Basi must beg a loan from Madame the Madame, who just spent a huge sum at a family funeral of her own and therefore rebuffs him with her catchphrase, "It is a matter of cash." Basi visits the bar owner Dandy, who insists—to spite his neighbor—that he will pay Basi's funeral expenses but not one naira before. Seeing that the well-to-do of Lagos would rather lavish thousands on a dead man than loan a few naira to a neighbor alive and well, Basi decides to fake his own death to teach his friends a lesson. He leaves for the village only to be brought back disguised as a corpse. News of his death spreads quickly, and the neighbors of Adetola Street begin to compete to outspend one another while Alali gathers their tributes to the deceased. The neighborhood gathers to celebrate the man they repudiated only yesterday, and as music is played, the episode ends with a visual punchline when Basi rises from his deathbed to dance at his own funeral.

In each episode of the series, the comic "situation," in one way or another, turns on money. As Basi and the other characters admonish in every episode, "To be a millionaire, think like a millionaire," a catchphrase that remains synonymous with the program to this day. Basi's motto speaks to the general perception of Lagos as a cornucopia of opportunity, while his continual failure to get rich quick underscores Saro-Wiwa's efforts to disabuse his national audience of any dreams of easy money in the big city. The situations thus created should not necessarily be regarded as enregistering certain circumstances of life in Lagos but instead be understood as the overt (didactic) response to—and implicit evidence of—how widely Lagos was associated with money and the speed and scale with which one could amass wealth from opportunities in the city. Furthermore, as Brunsdon notes, one crucial distinction between cinematic and television cities comes down to the mode of distribution and the regular schedule of network broadcast that create "television cities to which audiences return week after week, becoming familiar with places they have never visited."[27] Without overstating the credulity of audiences, the Lagos that Saro-Wiwa and company produced was meant not simply to evoke a place many viewers had not visited but often imagined but also to correct the fantasy of fast fortunes and easy living that Lagos excited in the minds of some viewers. Surely, most viewers had also heard stories of the spectacular misfortunes that the city metes out, and therefore the television program provided an ongoing point of contact, week after week, with the ambivalent popular discourse that I have argued surrounds Lagos.

Moreover, when the series aired, the transition of the capital to Abuja was still underway, which meant Lagos remained in many ways the national seat of government. Therefore, Lagos was simultaneously national and urban space in the way only a capital city can be,[28] making it possible for the program to delve into cultural and social dilemmas set within Lagos but pertinent to audiences elsewhere. For instance, the program's screenwriting often directed its humor at the Lagos elite, which also meant taking oblique swipes at the nation's ruling class. As Saro-Wiwa stated in a newspaper interview from London, he believed "many rich Nigerians, especially the political class, have the 'Basi' complex—they are hustling con men."[29] In "The Candidate," as Basi campaigns to become governor of Lagos, promising his close supporters high-ranking appointments and lucrative contracts, Segi remarks that "Lagos owes the world a lot of money. Who better to handle the finances than a man who knows how to dodge creditors." Thus, ultimately, the speculative manner in which the program represented Lagos drew in large part from and responded to established notions of the city within the national popular imagination—rather than topical events or circumstances specific to the city. Out of curiosity, I put this observation to Nkem Owoh, who earned fame as Osuofia but who entered entertainment through his work in multiple capacities on *Basi and Company* and is credited as the production manager in many surviving episodes. He remarked that the Church does not ask a priest to marry a couple before he can offer marriage counselling. He went on to explain that Nigerians from every walk of life and every region had a vision of the capital city, whether it was based on firsthand experience, secondhand stories, or nothing more than a dream. "Even if you are in Enugu, you had your imagination of what Lagos could be" (personal communication, July 24, 2018). The effort to create from Enugu a program about an urban trickster in Lagos was decidedly connected to this perception of Lagos as the place where the real money in the nation resides.[30]

It is important not to lose sight, in this respect, that like many characters in his company, Basi migrated to Lagos in search of his millions and continues now—ten years on—to make do while making the most of life in the city. Although the program remains diegetically fixed in place—and non-diegetically constrained to the recording studio in Enugu—it engenders an urban neighborhood of comings and goings, a crossroads of newcomers to Lagos and returnees from abroad. At the beginning of an episode, new characters enter the frame like newcomers to Adetola Street and move along to somewhere else after the resolution of the comic situation their presence introduces. Their thirty-minutes' appearance has the effect, nonetheless, of injecting some realignment of relationships that lends the televisual neighborhood of Adetola the material it needs to eat, digest, and sustain itself for another week. In this sense, it both captures the mixture of mobility and constraint that syncopates the rhythms of many Lagosians' lives and satisfies the situation comedy's generic demands for weekly variation laid overtop a recurrent arrangement of characters, motivations, and setting. As I discuss below, the return to this baseline itself stages a perpetual reintegration within the community such that the various individuals' struggles toward self-aggrandizement are continually foiled and no one member of the neighborhood overtakes the others. The neighborhood thus remains mutually—and comically—entangled (see chapter 3).

Following the genre conventions of a television sitcom, there is little need for characters to wander too far from a familiar setting. After all, it costs money to step outside in Lagos, both in the diegetic sense that Basi and Alali could not afford bus fare to somewhere more exciting or dramatic and in the non-diegetic sense that Saro-Wiwa's production company would incur unnecessary expenses for the program to venture outside the studios of ABS TV Enugu to capture a glimpse of city scenes. Instead, it is the script that augments these spaces, fleshing out the storyworld of the program with allusions to Mama Badejo's *bukka* and the *suya* seller down the street, landmark locations around Lagos, and even more distant spaces in Ibadan, the village, and foreign countries abroad. With a peek behind the curtains that cover the apartment windows, Basi can announce there are no customers congregating for food at Mama Badejo's just as he can peek into the pages of a newspaper to describe the foreign affairs that will impose themselves on Adetola Street that week. After all, as Doreen Massey reminds us, "'social relationships' don't only exist in intimate spatialities, or in face-to-face encounters, or even within cities. They also structure our imagination of the planet."[31] In this televisual sense of space, the narrative technique that places a food stand across the street differs little from that used to invoke more distant spaces—the village or abroad—that are nonetheless implicated in everyday life in the location on-screen. Ultimately, it is a diminished notion of space that fixes strictly on what is seen within the frame, a fact that *Basi and Company* makes surprisingly evident: set in the fictional Lagos neighborhood of Adetola Street and produced in Enugu by Saros International to be broadcast across Nigeria, the program commands a more complex network of spatial relations than first meets the eye.

TELEVISUAL SPACE

From the 1990s forward, the techniques with which television programs signified nominal setting came to entail more location shooting than was typical of the serial dramas and situation comedies of the previous years. Television decamped the studio to capture images of Lagos, even if only to more compellingly situate the interior settings that remained the principal space of narration. For instance, the title sequence of Amaka Igwe's *Fuji House of Commotion* (2001–13), further discussed below, commences with a rapid montage of expressway signs for specific destinations on Lagos Island, "Victoria Island," "Ikoyi," "Carter Bridge," "Adeniji Adele," and "Marina," and segues to a panning shot over Obalende motor park, followed by credits for the program's cast of characters, and finally an establishing shot of the family compound in a residential district of downtown Lagos Island. In more elaborate fashion, the opening sequence of Igwe's *Checkmate* (1991–94) features a striking montage of Lagos landmarks, beginning with a shot of Marina Road from the top of the NITEL building. The former colonial administration building and government printing press along Broad Street are dwarfed by the high-rise towers of the banks and corporate headquarters that form a powerful portrait of an African financial district. The editing proceeds rhythmically, in step with the stately timbre of the theme song. We cut to street-level shots of office towers with grand glass facades, which connote business on a corporate scale, the accumulated power and prestige of institutionalized commerce. We are made to understand that this is a city on the move, inhabited by a cast of dynamic characters, as we cut to the expressway over Five Cowries Creek to Victoria Island and the tunnel at Maryland, extreme long shots of the port leap to medium shots of a trawler heading out to sea. Subsequent shots pan across the edifice of Lagos City Hall and the suspiciously smooth flow of taxis and sedans along downtown thoroughfares. The camera seems drawn continually upward to admire how the light bounces off the high-rise columns of buildings and to prompt the viewer to envision the executive suite on the top floor.[32] Energy in motion characterizes this opening montage in a fashion that feels not just modern but perhaps even postmodern in the colloquial sense of a city at the cutting-edge of commerce, finance, and technology, a now dated corporate chic aesthetic. The sequence delivers an early imaginary of the form that glamour might take in an African metropolis, an urban imaginary since handed down to contemporary New Nollywood films, where it is upgraded with nighttime footage of the brightly illuminated Civic Center and soaring drone shots of Lekki Bridge, as I discuss in chapters 4 and 5.

Nonetheless, a fundamentally televisual mode of spatial representation—the fixed framing, the reliance on dialogue, the opportune arrival and departure of figures from elsewhere, readily legible interior settings—provided the techniques with which producers aesthetically situated video film diegesis within Lagos, especially given the practical constraints around filming outdoors on location. Few early video films employ a spatial "literalism," whereby screen space observes direct fidelity with the spaces of Lagos, and instead the city remains, by and large, a place formed from a few choice establishing shots and a series of interior settings. Generally speaking, the demands of the plotline govern the spaces depicted, and frequently it is the social relations between spouses, parents, children, relatives, neighbors, and friends that drive the plot forward rather than encounters with complete strangers or the anonymous crowds of the street, as I argue in chapter 3. As such, the household, an office, restaurants, a courtroom, a police station, and occasionally the hospital offer plausible spaces in which these relationships unfold. In this respect, Lagos of mainstream video films shares less in common with cinematic cities than televisual cities elsewhere in the world, in which "the city, and the look and sounds of the city, [are] often subordinated, formally, to the studio-shot conversations between characters so important to much of television drama."[33]

Nollywood expanded upon television's repertoire of spaces—producers work with much more than three set designs—but as with television, the function of setting in mainstream video films is often "primarily generic."[34] In other words, set designs create generic spaces that, I would argue, turn on an affective core, itself often entangled with the nexus of social relationships and interactions appropriate to the space: a church, university campus, courthouse, police station, boutique shop, face-me-I-face-you tenement, parlor, bedroom; these genres of space offer a map of the socially symbolic terrain of the city. The reference to specific place arguably matters less than the allusion to social, cultural, and moral values attached to this or that "genre" of space. In other words, Nollywood producers demonstrate an exceptionally vivid grasp of what Henri Lefebvre calls the affective attachments of representational space. "Representational space is alive: it speaks," Lefebvre writes. "It has an affective kernel or center: Ego, bed, bedroom, dwelling, house; or: square, church, graveyard. It embraces the loci of passion, of action and of lived situations."[35] Along the same lines, mainstream video films create settings that capture the condensation of the social, cultural, and moral values ascribed to a general kind of space: (the protagonist's) ego, (a stranger's) bed, (the conjugal) bedroom, (a modern) compound, a (raucous) public street, and so on. Given the fluidity with which space in Lagos is inscribed and reinscribed, used and repurposed, built up, physically overloaded and eventually worn down, screen media's generic spaces point to the affective core shared across similar kinds of space and speak to the durability of social meanings ascribed to such spaces despite the rapid pace of urban transformations.

In her exceptional formal analysis of urban space in Ghanaian screen media, Esi Dogbe identifies spatial patterns across numerous video films set in Accra and notes the frequent appearance of the airport; taxis; religious sites, such as churches and shrines; and entertainment spots, like beer venders, hotels, and chop bars. In a brilliant analogy, Dogbe discusses these sites as "mneumonic devices" that trigger preexisting associations given that, "in fiction and in reality," as she writes, "these sites invoke strong but varied forms of attachment, ambivalence, and emotional response within Ghanaian society."[36] In this fashion, such video films deliver readily legible narrative space, a recognizable location attached to audience expectations about the type of story, the social role of characters, and the likely scenarios to unfold in such a space.

Finally, the creation of "generic space" points to another way in which video films adopted a television sense of space. As Moradewun Adejunmobi argues, narratives that anticipate televisual spectatorship may often adopt an episodic structure, "topical immediacy" (stories ripped from the headlines), thematic repetition, and the "narrative accommodation for interrupted viewing."[37] Extending this argument, I would propose that just as certain narrative features afford greater "televisual recurrence,"[38] so too certain audiovisual renditions of place accommodate televisual narration. After all, narration necessarily engenders the space of its own diegesis—the story takes *place* somewhere—and as the example of *Basi and Company* demonstrates, some television programs displace the construction of space from the visual/

cinematographic to the scripted dimensions of the program. Each week the sitcom threw up a new Lagos "situation," which was staged across the same three set designs. The reliance on generic spaces and narrative scenarios allows for the viewer's immediate recognition of the dynamics at play. The spaces represented are not so singular and nuanced or so winding and expansive that one would lose their spatial bearings during casual and sometimes distracted viewing.

CITY SITUATIONS

Money troubles animated the weekly heartbeat of *Basi and Company* and parodied the popular perception that money comes easy in Lagos. However, the issue of ethnicity also signified the nominal setting of "Lagos" and structured the scenarios that were and were not possible to depict. The space of Lagos in *Basi and Company* is not bounded by ethnicity because, of course, the city does not belong to any one ethnic group. Although Yoruba, specifically Awori, migrants from Ilé-Ifè were the original settlers of the city and Yoruba remains the city's most widely spoken indigenous language—alongside English and Pidgin—Lagos cannot simply be regarded as ethnically Yoruba.[39] To illustrate this point, consider the contrast between Lagos and Ibadan, where Hausa families who have resided in the city for generations are not regarded as indigenes and where local government authorities require individuals to present an affidavit from a local community's *baalè* and even to demonstrate specific knowledge of the deep history of Ibadan to obtain an official certificate of origin, which itself is required for local government employment and admission to state universities.[40] In most states, bureaucrats within local government authorities have general discretion, and therefore considerable power, to define the requirements of indigeneity and the entitlements or responsibilities it entails, *except* in Lagos, where indigene associations protest the fact that, unlike other cities, jobs and entitlements are not reserved for indigenes of Lagos.[41] Furthermore, it is not in spite of Lagos's ethnic diversity but arguably in response to the city's exceptional multiculturalism that the consolidation of indigenous Lagosian identity takes place.[42] Similar histories of trans-ethnic multiculturalism are unique to a handful of Nigerian cities, but none more so than Lagos, and by extension, in Nigerian screen media, the selection of an ethnically diverse—or at least ambiguous—ensemble of characters can be enough to situate the narrative within Lagos. In this sense, a multicultural cast is a more relevant marker of place than the conventional signifiers of citiness, such as the architecture, infrastructure, or other urban material forms.

Television programs and video films deal with the ethnic diversity of Lagos in different ways, both playing up and playing down the relevance of ethnicity. For example, *Basi and Company* portrays the ethnic openness of Lagos, ironically, through the elision of ethnicity altogether. The program's recurring cast of characters defies an easy read of regional, ethnic, or linguistic identity, while ancillary characters of many stripes and stations in life pass through week by week. In reality, the initial cast comprised actors from Rivers State, Saro-Wiwa's own place of origin, with the exception of Albert Egbe and other actors later introduced. Curiously, the characters do not speak Pidgin English, the lingua franca of Nigeria that cuts across ethnic lines and is, in Lagos, perhaps as widely spoken as Yoruba. Instead, the program's dialogue passes in standard received English, as scripted by cowriter Tekena Harry-Macdonald and Saro-Wiwa, who retains international literary fame as, among other things, the author of *Sozaboy*, a novel in "rotten English." The program creator's own entrepreneurialism may explain the strict observance of standard English, given that his teleplays were repackaged as short books for adults and children and distributed by Saros International. The booklets are advertised during closing credits in some episodes and are presented as materials to improve literacy.

Ultimately, whether it was language, attire, names, or idioms, indicators of ethnicity remained pointedly ambiguous. In conversation with me, Nkem Owoh recalled that Ken Saro-Wiwa not only took special care not to denigrate ethnically marked characters but studiously avoided anything in his scripted treatments that might suggest ethnicity in order to avoid altogether the potential to touch off interethnic animosity (personal communication, July 24, 2018). In the episode "The Courier," for instance, a new character calling himself Mr. Gold Digger appears in Dandy's bar spinning a concocted story of an ailing relative in the United States desperately in need of particular "African herbs." He learns that Segi has plans to travel to Canada and manages to recruit her to carry his package of "African herbs," which is revealed to be a package of cocaine at the end of the episode. It should come as no surprise that the mischievous new figure is depicted as ethnically ambiguous in dress, speech, and appearance, which prevents the implication of any ethnic group in his individual crime. However, more notable is the fact the ethnic, cultural, and religious identity of the entire cast of characters is obscured to the same extent. Director Uzorma Onungwa expressed particular distaste for ethnic humor that pitted Yoruba, Igbo, and Hausa against one another and these three communities against ethnic minorities.[43] Moreover, as I argue below, sensitivity to inflammatory speech is itself particularly Lagosian, inasmuch as affective socialization in Lagos can be said to foster, if not demand, mutual tolerance.[44] Therefore, the producers effaced dimensions of ethnolinguistic difference while emphasizing humor that cut across demographics and dealt with themes to which all Nigerians could relate, aspects of life that were shared in common. As Nkem Owoh put it to me, "It is a Lagos setting, it is not a Yoruba setting, it was a *Lagos* setting and everybody, every section of the country, comes to Lagos the way the program's characters arrived in Lagos" (personal communication, July 24, 2018). In this respect, *Basi and Company* unsettles Yoruba claims to indigenous privilege in Lagos and instead postulates a Lagos that belongs not to one ethnic group but rather to a multiethnic nation.

In fact, arguably more important than the sheer fact of the ethnic heterogeneity of Lagos is the attitude of accommodation that permits so many people to share the same public sphere. For a rich, intriguing collection of documented instances of the "civic consciousness" of Lagos residents, one must turn to the research collaboration between Stephanie Newell of Yale University and Olutoyosi Tokun, John Uwa, Jane Nebe, and Patrick Oloko of the University of Lagos, who conducted individual and group interviews with Lagosians on popular perceptions of dirtiness among different ethnic, cultural, and religious groups within the city. Generally speaking, the city's residents are "proud of the cohabitation of diverse cultural groups in Lagos, and their way to preserve multiculturalism [is] to insist on individuality above ethno-regional markers," or as one resident explained to the researchers: "I don't assess people based on their size or their tribe or their color, whatever. I just assess them individually."[45] Notably, Newell summarizes that, "for our interviewees, multicultural toleration across mutually incomprehensible languages and behavioral practices took precedence over a liberal cosmopolitan desire for dialogue, translation, mutual understanding, persuasion, or rationalization, which are defining features of the public sphere in Western theorizations since Habermas."[46] The prevailing public sensibility is one characterized by mindful differentiation between individual and putatively collective behaviors among others residents, and personal discernment between the beliefs one shares openly and those one holds but does not utter publicly. "As neighbors in the vicinity of strangers, Lagosians adopt a policy of live and let live, involving scrupulous attention to the behavior of others and an equally scrupulous avoidance of critical public engagement with it."[47]

One finds in some video films and television programs the same combination of careful attention to cultural difference and circumspect avoidance of public criticism of others. Whereas Saro-Wiwa conscientiously erased markers of ethnicity from *Basi and Company*, other programs and video films that *do* signal characters' ethnicity arguably depict the multiculturalism of Lagos more effectively. A glimpse at Amaka Igwe's *Fuji House of Commotion* illustrates this point. The sitcom, a spin-off of the popular television drama *Checkmate* mentioned above, centers on Chief Fuji (Kunle Bamtefa); his three wives, Mama Moji (Toun Oni), Peace (Ngozi Nwosu), and Ireti (Sola Onayiga); the mistress-turned-fourth-wife Caro (Ireti Doyle); and their ever-expanding household of children in Lagos. The man of the house, Chief Fuji, is the owner and landlord of several properties around Isale Eko and an inveterate womanizer who continues to take on wives, mistresses, and children even as his ability to provision the family stretches ever thinner. In the episode "Family Census," Chief asks his three (official) wives to stand in a row before him and then commands the households' dozen children to form columns behind the woman who is their mother. The wives believe Chief has finally resolved to formally divide and bequeath his property to the different branches of the Fuji family. Instead, he explains that this activity will reveal the "ghost children" of "ghost mothers" in the room, and, indeed, it turns out that half the children do not belong to the wives present, which Chief remedies by arbitrarily assigning them to Ireti, his third wife, who does not yet have a child. This touches off an argument between the wives, who ultimately admonish Chief that he must eventually honor his obligation to share his property among the mothers of his children. Conceding defeat, Chief Fuji excuses himself briefly and returns with two more women from the neighborhood, mothers of various "ghost children" under his roof. The ensuing squabble between mothers allows Chief to evade the consequences of his peccadilloes for another week. The program's humor around Chief Fuji's remorseless philandering ultimately reflects upon the man himself and does not tarnish the personas of other characters who have their own comic shortcomings.

More broadly speaking, the situations the program dispatches with each week turn on the commotion of life within an interethnic polygamous household, but as I argue above, the multiethnic cast and the pragmatic, mutual tolerance the program preaches constitute key elements of a Lagos sitcom.

Chief Fuji is Yoruba, as are Mama Moji and Ireti, while Peace and Caro are Igbo. All the children have Yoruba names, whether their mother is Yoruba or Igbo. The light-skinned Peace is derisively referred to as "artificial yellow pawpaw," while Ireti is mocked for her disastrous experiments with Western cuisine; however, that is the extent of the open ridicule of identity. The ethnic identity of characters does not necessarily match that of the actors, such that the Yoruba actor Ireti Doyle plays the Igbo character Caro, for instance, a fairly common practice in Nigerian screen media. By comparison, the trilingual actor Ngozi Nwosu, who plays Peace, continually switches between Pidgin, Yoruba, and Igbo in a fashion that signals her Lagosian Igbo background and distinguishes her from Alika (Victor Eze), for example, the Igbo renter in the Fuji compound who recently arrived in Lagos, wears an Igbo cap, and never utters a word of Yoruba. Otherwise, dialogue includes frequent code-switching between snatches of Yoruba, Pidgin responses, and Peace's signature phrase, "Chineke!," an Igbo exclamation of exasperation in this context.

The theme song playfully characterizes the program as "Preaching practical solutions / Peaceful peace in confusion / And everybody in commotion," which summarizes rather well each episode's balance between comic disruption and pragmatic interpersonal accommodation. In the episode "New Wife, New Wahala," Bimbo Manuel guest stars as Chief Fuji's eldest son, Musa, who returns to Lagos from abroad with plans to marry the daughter of an elite Lagos family. The in-laws insist upon first visiting to inspect the Fuji household's habits, which Musa worries will appear too "bush" and not adequately "modern minded" for an elite family with such "exposure." The children must not kneel or bow to the parents in such an "ancient and anachronistic style of greeting," Musa insists, but rather should politely croon, "Hello! How are you?" When the prospective in-laws visit, the Fuji family's performance of civility descends into typical commotion, and the elites are run off the compound grounds. As the episode illustrates, the one thing the program cannot abide is Musa's "civilized" airs and the Western pretensions of his bride-to-be and her elite family whose affected English behavior stands intractably opposed to the "African" values of personal dignity and respect for one's seniors. In this fashion, the episode casts the condescension of the culturally "Westernized" elite as an intolerable constraint on the Fuji family, who observe purportedly traditional and modern practices simultaneously and without any sense of contradiction. In the same vein throughout the series, ethnic, linguistic, and religious differences are not suppressed but are acknowledge and presented as fully consonant with the multiculturalism of Lagos. In each episode, an ethos of mutuality ultimately diffuses the competing interests of wives, the rivalries among siblings, and the powerlessness of the father to assert control that threaten to upend the household week after week, and this repeated return from commotion to stasis reinforced the program's orientation toward pragmatic integration.

In her influential discussion of medium specificity and narrative television, Jane Feuer argues that "the self-replication of the episodic series depends upon a continual re-integration of the family."[48] With reference to American network television sitcoms, Feuer notes that the family members depicted on-screen—who are addressed to an implicit family seated before the television set—often personify divergent political perspectives and repeatedly confront an "enigma of the week" structured along generational, gendered, or racial divides. This pattern "politicized the basic sitcom structure of a return to equilibrium and a new dilemma which would proceed in an endless circle until the series was canceled."[49] Thus, television series, by virtue of aesthetic form and medium specificity, are inclined toward open-endedness rather than cinematic closure and the slanted equilibrium that allows the screenwriters to combine structure and variation in a fashion that grants a program the greatest duration possible. In the case of *Basi and Company*, repeated narrative reintegration ensures that despite how hard all the characters strive to "think like a millionaire," no resident of Adetola Street accumulates an obscene fortune or meets complete demise, and thus the struggle to make do in Lagos remains a *mutual* endeavor. By comparison, *Fuji House of Commotion* continually restores the quintessential interethnic polygamous household to equilibrium such that ethnic, cultural, and religious difference is both acknowledged and reintegrated into an urban "civic consciousness" of mutual tolerance.

Intriguingly, the social fault line most frequently emphasized in television and video films about Lagos is not ethnic, cultural, or religious difference but rather the distinction between newcomers, lifelong residents, and *omo Èkó*, the original inhabitants of Lagos Island. Population growth in Lagos, one of the fastest-growing cities in the world, stems overwhelmingly from migration, and as such a large number of residents are newcomers to the city. In village-to-city migration comedies, the figure of the "Johnny Just Come" stands in for popular ideas about the comic naivete of newcomers and the urban savvy of residents, as I mention below. However, multiple terms exist to differentiate between those who migrated to Lagos, those who were born and raised in the city, and the descendants of the "primordial" inhabitants of Èkó. According to Newell's research team, such terms include "'Ará Èkó' (non-Lagos-born people living in Lagos) and 'Ará Òkè' (uplanders, sometimes used to connote 'uncivilized' people) compared with 'Omo Èkó' (Lagos-born indigenes, lit. a child of Lagos Island)."[50] In addition, there is the phrase "*omo onílè*," which literally refers to the descendants of the landowner but also connotes those with customary rights over the community and therefore shares some semantic overlap with *omo Èkó*. "The only condition for becoming an Omo Onile is by birth or inheritance," as Rufus Akinleye explains. "The Omo Oniles oversee the affairs of the community since they are the custodians of the customs and traditions."[51] These categories have the effect of "complicating assumptions about a homogeneous Yoruba-Nigerian ethnic identity,"[52] in that identification with place of origin or duration of residence appear more primary than a shared ethnolinguistic identity among Yoruba in Lagos.

Along these lines, differences of ethnicity, culture, or religion matter less in screen depictions of Lagos than the distinctions between those who just arrived, those who have acclimated, and those who have always been in Lagos. Nowhere in Nollywood is this more evident than in the enduring genre of village/city migration comedies in which the humor hinges on the popularly perceived contrasts between urban and rural life, a juxtaposition staged by the journey of a rural character to Lagos or, in reverse, the return of city folk to the village. Kehinde Soaga's *Lagos Na Wah!!* (1994) is a notable example here, both for its comic portrayal of urban stereotypes and as an example of the migration of talent from television to video film. As Haynes explains, the video film "imported much of the Igbo cast of the Enugu-based classic television serial *Masquerade* to Lagos, where their characters encounter others played by an equally famous set of Yoruba comedians, the Awada Kerikeri Group."[53] One of the principal characters of *Masquerade*, Chief Jegede Sokoya, makes the transition to *Lagos Na Wah* with his characteristic arrogance and outsized preoccupation with money intact, as performed by the original television actor Claude Eke. However, whereas *Masquerade* unfolds in an unspecified town, this is Lagos, and the chief is thus cast as a landlord of Lagos Island, the city's oldest and densest district. Given the shortage of affordable housing, landlords throughout the city have strong bargaining power in lease agreements and are reputed to wield considerable authority over the lives of tenants. As such, it should come as no surprise that each of the texts discussed in this chapter features a landlord in some central role: Madame the Madame (*Basi and Company*), Chief Fuji (*Fuji House of*

Commotion), and Chief Jegede Sokoya (*Lagos Na Wah*). Moreover, in the two texts that openly mark ethnicity, the landlords are Yoruba, while Madame's background is elided, as discussed. The video film stages a contentious lease negotiation in which Chief Jegede demands three years' rent up front at an exorbitant rate, a contract signing fee of three thousand naira, and a bottle of beer to wash down the agreement. "Are we quarreling?" the prospective renter retorts, to which the chief replies, "No, we are not quarreling. This is the system here." He then adds, "You are meeting with the original landlord, and you are complaining?" The exchange is exaggerated for comic effect, but Chief Jegede's remark about being the original landlord is notable and might be construed as an allusion to his status as *omo onílè*. As Akinyele notes, "It is essentially through the control of access to land that the indigenes of Lagos have distinguished themselves from strangers and migrants as true Lagosians in a city that has often been described as 'a no-man's' land."[54] In one scene, Chief Jegede and Paulinuse venture out to survey properties along a stretch of downtown composed of rows of towering skyscrapers when the pair are accosted by a group of area boys who cajole the chief to settle them. With a portfolio folder under one arm of his flowing *buba*, the chief simply continues to saunter and point upward at skyscrapers with a contemplative scratch of his chin, ignoring the area boys' pleas, praises, and veiled threats. The scenario is performed not for the shock of danger but for the laughter that stems from a collision of high and low, the chief's pretenses and formal Yoruba at impasse with the vernacular street Yoruba and shabby attire of the area boys. Ultimately, Chief Jegede tires and departs with his assistant Palinuse's necktie in hand like some pet's leash, to which the area boys remark, "This guy no dumb at all," and give up hopes of earning small money through intimidation. The joke seems intended to cut both ways.

Indeed, *Lagos Na Wah* features, apart from Chief Jegede Sokoya, a range of typecast urban figures. "The Principle that organizes the resulting extensive fooling is not ethnic—no culture 'owns' Lagos and the transethnic medium of the film is prominently announced by the subtitled, 'A Pidgin Comedy'—but rather the distinction between those who know the ropes of the city and those who do not."[55] The narrative opens with the protagonist Solomon's voiceover describing the lack of opportunity in the village that has held him back from achieving his life's ambitions and the money that he believes can be had in Lagos. "Village dey dull. Everything dey for Lagos!" laments Solomon. After several expository shots of the village, the narrative rushes us off to Lagos, where we observe Solomon (Kayode Odumosu) disembark from his bush taxi at the busy Ojota motor park. An exception to the trend described above, numerous scenes in this comedy take place in the street, where the comedians' performances gain an edge from the spontaneous reaction of passersby. As Obododimma Oha asserts, Solomon embodies "the motif of the stranger—and the stranger-as-victim—in Nigerian culture."[56] Dressed in an absurd pair of "bakassi boots" with flamboyant high heels and barely able to conceal his bewilderment, Solomon stands out as a typical Johnny Just Come, a stereotype that the actor assumes to the amusement of onlookers in the motor park who become unwitting accomplices in the comedy. Passengers on the *danfo* chuckle and glance over their shoulder as Solomon pays the bus conductor not once but at every stop, apparently confused and intimidated by the young Lagosian boy's thick Yoruba accent as he spits out the conductor's favorite phrase, "*Owó dà?*" (Where's your money?). The newcomer's ineptitude is put on display so that the more sophisticated or streetwise viewer can share in the laughter of those on-screen who provide the spectatorial point of identification.

Solomon arrives in Ajegunle only to discover that his uncle has packed up his apartment and moved to Abuja, leaving Solomon no relations to help him and no roof over his head. Fortunately, he is taken in by the neighbors, Klarus (Davis Ofor) and Giringory (James Iroha), who are moved by his plight and offer to show him the ropes in Lagos. At this point the narrative only loosely follows Solomon's struggles in the city while it explores a string of comic episodes involving stereotypical city figures, each played by comic actors whose performances on Nigerian television programs had already ensured their popularity as household names. For instance, the gateman at the Ajegunle compound where the characters live, Papi Luwe (Sunday Omobolanle), engages in a "Who's on first?" skit with a prospective tenant named UK (short for Eucharia), whose nickname Papi Luwe mishears as U.K. Believing the man just returned from London, he demands five years' rent up front, but only after ensuring the man enjoys watching football, drinking local alcohol, and chasing young women, which are Papi Luwe's own pastimes.

The clownish Paulinuse (Lucky Edu), also called Pauly Pompo, embodies the comic rogue.[57] His laziness is only matched by his lechery. While his wife, Lovina (Gloria Obumse), and their troupe of children show the signs of chronic hunger in a household without a competent head, Paulinuse's own corpulent figure—supplemented by a false, padded belly—shows the signs of his gluttony. As he explains to Chief Ezego (Ralph Nwafor), his long-lost wealthy friend from the village, one day Lovina appeared at his doorstep in Lagos and informed him that his parents had "passported" her there to marry him. Unwilling to assume the responsibilities of marriage, he told her to pack up her load and return to the village, but when he turned his back for a moment Lovina "don carry belly" (was pregnant), Paulinuse explains, ignoring his own part in the pregnancy. Chief Ezego congratulates his friend, but Paulinuse retorts, "Carry your hand commot there! Congrats for where? I dey for Lagos. One cup of garri na twenty naira." (Take back your handshake. Congrats for what? I'm in Lagos, and here a single cup of garri costs twenty naira.) To avoid incurring further child-rearing expenses, Paulinuse makes all attempts to control himself, sleeping on a separate corner of the bed, refusing to share the same cup of water, and walking backwards into the bedroom for fear that even gazing at his wife might cause another pregnancy. He is hopelessly ignorant of family planning methods, as Chief Ezego points out, and the household swells to eleven children. In the final scenes of the narrative, Paulinuse receives his long-awaited retirement check from his employer Chief Jegede and, believing the check to be worth a million naira, immediately sets off to the bank to deposit his new fortune. He brings his eleven children marching along like some clownish parade and the scrawny family dog as "escort" in the absence of a police guard along the way. The punchline drops when the bank teller, a modern woman in pantsuit and educated accent, informs him his check amounts to a mere 500 naira. Like many other village/city comedies, the video film revels in rehearsing such stereotypes and makes little conscious attempt to challenge what is presented as commonplace ideas about rural and urban life.

CONCLUSION

An appreciation of the extent to which Nollywood grew from television is an important dimension of the historicization of Nigerian screen media, but I have argued here that it also presents important clues to the aesthetic conventions of video film that must be accounted for in formal analyses of screen representations of Lagos. Nigerian media urbanism demands new modes of interpretation, and in this effort, studies of televisual form prove especially useful. As I claim above, the dominant focus on cinematic cities tends to foreground particular signifiers of place, including architecture, historic sites, or other built spaces marked by the sediment of time and use, what Lefebvre would call "lived space."[58] However, in Nigerian television and video film, the referent is often not lived space, but what Filip de Boeck calls the invisible architecture of living space, which foregrounds the city as an "entanglement of a wide variety of rhizomatic trajectories, relations, and mirroring realities,"[59] which I discuss further in chapter 3.

When viewed as a televisual city, we find that the series of generic spaces with which television and video films represent Lagos work less as references to specific places than as scenes of symbolic and moral legibility. Television programs also illustrate the extent to which ethnic, cultural, and religious accommodation signifies place. Screen portrayals of trans-ethnic communities and affective socialization toward accommodation despite mutual uncertainty are crucial features of Lagos as a televisual city. These nuances are as much the substance of media urbanism as the city's material form, perhaps even more so, which has remained obfuscated by the dominant fixation on the cinematic representation of spatial surfaces. I contend, and the foregoing examination of Lagos as a televisual city demonstrates, that urbanism is not, in its final instance, only an essentially spatial phenomenon. Crucially, spatial theory has brought into focus the incessant intersection of things, people, and ideas that we often simply call the urban experience, but other frames of analysis are necessary to understand the social, affective, and aesthetic significance of these urban assemblages and their translation to screen representation. Perhaps, the great deal that we have learned about cities through the study of urban space has been to the occlusion of other urban experiences, such as the moral ambivalence that grants an elasticity necessary to grapple with the continual transfiguration of urban assemblages; or the affective socialization of mutuality across ethnic, cultural, and religious difference; or the ethical paradox of social entanglement, as I examine next.

CHAPTER 3

Narratives of Entanglement

The implementation of economic structural "adjustments" in the late 1980s, following pressure from foreign creditors, created unsettling consequences across Nigerian society and marked the beginning of an especially difficult period in Lagos.[1] The country witnessed the devaluation of the average person's effective purchasing power; unemployment resulting from retrenchments in the public sector; and escalating costs for food, rent, transportation, electricity, health care, education, and other social services.[2] Structural adjustment programs involved not simply a narrow reorganization of the economy but also a drastic restructuring of the lives of ordinary people forced to devise their own measures for coping and surviving. According to Eghosa Osaghae, these included "moonlighting and the creation of rent-seeking avenues by civil servants, withdrawal of children from school, a drastic reduction in food consumption, increased patronage of herbalists and 'traditional' or spiritual healing rather than hospitals and clinics, increased religiosity and the cultivation of fatalistic complexes which served to reduce the spirit of protest, crime, prostitution, drug use and so on."[3] The uncertainty was compounded, in the early 1990s, by the failure of a political transition to democracy to materialize.[4] Under the pretense of forging a path to elections, Ibrahim Babangida's military regime held onto power by engineering a protracted and intentionally convoluted transfer to civilian governance, which ended with the annulment of the 1993 election results, the imprisonment of Moshood Abiola, and Sani Abacha's seizure of power.[5] Stories of the ascension and demise of public figures were not uncommon under military rule.[6] Newspapers and magazines published accusations and counter-accusations of corruption fomenting alarm that no part of society appeared immune to the spreading of moral crisis.[7] As official institutions faltered, the public sphere collapsed, and ordinary life grew increasingly precarious, the majority of Lagosians turned to family, friends, and wider alliances to create what stability was possible, and as such social connections and collaborations among residents largely generated the collective force that held the city together.

To this day, social connections are arguably the most important dimension of life in Lagos. Especially amid generalized scarcity, enmeshment with others is necessary for most forms of individual progress, from minor advancements to the attainment of "that moral-intimate-economic thing" called "the good life."[8] However, even though most residents cannot thrive without social connections, these connections come with obligations, must be continually maintained, and can become overwhelming. As a result, the same bonds under different circumstances, or seen from another vantage point, may appear like social bondage. In this sense, city life involves entanglements, both unforeseen partnerships and unsought acquaintances, forms of mutual implication gained even if unwanted.

According to AbdouMaliq Simone, "There is a preoccupation on the part of many residents in African cities with the extent to which they are tied to the fates of others who they witness 'sinking' all around them. At the same time, they hope that the ties around them are sufficiently strong to rescue them if need be."[9] Furthermore, in large, heterogenous cities, shifting expectations and competing obligations loosen preexisting social norms and create intense contestation around who can do what with whom and under what circumstances: Will family ties hold under emotional and material hardship? Does one have the connections to gain employment? Might new affiliations provide the path to social advancement? Which friendships will prove lasting and fruitful and which threaten to create future liabilities? Such questions probe the uncertainties of urban entanglement, specifically the social, cultural, and moral ramifications that flow from the unavoidable mutual involvement that everyday city life requires of residents.

A glimpse at Kenneth Nnebue's *Died Wretched* (1998) illustrates my point. The narrative centers on two brothers in Lagos. The elder, Lucas, has established a successful trade in spare automobile parts but must sell everything he owns to save Chris, his less successful younger brother, from jail. Lucas cannot recover from the financial sacrifice and sinks into poverty even as Chris, by contrast, grows tremendously wealthy and influential. Will the material and moral debt that one brother owes the other be honored, or will the family fall apart? As the narrative drives toward an answer to this question, the cast of characters expands and brings into focus different moral perspectives, as well as a wider gamut of social ramifications, before closure and moral clarity are ultimately asserted in the final scene.

When the film begins, Lucas has gone without salary for two months and must borrow *garri* from the neighbor to feed his family. Poverty has forced him to withdraw his five children from school and place them with other families, where they work as servants. He approaches a friend to offer up his son as a shop boy, but the shocked friend asks why Chris cannot help. Lucas explains that his wealthy brother responds to his appeals with promises of assistance that he never fulfills, which causes Lucas to suspect the malicious influence of Sarah, his sister-in-law. "She seized Chris and chased every other family member away," Lucas laments, and then intones, "Oh Sarah, you came into my family. I accepted you and married you. Today you've turned to be my greatest nightmare." (Chris alludes here to an Igbo conception of marriage in which the bride becomes married to the husband's entire patrilineage.) Viewers, however, know this to be false because we witness Sarah regularly admonish her husband about the "debt" he owes Lucas. Chris repeatedly vows to send money but uses it instead to import a consignment of foreign goods, to take up with a mistress, to gift her a new car, and so on. The narrative allows several such deferrals before, finally, Chris resolves to give Lucas the money to rebuild his business selling spare auto parts. Alas, the elder brother's wife arrives to announce his untimely death, and part 1 concludes with a flood of tears. The web of social relationships expands in part 2, as the city's Igbo community gathers to make arrangements for Lucas's funeral. Unsure of what aid the selfish wealthy brother will offer, the elders decide Lucas should be buried in Lagos, rather than the village, and allocate the small sum of 7,000 naira to make it so. However, in his belated guilt, Chris decides that his deceased brother deserves the honor of an exuberant funeral, and the remainder of the narrative showcases the preparations to lavishly bury the good brother who died wretched. The funeral procession and ceremony are depicted in real time. In the final tableau with mourners gathered around the casket, the priest intones, addressing the large congregation and the implied viewer, "Your brother needs help, your neighbor is hungry. Help him! Don't wait until he dies," a lesson the dialogue and combination of characters on-screen make abundantly clear.

Because it requires a web of social supports to accomplish almost anything in Lagos, for many, everyday life involves continual concern for relations with family, friends, and wider acquaintances. As such, stories about the social bonds that ensnare individuals in the dilemmas of far-flung relations or lift them from destitution through an unlikely lifeline *are* narratives of the city. *Died Wretched*, the example in question, suggests that obligations between family members must not be allowed to erode under the pressure of acquisitive individualism that Lagos embodies. The narrative form reinforces this idea as it spirals outward to encompass a larger social horizon, beginning with a family torn apart by poverty and concluding with a lavish community gathering. Along the way, characters are periodically orchestrated into scenarios that stage sentiments of social friction: outrage at a neglected moral debt, remorse for acting belatedly, the shame of experiencing public reproach. In fact, the narrative arc appears organized primarily to convene different combinations of characters, scene by scene, that enact the moral principles the video film wishes to foreground. We might view this combinational mode of narration as a textual figuration of urban assemblages, which represents an additional register in which to examine video films as narratives of the city. In this respect, the video films in question call attention back to the importance of relationships between family, friends, and strangers and ultimately demonstrate the extent to which the city is the people.

As discussed in chapter 2, given the frequency with which Lagos is said to command a special fascination in Nollywood movies, early video films spend surprisingly little time amid the architecture, infrastructure, traffic, or general built environment of Lagos, the commonplace signifiers of urban form in cinema elsewhere. Instead, narratives remain indoors, where viewers can eavesdrop on dramatic conversations among family members, friends, neighbors, business partners, romantic partners, and all other manner of social acquaintances. Nollywood's production practices account in part for this. The same insecurity and infrastructural decay that make Lagos an inhospitable place for its residents to live make it a daunting space to represent on-screen. Area boys, property owners, police, or anyone appearing in the frame might object or demand compensation from a crew filming in the open streets. Perhaps as a result, Haynes explains, the camera typically hops over the insalubrious exterior spaces of Lagos in search of more photogenic settings, such as the interiors of palatial villas in swank neighborhoods.[10] However, this explanation is not exhaustive, and, as Haynes implies, the representational constraint that urban space imposes on producers should itself be interpreted as Lagos becoming inscribed, or enregistered, in Nollywood's particular mode of narration.

What I term "combinational narration" might best be understood in comparison with serialized television. The links between video film and television have been discussed elsewhere,[11] so I will underscore only several formal similarities germane to my argument. First, as Christine Geraghty notes, the soap opera format foregrounds "a set of characters and very often a place" and makes optimal narrative use of these minimal elements. Moreover, serialized programs conceived for continuous narration without episodic resolution tend to arrange narrative structure to foreground "the way in which a particular character fits in to the network of relationships" that populate the storyworld rather than to track a causal chain of events toward ultimate closure.[12] In fact, Christine Gledhill views individual narrative events and settings as "relatively incidental" in serial television, particularly soap operas, because "it is precisely the intervening social webbing of events through personal talk that constitutes their sphere of action."[13] Similarly, video film emplotment typically proceeds through intervals of characters assembled within the frame in combinations that provoke dialogue—or "personal talk"—that proves narratively generative, although not strictly subordinate to narrative causation. In fact, with the exception of B-roll footage to establish diegetic place, video films rarely include shots that are not anchored by at least one character's presence on-screen. In other words, this mode of narration traces a web of social ramifications rather than a clear sequence of events, and, as a result, narratives can expand, branch out, fold back, and intersect plotlines in unexpected ways that produce suspense, tension, and, most important, various scenarios of moral, cultural, or social legibility. The resulting tableaux of characters facilitate ready recognition and narrative participation for viewers engaged in "distracted viewing."[14] Both the aesthetics of exhortation that Akin Adesokan examines and the aesthetics of outrage that Brian Larkin discusses unfold within decisive scenarios of this kind, scenes that orchestrate weighty pronouncements of cultural values or stage scandalous transgressions of those values, often as the culmination of a moral dilemma.[15]

The claim is not that this mode of narration is inherently televisual. As Haynes and Okome remark, for instance, such "sprawling, rhizomatic plot structures, have affinities with oral narrative patterns."[16] Moreover, in his perceptive discussion of Nollywood's "character of recurrence," Lani Akande traces a related narrative technique involving the subordination of narrative progress to character performance from Yoruba theater and celluloid productions to early video films. Some actors, he explains, developed a signature character, such as Bàbá Sùwé, Mr. Latin, or Móládùn, who "recurs across numerous films, some of which share no production, creative, or narrative relationship," but who also retains "its uncontested character traits, which are superior to, and have priority over, the role it plays" in the narrative structure.[17] The recurrent character appears in scenes meant to showcase familiar traits and set pieces rather than advance narrative events, but the stylistic accommodation and audience recognition of recurrence itself also pertain to combinational narration.

The characters and circumstances of combination vary across video films, but some genres inherently call for certain scenarios that illustrate the mode of narration in question. So-called occult films, such as *Circle of Doom* (1993), *Rituals* (1997), and *Blood Money* (1997), are driven by a signature preoccupation with money rituals, which inevitably entails the depiction of the secret societies, outsider initiations, and magical practices performed, typically, at a hidden shrine under a malevolent high priest's guidance. In reference to occult scenes from *Living in Bondage* (1992), Haynes remarks that "it represented something that was widely rumored to be happening but naturally occurred in secret where it could not be seen or proved to be true. This was one of the kinds of stories people told that embodied the wickedness that seemed to be washing over the country."[18] The shrine scene in which Andy must sacrifice his wife, Merit, to unlock a magical source of wealth offers a quintessential scenario that combines setting, circumstance, dialogue, and characters into a culturally, socially, and morally significant assemblage. Another video film genre, exemplified by *Glamour Girls* (1994) and *Domitilla: The Story of a Prostitute* (1996), imagines the lives of women engaged in prostitution through narratives that repeatedly shuttle between the street at night and a dilapidated shared apartment where the clique of young women discusses the struggle to get by in Lagos. Onookome Okome argues that these female characters evoke the figure of "the good-time girl," which serves as a readily legible "social type" that the audience would recognize as part of the social webbing of the city. He also indicates that these video films turn a blind eye to another implied network, since "nothing is said of the men who patronize these women."[19] Numerous video film comedies delight in staging a newcomer's arrival in Lagos from the village or in mocking the pretentious attire and speech of those who have returned to the village from Lagos.[20] In dramas, by contrast, the village serves as a typical sight for more sober encounters between city people and family or in-laws, where the assemblage of urban and rural figures articulates more serious ideas about each space's cultural connotations.

This chapter examines the way video films released during the 1990s narrated urban entanglement or experiences of unavoidable mutual implication, especially through the orchestration of narratively consequential character encounters that stage the affective and moral significance of entanglement. I argue that this mode of representing Lagos illustrates that urban networks do not simply trace spatial connectivity but rather generate the combinational agency that, more than anything else, animates city life. This argument, furthermore, underscores the unusual ontology of cities, which as assemblages consists in this combination capacity but therefore leaves no singular feature of differentiation from towns, villages, or other kinds of communities. The so-called relational turn in urban theory suggests we must resolve to deal not with distinctions of kind but rather variations of the particularity, intensity, and circumstances of phenomenon. Approaching video films in this fashion overturns the primacy of spatial thinking about cities and challenges the inclination in film studies to privilege visual representations of space over other elements of city life enregistered in other formal features of film. My reading of Tade Ogidan's *Owo Blow* (1996/1997), which spans three parts (*The Genesis*, *The Revolt*, and *The Final Struggle*), forms the bulk of the chapter but is interwoven with examples from other video films with similar patterns in the hope that this dual approach will provide both a clear line of argument and moments to highlight variation and nuance.

URBAN NETWORKS

Intriguingly, the depiction of Lagos in early video films through narratives of social life rather than representations of physical space prefigures a much later shift in urban studies that Ash Amin and Nigel Thrift have termed the discipline's "relational turn."[21] This approach conceptualizes cities as composed of networks of circulation, the continual activity of recombination, and the assemblages that result, which in turn disrupts and disintegrates the common premise that cities exist as unified place entities. It envisions the city as "a force field of relational interactions" that "produce[s] immense combinatorial power and immense constraint," within which physical infrastructure and built forms—conventionally, the objects of cinema's visual attachment—are important but not definitive features.[22] This perspective redirects attention to the people, things, and ideas that cities bring together into unique configurations and how these elements change and are changed through continual interaction within what Doreen Massey calls the "throwntogetherness" of urban environments.[23] According to this framework, the coming together—the capacity to combine—is what explains the city, a claim that explodes conventional urban imaginaries of bound space and foregrounds instead the discontinuous eventfulness of ongoing rupture and reassemblage that the term "urban experience" is often meant to encapsulate.[24]

Interestingly, the poet Odia Ofeimun's famous essay about Lagos, "Imagination and the City," captured much of this style of thought decades prior.[25] More to the point, this multiplicity of movements and itineraries has profound implications for the social lives of urban residents and can leave people feeling "thrown together" in the sense of being implicated in various entanglements. For instance, possibilities for advancement and mobility still depend a great deal on the social connections one can mobilize. New migrants, for example, often room with distant relatives as they work to gain a foothold before overstaying their welcome in a notoriously overcrowded city.[26] University graduates seeking formal employment must marshal all their social connections to ensure their application has any chance of success. In some cases, the utilities and services provided to different neighborhoods depend on the chain of relationships between state government officials, local government chairmen, and party affiliates within the neighborhood.[27] In fact, in cities across West Africa, so-called economies of connection have come to fill the gap created where urban population growth outstrips economic growth.[28] Moreover, because social networks keep so much of ordinary life moving, they become the source of significant contestation. "How people are connected to each other is," according to Simone, "something that has given rise to great anxiety, conflict, and experimentation, particularly in urban Africa."[29] The volatility of urban life creates uneven accumulations and losses among neighbors, friends, and family members, which in turn generates competing claims about shared resources and responsibilities and ultimately places enormous pressure on relationships. Therefore, as much as urban residents depend on social connections, they must also mind the sudden gains and losses of others in their social networks because the ripples of such volatility may eventually reach them, for better or worse.

The contingencies of an urban environment also affect social networks beyond the family. There is the middle ground, so to speak, of "trust-based relations of voluntary friendship," which form the basis for "exchanges and obligations neither between strangers nor between close kin," where balancing what it takes to maintain social connections and what is gained by them can be no less fraught.[30] For instance, Sasha Newell describes how young men in Abidjan juggle a responsibility to one set of friends by establishing and drawing upon new sets of friends. "It is through the investment in social connectivity," Newell explains, "that people paradoxically overcome the anchoring obligations of their social networks."[31] In this way, social connections that come with material obligations are in turn fulfilled by recourse to other social connections, which underscores both the burden and the usefulness of having more of them. Filip de Boeck discusses a similar paradox of social amalgamation in Kinshasa through the figure of the knot, which stands for "interlinking, connecting" as much as "closure, blockage, and suffocation."[32] He further explains that individuals often succeed to the degree they can suture themselves into the social fabric of the city, "[to] knot yourself into as many networks as possible," but that, likewise, "the knot also expresses the possible dangers that every connection may bring."[33]

However, African urbanism does not simply strain conventional social relationships; it also creates fresh, sometimes unconventional, networks of collaboration. This perspective resonates closely with relational urban ontologies that conceive of cities as the eventful assemblages that result from the quintessentially urban activity of recombination. In Lagos, the pace of transformation far surpasses the ability of a central authority to govern it, and as a result, personal relationships, families, neighborhoods, and district organizations play the principal role in mediating the patterns of everyday life.[34] In fact, alongside Lagos's physical infrastructure of built forms exists an infinitely larger infrastructure of people, ensembles made up of countless actors, aims, and social arrangements. "These conjunctions become an infrastructure—a platform providing for and reproducing life in the city."[35] Residents' capacity to combine objects, spaces, people, and practices is what makes most things in Lagos possible, even as it remains an "invisible" urbanism predicated on minimal material traces and maximal social ramifications. I would emphatically underscore that Nollywood, the industry, embodies precisely this generative capacity of people collaborating to overcome an infrastructural dearth. Rather than state sponsorship, foreign funding, or corporate partnership, personal relationships between screen media professionals have proven the crucial catalyst in the formation and evolution of the mainstream video film industry.[36]

The network serves as an indispensable trope for understanding the actors, interactions, and overall combinational capacity of cities. The principal strength of this trope, arguably, stems from the ways it enables nuanced conceptualizations of extended and often complicated connections. In her study of aesthetic and social forms, for instance, Caroline Levine asserts that the network is a form that "first and foremost affords connectedness."[37] However, this emphasis on connection can prove limiting in several respects. First, the representation of networks as diagrammatic figures of nodes and edges, and the adoption of such language, privileges the static perspective of a mapmaker. Furthermore, these terms imply that the things connected exist as such prior to the connection that, post facto, we recognize as a network. Urban relationality can be understood more appropriately as a performative enactment in which nodes and edges do not exist except within continual relations of what Karen Barad terms "intra-activity."[38] Finally, the network trope implies, but often overlooks, the limits of connectivity. Recent scholarship in the humanities on networks in film, television, and literature tends to foreground contemporary—especially technologically mediated—connectivity and its implications without attending to complementary instantiations of disjuncture, and subsequently, from this perspective, urban environments appear thick with social connections, while obscured remain the barriers, gaps, and breakdowns that Brian Larkin insists are equally integral to urban experience.[39] Even with occasional nods to the limits of connectivity, textual interpretations of networks often remain animated by what could be called the network sublime, that spark of awe at the notion we live in a small world after all, each individually connected by n degrees of separation, sometimes across expansive physical distances.[40]

However, networked connection is not strictly synonymous with mutual implication. To understand the distinction and how it pertains to urban relationality, we must turn to Karen Barad's notion of entanglement, which she elaborates by rigorously examining the wider ontological implications of principles and evidence derived from quantum physics. To begin with, Barad's agential realist approach initiates a shift of primary ontological focus from objects to *phenomena*. This resonates impeccably with the pivot that Amin and Thrift describe in urban theory from instrumentalist approaches premised on the city as an object, especially one composed of built spaces, toward a view of the city as "a force field of relational interactions."[41] For Barad, the word "phenomenon" refers to "*the ontological inseparability/entanglement of intra-acting 'agencies.'* That is, phenomena are ontologically primitive relations—relations without preexisting relata."[42] In this fashion, Barad reverses the common perception that connections bring together things—or "relata"—that are there already and insists instead that we cannot presume the existence of what is thrown together prior to their differentiation—and, thus, inauguration—within entanglement. This is true because relation engenders relata through the performative enactment of connection, meaning that entanglement inaugurates what it brings into relation. As such, "the world is not populated with things that are more or less the same or different from one another. Relations do not follow relata, but the other way around. Matter is neither fixed and given nor the mere end result of different processes."[43] Barad could mean here that prior to the intra-action of relation, literally nothing exists—neither matter nor meaning—or rather that nothing exists from one moment to the next, except within the continual enactment of a sustaining relation of intra-action.

With regard to social theory and the matter of urban relationality, this line of thought unlocks the binary opposition between, on the one hand, social constructivist notions of individual subjectivity as passively formed by various external forces of determination and, on the other, the assumption of liberal humanism that individuals live according to self-generated, self-determined agency and intentionality. Barad's framework instead underscores the ontological (and semantic) indeterminacy that prevails prior to (and outside of) the phenomenon of entanglement between intra-acting agencies. Thus, entanglement describes something closer to the performative tension of subjectivation, Judith Butler's term for the "inauguration" of the subject through a formative resistance to the power of subjection,[44] and illustrates that our sense of ourselves, of the good life, of what lends life purpose, and of who we are for one another is grounded in the fact of our mutual involvement. "This is not a static relationality but a doing—the enactment of boundaries" between agencies that remain indebted to one another by virtue of an iterative, constitutive entanglement, and yet such enactment of what the material world *is* and *means* "always entails constitutive exclusions," which hold the potential of another possible intra-action that never was but could still be, nonetheless.[45]

This line of thinking underscores the dynamic of mutuality that a straightforward discussion of networks might view, and thereby risk overlooking, as simply another example of contemporary connectivity. Instead, as Sarah Nuttall eloquently explains, "Entanglement is a condition of being twisted together or entwined, involved with; it speaks of an intimacy gained, even if it was resisted, or ignored or uninvited. It is a term which may gesture toward a relationship or set of social relationships that is complicated, ensnaring, in a tangle, but which also implies a human foldedness."[46] In the context of Lagos, the idea that residents' social relations emerge performatively and require continual iteration becomes more evident after careful consideration of the emotional, political, moral, and cultural priority placed on relationships in many classic Nollywood narratives. These narratives illustrate the sprawling ramifications of entanglement, the innumerable possible answers to the question of who can do what with whom and under what circumstances, and the broad extent to which urban entanglement constitutes the primary dimension of city life.

OWO BLOW

Video films of the 1990s prioritized the narration of social relations over the visual presentation of built forms because, for popular audiences, the most prescient aspects of life in Lagos inevitably involved social change, the cultural norms undergirding it, and the competing moral frameworks with which to understand it. Even the occasional exception demonstrates the consistency of this prioritization, as with the opening montage of Ogidan's *Owo Blow* and its unusual attention to the streets, architectural exteriors, and public spaces of Lagos. The first shot takes us above the skyscrapers of Lagos Island for a panoramic view, and the camera proceeds shot by shot down into the streets, which are packed with traffic and pedestrians flitting across the frame. The camera directs our gaze to the hawkers dashing between cars to sell their wares, to *okada* drivers buying herbal remedies, to commuters embarking and disembarking buses, and to other glimpses of the banalities of urban existence. We are far from the action, and high up, but these long takes are cropped such that the entire frame is filled by the movement of bodies and vehicles.

The built structures of the city disappear behind and underneath the throng of activities in a pointed visualization of what Filip de Boeck terms built form as "living space."[47] Material infrastructure seems almost irrelevant as we watch a *danfo* hop the concrete median and cross into the oncoming lanes to circumvent a "no go" traffic jam. The camera never tilts up, since there is little curiosity for what is happening high up in the office buildings lining downtown Lagos Island. After all, the people to whom the film is dedicated, "the struggling masses of this country," as the epigraph calls them, are here in the streets. In this sense, the visual attention to public space illustrates exactly how little power the built city has over the bodies, activities, and agencies of residents and the extent to which they *are* the city.[48]

The camera eventually settles upon the narrative's young protagonist, Wole Owolabi, with the rest of the Owolabi family driving through go-slow

Figure 9. Lagos traffic in *Owo Blow*

traffic when their vehicle comes upon soldiers raiding a roadside marketplace. Heroically, Wole's father, Mr. Owolabi (Kayode Odumosu), intercedes on behalf of the market traders, which angers the soldiers, who maneuver to arrest him. In the struggle that ensues, shots ring out, several bystanders are killed, and the incident is pinned on Mr. Owolabi. At trial, he entreats the judge for leniency, explaining that as the sole breadwinner of his household, to punish him is effectively to punish the entire family. The impassive judge condemns him to ten years' imprisonment over the gasps of the courtroom as the weeping Owolabi family is torn apart. While the virtuous Mr. Owolabi languishes in prison, his family begins its slow descent into poverty. The remainder of the five-hour narrative is structured around Wole's struggle to save his family from sliding into poverty, his subsequent initiation into an alternative economy of social connections with which he secures and shares the good life with family and friends, and, ultimately, his ambivalent death after the return of a repressed past acquaintance.

At first, the Owolabi family's struggle to fend for themselves requires each member to make sacrifices in a series of dramatic blows. To pay Wole's school fees, his mother (Racheal Oniga) appeals to a wealthy relative, who offers only words of sympathy and an early indication of the unreliability of the support that familial bonds ought to guarantee. Subsequently, Wole (Femi Adebayo) abandons school in search of work to support the family and spare his younger siblings the same misfortune. The protagonist's commitment to hard work, it seems, might yet save the family: an upbeat montage frames his hands in close-up, washing buckets of laundry, carting away garbage, and ironing a large stack of clothes. A song celebrating the honesty of hard work bridges the sequence and suggests that, although sacrifices must be made, there is still hope the family will hold together.

Gradually, however, each family member must compromise even more to make ends meet. Wole's mother turns to the lecherous landlord (Sam Loco Efe), who offers to loan the family thousands of naira on the condition that she sleep with him. At first, she reluctantly bends to the pressure but ultimately rebuffs the sordid bargain, prompting the landlord to exclaim: "You and your family will experience the sharp fangs of suffering. The pain will gnaw you to the bone!" (*Ìyà tó ní eyín nla bàyìí áa je ìwo, áa je Wole, áa je gbogbo ebí e pátapáta. Ìyà áa je ìwo d'egun!*). The insult stings, but far less than eviction, a fate he spares the miserable Owolabi family. Meanwhile, the oldest daughter, Mope, begins to bring home generous gifts and concocted stories about their source. Her behavior attracts the attention of Mama Ojuju (Binta Ayo Mogaji), the neighborhood gossip, who discovers that Mope has an admirer twice her age. Mama Ojuju shares with Mama Jide (Lanre Hassan) the rumors that confirm what the viewer already knows: Mope's liaison with this generous older man only plants the seeds for future disaster, a development the narrative treats with forbearance for the moment. More important, at this point, is that the Owolabi family remains tied to the lives of neighbors and the shared concerns of the compound and that in spite of these tensions, the landlord, Mama Jide, and Mama Ojuju continue to regard the Owolabis as "*alajogbe* (a relationship based on neighborly existence)" even if the Owolabis' "*alajobi* (consanguinity or blood relation)" have eschewed their moral responsibility to provision support.[49] As Akin Adesokan explains, in shared residential compounds, "residents establish relations that transcend specific social categories, whether familial, ethnic, regional, religious, economic or political." The shared compound represents the sociality of neighborliness or, to borrow Adesokan's felicitous phrase, "the elasticity and the specificity" of community in transethnic Lagos.[50]

However, there remains the city at large, beyond the familiar neighborhood, where more unpredictable conditions of social entanglement obtain. One day, a neighbor's errand sends Wole across town aboard a *danfo*, one of the rusted yellow buses that crowd the frame in the opening montage of each of the film's installments as unmistakable signifiers of Lagos. When the conductor on Wole's bus—a youth who calls the route and collects the fares—absconds with the money that should be split with the driver, Wole steps up to replace the conductor after swearing solemnly never to steal. The work is dangerous, and, as other characters continually remark, it squanders Wole's innate intelligence, but the family must abide these small disgraces in order to keep the worst at bay. Therefore, he spends each day navigating the city's public transportation routes and returning to the motor park, thus becoming part of Lagos's vast infrastructure of people. In many West African cities, public transportation garages represent unique spaces that Simone calls "staging areas of anticipation," where innumerable activities jostle and overlap and where individuals and groups work out inventive "combinations of the many different actions, feelings, styles and functions" of the space in order to best anticipate the opportunities that unpredictably come and go.[51] In illustration of the fluidity with which networks form and disband in such spaces, Wole loses his bus conductor work as readily as he found it. He attached himself to the driver, named Akanni (Adewale Elesho), who in turn relied on an agreement with the vehicle's owner, but when the owner withdraws the *danfo* to give to a brother, the chain of social dependencies suddenly dissolves, leaving Akanni and Wole without a lifeline. The arrangement and its collapse exemplify the complexity, as well as the contingency, of social entanglements in the informal economy where job security, however provisional or tenuous, hinges upon personal relationships.[52] The driver decries the callousness of Lagosians, exclaims that "Lagos is just too tough for me," and resolves to return to his village where people can be trusted. But first, Akanni will "inform the [garage] chairman of my decision so that I won't be implicated if any crime is committed in the motor park," an inconsequential line narratively speaking—Akanni immediately walks off-screen and out of the narrative frame only to return much later—but one that expresses a recognizable, potentially familiar, fear of becoming unwittingly ensnared in absentia by events and accusations outside one's knowledge or control. Indeed, this preoccupation with ensnarement proves narratively significant when, in time, Wole's activities at the motor park do become the focus of collective suspicion.

Wole conceals his jobless desperation from his family and continues each day, returning to his staging area of anticipation in the motor park, to search of another job. Wole finds himself enduring the "enforced waiting of urban life" that Ato Quayson asserts is an increasingly chronic experience of time for young (male) urbanites who must form other social lives during this transitional period of un- and underemployment.[53] The protagonist waits in anticipation of some opportunity impossible to anticipate, seeking some way to become enmeshed in a new entanglement. By chance, he encounters a small team of area boys within the motor park, a fateful coincidence not unlike his accidental induction with Akanni, the *danfo* driver. The young pickpockets drop a stolen wallet in Wole's lap and flee with the owner close on their heels. The area boys later regroup and marvel as Wole, without paper or pen, quickly converts the wallet's pounds and dollars into naira. His naive inclination to help becomes his unwitting initiation rite as the other area boys declare him an official member and together they set out for the bus stops and motor parks, where they use clever deceptions to relieve unsuspecting passengers of their valuables. The small hustles pay, and Wole does not object when he receives his take, which the viewer witnesses with an escalating sense of shock. But no condition is permanent, and the clique of pickpockets is soon apprehended by a vigilant onlooker who pieces together each boy's role in disappearing the snatched purses and wallets. The scene crosscuts between the boys who relay a purse from one to the next and the attentive onlooker's eyes darting as he marks each furtive handoff from his surveillance point. This relatively sophisticated editing technique sketches the web of pickpockets embedded amid the throng of people, whose various itineraries the boys exploit to camouflage their ruse. But once rooted out, Wole is swiftly punished by the motor park crowd, who strip, beat, and prepare him to be lynched. At this point, an intriguing example of combinational narration ensues as Wole's neighbors, Mama Jide and Mama Ojuju the gossip, miraculously arrive upon the scene and intercede to claim him. "He is my child!" Mama Jide pleads. The two women who have saved him from the lynch mob scold him: "Wole, see your life? Why do you behave so unruly?" However, the words are almost redundant, as the image of Wole's body conveys the moral consequences inscribed on—literally beaten into—his physical figure.

Our gaze is directed to Wole's body, centered in the frame, bare chested, beaten, shoulders slouched, with traces of blood still on him. Both the lashings on Wole's body and our physical reaction to them participate in what Peter Brooks terms melodrama's "aesthetics of embodiment, where the most important meanings have to be inscribed on and with the body."[54] Having lost everything—father, school, employment, neighbors, and family—the young

Figure 10. Wole stripped and beaten in the motor park in *Owo Blow*

man finds himself, literally and figuratively, stripped bare. Too ashamed to face his family or perhaps wishing to save them disgrace—his petty theft supported the family, after all—Wole refuses to return home and instead wanders into the streets as the screen fades to black, concluding the first installment in the *Owo Blow* trilogy.

SCENARIOS OF ESTRANGEMENT

The various networks that structure the narrative should be evident, including the motor park where the public jostles together, the residential compound full of neighbors, and, at the heart of it all, the Owolabi family itself. Family is consistently at the center of video film narratives, which should indicate the tremendous gravity that surrounds familial relations both in video films and in Nigerian society writ large.[55] However, focus on family does not always represent a turn away from the disorder of the public sphere toward the security and stability of familial bonds, as one might expect, given that intimate relations appear as figures of betrayal as often as they stand for trust and comfort.

To illustrate this point, we must return to the shared compound where the Owolabi family, their neighbors, and the landlord all reside. As emphasized by the zoom of an establishing shot, the residential building is known as "Great Inheritance," a phrase prominently inscribed on the edifice. Intriguingly, when Wole's mother visits the landlord to plead for money, he boasts between sips of beer of the comforts his wealth could provide her and then exclaims, "I am the inheritor." He continues, "My younger brother simply died. I did not kill him! His wife had no children, so I inherited [this property]. Now my tenants shout, calling me 'Inheritor! Inheritor!' But if their father died, can they inherit anything? They are jealous of me." (*Èmi, inherita. Àbúrò temi ó kú. Èmi kò ló pa. Ìyawó e kò bímo. Èmi wa inherit. Àwon tenant wón n pariwo mi, "Inherita! Inherita!" Tí bàbá ti won ti o bá ti kú, sé wón lè inherit? Wón jealous mi.*) The landlord delivers this outburst unprompted, and one has the distinct sense he doth protest too much. In fact, his fervent protestations are the only narrative indication that the neighborhood suspects he killed his brother in order to acquire the Great Inheritance compound. The allusion to fratricide remains confined to these lines alone, which Sam Loco Efe may have improvised given the mode of delivery and the imperfect Yoruba phrasing (Efe performs in Yoruba fluently but is not ethnically Yoruba), but the implied scenario, however minor, contains revealing echoes of other early video film narratives in which the most intimate relationships pose the acutest threat. This imagined situation addresses potent misgivings about familial relations and specifically the perception that intimacy entails exposure to vulnerability. I will call these scenarios of estrangement and propose that the frequency and similarity with which early video films envision such scenarios speak to an apprehensive structure of feeling attached to intimate, or even proximate, relations.

A remarkably similar scenario initiates the storyline of Amaka Igwe's influential feature *Rattlesnake* (1995/1996). Louis is a consummate professional, the head of a middle-class household, and a caring father to his son. When his monthly salary fails to come through, the family practices patience while he remains diligent at the office, which earns Louis a promotion and reimbursement of his lost salary. Just as Louis delivers the good news to his family, he suffers a heart attack that proves fatal. With his dying words, Louis instructs his son Ahanna (Okey Igwe) that, first, he should attend university and, second, he must remain ever vigilant because "it's the person closest to you that can kill you." This advice succinctly captures the affective posture in question, the mixed feelings that stem from constant, wary attentiveness to intimate relationships, the exhausting awareness that the closer one depends upon another, the greater the disruption the relationship could pose should it fail. At this point in the narrative, appropriately enough, Louis's covetous brother, Odinaka (Nkem Owoh), who has sought to feed off his relative's prosperity from the outset, begins maneuvering to appropriate his brother's wealth and wife, Nancy (Ebele Ozuchukwu). The virtuous brother's death finally creates the opportunity to do so. Odinaka is deceitful and coercive, with a long list of vices—gambling, drinking, smoking, and womanizing—that cast him as a man deeply corrupted by the big city and its crass materialism. The whole group returns to their village in the East for the burial ceremony, but Odinaka eagerly presses for a return to Lagos, where he will take up his brother's estate. He coerces Nancy to accompany him to the city, which means both abandoning her children in the village and foregoing the mourning period customarily observed by an Igbo widow. This also means that Louis's son, Ahanna, inherits nothing. Ultimately, customs of inheritance are perverted by the acquisitiveness that city life instills in some men, and herein lies the clearest parallel with the fratricidal scenario that in *Owo Blow* hangs over the Great Inheritance compound. The connection that the line of inheritance represents reemerges as the trajectory of an imminent threat because "it's the person closest to you that can kill you."

Similarly, recall that the central narrative conflict of *Died Wretched* turned on an unfulfilled debt between brothers. Not only does the wealthy brother, Lucas, betray his familial obligation to his poor brother, Chris, but, as the narrative reminds viewers, the debt is material, a matter of life and death, in fact. When roles were reversed, Chris sold his business and property to bail Lucas from jail, and in this sense the virtuous brother's destitution and eventual death are presented as the result of Lucas's active negligence. One brother honors fraternal bonds and suffers, while the other brother ignores them and prospers at the cost of his brother's life, which once again stages the anxious possibility that intimate connections, presumably grounded in trust, hold the potential to harm. However, the matter of betrayal can cut both ways.[56] When Lucas neglects his moral and familial obligations, Chris initially suspects the malevolent influence of his sister-in-law, Sarah, and laments the day she married Lucas and, by extension, the family. Sarah suffers her in-laws' misplaced suspicions even though viewers witness Sarah repeatedly admonish her husband to help his brother. Sarah is never absolved of these allegations and even endures the insults of her in-laws when she attends the poor brother's funeral. The intimate proximity of family, the entanglement of family members' lives, is precisely what makes such recriminations especially consequential and thus a source of anxiety in the narrative imagination.

Likewise, in Amaka Igwe's *Forever* (1994), after Nnedi suffers three miscarriages, a doctor informs her and Ogbabi, her husband, that she carries a congenital blood disorder that caused her body to reject the pregnancies. Following this news, Ogbabi turns on Nnedi and accuses his brothers-in-law of arranging a marriage with a witch who bears *ogbanje* children. He abandons Nnedi, and the narrative traces her hardships raising the only female child to survive their marriage. Similarly, in Chico Ejiro's *Scores to Settle* (1998), when the protagonist Sade's husband dies in a car accident, her mother-in-law arrives from the village with accusations of witchcraft and the intention to take ownership of her deceased son's mansion, business, and wealth. Ousted from her late husband's home, Sade (Liz Benson) wanders the streets of Lagos in search of work, hand in hand with her two young sons, but discovering none, the three take refuge under one of Lagos's several bridges and sleep on wooden benches amid thieves and malarial mosquitos. Eventually, the family escapes this ordeal and lives modestly together until, many years later, a motorist strikes and kills Sade's youngest son, Richard, a tragedy with eerie echoes of his father's fatal car accident, which raises the haunting suspicion that some occult force could be working against the family. Nevertheless, her eldest son, Charles (Richard Mofe Damijo), survives, matures, prospers, and invites Sade to live with him. That is, until he becomes engaged and his fiancée also accuses Sade of witchcraft, after which Charles repudiates his own mother, sending her back onto the streets. As Sade, once again, shelters under a bridge at night, she questions her faith aloud: "Where do I go? What do I do? My parents denounced me because I married the man I loved. My mother-in-law rejected me for no just cause. You took away my loving husband; you also took my son Richard. And now, my only hope, my only remaining hope, a son I suffered all my life for, has thrown me out, calling me a witch!" The pronouncement punctuates one of the narrative's several scenarios of estrangement in which intimate ties leave characters embroiled in mutual suspicions, stigmatized by accusations, or defenseless against betrayal.

Importantly, however, the alternative to this enmeshment in ambivalent relations is, in many video films, envisioned as far worse. The most potent representation of this fear tends to involve the neglected character living destitute on the streets of Lagos. As Haynes observes, among the hardships that afflict characters in structural adjustment–era video films, which include unemployment, loss of class status, and the crumbling of the family, the worst to suffer was homelessness.[57] As such, the greatest fear the city provokes is not embodied in some urban multitude of anonymous figures with unknown motives but rather turns on social abandonment and the risks and deprivations that follow the loss of social connection. Of course, notable examples of spectacular violence committed by strangers do exist, as with the terror of armed robbery (*Rattlesnake*, *Onome* [1996], and *Silent Night* [1996]), kidnapping (*Terror* [2001]), and sexual violence (*Violated* [1996], *Domitilla*). However, tellingly, the assailants are sometimes later revealed to be known acquaintances (*Rattlesnake*, *Violated*, *Silent Night*, and *Terror*). In fact, the generic conventions of blood money ritual films seem to demand specifically the violent sacrifice of a family member or loved one (*Living in Bondage*, *Blood Money*, and *Rituals*). As such, the fear of urban strangers is arguably outstripped by that of becoming the stranger without any—or only the most tenuous—attachment to the social relationships that afford support and belonging.

Unfortunately, *Owo Blow* situates Wole in precisely these circumstances between the conclusion of the first and the opening of the second installment. Unable to face his family after the catastrophe in the motor park, Wole sleeps under a bridge in the unlikely company of a married couple, a civil servant, and a refugee displaced in the notorious demolition of Maroko, who together represent a cross-section of those afflicted by post–structural adjustment program (SAP) poverty. Although not overtly didactic, the mode of address here steers toward explicit social commentary on the devastation that structural adjustment and inept governance inflicted upon ordinary Nigerians of all walks of life. As a dramatic depiction of social abandonment, more broadly, the scenes under the bridge draw upon a particular reservoir of urban anxiety, namely, the fear of becoming an anonymous individual within an urban context in which anonymity exacerbates vulnerability and powerlessness.[58] When accidents, accusations, or unforeseen crises arise, as easily happens in the volatile environment of the city, anonymity can mean greater exposure to exploitation, punishment, or the censure of public opinion. For some residents, to insinuate oneself into some neighborhood milieu may be motivated by nothing more than "the struggle against anonymity which menaces the weak, the anonymity which permits anybody to accuse you of doing anything, or of doing [*sic*] anything to you."[59] As such, the representation of homelessness or social abandonment within Lagos does not evoke wariness of the city's countless unknown faces as much as fear of anonymity and its ramifications. Worse than scenarios of estrangement and the encumbrances of fraught intimacies is the loss of attachments altogether, which leaves characters without any social strand with which to suture themselves back into the social fabric of the city.

ECONOMIES OF CONNECTION

According to Levine, "networks afford connection and circulation,"[60] but I would assert furthermore that circulation—of material support, gestures of care, or demonstrations of trustworthiness, for instance—is often what forms and sustains connections. In both Nollywood and Lagos, moral concerns are bound up with material concerns, and relationships matter because they inflect the allocation of material abundance and scarcity, as well as recognition of belonging, according to particular "economies of connection."[61] For instance, Newell describes how extravagant performances of prosperity and generosity that exceed one's financial means to continually maintain may ultimately serve to rearrange social supports and, thus, one's social reality in a manner that enables one to sustain the exuberant identity initially performed.[62] Furthermore, circulation should not be narrowly construed as pertaining to money or merchandise—what James Ferguson calls the "cash nexus"—to the exclusion of "solidarities and mutualities that sustain rich lives under adverse circumstances,"[63] but rather should include the circulation of material resources among urban residents that enfolds within performances of social relations, such as buying round after round of beers for the table, linking a friend to a bit of work, or sharing useful information with an older friend in hopes the favor will be returned later on.[64]

Moradewun Adejunmobi asserts, in her discussion of social performance and moral economy broadly conceived, that "kinship involves obligation and in that respect, performance," and describes the individual's fulfillment of social obligations as "the performance of one's social self." She explains further that social obligations must be

> *regularly performed* irrespective of one's feelings about this or that member of one's extended family. Interactions with kin in Africa were and often continue today to be defined by obligation rather than by sentiment. And because these interactions are founded on obligation, members of an extended family

are aware that they are bound together as kin by *repeated performances* intended to safeguard the individual and the community. They recognize their actions towards kin as a performance.[65]

While the social self originates in the regularly repeated performance of connection, trustworthiness, and good character, the fact that repetition sustains connections and social identity over time implies that the social self remains vulnerable to contingency, that bonds can become brittle if left neglected, that trust might extend only so far, and that moral consequences might follow if obligations are not regularly honored. In other words, social entanglement and the trust, loyalty, and connection that underpin it are constituted through performative acts that Barad might term "iterative intra-activity." I should note here the distinction between performance, understood as acting out a social role, and performativity, as the enactment of relationality, but there still remain parallels with Barad, who explains that "intra-actions are agentive," in the sense that "different material-discursive practices produce different material configurings of the world."[66] From this perspective, the social self is inseparable from the material practices of its production in the same way that "subjects and objects do not preexist as such but are constituted through, within, and as part of particular practices."[67] Moreover, within urban environments with overwhelming ethnic and cultural diversity, like Lagos, the norms governing social performances undergo inevitable contestation, revision, and reinvention. As these shifts occur, they confront urban residents with ethical dilemmas concerning which social bonds enable greater freedom and which present undue constraint, which relations "call for moral judgement rather than mere choice" of association, and, to paraphrase Elizabeth Povinelli, how different social connections "distribute life and death," endurance and exhaustion.[68] These questions get at who urban residents are for each other and, in the broadest sense, what shapes the material world of the city.

The Genesis concludes as Wole wanders into the night. The next chapter in Ogidan's saga, *The Revolt*, chronicles the protagonist's life on the streets, his mixing with networks of other young men, and his subsequent transformation of character. Although the Lagos streetscape provides the staging ground for scenes of homelessness, as discussed above, these streets are also always animated by "the chance of space that may set us down next to the unexpected neighbor," to borrow Massey's phrasing.[69] The narrative thus far bears this out, given that the pivotal events in the protagonist's journey, includ-

Figure 11. Wole's chance encounter with Jeje on the street

ing being hired as a bus conductor, initiated as a pickpocket, and rescued from public lynching, all result from accidental encounters on the street. In this sense, the narrative trope of the chance encounter—and its recurrence—describes one effect of the combinatorial quality of city life: frequent unintended interaction. The storyline of *The Revolt* commences with a fortuitous encounter that yet again redirects the protagonist's trajectory. Having fled his family's home in shame, Wole shelters under a bridge by night but begs along downtown Lagos Island by day. Most passersby ignore him studiously, but, in another staging of the "throwntogetherness" of urban space, an area boy named Jeje (Bayo Bankole) recognizes him immediately as a former schoolmate and friend.

He guides Wole to the neighborhood *buka* and introduces him to a large group of area boys and their leader Ebosa, the "*baba alaaye*," or area father, which thereby returns the protagonist to the fold of "family," even though the area boys' drinking, drug use, and other vulgarities pervert the adopted idiom of family bonds. Other video films, notably *Ayo Ni Mo Fe* (1994), *Rattlesnake*, and *Silent Night*, elaborate on the same theme of the promising male protagonist falling in with a gang of area boys, and area boys figure prominently in the popular perceptions of certain Lagos neighborhoods.[70] Wole's sense of responsibility to his consanguineous family remains uncompromised, and while the other area boys squander their money on strong drinks and drugs, he hustles and saves a generous sum to offer his mother and siblings. When he returns home with this gift, however, he discovers the Owolabi family has all but collapsed beneath the crush of misfortune. His father has perished in prison, and his sister, abandoned by her wealthy older suitor, has died in an attempted abortion. Despondent and aimless, Wole returns to the den of area boys. He wonders aloud how his street life is different from that of thieves and bandits, an insinuation that angers the other area boys and incites an argument. Friends turn on each other, exchange blows, break bottles, and upend tables, and as the chaos consumes the gang, Wole once again walks off sullenly into the shadows of downtown Lagos. Importantly, although Jeje disappears from the narrative at this point, the character resurfaces much later with crucial information that unwittingly ensnares the protagonist.

An intertitle moves the narrative ahead three years. In that time, Wole outgrew petty street crime to become the head of a formidable group of armed robbers, a transformation of character embodied by the replacement of the youthful actor Femi Adebayo by the more mature Taiwo Hassan in the lead role. Their violence is depicted spectacularly. We see the men hijack cars in broad daylight, burglarize homes by cover of night, and retreat to their hideout to divide heaps of loot. However, Wole insists that ground rules must be observed: create fear but shed no blood.[71] The narrative can still in good conscience frame armed robbery, in contrast to cold-blooded murder, as a crime of necessity, a tendency also found in popular Nigerian crime novels. As Wendy Griswold contends, tales of armed robbery and vigilante retaliation do not compel condemnation of the young male perpetrators for breaking the law because it is the law, and the social order for which it stands, that is in fact broken.[72] Such narratives—including the video film in question—shift affective and ideological investment away from the civic public toward what Peter Ekeh terms "the primordial public," which is governed by moral imperatives and wherein "the individual sees his duties as *moral* obligations to benefit and sustain a primordial public of which he is a member."[73] In other words, the moral expectation that characters, when faced with untrammeled corruption in governing institutions, will observe the authority of the rule of law gives way to other, more reliable moral attachments, such as the fulfillment of obligations to the character's family, friends, and wider social circle.

Intriguingly, *Owo Blow* exploits this tension by envisaging a situation wherein the protagonist's turn to crime enables him to fulfill—and far exceed—these various responsibilities to the people who surround and depend upon him. The gang accepts Wole's terms, and—trust among thieves being what it is— all swear an oath that binds them together. The oath will, of course, return to haunt Wole.

At this point, Wole stands as the conduit between two social realms, the Lagos underworld with its illicit accumulation and circulation, and decent society where attainment of the good life includes having the material means to provide for family and friends and, thereby, to be as rich in people as in things, so to speak. In other words, he becomes a "hinge" that joins otherwise separate groups.[74] However, the hinge is an ambiguous position, as here it functions to connect discrete networks even as it ensures the two remain unconnected and mutually unknown. In fact, the network hinge resembles the figure of "the intermediary," increasingly discussed in scholarship on African urbanism, who derives advantage from position, often by virtue of getting literally in the middle of things.[75] It remains unclear whether the narrative intends to underscore this fact, but a tremendous amount of money and stolen goods passes through Wole's hands into the wider community, including his family, friends, employees, and charities. The resulting arrangement, in which Wole translates his "good fortune" into performances of good moral character, almost precisely recalls Ekeh's remark that, within the popular Nigeria moral economy, "a lucky man would not be a good man were he to channel all his lucky gains into his private purse. He will only continue to be a good man if he channels part of the largesse from the civic public to the primordial public."[76]

The remainder of the narrative arc of *Owo Blow: The Revolt* works out a familiar didactic pattern, one that echoes the moral dualism of Yoruba popular theater's narrative construction, discussed in chapter 1. While his accomplices squander their stolen wealth on fleeting crude comforts, Wole uses it to create an alternate life for himself, with a thriving business, a house for his mother and siblings, and a bride-to-be named Bimbo—the life he should have had if fate had not dealt with him so harshly. The contours of this middle-class life are sketched in some detail because they represent the attainment of the good life, something that, following an underlying melodramatic logic, Wole and his family have long deserved, almost as moral compensation for their years of virtuous suffering, beginning with the first paroxysm of tears at the news of his father's unjust imprisonment. Importantly, the misfortunes of life have taught Wole to be generous and, in his words, to "invest in people, not material things." Despite his wealth's illicit source, Wole exemplifies the moral management of it when he channels his money into his social connections and thus fulfills his obligations to family, friends, and acquaintances.

As Wole invests in his people, the narrative reconnects the protagonist to a raft of characters from his youth in a manner almost meant to remind the viewer of the numerous social connections Wole has accumulated over his lifetime. He calls old acquaintances into his executive office to dole out generous portions of his wealth, advice, and goodwill. He shares his good fortune with past allies, like the *danfo* driver Akanni and the motor park chairman, as well as past adversaries, such as Ebosa, head of the area boys, and the lecherous landlord. Everyone he knew is brought into the fold, but Wole does not stop there. He donates to an orphanage, constructs new housing for hundreds of the homeless living under Lagos's bridges, and grants scholarships to promising university students in need, and this philanthropy earns him admiration. His acts construct for him a new public persona. In newspaper headlines and on the lips of ordinary Lagosians, his nickname—"Owo Blow"—becomes synonymous with charity and goodwill. "Wole wisely invests his money, transforming himself into a philanthropist and chief executive officer of Owolabi Multi-Investment Limited, and thus a respectable member of society."[77] The charitable expenditure narratively shifts the protagonist from the social fringe to the center and enacts his performative transformation from street urchin to beloved public figure. Of course, the other thieves, who consume their wealth with selfish enjoyment, also call themselves businessmen; discuss foreign currencies; and mention trips to Chicago, New York, and London; but these are mere words viewed by all as plain deceptions. Their guises have no performative force because nothing is enacted through the mere fact of holding wealth; rather, what matters is what one does with it, and for Wole that includes marriage.

Poignantly, Ekeh asks what the individual gets in return for material contributions to the primordial public and concludes that "although the African gives *materially* as part of his duties to the primordial public, what he gains back is not material. He gains back intangible, immaterial benefits in the form of identity and psychological security."[78] As the narrative proceeds, the protagonist's connections to his community expand, appropriately enough, with the introduction ceremony that customarily precedes Yoruba marriages. Wole's extended family now includes his neighbors and friends, the *alajogbe* having effectively become *alajobi*, who together visit the village of his fiancée

Bimbo's family.[79] The occasion, which represents the formal marriage proposal, calls for a large entourage of the groom's family to visit the hometown of the bride's family to make his intentions known, to offer an engagement gift, to allow the bride's family to take their measure, and, ideally, to celebrate the couple's engagement. It involves certain customary gestures, which in *Owo Blow* include a series of questions posed to Wole's family: "Who do you seek? Where have you come from? What do you want?" The answers to these questions locate Wole and his family both geographically and genealogically: "We are the family of Mr. and Mrs. Ishola Owolabi from Oboto in Ondo"; the utterance of Wole's father's name is accompanied by the *dundun*, or "talking drum," which sounds the intonations of Ishola Owolabi, thus lending even greater thickness to the scene's sense of cultural specificity and belonging. The scene showcases a glimpse of Yoruba culture, and although an exhibitionistic mode lightly marks some moments, there hangs over the scene the playful warmth of genuine enjoyment, which affectively underscores the intangible dividends of Wole's material performances of social responsibility: recognition of belonging.

More broadly, to the extent that Nollywood tends to translate intangible values into tangible figurations—for the sake of moral legibility, for instance—the village often serves as the embodiment of the belonging that Lagos cannot afford characters in early video films. To illustrate this point, consider the roll of the village in *Living in Bondage*, whose protagonist Andy, after years of fruitless struggle to get ahead in Lagos, sacrifices his dedicated and loving wife, Merit, as a rite of initiation into a billionaire's club that uses occult powers to enrich its members. Haynes asserts that the video film established the foundations for many of the enduring conventions of Nollywood, including representations of the spatial, moral, and material relations between city and village. "Andy has left his village to come to the city, measuring himself against the city and facing its temptations as he seeks to find his place in life, but he is still surrounded by his family, which is to say his village society, held to account by it, judged by its standards, enmeshed in its texture, navigating by its landmarks."[80] That moral accounting comes due when, following Merit's inexplicable death, Andy suddenly becomes immensely wealthy and suspicions arise in his village in the East and among the Igbo community within Lagos. (It bears mentioning that the film is in Igbo language and features a largely Igbo cast.) When Andy returns to the village in his new Mercedes to announce his intention to marry another woman, his own family reminds him of the customary mourning period for Merit's passing, which they will observe out of love for their daughter-in-law, even if he will not. In this way, Andy's willingness to extract wealth by killing an intimate relation—to transform Merit's closest intimacy into her greatest vulnerability, to echo Louis's dying words to Ahana in *Rattlesnake*—is juxtaposed with his family's love for Merit and commitment to honor their obligation to their daughter-in-law even in death. Thus spurned, Andy rises to go, presents a wad of cash, and offers 20,000 naira to help take care of his family, which insults his father. When Andy instructs a young relative to pack quickly and come with him to Lagos for proper schooling, his father retorts, "You want to take someone else to Lagos. Where is Merit whom you went with?" The scene is pivotal. The depiction of the village "does not aim at showing us a rural idyll," as Haynes notes, "but this scene powerfully conveys the dignity, deep emotion, and unshakeable principles of the family. They cannot be fooled or bought."[81] As Andy's family ties in the village thus fray, he grows more stubbornly ensnared by his in-laws. Merit's family demands an explanation for her death and sends representatives to Andy's village and to Lagos, ensuring the protagonist is held socially accountable to—bound to—others around him, including those in the village who can appear unannounced at his doorstep in Lagos.

The encounter between a wayward individual in Lagos and the community of the village is, as mentioned at the outset, one common example of combinational narration's culmination in scenarios of social, cultural, and moral legibility. Similarly, in *Rattlesnake*, the death of the virtuous father prompts the family, including his deceitful brother Odinaka, to return East to the village where he is interred. Ahanna, in scenes of "righteous agricultural labor," toils sunup to sundown on the village farm to sustain his siblings, a narrative demonstration of his impeccable moral character and work ethic, in subtle contrast with *Living in Bondage*, where the dignity of village life is a matter of course without need for romanticized display.[82] In *Died Wretched* as well, characters are surrounded in Lagos by community members from their village, and the "village" elders who convene to discuss burial rites for the good brother, Lucas, do not journey from the East, as they are all apparently already leading lives in Lagos. The group acknowledges that Lucas deserves a burial at home in the village, but with money among them being scarce, they decide with resignation to bury him in Lagos. The half measure signifies the extent to which Lucas fails his deceased brother and further articulates the narrative's moral implications.

Therefore, the village is in the city, and the city is in the village, such that the two remain contemporaneous in tense. As such, the village does not simply stand for "the governance of the prior," wherein moral force is grounded by an authentic connection to past tradition or some unchanging inheritance.[83] (In fact, such a vision of the village serves as the source of humor in a comedy like *Ikuku: Hurricane* (1995), in which urbane Raymond Ezigbo—with a doctorate in nuclear physics—is called home from Lagos to become the village oracle's priest.) This owes, in no small part, to the continual migration between city and village: journeying to Lagos to find work, for instance, or traveling from Lagos to home for celebrations and important life events—such as marriage engagements—to keep up ties.[84]

PERIPETEIA, OR NO CONDITION IS PERMANENT

The simplest conceptualization of networks as configurations of nodes and links adopts a spatial vantage point that obscures the fact that social connection unfolds within time. Attention to time is central to Barad's concept of entanglement, especially the principle of reiterative enactment, which, like social demonstrations of trustworthiness and dependability discussed above, involves performative rehearsal. In contrast with the static mapping of networks, narration entails the organization of information over time and, in this respect, is especially suited to capture the eventfulness of cities, or the city as an event undergoing ceaseless elaboration. I have argued that video films narrate through combinational scenarios that assemble characters in ways meant to create action, or in other words, narrative events. Effectively, video films tend to narrate Lagos through social webbing rather than spatial mapping. In *Owo Blow*, the narrative culminates with a dramatic reversal of fortune for Wole, brought about by the revelations of his enmeshment within various social connections, and a deeper understanding of the ironies of city life.

Owo Blow: The Genesis traces the attenuation of Wole's social life to the point of abandonment, while *Owo Blow: The Revolt* recounts Wole's efforts to restore his relations within decent society. That others now rely upon him and that he enjoys the intangible dividends of belonging are evidence of this achievement. However, there remains the matter of his ties to crime, a set of social associations that enabled his rise but now jeopardize his good name, social standing, and freedom. Wole attempts to disentangle himself from the gang of thieves who squandered every kobo of their stolen wealth, but they resist and even maneuver to draw him into deeper involvement. In the smoke-filled hideout where the robbers strategize their largest heist to date, Wole refuses to participate and attempts to dissuade his accomplices with offers of money from his own pocket. Instead, the gang threatens to expose his criminal connections if he refuses to join the heist. In this closing scene of *The Revolt*, the gang members invoke the oath that initially bound them together. The threat is not lost on Wole, who complies but insists the armed robbery will be his last. The premise of this conflict is patently implausible, but sensationalism is the idiom with which Nollywood articulates larger social and moral pronouncements.

In *Owo Blow: The Final Struggle*, the video film's third installment, Wole moves ahead with the good life he has built from a troubled past. As he luxuriates in his mansion, his new wife, Bimbo, excitedly brings a letter from his correspondence education program announcing he had earned his diploma. He builds a house for his mother, who will never again live under a landlord's roof. Years of happiness pass before inevitably, one day, the police arrest and interrogate two members of the old band of thieves, including Jugnu (Yinka Quadri), who names Wole as an accomplice. Wole repudiates any connection to the criminal network and counters that Jugnu's true aim is extortion. Given Wole's public identity as an entrepreneur and philanthropist, the police are skeptical, but the accusation initiates the (prolonged) investigation and trial that guide the narrative to its conclusion. Spontaneous protests erupt outside the courthouse in support of "Owo Blow," the kind-hearted philanthropist, while inside the courtroom the narrative depicts the trial as narrowly adjudicating the question of acquaintances—who is connected to whom rather than what crimes have been committed—staged decidedly within melodrama's theatrics of recognition.[85] For instance, Jugnu calls as a witness an area boy with no fixed place of employment, no formal place of residence, and no name other than Bantam Weight, who replies to the attorney's questions in the first-person plural, as if speaking for area boys generally: "*Káàkiri káàkiri l'awa n se isé tiwa!*" (We do our work everywhere in the city!). He assures the court that "I'm known all over! From Isale-Eko to Oke-Arin, everywhere. Just ask my name." The court attempts but fails to recognize this man by name, place, and profession, even struggling to comprehend his "street"-inflected Yoruba, while Bantam Weight, in turn, states he does not, as Jugnu had hoped, recognize Wole with his luxurious robe and new stature.

As the trial moves forward, the protagonist mobilizes his extensive network of friends, including Akanni, Ebosa, and the landlord, to aver his integrity. "I can't let my image be tarnished. That is why I don't have many friends," he remarks in echo of the idea that intimacy bleeds into vulnerability. As Adesokan notes, "Wole makes the significant statement that 'I have no other relatives than you,' thus binding the disparate individuals into a familial structure on the basis of good deeds turning both ways."[86] Here, intriguingly, an odd narrative complicity stirs the viewer to hope this mutuality that "turns both ways" can hold out against the recriminations of Wole's former partners in crime, whose *truthful* testimony jeopardizes the narrative's drive to deliver the good life for its protagonist in a melodramatic offer of reward for his lifelong embattled virtue. To evade incrimination and protect his good name from tarnish, Wole insists his past lives—as bus conductor, pickpocket, homeless beggar, and area boy—must be concealed from the public and the authorities and accordingly implores each man to deny the nature of their past connection to him. Thus, "the purpose of the gathering, oddly enough, is to encourage the men to deny any previous association with Wole."[87] The plan succeeds, and Jugnu is unable to convince the court that the well-known philanthropist businessman was once the leader of a gang of armed robbers, whose true source of wealth was plunder. Again, intriguingly, despite having witnessed these facts ourselves, the viewer's close identification with the protagonist permits a willful amnesia, a passive disavowal of the character's past identities and actions that parallels the well-intentioned disavowal that Wole's circle of supporters offers. Viewers, like those characters elevated by their connections to the protagonist, do not doubt that Wole deserves his freedom and good fortune. At this juncture, the narrative operates under the abiding ambivalence that, as discussed in chapter 1, defers judgment and preserves a moral, ideological elasticity.

Of course, video films can only offer representations of performative enactments, which are not themselves performative, strictly speaking. However, to position viewers to sympathize with—to give recognition to—the social self that the protagonist has created through generosity and virtuous deeds brings the narrative quite close to effecting such an enactment. The trial scenario prompts the staging of recognition, as it provides the occasion for multiple characters to assemble in the courtroom in orchestrated encounters that, in keeping with combinational narration, generate narrative eventfulness. The courtroom serves a similar role in *Hostages* (1997) and *Domitilla*, wherein the protagonist's vindication is underwritten by the interrogative procedures of a trial, even as judicial principles are left blurrily in the background. Still, Okome characterizes this pattern as narrative recourse to reason as opposed to the religious retribution of the church or prayer circle, which provides the setting for similar scenes of recognition in a number of video films.[88] Thus, we have another recurrent scenario in Nollywood's combinational mode of narration. In another context, these scenes would be said to involve peripety, or the reversal of fortunes (which is followed by anagnorisis, or the removal of non-knowledge), a technique that inflects the narrative arc and, I would add, taps into the temporality of Barad's iterative enactment. Who characters are for one another remains contingent upon the entanglements in which they are held together, and by narrative design, sudden reversals change characters in ways that have wider ramifications and moral import. Interestingly, in *Owo Blow: The Final Struggle*, Wole's reversal of fortunes is triggered by the abrupt return of the character Jeje, which itself stages the liabilities inherent in social connections.

Once Wole is vindicated in court, an intertitle moves the story two weeks forward, at which point the nearly forgotten Jeje returns to Lagos enriched by spurious dealings in Port Harcourt, he scuffles with an envious friend at the area boys' old gathering spot, and all are promptly arrest. In police custody, Jeje attempts to talk his way to release, alludes to friends in Port Harcourt who will put up bail, which the police ignore, and finally demands a call to Owo Blow, his powerful friend in Lagos. The police inspector on duty—implausibly, the same officer previously assigned to investigate Wole—pounces on this lead, ushers Jeje from his cell, entices him with food, and extracts the entire tale of Jeje and Wole's friendship, which he records as evidence. "Now you're jittery because I mentioned the name of an important man," Jeje remarks, himself unaware of the events of Wole's trial in Lagos. This is the same Wole Owolabi who owns the Owolabi Multi-Investment Limited, the inspector inquires, which Jeje affirms, boasting that, in fact, he introduced Wole to the "business" of area boys. Like the return of an irrepressible entanglement, this revelation puts in motion the final machinations of the three-part saga. Although the police resurrect the case and ask to introduce Jeje as a new witness, Wole's attorney maneuvers to quash the request and advises Wole not to worry, dismissively adding "I will handle the rest." The viewer must trust that the attorney will handle Jeje's testimony as easily as Jugnu's, because unlike the previous court challenge, the narrative does not reroute to depict the protagonist's defense, vindication, and attainment of the good life. The court may absolve Wole, but the narrative has other business to settle. It veers obliquely toward a tragic conclusion: the news of Jeje's return initiates the prolonged final sequence of Wole's suicide. But if the case can be won, what necessitates the protagonist's death? In a series of flashbacks, a remorseful Wole recollects his lifetime of misfortunes and the people who saved him. Among other memories, the story returns to the moment Jeje discovers and *recognizes* his friend Wole as the beggar on the street. The fateful moment parallels the narrative present, but faced with the same choice, Wole decides to repudiate his friend because the hand that helped lift him from destitution, ironically, now threatens to pull his life crashing down. He denies Jeje in order to forestall the discovery and recognition of his full identity by his family, friends, and the wider public, and this moral crisis suggests, in an imprecise way, what necessitates the protagonist's death. Wole's suicide note to Bimbo attempts to tie up these ambiguous threads of the narrative and to put in words a moral lesson ("The little help you render today will go a long way to help others") that the larger narrative structure does not quite manage to articulate clearly.

In one sense, character reversals and returns fit comfortably within video film's aesthetic of outrage as subordinate narrative devices intended to generate scenes of astonishment and moral reckoning. Brian Larkin coined this term to designate video film's ability to scandalize viewers and thereby reinforce moral principles through intense affective experience.[89] "The negation of morality [depicted] in the film is designed to stimulate it in the audience," Larkin argues, "vivifying social norms and making them subject to public comment."[90] The argument is indebted, in part, to Peter Brooks's widely influential study on the melodramatic imagination, including the notions of recognition and the moral occult, which dramatic reversals and unlikely returns brought to light. As Brooks notes, "Melodrama needs a repeated use of peripety and coups de théâtre because it is here that characters are best in a position to name the absolute moral attributes of the universe, to say its nature as they proclaim their own." In Brooks's view, melodrama responds to the unmooring of old certitudes in a world dramatically upended by rapid historical change, and in this sense its drive toward moral recognition addresses, almost in a compensatory fashion, the uncertainties facing the individual subject in emergent circumstances of social and moral disarray.[91]

However, dramatic reversals and the return of past acquaintances are also common conventions of televisual melodramas, such as the telenovela and the soap opera. In this context, "rather than engineering symbolic confrontations," Gledhill posits that "soap opera's sudden reversals or coincidences may render life's habit of disappointing expectation or of throwing up undesirable complications."[92] In a similar vein, as I have argued, Nollywood's staged return of long-lost characters speaks to the perseverance of social connections, for better or worse, which the narrative can frame as a symbolic confrontation—moral accountability embodied in the figure of the neglected social relation—or as a reminder of the vexing potential for unsolicited entanglements to intervene and frustrate one's path toward some deserved attainment, the thing that will have made one's strivings worth it. Unresolved remains the question of what one ought to do about the inevitable mutual dependencies that hold life up in Lagos.

CHAPTER 4

New Nollywood and the New Image

The story of Nollywood's unlikely origins has by now been thoroughly detailed in scholarly and journalistic accounts that often frame the Nigerian film industry as perpetually on the rise. It is true that in its first decade Nollywood thrived by releasing thousands of films directly to video markets and networks of petty commerce that carried the films across West Africa. However, by the mid-2000s, signs within Nollywood suggested that the industry had entered a period of generalized fatigue, both among audiences hungry for new stories and more refined images and among producers disheartened by the race to the bottom in revenues triggered by the industry's unchecked expansion. Piracy and high levels of competition perpetually eroded dwindling earnings. Nevertheless, Nollywood's regional cultural dominance remained and spurred the search for alternative avenues of distribution. Along these lines, a number of filmmakers began to experiment with high-stakes, big-budget films explicitly intended for exhibition at national, regional, and diasporic cinemas. The hope was that Nollywood might find renewed life on the big screen in multiplex cinemas that continue today to multiply in major cities across southern Nigeria.

New Nollywood has come to describe the top-of-the-line films that have since emerged from this ongoing process of industry segmentation. For industry insiders, this new brand of film satisfies the anticipation that the industry will gradually rise to achieve so-called international standards and to access broader regional and diasporic cultural flows, extending Nollywood's reach to wider audiences, with the hope that in turn this will propel even more growth and improvement. But the films themselves remain scarce in local video markets, such as Alaba and Oshodi, in part because producers must safeguard their films—and the large financial investment each represents—from exposure to the piracy that attends wide-scale DVD circulation. As such, more than anything, theatrical release and high production values set New Nollywood films apart from the straight-to-disc video films. With respect to depictions of Lagos, New Nollywood films portray both the glossy and the gritty ends of the urban spectrum, but always through a lens that is markedly aestheticized. In particular, they adopt a visual style that Carmela Garritano describes as "an assemblage of desires, bodies, objects, and intensities that presents spectators with pleasurable, affective encounters with new urban consumerism."[1] This chapter examines how New Nollywood and its spaces of exhibition lend fuller texture and density to screen representations of urban life and have driven production practices that illustrate the increased value placed on polished images and refined production values. Thus far, a recurrent assertion of this book has been that, in television programs and video films, narrative bears the representation burden of depicting city life, which is itself instructive. This changes with New Nollywood and its attentiveness to technical sophistication, which has encouraged the generation of new images of Lagos and new modes of envisioning the city.

Nevertheless, the most definitive measure of the divide between mainstream Nollywood and New Nollywood remains their distinct circuits of production and distribution. New Nollywood reaches audiences by bypassing the grassroots home video market in favor of new distribution windows, including satellite television, streaming video websites, video on demand, in-flight entertainment, and theaters in West Africa and the diaspora. While not every Nigerian film that appears in cinemas is a New Nollywood film, the titles most often cited as illustrating the emergence of a new trend all had premieres in theaters before ever appearing on DVD. The theatrical release in 2010 of four Nollywood films—Chineze Anyaene's *Ijé: The Journey*, Kunle Afolayan's *The Figurine*, Jeta Amata's *Inale*, and Lonzo Nzekwe's *Anchor Baby*—signaled a coup for the industry in view of local producers. These were followed in 2011 by Mahmood Ali-Balogun's *Tango with Me*, Obi Emelonye's *Mirror Boy*, and Funke Akindele's *The Return of Jenifa*, among others since. The following year saw the theatrical release of more than twenty Nollywood films as the slotting of Nollywood movies alongside Hollywood and Bollywood fare became a normal arrangement.[2] In this sense, the cinemas serve as both the first window in a tiered system of release and a starting point for gauging what is new—and not so new—in Nollywood.

Although box office revenue is rarely strong, and most movies shown at multiplex cinemas are not Nigerian, these venues have become integral to New Nollywood. Without mechanisms for formalized estimation of value, theatrical release becomes one mark of distinction with which producers distinguish their film from numerous other available titles. As Adejunmobi illustrates, theatrical exhibition seems to increase the prospect that a film will be licensed by video streaming services dedicated to Nigerian movies.[3] In other words, cinemas lend the perception of success amid an informal distribution terrain that long evaded measurement. Furthermore, I highlight these networks of distribution because they reveal Nollywood's material emplacement within Lagos and other major cities throughout Nigeria. Multiplex cinemas symbolize the screen media industry's association with Lagos and should be understood in relation to Nollywood's other physical spaces, such as the National Arts Theatre, the video marketplace on Lagos Island, the producers' offices in Surulere, and the film sets in Lekki.

TRENDS IN SEGMENTATION

In the mid-2000s, the industry experienced the growing pains of a distribution crisis that exposed the constraints of its informal organization, as well as the impossibility of simply imposing formal distribution structures from the top down. Subsequent shifts in film production and distribution methods have responded to the overproduction of low-grade movies that continually saturate the video market as well as the unlicensed television broadcast of Nollywood movies, which has created a new puncture in an already leaky distribution system.[4]

In 2007, the Nigerian Film and Video Censors Board (NFVCB) pushed to implement its New Distribution Licensing Framework, a combination of measures that sought to regulate participation in video film distribution, to encourage the consolidation of distribution around fewer marketers operating with a larger capital base and supply networks with national reach, and to introduce mechanisms to generate formal documentation of the film industry's scale of economic activity. Such documentation, it was believed, would substantiate the industry's value and growth and attract investment by regional and international media companies. But it also directly jeopardized the livelihood of the marketers who prefer the business of the film industry to remain ensconced within the informal relations of the video marketplace, where lack of transparency allowed numerous small operators to thrive, as Jade Miller's work astutely shows.[5] In response, the marketers rebuffed the NFVCB's intervention and succeeded in watering down the framework's new provisions, thereby muting its impact on video disc distribution.[6] Nonetheless, piracy and overproduction continued to drive down the returns on physical disc sales and create an increasingly desperate situation for production. The industry needed to develop new ways to deliver Nollywood films to audiences.

In response, producers have adopted a range of strategies. Some continue to push the limits of how swiftly and cheaply a film can be shot, pressed to VCD, and disbursed to video markets, a process that appears today more like the assembly line of a factory or even "subsistence filmmaking," to borrow veteran director Bond Emeruwa's phrase (personal communication, June 15, 2014). These sensationalist films rip stories straight from the headlines of local tabloid publications and even borrow the images printed on disc jackets directly from video tabloids.

Another trend has been to foster niche markets in indigenous-language films that appeal to audiences based on shared language, experiences, and attention to topical issues. Yoruba-language filmmakers have quite successfully operated in this way for years, addressing a loyal ready-made audience on perennial themes, with actors whose presence alone implies a welcome predictability for viewers familiar with their screen personas and performance repertoires. Carmela Garritano has observed a similar trend in Ghana's video film industry, where she identifies a pattern of Akan-language films that are "topical in focus and made and consumed quickly [and that] dialogue directly with local publics."[7]

The most successful production companies employ a strategic combination of high- and low-end film practices. Emem Isong's Royal Arts Academy, for instance, is organized so as to allow the production unit to work simultaneously on four or five films in different stages of completion and to release no fewer than six features in a year.[8] Like a major film studio, Royal Arts can anticipate that a few features, like *Okon Lagos* (2012) or *Nollywood Hustlers* (2009), will sell exceptionally well, allowing Isong to recuperate revenue losses on other films. This method gives Royal Arts the advantage of maintaining continual forward momentum, since Isong does not depend on turnover from one film to bankroll new films. As she explains in an interview, "I don't wait for the turnover, but I know eventually it's going to come."[9] New productions and releases are lined up so that they overlap, meaning that Isong does not need to wait for one film to peak in sales before putting money into a new production. This affords her producers and directors the leeway to tailor different filmmaking practices to low- and high-end markets in an overall strategy for attenuating financial risk. For instance, Isong asserts that her Ibibio-language films, produced quickly and inexpensively, are so popular with audiences in the Southeast that they bring a larger return than her high-budget English-language films that can circulate across West Africa. In this sense, Royal Arts employs a logic of translocal cross-collateralization that, according to Simon During, was common among the first movies consciously aimed at transnational film markets.[10] The difference is that Isong's company makes this model workable across the ethnic, linguistic, and regional lines along which the industry has witnessed growing segmentation. The fact that this sort of differentiation occurs within a single company, almost like Hollywood's tiered system of "A" and "B" productions, indicates that Nollywood's recent hodgepodge of films does not arise from a gap in technical capabilities or competency as much as it reflects different filmmakers' strategies for contending with an unwieldy video market.

Importantly, the sustained success of indigenous-language films should not be overlooked. Despite the eye-grabbing publicity campaigns of New Nollywood and corporate Nollywood theatrical releases, indigenous-language video films broadcast on television seem to remain the most widely viewed screen media in Nigeria.[11] It cannot be repeated enough that straight-to-disc video films, whether purchased in video markets, viewed free on television, or streamed from YouTube, remain the bulk of Nollywood content released and consumed within Nigeria. In fact, straight-to-disc releases—and their unregulated redistributed formats—still represent what we might call "mainstream Nollywood," a term that indicates both their numerical majority and their popular aesthetic and cultural sensibilities. Furthermore, "New" Nollywood implies an "Old" Nollywood, but such language inaccurately frames the distinction in temporal terms, which imposes a developmentalist narrative onto the industry that erases the producers and productions that make up its popular center of gravity and whose works are not only contemporaneous with theatrical and streaming service releases but also socially and culturally revealing points of comparison.

JENIFA

Among the titles released from 2010–11 marking the beginning of a new phase in Nollywood, *The Return of Jenifa* represents a noteworthy anomaly in the narrative of New Nollywood's rise. The film was an unlikely box office success, earning 38 million naira to become the highest-grossing Nigerian film on record at that time, but its tremendous success arguably turned on the preexisting popularity of Akindele's on-screen persona rather than the fulfillment of "international standards" of filmmaking. First appearing in the Yoruba-language video film *Jenifa* (2008), Akindele's eponymous character inspired a small franchise, following the release of *The Return of Jenifa*, that includes the long-running televisual series *Jenifa's Diary* (2015–present) on iROKOtv. Therefore, the full trajectory of Funke Akindele's *Jenifa* film and television series has endured several historical moments of structural change that also spans straight-to-disc, theatrical release, and streaming service distribution platforms. The series brings into focus several important dimensions of this transition, especially the pivot toward "cinematic" production values, new technology and production practices, brand sponsorships, and windowed distribution, but also demonstrates the persistence of what Lani Akande calls the "character of recurrence," a performance style rooted in video film and Yoruba theater,[12] as well as the telling popularity of a character type premised on an ambiguous identity of local and global amalgamation.

The original *Jenifa* (2008), released on VCD by the Yoruba-language marketing company Olasco Films, begins as a campus-based comedy centered on Jenifa's (Funke Akindele) transformation into a Lagos "big girl." The young protagonist leaves her village to attend the University of Lagos, a school with connotations of privilege and prestige. Her fashionable new friends at university insist she "blend," by which they mean replace her local appearance, mannerisms, and name (Suliat) with a new name (Jenifa) and persona meticulously styled after trends in global popular culture. The humor turns on the characters' embodiment of "local" and "global" culture and the resulting play upon familiar stereotypes about those with and without "exposure" to cosmopolitan sensibilities. The narrative proceeds in comic episodes that showcase incongruities in style of dress, accent, grasp of English slang, and sensibilities toward men and money. The group of friends, who describe themselves as "big girls," attracts the attention of "big men" willing to pay for the company of young, beautiful, and stylish women. The university students oblige, meet these men for liaisons at swank hotels, enjoy their largesse, and eventually grow overconfident, unwilling to heed the warning signs of danger ahead. Ultimately, each friend in Jenifa's clique meets with demise in a manner that illustrates the consequences that follow from a life lived frivolously. Jenifa learns she contracted HIV from her sexual encounters with wealthy men. The conclusion, marked by troubling, misogynist overtones,[13] remains in keeping with Nollywood's tendency to bend the final narrative arc to meet a desired moral endpoint.

Intriguingly, the first events of the sequel, *The Return of Jenifa*, effectively reverse all of this. Jenifa wakes from a nightmare—the same footage of the original diagnosis scene—and is thus released from the consequences and closure of the original narrative, free to pick up where she left off. The story reestablishes her character and the ground rules for the film's particular variety of comedy. Jenifa never quite sheds all traces of her local, village girl mannerisms, which are now presented as endearing and innocently humorous. Her renewed effort to become a fashionable Lagosian woman is depicted in more exaggerated episodes than the original production's budget could afford. The cinematography, marked by tracking and craning shots in high resolution, seems intent to showcase equipment rarely used in previous productions, while heavy-handed product placement throughout heralds on-screen a new political economy of finance and production at work off-screen. Jenifa carries the latest smartphone, visits a shopping mall, relaxes in the airport's first-class lounge, and casually encounters young Nigerian pop icons like Wizkid, eLDee, and Kaffy. Ultimately, in the gap between the release of *Jenifa* and *The Return of Jenifa*, an unmistakable turn in the aesthetics of video film took place.

The original *Jenifa* was produced for straight-to-disc release within the informal sector of the video film industry. As Jade Miller importantly notes, in mainstream Nollywood, personal connections and a track record of successful coproductions are the strongest basis for trust and collaboration.[14] Funke Akindele is credited with the story concept and receives co-credit for screenwriting. However, the cast and crew indicate the strong influence of the financier and distributor Olatunji Balogun and his company Olasco Films.[15] Olasco Films brought on board Muhydeen S. Ayinde, the director of many of the company's other video films. The cast features actors familiar to Yoruba audiences, including Akindele, Yinka Quadri, Odunlade Adekola, Yomi Fash Lanso, and Eniola Badmus, niche celebrities within the star system of the Yoruba video film industry. Stylistically speaking, *Jenifa* is an artifact of the Yoruba-language video film industry based in Idumota, Lagos, and the video film, with its linguistic humor, narrative structure, genre conventions, and didactic mode of address, exemplifies this sector's orientation toward direct dialogue with the local public of Yoruba-speaking audiences in the nation's Southwest region. All of this situates *Jenifa* comfortably within the wider milieu of the mainstream video film industry of the mid-2000s.

The sequel was produced for theatrical release, to be followed by disc distribution, and signs of this production and distribution strategy are in the film. The mark of Akindele's own creative control is more evident, beginning with an inspirational epigraph in her own words. New Nollywood tends to have a central creative figure behind the scenes, typically the director but occasionally the producer or screenwriter. The financing for *The Return of Jenifa* was raised through brand sponsorship deals and support from the Lagos state government, both of which surely entailed formal contract arrangements. The first fifteen minutes of the film showcases a slew of thinly veiled product placements, while various brand logos appear along the bottom frame, similar to a television sponsor's digital on-screen graphics, throughout the rest of the narrative. Akindele poses in the bathroom mirror and admires aloud her new brand of toothpaste. Phone credit vendors hold an implausibly detailed conversation about the advantages of service with the sponsoring telecommunications company. As mentioned, the film's theatrical release launched Akindele's persona from a Yoruba-language video film character into a new brand entity in its own right. National newspapers reported this as a significant development for all of Nollywood, and this trope of a pioneering success story remains part of New Nollywood's discursive formation. Since 2015, Akindele's spin-off television series, *Jenifa's Diary*, has released 105 twenty-minute episodes on the video streaming platform iROKOtv. Having traversed the gap between mainstream Nollywood and New Nollywood, Akindele's character points up the recent segmentation of the industry but also demonstrates, by the same token, the continuities that mark these distinct but contemporaneous segments of the screen media industry.

MULTIPLEX CINEMAS

In 2004 Silverbird Group, a private media house with holdings in radio, film distribution and exhibition, television, and real estate, opened a five-screen cinema on the top floor of the company's newly built shopping center in the posh seaside commercial district of Victoria Island.[16] The construction of the country's first multiscreen cinema in an affluent pocket of urban development signaled a departure from the cinema culture of the 1970s and 1980s, which flourished around the National Arts Theatre and some thirty cinema halls located across Lagos that brought American, Chinese, Indian, and some Nigerian films to broad urban audience until these theaters closed in the early 1990s.[17] The success of the Silverbird franchise sparked renewed interest in cinema exhibition, which seemed more viable given the return of relative security and stability to Lagos. City Mall Cinemas in Lagos Island began operating in 2007 but has since closed. Two others founded in 2008, however, remain mainstays of Lagos cinemagoing, Genesis Deluxe Cinemas in Lekki and Ozone Cinemas in Yaba, which is owned by the Silverbird Group and was established as the first multiplex on the mainland and is especially popular among nearby university students.[18] The founder of Filmhouse Cinemas, Kene Mpkaru, had a more ambitious business strategy that involved the simultaneous construction of multiscreen cinemas in cities across Nigeria to establish a sustainable chain of theaters all at once rather than build incrementally. By 2021, the company was operating five cinemas in Lagos, two in Ibadan, and others in Akure, Benin City, Kano, and Port Harcourt. Smaller cinema operators have also arrived on the scene, including Lighthouse Cinemas (Warri and Jibowu), Mcrystal Cinema (Abeokuta and Ijebu), Viva Cinemas (Ibadan, Ilorin, Enugu, Ikeja, and Ota), and Kada Cinemas (Benin and Port Harcourt). However, three companies—Silverbird, Genesis, and Filmhouse—control the majority of multiplex cinemas with a strong combined presence in many of the largest cities: Lagos, Abuja, Ibadan, Kano, Port Harcourt, and Uyo. These theaters represent an immense capital investment and a rapid reconfiguration of the distribution landscape, but, interestingly, multiplex cinemas also appear to be gaining ground in Nigeria at a time when such venues serve a greatly diminished role in distribution elsewhere in the world.[19]

Nigeria's cinema operators envision their theaters as leisure destinations for those seeking entertainment and an escape from the enervating grind of the city. "It's an excursion," as Jonathan Murray-Bruce, the general manager of Silverbird Entertainment, put it to me during a conversation about the galleria's opening.

> If you have a cinema alone, then people just come and go. We want to have an entertainment area, a mall where people will come to the cinema, go to shops and [partake of] everything. When you have a mall and a cinema together, you have a lot of people coming, but you want them to stay around. Those same people will want to go to a movie, will want to eat, will want to shop. . . . It's interrelated. They play off each other. And soon it becomes a destination, a full day event—especially considering traffic and how hard it is to get anywhere [in Lagos]. You want a place where it's convenient for people to come, enjoy their time, and then they go home so they aren't going from one place to

another. It's more incentive for them to come out. (personal communication, March 20, 2013)

The boundary between the chaotic streetscape and the galleria's highly controlled interior is marked by a security gate manned by a detail of private security guards. Beyond the entrance, one immediately confronts large advertisement banners draped from the top to the ground floor, bearing the brand images of telecommunications companies such as MTN, Airtel, and Etisilat, as well as those of Airk Airlines, Coca-Cola, and regional banks. The images encourage one's identification with a lifestyle of pleasure and enjoyment, of high technology, high fashion, and the idea that one must, as the motto above one retail clothing store exhorts, "Wear it, Love it, Live it." Within the building, screens are pervasive. A digital projector casts a video image across the floor before the circular central plaza, while dozens of smaller video screens are perched around the mall showing advertising images. The Union Bank on the ground level features a twelve-by-eight-foot flat-screen television that cycles through trailers for films currently showing at the cinema on the fourth floor. Small-screened consoles beam image and sound from atop small kiosks provided for patrons to charge their mobile devices. The mall's dedicated private generator, an expensive but essential infrastructure given the unreliable public grid that subjects Lagos to daily blackouts, produces the electricity that powers all of this.

The configuration of shops and attractions gives one the sense of an array of global spatial imaginaries drawn together, enframed within the structure of the shopping mall and composed to suggest their immediacy and accessibility. As Amit Rai argues of multiplex cinemas in India, "Middle-class habituations connect buying in the space of the [multiplex] to movement and modernity through technologies of the global (credit cards, privatized devoted energy generators, cell and land phone lines, wireless and fiber optics, English-speaking salespeople, regularized quality control, standardization . . .)."[20] In this way, the material organization of the multiplex cinema conscripts the body in the constitution of "modern" subjectivity and foregrounds the illusion of free and infinite mobility in the experience of that modernity.

Carmela Garritano recalls that when she entered the Silverbird franchise branch at the Accra Mall in Ghana, "though many of the specific stores were unknown to me, the mall seemed an utterly familiar place, its geography and atmosphere replicating any shopping mall I might find in the United States.

And this, of course, is precisely the point."[21] Be it Accra or Lagos, the mall promises the same pleasures that a clientele, who may have enjoyed a level of cosmopolitan "exposure," comes to expect from similar encounters abroad. To produce this effect, Silverbird Galleria in Lagos imported specialized technology and equipment and enlisted expert consultants from Universal Cinema Services, according to Patrick Lee, general manager of Silverbird's sister cinema, Ozone, and a member of Silverbird Group's board of trustees. Based in Texas, Universal Cinema Services functions something like a one-stop shop for cinema franchises from Japan and Italy to Ghana and Nigeria. The company provides consultation on architectural and spatial design, specialized labor for outfitting the cinema, and procurement of technology and equipment—from the film projector and sound system right down to the seating, popcorn machine, wallpaper, and tiles. It should, therefore, come as no surprise that for any well-traveled cinemagoer, entering a cinema hall provokes an experience of the uncanny.

The shopping center thus caters to the city's most elite consumers and explicitly brands itself as a landmark of exuberant leisure. It is precisely because of this overt coding that the Silverbird Galleria served, at this time, as a symbolically charged reference point for all Lagosians. In one scene from *The Return of Jenifa*, for instance, Jenifa enjoys an afternoon of shopping and spa treatment there. The sequence, otherwise insignificant to the plot, moves from establishing shots to interior shots so as to follow the character as she crosses the mall's threshold and marvels at the change of scenery. The sequence suggests a fascination with the ability of the mall, like that of the cinema, to create a lifelike world of its own. The shopping center provides the enhanced allure of environments that Achille Mbembe calls "synthetic spacetimes" or "constructed tableaux on which disparate images are grafted": environments "through which late modernity and the globalization of capitalism have transformed human [sensory] perceptions."[22] This stimulation of visitors' sensory perceptions and the mall's commodification of leisure time are integral to the space's construction of modern subjectivity, as we glimpse in Jenifa's orchestrated passage through the mall's threshold.

Silverbird's architecture and decor are a local iteration of a spatial form that is reproduced around the world, a globalized sensorium providing a unique affective experience and promising to insert spectators, as if seamlessly, into an immersive space of consumption that is shared around the globe. Significantly, the theater and cinematic experiences around which it is constructed promise similar pleasures: the illusion of freedom, as Amit Rai argues, in the form of choice from a plethora of options and the complete immersion of the body in "image-commodity consumption through the simulation of reality as its intensification."[23] The cinema's sensorium, furthermore, is as much temporal as it is spatial. In fact, the fantasy of immediacy and perfect contemporaneity with global media flows is so integral to Silverbird cinema's aura that the company petitioned (successfully) for the rights to premiere Hollywood blockbusters in tandem with their American premiere. Closing the temporal gap has enhanced the cinemagoer's fantasy of partaking in a global consumer culture in real time. The ritual of cinemagoing is made all the more dramatic by contrast with the backdrop of Lagos, its generalized condition of economic scarcity and fundamental spatial discontinuity, from which one retreats into a decor of continuity, mobility, and immediacy.

New Nollywood gravitates toward such venues because they bear the imprint of global consumerism and because releasing a film at the multiplex cinema can be imagined as tantamount to injecting Nigerian film culture into the global slipstream of image commodities. With screen images styled after sleek advertisements and its seamless storyworlds partitioned off from malfunction or disruption, New Nollywood appears comfortably at home in the space of the multiplex, striking an eerie visual harmony with the cinema sensorium. On another register, the films and theaters both demonstrate a deep preoccupation with real and imagined mobility, as evident in the films' narratives, which traverse national, cultural, and economic borders, and in the confines of the multiplex, where the fantasy of having the world in one's grasp comes alive through a complex assemblage of semiotic and sensory stimulations.

Multiplex cinemas of this sort do not succeed by catering to the biggest audiences possible but rather by drawing an urban consumer class willing to pay 1,500 naira (US$9.50 in 2013) per ticket and a loyal cadre of university students able to scrape together 500–1,000 naira for a discounted ticket. Initially, reluctant cinema operators began scheduling local films to appease tacit pressure from the NFVCB and public comments by Nollywood stakeholders. The move was viewed as a small concession to avoid a publicity battle over the cultural content of films appearing at the new cinemas and had by 2013 formed a status quo that required no long-term commitment from exhibitors, expanded their film offerings, and attached their brand image to the aura surrounding New Nollywood. Cinema operators did not, at that time and with the exception of Filmhouse, envision themselves as a distribution branch within the local film industry, but they have quickly reversed strategy as evidenced by the multiplication of screens, notably in cities beyond Lagos, and the scheduling of more Nigerian films. The case has been made that what Nollywood and the average Nigerian truly need is an extensive network of single-screen community cinemas in low-income, high-density neighborhoods. Proponents envision something similar to existing cinema venues in Kenya and South Africa and more formal than the once ubiquitous video parlors.[24] Such venues might also enable a certain public sociality around film that, as Añulika Agina insightfully notes, seems missing in multiplex theaters. Drawing comparison with Onookome Okome's memorable essay on video parlor spectatorship,[25] Agina remarks that unlike "street corners and beer parlors, where viewers engage in animated conversations, laughter or lamentations during and particularly after the film, it is worthwhile remembering that modern cinemas do not afford audiences the luxury of keeping up extended conversations with other non-familiar audiences," particularly because employees have ten minutes between screenings to clear and prepare the hall.[26]

Among producers, cinema distribution has prompted excitement owing, in part, to the belief circulating within and outside the film industry that New Nollywood movies do not suffer financial losses. Speculation has further fostered the belief that any theatrical release, even a short run at a handful of screens, will generate at least modest revenue for the producer, while some dream of making back their money before their film ever hits the video markets. But appearances are not what they seem, given that, in more cases than not, local films lose money on theatrical releases.[27] Federal and state entertainment taxes on exhibition venues remain punitively high, at as much as 20 percent of a film's net box office earnings. The remaining revenue is shared between the cinema operator and the producer according to a prearranged sliding scale that, under the most equitable contracts, begins at an even fifty-fifty split and slides each week in favor of the cinema operator. In a film's final week in theaters, as much as 70 percent of the revenue could go to the exhibitor, but few Nigerian films remain in theaters for long. Finally, producers who contract with a film distributor, like Blue Pictures, Silverbird Film Distribution, or FilmOne Distribution, forfeit a percentage of their film's earnings to the distributors in commission fees. When all is settled, the producer collects between 30 and 35 percent of the gross box office earnings, and 30 percent of next to nothing is still next to nothing. This means that all but the highest-performing films will fail to meet expected earnings and others will sustain colossal losses.

Furthermore, relations between producers and exhibitors are still not perfectly transparent. The decision concerning which time slot a film is assigned is a common point of contention, and distributors can stick producers with additional costs for what they term "consulting" on publicity and advertising, as well as for the printing of the materials themselves. To bankroll the cost of the theatrical release for *Maami* (2011), Tunde Kelani had to seek a loan, the repayment of which exhausted a large part the revenue earned at the cinema. Finally, producers are aware that, because exhibitors share a percentage of box office revenue on a sliding scale, a potential incentive exists for underreporting ticket sales, and while a producer can request a printed record of a film's weekly performance, no independent verification system is in place to ensure the accuracy of these figures. Still, revenue is not the only advantage that a film's theatrical release has to offer.

There has never been a time in the Nigerian screen media industry when predicting, quantifying, and verifying a film's performance has been a straightforward, transparent process. At the very least, a producer's record of continual releases indicates their personal acumen concerning which practices do and do not work within the generally opaque landscape in which movies are made and sold. A lack of exposure to measurement is a primary defining feature of informal economies of film production and distribution, especially insofar as reliable documentation and record keeping represent important prerequisites for regulation, taxation, proprietary enforcement, and other aspects of formalization.[28] Video film marketers have used the opacity of informality to their advantage, as Jade Miller illustrates.[29] However, it creates an imperative for producers working independently of the marketers to cultivate markers of success other than hard figures as, given the absence of measurement, something else must serve to ratify the performance of a film. For most New Nollywood producers, a theatrical release accompanied by a high-profile premiere event offers one such marker, and in this respect, box office numbers do not simply hold constative value but also performative value.

As Tejaswini Ganti argues regarding the blurry figures that film producers and cinema operators in India must work with, "ambiguity about commercial transactions is actually generative and productive."[30] When "fuzzy numbers," as Ganti calls them, are the only numbers available to gauge the outcome or the popularity of a film, it is sometimes merely the image of success that can attract deals with those entities that actually do pay, and in Nollywood today that includes sponsors, online distribution, video on demand, and television distribution. "Not being able to accurately measure outcome, rather than curtailing commercial activity . . . is generative—leading to certain contracts, business practices, performative displays, and discursive mechanisms that attract new capital as well as enable others to persist in the industry."[31] Kunle Afolayan clearly grasps this principle, as his fascinating comments on piracy at a public lecture in Lagos in 2013 illustrate. Of course, video piracy and unlicensed television broadcast are two reasons for the lack of firm figures on Nollywood's viewership. However, in sponsorship negotiations, as Afolayan explained, he emphasizes rumors of the industry's struggle with rampant piracy to bolster the legitimacy of the proposed estimated viewership for his films. He reminds prospective sponsors that "there is no way [this film] is *not* going to be pirated. In fact, it will be pirated the day it is released. And as soon as someone pirates it, it gets to Ghana, Togo, London, America, everywhere!" (personal communication, December 6, 2012). This narrative helps construct an image of high demand, where there is largely no way of accounting for demand.

As yet, theatrical release alone does not allow a film to recuperate its cost of production and marketing, meaning that producers cannot do without sponsorship or the distribution agreements that can follow a high-profile run at cinemas. In this sense, publicity for strong box office performance is almost as valuable to the individual producer as the box office revenue itself, and this in turn speaks to the industry's emerging spilt that Jedlowski identifies between tangible and intangible distribution.[32] It demonstrates a crucial divide between the outlook of mainstream producers, who make video films destined to be sold on disc, and those who can obtain contracts for formalized distribution. It is the distinction between a short-term and long-term outlook, which each runs in parallel, respectively, with the materiality of the disc and what one might call the promise of a deal. The logic of the former is that it is safest to rack up direct sales as *quickly* as possible, while the logic of the latter views a film as "content" whose value is much less attached, if at all, to DVD sales and more dependent on the windows of distribution it can reach, with cinemas representing the first step in the process.

PRODUCING THE NEW IMAGE

Today, a mere five-minute walk south of Silverbird Galleria, the largest urban development project in Lagos's recent history is underway. Eko Atlantic

City, this newest expansion to the Lagos metropolitan area, is a spit of luxury real estate that extends from Victoria Island directly into the Atlantic Ocean, appearing like some Dubai-style paradise risen from sea but in fact is the product of immense sand dredging. This monumental private construction project has consequently erased—or, rather, buried—the historic Bar Beach, where urchins and tourists, drug peddlers and Pentecostal prayer warriors, suya sellers and families on holiday were once free to congregate. The way in which Victoria Island and its surrounding districts (Lekki and Ikoyi, in particular) have developed into a world onto itself with shopping malls, towering luxury apartments, corporate headquarters, a Porsche car dealership, and countless nightclubs calls to mind James Ferguson's oft-cited contention that in Africa today "capital is *globe-hopping,* not *globe-covering.*"[33] Capital, in other words, tends to connect discrete locations rather than bringing whole locales into economic confluence in some flat world fantasy of neoliberal ideology. The curtailed traffic of commodities and people within specific sedentary urban spaces brings into focus the degree to which a similar disjuncture reproduces itself in the megacity. But images, especially digital images, have a more kinetic circulation, and they are able, therefore, to flood an array of surfaces and screens, flow in a viral—rather than formal, regulated—manner, and take hold as one of the most flexible and supple commodity forms available in Lagos.

In Lagos today, one also notices an uncanny parallel between New Nollywood films and the advertising sensorium that is reproduced across the surface culture of the city as corporate advertising targets Lagosians with ever more sophisticated marketing. The most felicitous examples include billboards for celebrity endorsements in which Nollywood stardom and corporate marketing directly converge, in unsettling signs of the "globalization" or "democratization" of desire whereby urban residents are everywhere invited to embrace their yearnings and longings while the means of fulfilling desire have been segmented, confined, and reserved for specific zones of development. In such cases, the distinction between mainstream Nollywood and New Nollywood turns on the fact that while the former carries on as an index of popular reactions to the fraught and corrosive effects of contemporary capitalism on social life, the latter serves more and more as a direct demonstration of capitalism's production of social life in the city.

A consensus within Nollywood studies holds that the formal qualities of a film bear an important relationship to the places where it is circulated, sold, and viewed. In the case of mainstream Nollywood, the images that adorn videocassette jackets and VCD slips are often a tableau of celebrity actors whose faces alone signify certain expectations about the genre, story, and acting style, arranged according to unstated but habituated codes that promise something about the drama and imagery contained inside. These videos then flow through street settings that resemble a dense shopping center turned inside out, presenting to the public commodities marked by little or no aestheticization. The images compete with one another for attention in saturated urban markets, neighborhood video shops, and the piles of videos wheeled about in carts by mobile vendors. In short, the industry has grafted itself onto the existing media circuits and engendered new social spaces of its own, which have effectuated "the re-mapping of the visual and aural landscape of the city."[34] However, the images created with small amounts of capital in this decentered field of competitors are dramatically different from the media environment of the shopping-mall-cum-multiplex-cinema, where images make direct appeals to one's affect and immerse the senses in an aesthetic designed to stimulate and channel desire.

In New Nollywood's endeavor to standardize its trade and foster a glossy visual style, considerable effort has been put toward the mastery of cinematography and production design such that the image itself directly expresses value rather than merely providing the frame or container for some valued object. For many producers, well-crafted visuals attest to the industry's adoption of so-called global best practices, and the public's wide praise for New Nollywood's heightened production values suggests their satisfaction with the industry's new look. One might consider, as Alessandro Jedlowski does, the reflexive glimpses the industry offers of itself in the "making-of" videos that now commonly serve as an online promotions tactic.[35] Such videos showcase the technical skill of the filmmakers, the costly state-of-the-art equipment, the trendiness of the celebrity actors, and the fashionable aura that surrounds Nollywood. These producers are keenly aware that they have a unique purchase on the personal and collective desires of African audiences, and this awareness seems, in recent years, to have motivated producers to pour resources and effort into creating ever more sumptuous representations of those fantasies and fears. As a result, New Nollywood has become synonymous inside and outside the film industry with high production values.

The budget of New Nollywood has generally grown beyond anything home videos could ever manage: US$100,000–400,000 in 2013, or nearly ten times what mainstream producers allotted for production costs at the time. More than anything else, a budget of this size buys the filmmakers time—

meaning that the gestation period for a film may now stretch into months rather than the weeks or days allocated to the more slapdash productions associated with Nollywood. With time and money, filmmakers have also begun to scout locations that before were out of the question. By necessity Nollywood movies have always been shot on location, either behind the compound gates of a villa in the city or at more modest homes tucked away in rural locales. With larger budgets available, some producers have begun to build sets and shoot at sound stages around Lagos, where once only television and music video producers could afford to shoot.

With the advent of private satellite television and a corresponding rise in demand for Nigerian advertisement, television, and music video content, private investors began building commercial sound stages in converted warehouses.[36] For example, Dream Factory Studio, which features two separate sound stages, was founded in 2010 by Yinka Oduniyi, a television producer who shoots high-end advertisements for multinational corporations and local companies. The studio has all the equipment needed to shoot a film: a full lighting workup, grips, microphones, dollies, and tracks, as well as Panasonic camera equipment. Oduniyi also keeps an editor and sound engineer on contract so that postproduction sound mixing and editing can take place under the same roof. Spaces of this type offer producers a great deal of control over the lighting, sound, setting, and camera movements that produce the cinematic features that viewers recognize as defining high production values. The price tag is high, between 200,000 and 300,000 naira (US$1,200–2,000) per day, but this has not deterred producers like Mildred Okwo, who shot her romantic comedy *The Meeting* (2012) almost completely within the Dream Factory sound stage. The same studio provided the art director of Kunle Afolayan's *Phone Swap* (2012) the necessary facilities to construct a replica airplane interior for a key scene of the film. The plane was fabricated entirely from scratch, including the addition of decals to give the illusion of details where none existed. To create the overhead console, its dials, and the overhead storage compartments, for instance, the art director photographed the interior of a real airplane, printed the images onto laminate, and pasted them onto the structure like an artificial skin.

As one can surmise, such a feat demanded a great deal of space, a meticulously constructed set, a precise lighting design, and considerable effort put into production design and cinematography. On Afolayan's set, those duties fell to art director Pat Nebo and director of photography Yinka Edward, who together are responsible for the hallmark naturalistic realism of Afolayan's

Figure 12. Akin boards the wrong airplane

films. A veteran from the earliest days of the video film boom, Nebo trained professionally for interior design and today builds sets for advertisements and publicity events for major Nigerian companies. Edward is likely the most esteemed Nigerian cinematographer today, having also shot Kenneth Gyang's *Confusion Na Wa* (2013), Izu Ojukwu's *'76* (2016), and Genevieve Nnaji's *Lionheart* (2018), and as such makes his primary living as director of photography for advertising segments. In conversation, Edward explained to me that Afolayan's crew shoots at a very deliberate pace, capturing an estimated five minutes of usable footage every day, a glacial pace compared to mainstream Nollywood (personal communication, May 20, 2013).

Branding and cross-promotional strategies are favored by producers who must mount formidable publicity campaigns to increase the likelihood their film will gain the momentum to reverberate across multiple media spheres. When Afolayan was still conducting preproduction on *October 1st* (2014), he directed a music video for the acclaimed singer-songwriter known as 2face Idibia and the trumpeter Victor Olaiya that showcases the highlife modernity of post-Independence Nigerian that Afolayan would develop more fully in *October 1st*. A promotional "making-of" documentary about the video that appeared on YouTube mentions the state-of-the-art film equipment and the fact that Afolayan flew the final edit to London for color correction, implying professionalism and prestige. Afolayan himself comments that although his crew had never before shot a music video, he believes the finished product demonstrates that today's film professionals can deliver high production values. The ripple effect of cross-promotion means Afolayan's upcoming feature film is felt across local screen media, given that the promotional video represents a spinoff of the music video, which is itself in its aesthetic concept a spinoff of *October 1st*. Furthermore, it permits the director to amplify his popular persona and strengthen his relation to parallel spheres of popular culture, as Nollywood celebrity actors do, by channeling what Noah Tsika calls "the simultaneity of various modes of transmedia publicity."[37]

From a producer's perspective, formal finance partnerships and corporate sponsorship grow more central to filmmaking as, on the one hand, the costs of production rise, and on the other, as the financial returns continue to be eroded by piracy. In this regard, Kunle Afolayan leads the way in securing sponsorship deals from major Nigerian corporations like the construction and food processing company Dangote Group and the telecommunications company Globacom, not to mention multinationals like Honeywell, GSK Luzocade Sport, and Toyota. In fact, his 2012 film *Phone Swap* was conceived and scripted to meet a call by Samsung for a feature-length Nollywood film that would go beyond product placement and integrate Samsung phones directly into the premise of the narrative. The measly 5 million naira budget they offered was not enough for Afolayan, who chose to produce *Phone Swap* on his own and later landed sponsorship contracts with Blackberry, Honeywell, and Globacom (Glo). With this type of attention from formal-sector investors on the rise, a third of a film's budget can derive from sponsorship deals, although the relationships forged are far from fair and equal. Major companies see the opportunity for cheap publicity in movies that, in a sense, autonomously reproduce and distribute themselves across Africa and the diaspora thanks to the uncontrollable shadow industry of video piracy.

Even when corporate sponsorship does not leave a heavy footprint on the film itself, it often manages to position itself in the interface between the film and the audience through celebrity endorsements, social media marketing, and event marketing. In Lagos in 2013, one could find a film premiering at cinemas almost every weekend. Producers have turned these red-carpet events into an opportunity to draw additional funding for the film by selling advertising rights. According to Afolayan, the mobile phone company Blackberry paid twice the amount it paid for its product placement within the film itself simply to advertise the brand at the hotel where he held the red-carpet premiere of *Phone Swap* (personal communication, June 20, 2014). On occasion, the red carpet itself can bear a sponsor's brand image. In short, the growing penetration of Nollywood by marketing and advertising finance leads to a scenario in which the capital gap closes, and to follow Anastup

Basu's provocative suggestion, the flashes of words and images on and around the theater screen become "capital itself (and not the reflection of it) precisely because it acquires a 'life of its own' by virtue of being value in serial flow."[38]

PRODUCTION "VALUES"

Broadly speaking, what sets New Nollywood films apart from mainstream video films is the combination of higher production values and, typically, an initial theatrical release. However, as time has demonstrated, other commonalities among New Nollywood films, such as an orientation toward global consumer culture, may be subject to fluctuations across audiences with different tastes. For instance, I have argued that an initial cycle of New Nollywood films inhabit a metropolitan vantage point that assumed audience familiarity with airline travel, global popular culture, lifestyle brands, and cutting-edge technology. I have also noted that air travel emerges as the supreme expression of free mobility, and consequently, the international airport at Lagos becomes an ever more common sight as films orient themselves in relation to life elsewhere, as with characters who freely travel abroad (*Flower Girl* [2012]), who have established lives abroad (*Ijé, Anchor Baby*), or who embark on a journey home after years abroad (*Mirror Boy, Maami, Doctor Bello* [2012], *Streets of Calabar* [2012]). In fact, Afolayan has gone as far as to orchestrate an in-flight premiere of his film *The CEO* (2016) aboard an Air France aircraft in fulfillment of a sponsorship deal. With its ensemble cast, drawn from across the continent and diaspora, performing as regional branch executives competing for leadership of a trans-African corporation, and the involvement of internationally acclaimed Beninese musician Angélique Kidjo, the film had the blueprint to become a regional blockbuster, but it reportedly struggled to earn returns. Subsequently, Afolayan released three films commissioned by Multichoice Nigeria, including *Mókálìk* (2019), a Yoruba-language film with a cast of top-tier actors from the Yoruba video film industry's star system, including Lateef Adedimeji, Fathia Balogun, and Femi Adebayo, as well as Nigerian singer Simi. The film's perspective is focalized through the experiences of Ponmile, the eleven-year-old protagonist who is apprenticed to a car mechanic for a day to absorb the life lessons that the autobody workshop offers. The narrative and camera never depart the cluttered space of the workshop with its rusted chasses, oil-stained rags, and rapid Yoruba dialogue, but we do periodically gaze upward, along with the child protagonist, at the white vapor trails of airplanes carrying passengers to and from the nearby Murtala Muhammed International Airport. At these moments, Ponmile recites the airline and destination of each flight, the trivia learned from living in a neighborhood directly below the airport's flight paths. But the child also shows a fascination with the mechanical engineering involved in flight, which the narrative cleverly connects to the underappreciated expertise of the mechanics. In short, the film creates a vantage point "from below"—figuratively and literally—and elaborates from this ordinary storyworld a number of themes that stand in distinct contrast with the trends of New Nollywood described above. The film undercuts the very notion of a "metropolitan" vantage point and should remind us that Lagos is large and contains multitudes. The choices of language, casting of Yoruba video film stars, and inclusion of a locally admired musician attest to this fact, perhaps even more powerfully than the film's characterization and diegetic focalization do. Other notable titles in the same vein include Ema Edosio's *Kasala!* (2018), a caper involving four teenagers in a recognizably working-class neighborhood, and Abba Makama's debut *Green White Green: And All of the Beautiful Colours in my Mosaic of Madness* (2016), which offers a self-reflexive satire of Nigeria in which the teenage protagonists create a movie that captures their generation's perception of the nation's abiding contradictions. Ultimately, this segment of the industry has the capacity to generate multiple visions of life in Lagos and may even become inclined to elaborate alternative storyworlds as genre cycles and audience preferences evolve.

It must be emphasized that technical excellence and ideological outlook do not follow one upon the other in a deterministic relationship. As I assert above, New Nollywood's capacity to create sophisticated images is what embodies value for audiences and producers rather than some desired object they may depict. There is nothing surprising, therefore, in the fact that higher production values are now employed to depict many facets of life in Nigeria, from the shimmer of a shopping mall to corroded textures of a mechanic's workshop. For example, in the production of *Phone Swap* described above, Afolayan's crew went to great lengths to erect the rural domestic compound where Mary's family, in the course of resolving their grievances, gradually humanize the callous Akin and expose him to what the narrative frames as the authenticity of village life, which we perceive in the beautiful visuals of the cornfield or family parlor at dinnertime.

Kelani's *Maami*, similarly, portrays a tight-knit neighborhood in Abeokuta reproduced by the filmmaker from his memories of childhood. Here

Figure 13. Akin at the village homestead of Mary's family

the protagonist's memories of the city come to us by way of visually sumptuous flashbacks of the child hunting for fruits in the bush, marveling at the *egungun* masquerades, reading Yoruba novels to his parents and grandparents, and learning the moral ideals of the community. The formal qualities of portrayal here bring to mind Basu's observation that "in a new dispensation of the image as a direct expression of value, the home has to acquire a cinematic plenitude of colors, textures, bodies, and objects in order to upgrade its affective strengths and emerge as an exemplary exhibit of a national-cultural heritage."[39]

New Nollywood's refined production values do require particular equipment, technical training, and more time on set to create, and in this specific sense, they do represent a direct expression of capital. However, as Brian Larkin compellingly argues, "The desire for technical excellence must be analyzed in the context of the structural violence of infrastructural breakdown that haunts much of Africa. Breakdown in many parts of Africa is an everyday fact of life. In a world where access to technology has long been a powerful index of the modern and denial of that access a form of abjection, the insistence on making films of superior technical quality carries a political charge." This political import includes "[the] demand that African film be taken seriously on an equal footing with international standard cinema."[40] I largely accept this important intervention, which Larkin makes in response to a perceived ambivalence in scholarship on New Nollywood concerning this sector's links to neoliberal capitalism, on the one hand, and its genuine achievement of aesthetic success, on the other. In concluding this chapter, I would like to draw out, rather than resolve, this ambivalence and redefine it in comparison with Nollywood's larger historical perspective on Lagos, where ambivalence has provided the industry and its films with the affective, moral, and ideological elasticity to confront the unforeseeable changes the city itself embodies. I wish to underscore that this not only entails a dissonant embrace of contradictory perspectives but also demonstrates the generative force of leaving things unsettled, which in urban studies is known in shorthand as provisionality. In fact, we might adopt ambivalence as a manner of "learning" the films in parallel with Colin McFarlane's notion of learning the city, which involves residents understanding and exercising the affordances of their surroundings through a continual process of dwelling within a place. If we dwell with these films for some time, they may come to afford us unexpected insights, a possibility I further explore in the next two chapters.

CHAPTER 5

Love and Work in Lagos

The term "creative" and its variations have become watchwords for a particular imaginary of urban life. The creativity of cities is presumed to arise from an inherent inventiveness of urban environments, but it also increasingly serves as an element of the brand image that cities develop and claim for themselves. This impression of urban creativity, whether organic or engineered, informs the way cities *feel* and becomes constitutive of the affective identity of a place.[1]

In the creation story of Nollywood, the film industry emerged from the broad field of popular culture that preceded it, including theater, market literature, television, and local film. This view of the industry brought with it a powerful interpretive model geared toward understanding the relationship between these cultural forms and the social milieu in which they were made, sold, and viewed. It illustrated the embeddedness of the films in everyday life and the extent to which they relied on countless individual artists opportunistically drawing from the full gamut of everyday cultural resources.[2] It underscored the collective intellectual, cultural, and creative inputs that made these films "popular," meaning vibrant expressions of shared local life, and set them apart from the mass production, marketing, and consumption of cultural industries elsewhere in the world. The ingenuity of Nollywood, the collective creativity that lends these films unique value, is also what makes the industry appealing to formal media companies looking in from the outside, to whom Nollywood appears as an abundant but intractable field of cultural activity.

The advent of corporate investment in Nollywood—characterized in shorthand as the "corporatization" of the industry—is described and interpreted elsewhere from the perspective of media anthropology, media studies, and production and distribution studies.[3] Rather than reprise the intriguing findings of this research, I will instead highlight several conclusions pertinent to my argument. To begin with, like screen media industries elsewhere, the technology and economy of Nollywood's distribution are "increasingly moving from tangible to intangible forms of circulation," which has prompted fundamental changes in the way Nollywood films move through space and time to find their audiences.[4] It is not that films no longer circulate on video discs but that video disc sales generate smaller profits than before, meaning film productions of a particular scale must cut distribution deals for television broadcast, internet streaming, and, if possible, theatrical exhibition. Moreover, cinema, television, and streaming services have introduced new forms of revenue: ticket sales, subscriber fees, advertisements, and sponsorships. As Alessandro Jedlowski observes, one result of the migration toward new distribution platforms has been "the concentration of capital and resources around the activity of a small number of big media corporations."[5] A small but well-resourced share of the industry is now consolidated around a handful of companies: Filmhouse/FilmOne, iROKOtv/ROK Studios, Multichoice, and EbonyLifeTV. No longer content to merely distribute Nollywood, these companies have made the foray into production, hoping to feed these new formal media networks with their own content, and contract work for EbonyLifeTV or iROKOtv has become a sought-after opportunity for the young generation of Nollywood producers coming up the ranks.

These corporate distributors aim to channel the industry's creative activities and audience engagement into formal structures and practices where the cultural generativity of Nollywood is more readily subject to logistical management. This is not the same as a corporate takeover but rather represents the introduction of management techniques that rely on the creative labor of Nollywood producers and that of audiences to generate "cultural and artistic standards, fashions, tastes, consumer norms and . . . public opinion."[6] Corporate distributors seek to harvest the fruits of this cultural creativity by either buying it up for television broadcast across Africa or commissioning more films from Nollywood producers to draw audiences to original content on formal subscription platforms. This arrangement represents an exceptionally flexible mode of accumulation, one that safeguards formal investors from the messy business of dealing with partners in the informal sector. Meanwhile, the producers and media professionals who generate this content and sustain the engagement of popular audiences continue to practice their creative trade under conditions of precariousness.

Such developments within the Nigerian film industry illustrate local manifestations of global trends within so-called creative industries, including the growing force of logistical management, which Hockenberry, Starosielski, and Zieger view as "systems of coordination [that] modulate flows across infrastructure, [and] reinforce the dominance of some companies," and argue should therefore be interrogated for "the forms of power latent in its techniques."[7] I argue that in corporate Nollywood we find what Stefano Harney more pointedly describes as the commodification of the arts through the commodification of those who produce them.[8] This commodification does not apply narrowly to the producers themselves but also to the audiences whose strong rapport with Nollywood engenders its value from the perspective of formal capital. From this perspective, the corporate media networks based in Lagos are not the creators but rather the managers of popular culture. To be clear, the vast majority of Nollywood films continue to be produced on relatively small budgets, with little documentation, regulation, or transparency and a tremendous amount of ingenuity by cast and crew, who pull together the various resources needed. Producers have always faced challenges of this sort, but the personal relationships that hold the industry together mitigate the uncertainty and financial strains. However, once a film is complete, its circulation is increasingly governed by formal protocols that, in the main, work to the advantage of corporate distributors. In this sense, I argue that the precariousness of creative labor has been formalized, made an integral feature in the new structures and practices of filmmaking in Lagos. To illustrate this claim, I will draw on discussions with filmmakers who work on commissioned projects for iROKOtv's production arm, ROK Studios.

However, the same conversations make clear to me that, despite the asymmetrical arrangement, corporate collaboration enables many individual filmmakers to accomplish other important aims. After all, for most producers the hope is not simply to secure a steady flow of contract work with a corporate outlet. Most have original film projects in various stages of gestation, and they work hard hours on commissioned projects in order to amass the financial and social capital to eventually shoot an independent film of their own. Relatedly, as Moradewun Adejunmobi shows, some filmmakers with noncommissioned productions strategically withhold their film from streaming platforms to increase the perceived value of their work by virtue of its scarcity.[9] Therefore, the precariousness of these new flexible relations of media production can be tolerated in service of personal calculations about the probabilities of future opportunity, which describes the conditions today of below-the-line media work around the world.[10]

While some producers leverage their close contact with corporate partners to garner support for their original projects, for others the commissioned work pays the rent and school fees for children, keeps the lights on, and puts fuel in the tank. It keeps filmmakers going until the right opportunity arises, the necessary resources can be drummed up, and personal contacts are assembled to shoot an originally conceived project. Furthermore, intriguingly, partnerships with formal distributors appear to have created a space in which female filmmakers exercise more power and participation than was possible in the informal mainstream. Whereas the marketers of mainstream Nollywood—who are by and large men—have historically used the personal relationships of the informal sector to retain control over video disc production and distribution, female filmmakers appear to find opportunities for creative control and power over production by circumventing marketers in favor of partnerships with formal distributors.

However, where neoliberalism structures the conditions of work, including that of the creative industries, it has proven creative in another regard: by recasting the space of work as one of self-making, such that a job is no longer simply work but a calling that both defines and is defined by the personal beliefs, values, and aspirations of the individual worker. Within this neoliberal work ethic, the drive to discover one's professional calling appears natural, a path toward becoming a better version of oneself. The goal of satisfying material needs and the dignity of working to support oneself are replaced with an existential search for work that is "meaningful." Part of the appeal of so-called creative industries, and the allure of cities as the ideal home for young "creatives," is the notion that "creative" professions allow one to pursue work that is personally fulfilling, and indeed for some this is true. Therefore, this chapter begins with the premise that work does not only produce goods and services; it also produces social subjects.[11] This observation pertains in part to the developments within Nollywood I describe above, but it finds more definitive expression in the films distributed by corporate networks and platforms, especially recent romantic comedies. The organization of this chapter attempts to suggest the contrast between representation of urban professionalism in these romantic comedies and the material circumstances of many media professionals' work in Lagos. Such an approach models how the constructive combination of representational and nonrepresentational analysis allows for a more nuanced critique of the relationship between labor, media, urbanism, and subjectification.

My reading of these films illustrates that work and workplaces create particular forms of subjectivity, such as the young Nigerian urban professional, as well as new ideas about love, marriage, family, and gender. Indeed, as discussed in previous chapters, work figures centrally in depictions of life in Lagos, beginning with the Yoruba theater films of the 1970s and throughout the classic video films of the 1990s. One can always find work in Lagos, or so some suppose, whether or not this is true. Narratives of those periods—and of today's mainstream productions—dwell on the moral virtues of honest work, the struggle to work one's way out of poverty, or the social bonds supported by the fruits of one's labor. Lagos and labor were both subjects of anxiety in those narratives. The films discussed here, by contrast, are vigorously optimistic about work and its promises to transform the individual, the city, and even society at large. These romantic comedies are unabashedly aspirational films, narrowly focused on urban professionals to the exclusion of all other forms of work that keep the city moving. Indeed, such optimism and the promise of transformation are ingrained features of the genre, wherein transformation refers not merely to a new vantage point that envisions Lagos in a new light but more fundamentally to a change of atmosphere, a new feeling of anticipation associated with the space of the city. This atmospheric shift releases the intense pressures associated with the megacity in prior screen depictions and renders Lagos instead as more permissive and pleasurable than in other urban genres, more accommodating to the fulfillment of various aspirations. Such embellishments are obvious to most viewers, who may nonetheless appreciate the films for envisaging how Lagos *ought* to be. After all, if film genres are stories that society tells itself about itself, then Nollywood romantic comedies are narratives about life getting better in Lagos.

Does this serve to remind us that Lagos is, in the minds of many, a place where sincere dreams can be actualized? Perhaps. But a reading of this sort strikes me as too optimistic, especially given how frequently the aspirations of characters conform to global urban middle-class normativity. Rather than foster a critical standpoint from which to critique or refuse the middle-class normativity of urban professionalism, this cycle of romantic comedies largely rehearses the mantra of a neoliberal work ethic, namely, that self-fulfillment is found at work. In the process, the foundational constraint of subjectivation is erased,[12] and viewers witness only the enabled individual, the figure of the self-made subject. Given this ideological erasure of constraint, characters achieve their desires without any need to make concessions to the moral and cultural proscriptions of the family, the community, or society at large.[13] Furthermore, the norms of middle-class professionalism, which characters adopt for themselves and through which they "become" themselves, are not represented as a constraint in itself, as entailing the sacrifice of other elements of one's identity, for instance.[14] Finally, the films seem to imagine that this optimistic becoming will naturally radiate outward from the individual to produce uplifting ripple effects for the family, community, city, and society. My discussion of these films below provides a critique of this vision of life getting better in Lagos.

GLOBAL DISTRIBUTION, LOCAL PRODUCTION

As Nigeria's screen media industry today transitions into some as yet unknown iteration of itself, it seems likely that global distribution will become an increasingly important element of the industry. The source of Nollywood movies for audiences outside of Nigeria is no longer the informal trade in physical discs alone but also includes primarily satellite television and video streaming services.[15] Today local television markets in other African countries are saturated with relatively lower-cost Nigerian content, effectively blocking local producers from the airwaves.[16] Moreover, those dubbing Nollywood into French have extended the circulation of these films to Francophone Africa.[17] There now exists a healthy business in content brokerage that entails bundling Nollywood films for sale to television networks in Europe, Africa, and China.[18] The video streaming service iROKOtv lists the United States, Canada, and the United Kingdom as its top three locations of distribution on its advertiser factsheet.[19] "Internet distribution has until recently been almost exclusively to the diaspora, itself an envied, elite group," Haynes explains, "and the films may remain forever gated behind subscription or video-on-demand barriers."[20] Meanwhile, new forms of unregulated distribution—piracy— chip away at these platform enclaves, especially where YouTube represents an alternative access point for an even larger portion of Nollywood's global audience. The snack vendor outside my office at the University of the West Indies views "African movies" on her mobile phone using the campus wireless broadband to connect to YouTube, while the pirate DVDs for sale on the sidewalks of Halfway Tree bus stop in Kingston are not reproductions of an original disc purchased from a Nigerian marketer in New York City, as one might expect, but simply content ripped from YouTube and burned to disc. However, even though distribution has grown in scope, film production for the new corporate distributors takes place by and large within Lagos. Beginning in 2018, filmmakers expressed, in conversations with me, the sense that mainstream Nollywood—barring the Yoruba-language industry—had definitively relocated to the East and that the only films still made in Lagos were destined for cinema, satellite television, or online streaming services. What makes this all possible is the arrival in Nollywood of formal institutions and investment, linked to formal global networks of distribution but concentrated in Lagos.

Jade Miller argues that the gap between mainstream and corporate networks of cultural production persists even as formal practices take root in some corners of Nollywood and that this gap constitutes a genuine source of cultural creativity.[21] I propose that much of the formalization and corporatization of Nollywood is, as yet, relegated to the realm of distribution, while the actual sites of production remain marked by the persistence of informality, uncertainty, and risk. A company like the video streaming service iROKOtv must operate at the intersection of informal and formal conditions, and that intersection regularly divides along the lines of production and distribution. In this respect, there is a comparison to be drawn between Nollywood and other screen media industries where media globalization has coincided with—even come to depend upon—the localization of media labor. Moreover, the globalization of creative industries like film and television has resulted in the untethering of creative labor from place, as film studios increasingly seek out more favorable production locations, generally to the detriment of creative workers.[22] By contrast, the financialization of screen media industries has opened a dramatic gap between the sites of decision-making and creative practice.[23] Michael Curtin and Kevin Sanson view these developments as "a distinctive phase of flexible capitalism in the screen media industries, since it is characterized by a mobile regime of socio-spatial relations that entail a more protean mode of production, one that involves a constant refashioning of relations and resources across locations."[24] In their work on creative labor, Curtin and Sanson foreground interviews with below-the-line media workers and from this position fashion a framework to conceptualize new global configurations of financing and distribution that thrive upon easy access to localized creative labor.[25] The way this respatialization of finance, distribution, and production has unfolded in Nollywood is here the question at hand.

Examining this divide between global distribution and local production in Nollywood is important because the gap loosely maps overtop the divide between spaces where formality or informality operate. For example, sanctioned international distribution of Nollywood films requires documentation, regulation, and other formal practices, even though the films that circulate internationally are often scripted, shot, and edited by media professionals who do not enjoy the protections of regulation, union representation, transparent documentation, or legal recourse. Local production remains best accommodated to shooting quickly and inexpensively, at which Nollywood excels, owing in part to its informal organization.[26] The use of data is another example of this divide. Companies like FilmOne, Multichoice, and iROKOtv succeed to the extent they can anticipate and fulfill audience tastes, which can be measured in box office figures, viewer ratings, and online interactive engagement and itself represents an enactment of formality. The ability to document and report a growing number of subscribers to investors, for example, is a formal practice that underwrites their ability to attract more investors. Some of the same data—especially subscriber traffic on video streaming services—can often determine whether or not a producer is commissioned for future work.

Streaming services and satellite television networks, which must offer subscribers a plethora of program choices, generally seek to acquire as much content for as little cost as possible, and, directly or indirectly, they count on the informality of production to achieve this. The resulting balance aims to ramp up content creation and simultaneously drive down content producers' compensation. Given the surplus of media professionals in Lagos, producers can be inexpensively commissioned to create original film and television series under the distributor's brand, as is the practice with EbonyLifeTV, which disburses a fixed sum of funding to a producer but remain otherwise removed from production. It is even more economical to buy broadcast rights for existing films, which is how Multichoice sustains its Africa Magic channels, vacuuming up the inexpensive leftovers of Nollywood's endemic overproduction.[27] Therefore, even as the Lagos-based screen media industry becomes more formal and contractual, it continues to depend upon preexisting informal practices. In this arrangement, media companies are empowered by virtue of their position at the intersection of the informal alternative and formal global networks of production and distribution centered in Lagos.

CREATIVE CONTROL

Michael Curtin argues that media capitals evolve in step with the changing regimes of accumulation that bring together a media industry's human, creative, and financial capital.[28] This section examines the methods by which

Nollywood's new corporate distributors assemble resources, in particular around their original productions, and the place of Lagos as a production and distribution hub within this emerging assemblage. At first glance, the position of the corporate distributors is not unlike that of its marketers. Both wield powerful influence within the industry by virtue of acting as the conduit between producers and audiences. Marketers combine commercial instinct with the knowledge of what last sold best in order to predict the themes, genres, and actors that will appeal to viewers. Such knowledge comes naturally from living on familiar terms with the same circumstances as their audience. By comparison, formal distributors also seek to know their audiences on intimate terms. They accomplish this by using management strategies and data analytic tools designed to predict audience preferences and retool their content production as rapidly as possible.

More than ever before, companies like FilmOne, iROKO, and Multichoice have the means to learn the tastes and desires of the most sought-after segments of Nollywood's international audience.[29] iROKO is in a unique position to continually gauge the desires of viewers on its streaming platform, especially given that the platform not only distributes films to subscribers around the world but also receives back valuable data on individual viewing habits. There is good reason to question how this mass of data drives iROKO's new acquisitions and original productions; however, the company guards its policies as carefully as the data itself. In fact, what iROKO knows about the activity on its video streaming platform remains off-limits even to filmmakers who create the content that appears there. This is because, contrary to what one might expect, information about audience preferences is not shared with producers working under contract with iROKO. For producers, access to such information could inform creative decisions about genre, setting, characterization, casting, length, and soundtrack. Instead, producers are left to conjecture about what the company is likely to acquire or commission.

This arrangement results from iROKO's adoption of a flexible mode of production informed by proprietary data, whereby viewer data is combined with an in-house ratings system to indicate which films fare best at the moment and thus which individual producers to keep and to cut. I can describe this process only from the perspective of the producers with whom I spoke, but, in and of itself, the positionality of this perspective yields valuable insights.[30] After a screenplay is submitted for consideration, the producer receives a report from the acquisitions department evaluating the screenplay in terms of narrative structure, characterization, originality, and moral orientation. The report also assigns the screenplay a letter grade, and the project is accepted or rejected accordingly. Commissioned producers offer iROKO a prospective cast list for vetting. (Note that given the powerful appeal of Nollywood's star system, iROKO's streaming service allows subscribers to browse films by actors, with dozens of Nigerian and Ghanaian stars listed.) Budgets follow a three-tier structure ranging from approximately US$11,000 to $28,000. Top-tier budgets are reserved for producers who command a degree of celebrity in their own right. The commissioned film undergoes a second round of evaluation and ranking once the final cut is submitted. A third ranking is drawn from the iROKO website itself, where the interface invites viewers to like or dislike a film and where the comments section supports an ongoing discussion of the film's merits and demerits. Producers are keenly aware that continuing to work under commission with iROKO demands that they sustain a high viewer approval rating. Audience ratings are expressed as a percentage and continue to fluctuate as audience feedback accumulates as long as the film remains on offer. One producer, unprompted, recited to me the rise and fall of percentage points his films experienced while on iROKO's platform.

While iROKO earned its foothold as a distribution company, it established a production arm in 2013 called ROK Studio, although it would be more accurately described as a commissioner of content, given its general removal from the actual process of film production. The company offers commissioned producers two things: a budget and a deadline. There was no direct supervision by company representatives at any of the film productions I visited, and producers confirmed that no such oversight takes place. (The producers I interviewed who had worked on productions for FilmOne and EbonyLifeTV distribution did report some degree of creative guidance by the distributor, such as preproduction revisions or on-set supervision.) The company can insist that a producer cast a specific celebrity actor for the lead, and they may offer an estimate for the actor's fee, but they play no part in the subsequent negotiations. In this regard, their role is not unlike that of the marketers within the mainstream industry. ROK Studio avoids becoming bogged down in the production process proper, including, for instance, the work of bringing together a crew, scouting locations, and hiring equipment, all of which the producer undertakes independently. This leaves the individual filmmaker and his or her production company assuming the bulk of the risk because the sum offered by ROK Studios is a flat rate, and it must cover all eventualities that arise during a shoot. If a producer loses a day of filming due to flooding—a frequent obstacle in Ajah and Lekki during the rainy season—she may ultimately operate at a loss. If the recommended lead actor abandons the shoot for a competing production—which occurred on one production I visited—there is no recourse to ROK Studios (who insisted she be cast) or any chance of compensation for the material that must be reshot. Conversely, this arrangement affords the filmmaker no additional revenue should the film prove exceedingly successful. "The only compensation that you get is that you get more films to do" (personal communication, August 16, 2018). Contracts make no stipulation for producers to receive residuals, and I was made to understand by one producer that to expect it was naive of me. This producer discussed scrapping plans to shoot a sequel of one of his most successful features when he learned that, in his initial contract with iROKOtv, he had signed away his rights to any subsequent spinoff.

The margins are extremely tight for producers who must eke out their own earnings from the budget offered, either by assuming and paying themselves for several production duties or by stripping down costs in hopes of keeping what remains. Some producers opt to premiere their films in theaters and reserve the rights to box office earnings. However, these producers must inevitably supplement their commissioned budget with personal funds to make something suitable for cinemas. The filmmaker also foots the cost of the publicity required for a film to make money—or break even—at cinemas. A theatrical release lends the film publicity and prestige before it lands on iROKO's streaming and satellite platforms, so the company has incentive to oblige. In part, this accounts for iROKO's continuum of televisual and cinematic fare. In this way, iROKO enjoys almost unlimited flexibility to respond to the trends it discerns among audiences while displacing elsewhere the costs a production outfit would typically incur to continually retool itself. But once again, it is important to recall that the marketer-producer relationship elsewhere in the industry is premised on a similarly asymmetrical distribution of costs and benefits.

This process of commission and acquisition is structured to enhance flexibility and strategically displace costs. Within Nollywood, such a method of creative control is only possible within the formal distribution networks that have taken root in Lagos and now connect producers from across the industry to audiences around the world. Yet in many respects, this mirrors recent developments in screen media production in much of the world. Needless to say, cinema is no longer the assembly line of specialized labor manufacturing a commodity for mass consumption. Studios today commonly contract with a production company that in turn assembles individual freelancers. Nevertheless, Curtin and Sanson offer a crucial observation about the limits of flexible relations. In regards to the emerging global matrix of media finance and production, the authors remark that "the system functions not because it grows the value of its existing human capital but because it constantly harvests an influx of eager aspirants, replenishing its labor ranks with those amenable to a mobile and excessive regime of production."[31] They argue that, combined with the general casualization and irregularization of labor, these transformations make creative industries especially precarious places to work. When it comes to Nollywood, the politics of production is exceptionally tricky to parse because the stakes vary so dramatically between the new corporate managers, the relatively privileged—but exploited—producers and production companies with whom they contract, and those producers and marketers outside this segment of the industry altogether, who operate in purely informal conditions that are the most prone to the attendant risks. However, it is clear that corporate distributors enjoy a relationship of selective entanglement with the spaces of Nollywood's production, one that mitigates their exposure to the risks of filmmaking under conditions of informality. Furthermore, the flexibility that keeps the cinemas, video streaming, and television profitable and responsive to audience tastes also leaves the filmmakers themselves in a tenuous position that could slowly jeopardize the long-term health of the industry. The "harvesting" of Nollywood's creative talent may have its limits.

CREATIVE LABOR

There is another approach to understanding the new ecology of screen media production that has taken root in Lagos, an approach that examines media work as more than strictly a question of the political economy of creative industries. There are also what Kathi Weeks terms the "extra-economic" effects of work to consider, in particular, the ways in which creative labor shapes the subject performing the work. She also calls this the "subjectification function" of work, referring to the ways in which "work produces not just economic goods and services, but also social and political subjects."[32] Weeks goes on to theorize the constitutive effects of work on the one performing it, including the way work genders, racializes, and classes workers. Her critique of work thus overlaps with a critique of subjectification and demonstrates that all labor is "creative" insofar as it engenders and sustains particular subjectivities. Similarly, as Nollywood comes to accommodate several different modes of media production, it seems appropriate to ask how such work creates and shapes the subjectivity of those performing it. In other words, I am interested in the difference between the ways the informal and formal spaces of Nollywood call upon a filmmaker to put him- or her*self* to work.

To illustrate this point, it is useful to consider first the work habits of mainstream Nollywood where personal relationships take precedence over formal contracts. As Jade Miller observes, entry into the industry often requires the newcomer to leverage family, ethnic, or other preexisting social ties or to apprentice into the industry under a mentor.[33] Similarly, marketers in particular are positioned either to elevate an actor or producer or to hold them back. Given the small amounts earned per project, individuals must work especially frequently, as Miller notes, which means continually locating new projects, often through a social network within the industry. Under such circumstances, trust, personal relationships, and a history of successful partnership are paramount, while a simultaneous incentive exists for a producer to work to expand and sustain his social connections, which illustrates one of the ways in which creative work entails working on oneself. Consider also the locations where this kind of work takes place. Certain offices in Surulere—often belonging to a guild leader or notable producer—serve as the confluence point where producers, editors, actors, and marketers meet, socialize, argue, and network. Alternately, O'Jez's Bar at the National Stadium is a longtime industry hangout where marketers, producers, and talent convene to socialize and do business. Miller writes,

> [O'Jez's Bar] provide[s] the chance to see and be seen, and people make an effort to hold personal meetings there, in order to be observed by others in the industry. In such instances, industry aspirants may find themselves only a few degrees removed from a critical phone number; personal introductions are common occurrences in these locations, helping novices connect with senior players in the industry.[34]

As such, this location also represents an exemplary site of subjectification, where the professional, cultural, linguistic, ethnic, and gendered codes of conduct of the industry are forged and put to work. If it is hard to appreciate the fact that work and subjectification take place in this setting, it is because both are indistinguishable from the activity of sitting down to enjoy a beer and talk shop. To ingratiate oneself with established industry players, to learn the social terrain, and to insert oneself within that terrain are as fundamental to the work of media production in Nollywood as performing labor on set.

Bearing this in mind, we turn our attention back to iROKOtv and its commissioned producers. Here, by contrast, contract arrangements take precedence over personal interactions. The company's presence within the industry is generally felt at a distance, given that iROKOtv officials keep a low public profile within Lagos. The company has little presence in the social spaces of mainstream Nollywood such as the bars and offices of Surulere, meaning that no comparable point of contact exists between iROKOtv's representatives and the producers they commission. In fact, almost a minimum of contact is maintained.

Contract negotiations, script evaluations, postproduction revisions, and final cut submissions take place electronically. Alternately, filmmakers may drop their final cut on an external hard drive at iROKOtv offices in Anthony Village. However, some producers with whom I spoke did not know the location of the iROKOtv offices in Lagos, nor did they need to know the physical offices given these immaterial channels of workflow. It bears emphasizing that no one I spoke to had ever been inside iROKOtv's offices. More to the point, as I note above, producers do not know the team that reviews and ranks their films or those who compose the feedback report about the formal elements of the submitted film. The producers with whom I spoke learned the names of these iROKOtv "collaborators" only because they appear on the credit sequence after the film is posted to the video streaming website.

For this sector of the industry, we might ask what takes the place of the personal relationships that bind mainstream Nollywood and allow filmmakers social avenues for advancement. Among the young producers I spoke with, there was a more acute sense that one must establish a degree of individual prominence as a filmmaker. In contrast to the mainstream, where the producer or director is not required to have a signature style, these producers fashion themselves as the creative component in the production process and envision their personal talent as a more reliable resource than a long-standing relationship with a marketer, mentor, or more senior producer. This is not to suggest a hard distinction or that personal relationships do not matter in this branch of the industry or that mainstream producers lack creative talent, quite the contrary. As with project-based work in any other creative industry, relationships and a reliable professional network are still essential to assembling the financial, technological, and human capital needed to create a film.[35] My claim is that even as young producers forge connections with other media workers, they also stake out claims to a certain exceptionalism because the film industry is a crowded space and the need to distinguish oneself is palpable.

In response, some filmmakers engage in nuanced examples of "boundary work," a term with which Tejaswini Ganti characterizes the aesthetic practices and professional rhetoric that Indian filmmakers cultivate "to establish criteria for expertise, authority, and legitimacy" and thereby define what makes their work distinctive in relation to a large field of similar films.[36] One of the most memorable examples of boundary work I can recall arose in conversation with Ema Edosio, who compared film production to the manufacture of "pure water" sachets. To invoke the so-called pure water effect typically suggests a successful business enterprise, or other endeavor, that encourages an influx of shoddy imitators. As she remarked,

> I feel like there is a generation of filmmakers coming up who will set a new benchmark. Nigerians are like this. If there is pure water and they see that this person is making millions off pure water, everybody goes to that pure water. And it happened with Nollywood, and everybody rushed into Nollywood and created a lot of things. A lot of people are really tired because they only have that pure water to drink. There are those wait for something new, something fresh. (personal communication, August 6, 2018)

Here Edosio points to the monotony of mainstream productions and proposes an audience appetite for something more flavorful than the usual fare, which bolsters her claims about the distinctive creative energy of the upcoming generation of Nollywood filmmakers. Such comments are part of the discourse of boundary work.

To produce a film on commission with iROKOtv or EbonyLifeTV or in coproduction with FilmOne represents one such practice of professionalization with its accompanying discourse of distinction. Despite the excessive work regime and the marginal gains, to produce a film for the corporate distributors allows a producer to partner with an emerging power in the film industry. It also lends a filmmaker favorable visibility. One producer I spoke to about iROKOtv explains her reasoning this way:

> I would rather take that because this is an industry where you're working, people are seeing you, and it gives you more work. As against not working

[because] you're waiting for a lot of money to come, people will forget you. I would rather remain consistent and remain in people's faces. You know, just be consistent, and that is what those commissioned projects do for you as an independent producer. (personal communication, August 12, 2018)

Some filmmakers described their commissioned projects as "resume builders" or part of a growing "portfolio" that would lend them the professional prestige or the symbolic currency to realize an independent project. As Ema Edosio once remarked to me, "EbonyLifeTV, once you work with them, your name travels." She produced serialized content for EbonyLifeTV while raising the funds to independently produce and release a feature film titled *Kasala!* (2018). The notion of a resume is a clear piece of boundary work. However, more importantly, the difference between resumes and relationships also demarcates the difference between two modes of subjectification within the screen media industry outlined above.

With this in mind, one crucially important implication of the "corporatization" of Nollywood must be underscored. The creation of a path that circumvents the marketers of mainstream Nollywood seems to have opened the way for the advancement of women in the industry. When iROKOtv first sought, around 2012, to transition from the distribution to the production of commissioned content, which would directly compete with the marketers' networks of influence, they approached and partnered with Emem Isong, the founder of Royal Arts Academy and one of the industry's strongest producers at the time. The partnership laid the groundwork for other female producers to circumvent the mainstream marketers. For a sense of the gender power at work on Nollywood sets, we can turn to Tope Oshin's documentary *Amaka's Kin: The Women of Nollywood* (2016), which sheds light on the subtle and explicit efforts to marginalize female media professionals.[37] The film includes interviews with Omoni Oboli, Mildred Okwo, Stephanie Linus, Michelle Bello, Belinda Yanga-Agheda, Dolapo Adeleke-Lowolade, Ema Edosio, Blessing Effiom-Egbe, Adeola Osunkojo, Jade Osiberu, and Patience Oghre-Imobio. Almost all entered the film industry in a capacity other than director or producer—such as actor, screenwriter, makeup artist, and so on— and drew the same conclusion: roles of authority on set are tacitly reserved for men, the concern being that a woman could not command the respect of male cast and crew. As Oshin herself remarks, "The Nigerian woman is not supposed to be a leader, [especially] a leader of men. You should not be allowed to yell at anyone, let alone 'action' or 'cut.'" Some share anecdotes about male crew, unaccustomed to taking cues from a woman, explicitly disregarding directives. However, gender bias pervades not only the spaces of production but also those of distribution. One might recall the example of O'Jez's Bar, where social practices like drinking, smoking, and sometimes lewd talk make up part of the work of producers and directors. By contrast, I would argue that the new formal networks of production and distribution permit women to circumvent the influence that marketers have retained by virtue of opaque personal relationships with one another. This would explain why the most powerful individuals in corporate and New Nollywood are women, including EbonyLifeTV founder Mo Abudu, Royal Arts Academy founder Emem Isong, and African Movie Academy Awards founder Peace Anyiam-Osigwe, as well as actor/producers Genevieve Nnaji, Omoni Oboli, and Funke Akindele.

Therefore, the corporatization of Nollywood cannot be reduced to a simple narrative of the exploitation of producers or a triumphalist tale of the unlocking of untold potential creativity. For producers, the upshot has been unclear, but I hope to underscore that some producers have discovered new opportunities, albeit amid larger developments that are outside their control. And this is the bargain the creative industries paradigm ultimately puts to media professionals. The work ethic that motivates many media professionals within the screen media industry in Lagos keeps the cameras rolling, even as the precariousness of the work takes its toll. At the same time, the sense of pursuing a creative calling can make the sweat of filmmaking in Lagos—scarce resources, long hours on set and in traffic, arduous negotiations over payment, and so on—genuinely worth it.

In this respect, work both constrains and enables the individual who performs it and as such should be understood as a mode of subjectivation.[38] Once we recognize that work produces subjects, the politics of work becomes clearer. It reveals the workplace and work activities as sites for the negotiation of subjectivity, especially with attention to "the possibility of becoming different."[39] It allows for the examination of various workplace practices as the grounds for a critical standpoint toward a potential self as opposed to a true or essential or normative self.[40] For the urban middle class and elite, the path toward becoming different by shifting the norms of middle-class urbanism would begin with a recognition of subjectivation's inherent ambivalence between subjection and agency. However, insofar as New Nollywood and corporate Nollywood produce films that reflect and address the Nigerian middle class in Lagos and the diaspora, we find that the allure of a global urban normativity remains a strong influence in optimistic depictions of an upwardly mobile Lagos.

ROMANTIC COMEDIES

To illustrate my point, I turn to *The Wedding Party* (2016), which tells the story of the "matrimonial merger" of two families headed by wealthy businessmen. It chronicles the wedding day of Dunni Coker, the daughter of a Yoruba oil tycoon, and Dozie Onwuka, the son of an Igbo electronics magnate. Each family harbors deep reservations about their prospective in-laws. The Coker family is presented as close-knit and loving, although their future in-laws also view them as loud, uncouth, religiously zealous, and too "village," oddly, in spite of their tremendous oil fortune. By contrast, the Onwukas are a discerning family who earned their wealth through shrewd management of their trade. And yet, ironically, the family business seems to have sucked both love and life from the household and left the family distant from one another. The film's comic plotline throws up, and quickly dispatches with, a series of mishaps and petty rivalries that jeopardize the marriage ceremony. Meanwhile, a subplot develops around a threat confronting each family business. With their oil investments faltering, the Cokers are frantic to maintain the charade of lavish wealth. Among the Onwuka family, the impending retirement of the father sets up a struggle over the line of succession. The father, played by Richard Mofe Damijo, doubts the dedication, management skills, and personal responsibility of his sons and therefore hesitates to name either heir to his electronics empire.

Of course, the drive toward happy endings characteristic of romantic comedies ultimately subsumes and resolves each family's subplot, and, before relinquishing the family business to his younger son in the closing scene, Richard Mofe Damijo stands and intones a blessing for the newlyweds: "The two of you are an inspiration to us all, because you have taught us that family is the most important thing and that life can be a lot better if we all would just follow our hearts." A perfectly predictable sentiment. And yet happier lives are the animating promise that runs throughout many recent New Nollywood films and their particular vision of a better world. The romantic comedies I examine in this chapter offer aspirational stories that cultivate an ethical imaginary inclined toward self-transformation, flexible family relations, professional accomplishment, and the notion that "life can be a lot better" when individuals discover and pursue their own interests.

In what follows, I want to interrogate the development of the urban professional as an ethical figure that points to the moral underpinnings of the New Nollywood aspirational imaginary. My discussion is grounded in a selection of romantic comedies, including *Phone Swap* (2012), *The Meeting* (2012), *Flower Girl* (2013), *When Love Happens* (2014), *The Wedding Party* (2016), and a number of other minor films, including *Kiss and Tell* (2011), *Weekend Getaway* (2012), *Alan Poza* (2013), and *3 Is Company* (2015). Interestingly, Ghana witnessed its own cycle of romantic comedies during this period, including *Single and Married* (2012), *Contract* (2012), *Jack and Jill* (2014), and *Husband Shopping* (2015), all of which received distribution beyond the domestic Ghanaian market. These films were available to Nigerian audiences, even appearing alongside Nollywood romantic comedies in theaters and on streaming platforms. The cycle coheres around stories of the lives of young, urban professionals caught up in various pursuits of self-actualization. Narratives pair an unlikely couple, often as dissimilar in social status as they are in personality, whose romantic bond falters, giving rise to a prolonged sequence of indecision before the relationship is ultimately—inevitably—consummated in a happy ending.

In New Nollywood romantic comedies, oriented as they are around personal freedom and self-actualization, the conduct of characters is often informed by the pursuit of a better self and subsequently a better society. Such pursuits are possible within the generic space of the romantic comedy, which Celestino Deleyto characterizes as "a magic space of transformation." The transformation concerned here is not only, or even primarily, the character development through which protagonists emerge wiser and happier, although that is consistent with the genre. More fundamental is the transformation of the fictional space itself, the creation of a storyworld more open and permissive than is plausible relative to other genres. According to Deleyto, this transformation of fictional space "allows the spectator to glimpse a 'better world,' a world which is not governed by inhibitions and repressions but is instead characterized by a freer, more optimistic expression of love and desire."[41] Of course, Nigerian narratives of love and desire are rarely isolated from concern for family, work, money, and morality. It is important, therefore, to ask of each film what types of optimism it expresses, inhibitions it assuages, and freedoms it affords. In what follows, I claim that New

Nollywood offers a glimpse of Nigeria unencumbered by family obligations, interethnic distrust, political powerlessness, social immobility, economic instability, or material deprivation. The removal of such external constraints enables the search inward for self-knowledge and the proper exercise of personal freedom, which is the principal drive of these narratives, especially in sequences of romantic and professional indecision.

The themes of romantic love and professional success promise audiences rather predictable pleasures and trade heavily in cliché. However, here cliché may be an asset. Recognition of the rom-com's typical pattern of emotional twists and turns is part of the appeal for audiences seeking markedly *global* genre films. By the same token, recourse to cliché also signals a filmmaker's self-awareness and proficiency in the conventions of dominant global film genres.[42] Genre is, in this sense, the performance of professionalization.

PROFESSIONALISM

Almost as a rule, the films intertwine their central plotline of romantic courtship with a subplot dramatizing some form of corporate intrigue, whether it be a hostile boardroom takeover (*Phone Swap*), the competition for promotion to top management (*Alan Poza*), or outright corporate espionage (*Weekend Getaway*). Interestingly, though, we do not need to see work take place, since the professional class—whose social horizon this genre adopts—does not specialize in tangible forms of work. The type of work portrayed is invariably what Michael Hardt terms "'immaterial labor,' or "labor that produces an immaterial good, such as a service, knowledge, or communication" or I might add, an experience, such as emotional intimacy.[43] In *Flower Girl*, for example, Kemi creates ornamental decor for the lavish weddings of wealthy Lagosians while her own love life drifts indecisively between her fiancé, Umar, a lawyer up for promotion, and Tunde, a movie star who revives her sense of excitement for life. Similarly, *When Love Happens* centers on Mo, a wedding planner called upon to organizer her best friend's wedding, which underscores her own struggles to find a suitable relationship. The entire cast of *Alan Poza* works for Scorpio Movies and Records, an entertainment company that also engages in "media consultancy and the brand building business," as the board chairman explains. The male protagonists of *Kiss and Tell* are public relations officers by day and sweet-talking Casanovas by night, their professional powers of persuasion put to work in their romantic lives. By contrast, *Phone Swap* develops an elaborate scheme between competing factions within a single company without ever detailing the nature of that company's work. The narrative requires no more than a generic corporate setting to create a plausible environment for Akin, the consummate urban professional. Even though careers of this sort are exceptionally few in Nigeria, urban professionals occupy an oversized place in the popular imagination as figures of success, upward mobility, and modernity.

Many of these narratives are set within corporate offices, boardrooms, and retreats, as well as the nightclubs, where colleagues who work hard then play hard. We should view these spaces of work as important sites of subjectification because, as these films illustrate, work is about more than the production of commodities, services, and revenue. Work also entails the production of particular forms of subjectivity.[44] As my opening discussion of *The Wedding Party* illustrates, professional advancement is one of the ways in which New Nollywood envisions life getting better. At the same time, the possibility of a better world seems to hinge on the willingness of individuals to work for it by working on themselves.

In these films, professionalism entails not only achievement at work but also the fostering of particular practices that come to shape oneself in ways seemingly unrelated to work. Kathi Weeks discusses the category of the professional as a disciplinary mechanism, "one that can induce the effort and commitment, entitlement and identification, and—perhaps above all—the self-monitoring considered necessary to a profession's reproduction as such."[45] The pleasures of self-realization follow from the pains of self-discipline, which we glimpse in characters' scrupulous attire, physical self-care, personal conduct, choice of language, and manner of speech. While these practices pertain to the workplace, they also describe the fashioning of a character's professional persona. In this way, professionalism becomes "a specialized knowledge of how to esteem ourselves, to estimate, calculate, measure, evaluate, discipline, and to judge our selves."[46] In this respect, it is within the workplace that characters learn self-management, self-discipline, and self-improvement. They learn, in short, to work on themselves in subtle discursive practices that Moradewun Adejunmobi terms "the arts of the self."[47]

Professionalism is defined not simply by the content of one's work or a mode of socialization within the workplace but also by the style, affect, and attitude one assumes in order to perform a job. In New Nollywood films, men wear stylish suits and luxury brand accessories, sport immaculately groomed hairstyles, and carry the latest mobile phone. Women are attired in designer dresses and shoes and expensive-looking jewelry, wear their hair in elaborate styles, and, of course, carry the latest mobile phone. The films showcase the attire, technology, and social habits of urbane young professionals, thereby transforming the world of work into a domain of pleasures. According to Weeks, part of the appeal of so-called professional work stems from the modes of consumption that are subtly folded into the practices of production. Similarly, the ways in which film producers foreground the commodities and consumer habits associated with professionalism close a discursive loop that links "the practices and identities of production with those of consumption."[48] In this respect, the representation of professional work folds neatly into the romantic comedy's transformation of the storyworld into a permissive space of possibilities rather than constraints.

For example, several films portray female characters undergoing makeovers as their transformation into figures of female professionalism. In *Flower Girl*, for instance, we follow the protagonist Kemi to an upmarket boutique called *Le Space*, where the camera hovers in close-up over *ankara* print purses, shoes, and fashion accessories. In keeping with a cliché of Western rom-coms, Kemi presents herself before the camera in a montage of outfits to illustrate the playfulness of her self-fashioning.

The audience's attachment is stimulated by both the fantasy of effortless self-transformation and the visual consumption of the commodities placed on display. Carmela Garritano discusses a similar pattern of vicarious consumption in Ghanaian video movies.[49] Fusing professional status to practices of consumption thus taps into notions of style and dress as statements of individuality, markers of status, objects of pleasure, and sites of aspiration. A professional look—and by extension the time and resources to maintain it— "tie[s] us not only economically and socially but also aesthetically and affectively to work."[50] New Nollywood films bring these aesthetic and affective dimensions of work into vivid focus, while the duress of work and the power relations of the workplace fade from view. Makeover montage sequences, which also appear in *Weekend Getaway* and *Phone Swap*, connect narratives of professional development to the pleasure of window shopping, while it also activates deeper aspirational notions of self-mastery and the pleasure of fashioning a better version of oneself.

While the body is the site of pleasurable refinement, so too is the space of the workplace. Offices are clean, orderly environments where the electricity supply never fails. They are furnished with new chic decor, glass tables, leather chairs, and personal computers. Screen technology, such as laptops,

Love and Work in Lagos • 169

Figure 14. Makeover montage from *Flower Girl*

Figure 15. Young professionals commuting to the office in *3 Is Company*

PCs, and mobile phones, represents workplace pleasures while also enhancing the aesthetic gratification of the office setting.

Often the space of labor spills over into spaces of leisure, because professionals are not required to toil in place; they are free to take work with them. In a number of films, the characters meet at a lounge or nightclub for drinks after work (*When Love Happens, Kiss and Tell, Weekend Getaway, The Meeting, Flower Girl, Alan Poza, 3 Is Company*), dine with colleagues or a boss at upscale restaurants (*Flower Girl, Weekend Getaway, When Love Happens*), and attend a work retreat at an all-inclusive resort hotel (*Weekend Getaway*).

Overall, this aesthetic makes professionalism palpable and even sensuous. Such pleasures become a part of the rationalization of work that might be otherwise unsatisfactory, as well as the inducement of the individual to accept self-discipline as one's own ambition. In other words, the office worker becomes more inclined to take up the goals of professionalism as their own and the vision of a professional life as the basis of the good society. In this way, the urban professional becomes an ethical figure, one who embodies the "ethic of self-sufficient citizenship," by which responsible individuals govern themselves "through freedom, not control."[51] Viewed as a disciplinary category, professional comportment establishes a norm of "modern" subjectivity, and by extension the becoming modern of New Nollywood's urban professional characters stands as part and parcel of contemporary Nigeria's national becoming, a claim I will return to shortly.

The notion of professionalism elevates certain jobs above others, distinguishes them as more prestigious, and ascribes the individual jobholder a degree of distinction. As I discuss above, professionalism is both a product and a performance of boundary work, a combination of sentiments and social practices that police the boundaries of legitimate and illegitimate forms of work. A professional occupation ostensibly demands more emotional, imaginative, and creative investment by the professional, even as those intimate investments are refigured as self-expression.[52]

Kunle Afolayan's *Phone Swap* notably toys with this conceptualization of professional identity. The main characters, Mary the tailor and Akin the businessman, are cast as different in social class, ethnic identity, lifestyle, and line of work. Mary's and Akin's divergent social worlds are defined as much by their occupations as anything else. In the opening sequence, the camera wanders, in extreme close-up and shallow depth of focus, over the objects in each character's room, studiously picking out and ascribing significance to the volumes of books, trays of designer watches, and silk ties in Akin's room and the Singer-style sewing machine, mannequin, and piles of colorful ankara cloth in Mary's. Before we ever see the characters themselves, we are introduced to these tokens of their trades, with the camera bringing the spectator's eye right down into the minute details of the mise-en-scène. Later, when the two physically collide in the airport on their way to pressing engagements, they accidentally swap phones and end up being routed to the wrong destinations. Mary arrives in Abuja, where an important shareholders' meeting that could decide the fate of Akin's career is scheduled to take place, and Akin arrives in Owerri, where Mary's family has called an urgent meeting to resolve a marital dispute. The story is animated by the personal transformations that Mary and Akin undergo as they work in cooperation to resolve the disparate conflicts, which also correspond to each character's personal weaknesses. The fastidious Akin must shed his Western pretensions and learn humility in order to counsel compromise within Mary's family, and in the process, he realizes the need for reunion with his mother. Meanwhile, Mary must become more assertive in order to represent Akin at a corporate retreat. At the same time, the film celebrates Mary's transformation from a mere tailor—engaged in the hard, physical labor of assembling garments—into a fashion designer, a change of mindset more than anything else. But this is not merely a distinction without a difference, as the profession of fashion designer revalorizes the creative component of her labor. Presenting herself in this new light, Mary sees that her once unrecognized talents take on new value, and subsequently her services attract upmarket customers as well as the romantic attention of Akin. The same trope of recognition appears in *Alan Poza, Weekend Getaway,* and *Flower Girl*, wherein the discovery of overlooked creative talent mirrors the development of an unrecognized intimacy into an undeniable love affair.

LOVE, MARRIAGE, AND FAMILY

In New Nollywood romantic comedies, the effects of the urban professional's subject formation ripple outward in concentric circles that come to encompass the family, community, and society at large, even as the individual remains the central focus and the locus of agency. In this radiating chain of dependencies, the family's happiness and even the wider civic well-being hinge on the individual's responsibility for their own conduct and self-actualization. To make this leap possible, the films often mirror a struggle in the protagonist's professional life with some obstacle in their romantic life and even suggest that the attitudes and practices that secure success in one sphere will unlock happiness in the other. For instance, characters in these films espouse what Rachel Spronk calls a "therapeutic ethos" of love, or the idea that "emotional investment and sexual intimacy in relationships is a means of individual development and self-fulfillment."[53] This ethos also comprises "the art of emotional openness and intimacy" that permits one to better "manage" one's relationships.[54] From this vantage point, the moralizing advice of others cannot substitute for the endeavor to know better oneself and one's heart. In Emem Isong's *Weekend Getaway*, for instance, on the advice of a pastor and marriage counselor, one couple sets off on a romantic excursion in hopes of rediscovering the connection that first led them to fall in love. By comparison, in Seyi Babatope's *When Love Happens*, a similar therapeutic ethos arises in the form of a confessional video blog that the protagonist Moduroti creates to discuss her hopes and fears about online dating in Lagos. The video blog entries are shot with Moduroti speaking directly into the camera as she alternately offers intimate confessions and dating advice, and the video blog thus serves as a substitute therapy for the lovesick protagonist. In these films, the search for love and partnership has more to do with notions of healthy and unhealthy relationships than with consideration of the prospective partner's family background, social standing, moral character, or ethnic identity.

The role of the family in New Nollywood offers an especially significant measure of the shift away from the social and cultural orders that undergird mainstream video films in which romance, family bonds, marriage arrangements, and the moral character of the betrothed were matters involving the family. In Nigerian family dramas of the 1990s, for instance, the moral authority of the family carried a weight that was never in doubt, even if the film depicted the individual's obligations to relatives as an unwelcome restriction placed on his or her conduct. Characters still married against the wishes of the family or decided not to send remunerations to the village after experiencing a financial windfall in the city, but the character's responsibilities to family—even when left unfulfilled—remained part of the narrative frame. By contrast, the same cannot be said of many New Nollywood films, including the romantic comedies discussed here, which eschew the moral economy of family bonds in favor of an imaginary of individual freedom, especially in matters concerning love.

An unexpected upshot of this permissive vision of romance and marriage is that depictions of interethnic intimacy have become rather common in New Nollywood films. Ethnicity was reason enough for families to come between young couples in early Nollywood.[55] However, in a number of the romantic comedies in question, characters who voice objections to a romantic bond between characters of different ethnic backgrounds come off as ill-willed "tribalists" and thus objects of the narrative's scorn. As I mention above, *The Wedding Party*, perhaps the most financially successful romantic comedy discussed here, centers on the interethnic nuptials of the Yoruba bride, Dunni, and the Igbo groom, Dozie. One of the obstacles to the film's inevitable happy ending is the groom's ill-tempered, condescending mother, who views her future in-laws as little more than up-jumped villagers, despite (or perhaps because of) their immense fortune in oil. In one scene, she presents her friends with a magazine article featuring the city's most eligible bachelorettes and remarks on the shortcomings of each, only to then quip that at least their fathers are powerful leaders of major companies. Why couldn't her son bring one of these young women into their (Igbo) family, she wonders aloud, "but no, my son brings me a native housegirl from Ekiti State." The reference alludes both to her perceived station and her (Yoruba) ethnicity and prompts her husband to slap the dinner table in frustration as her friends muffle their laughter. These remarks about ethnicity are used to underscore the wickedness of the mother more than anything else and can be viewed in contrast to the "noble" father's recognition that his son has found a soulmate.

How to situate the matter of ethnicity is complicated and requires attention to the distinction between corporate and New Nollywood. In corporate productions like *The Wedding Party* or *When Love Happens*, the theme of interethnic marriage comes across as a corporate appeal to multiculturalism and, I would argue, cannot be mistaken for a sign of shifting attitudes among audiences. The interethnic marriage at the center of *The Wedding Party* feels, in particular, like a market-tested statement about Nigerians putting aside differences in order to take pride in national identity. Furthermore, the venue in which a film is viewed can dramatically inflect whether and how audiences receive, recode, or refuse such messages,[56] and ethnicity is a lens through which audiences view and translate the narrative conflicts of mainstream Nollywood.[57]

Nevertheless, the romantic couple's union often doubles for the joining together of some other social or cultural dissimilarity, whether that be a difference of ethnic identity, wealth, age, or place of origin. The genre lends itself to this vision of the reconciliation of difference. In a society of exceptional cultural, linguistic, and regional diversity—as well as deep social inequality—these romantic plotlines imagine the marriage of old and new, local and foreign, and traditional and modern ways. Of course, in the process, complex identities are translated into readily recognizable signifiers, such as language, cuisine, or clothing, New Nollywood's shorthand for ethnic and cultural identity. In this way, Nigeria emerges as a compatible assemblage. And in this narrow sense, the films ask to be viewed as more than just love stories but also as commentaries on new ways of understanding what it means to be Nigerian.

To flesh out this point, I return once again to Afolayan's *Phone Swap*. Like many other New Nollywood romantic comedies, *Phone Swap* develops a world of complementary binaries that it seeks to resolve by binding one to the other. What is striking is the role of mobile phones in the film, which represent the technological connectivity that enables romantic and familial connectivity and overcomes challenges of physical distance as well as social and economic boundaries. The opening sequence of the film is once again illustrative. Mary awakes to a call from her employer on the other side of town and another phone call from her father from his cornfields in Owerri, who greets her in Igbo. A jump cut from Mary's bedroom to a high-angle panoramic view of the fields at the precise moment the phone rings punctuates the distance, and as Mary enters the streets of Lagos, the film cuts between golden cornstalks of the village and the buzzing *okada* motorcycles and pungent LAWMA garbage trucks of the city. The sequence concludes in parallel fashion with Akin and his Yoruba-speaking mother. The camera recreates the same high-angle panoramic shot over the mother's lush compound, depicting her phoning her son as he is chauffeured to company headquarters in a private vehicle, the Lagos traffic shunting by outside the window of the car. When Mary and Akin find themselves holding the phone and inhabiting the life of the other, they are displaced from their natural element, the confines of their everyday lives. The film resolves the situation by bringing about a new balance in each character's life and forging a romantic bond between the two. The assemblage depends on the mobile phone and its publicized ability to suture together vastly disparate spaces and times. The phone motivates the narrative drive toward closure in which Mary's and Akin's detours lead back to the site of their first hostile collision, this time as a romantic reunion. On the level of aesthetic form, the cinematography and editing do the work of stitching together these divergent worlds, visually producing the connectivity that mobile phones promise.

In another genre—and another context of subjectivation—the families would bar the pairing for any number of reasons, such as ethnicity or Mary's low social status. Honoring obligation to the family would be portrayed as both a moral duty and an obstacle to the character's pursuits of the heart. By contrast, in *Phone Swap* the families are perfected by the romantic connection between Mary and Akin, and by extension, the community and wider society are perfected by families setting their affairs in order. The self-realization of the individuals heals the family; the family does not set straight the wayward individual, which returns us to that notion of "life getting a lot better."

THE WORLD-MAKING ETHIC OF NEOLIBERALISM

In this final section, I would like to return to the notion of capitalism as a world-transforming project that the individual experiences in intimate terms. To illustrate my point, I turn to Mildred Okwo's *The Meeting*, which centers on Makinde (Femi Jacobs), the representative of a company seeking government approval to construct new telecommunications masts across the country. The DVD jacket captures the gist of the story: "A Lagos-based corporate executive finds himself at the mercy of political patronage, bureaucratic red tape and his tender heart." The film's title alludes to the protagonist's meeting with the minister of land to secure federal licenses to build new masts, an appointment that is repeatedly postponed by the minister's secretary, Clara (Rita Dominic). The telecom infrastructure his company hopes to erect would service the country's burgeoning information and technology needs, which places the question of economic progress at the center of the protagonist's struggle. Meanwhile, intermittent crosscutting with the corporate headquarters in Lagos reminds us that the fate of the company hangs on whether Makinde can bypass the buffoonish secretary and speak with the minister. An afternoon business trip to Abuja to secure the licenses becomes a weeklong fiasco involving, for the most part, a great deal of sitting and waiting.

Abuja and Lagos stand as the political and economic capitals of Nigeria, respectively. The opening panoramic of Abuja is intercut with establishing shots of the National Mosque followed by the National Church of Nigeria, thereby locating the story in the political seat of power while gesturing also to two seats of spiritual governance. From here the narrative settles on Nnamdi Azikiwe Airport as Makinde deplanes and calls his managing director at company headquarters in Lagos. He soon after telephones his daughter at the Ikeja City Mall, an elite Lagos shopping center. This constellation of iconic sites of national identity is fleshed out further during Makinde's tribulations at the Federal Ministry of Land, where citizens of different ethnic groups wait patiently to petition the minister. The government office lobby serves at once as a cross section of the body politic and a commentary on the welfare of the nation, signaling the film's encompassing notion of national identity and its thematic preoccupation with public and private management of civic welfare.

The satire of political chauvinism and ethnic animosity is confined strictly to the waiting room of the Federal Ministry of Land. The film offers a gentle mockery of interethnic rivalry by playing off stereotypes Nigerians hold about one another but reserves its strongest ridicule for the political class. Clara stands as a caricature of the venal gatekeeper and thereby taps into a sentiment that unifies Nigerians of every stripe. She rebuffs the attempts of individuals in the waiting room to have their meeting with the minister but boisterously celebrates the wealthy men who arrive periodically with full entourage and are promptly granted access to minister. First is the Igbo Chief Omego, whom Clara ushers directly to the minister, followed by the Yoruba Oba Adeniyi, whom she greets with a drawn out "Kabiyesi-o," and last is the Hausa party chairman. In each instance, the secretary proffers some threadbare excuse in response to the objections of ordinary citizens who sit and wait.

Of course, the continually deferred business meeting creates the opening for a romantic meeting, in which Makinde encounters and develops a relationship with Ejura (Linda Ejiofor). The initial connection is strictly platonic. Ejura is a significantly younger woman serving in the National Youth Service Corps (NYSC) as an aspiring civil engineer, although we see virtually nothing of her work. References to NYSC and civil engineering read like allusions to an ideal of citizenship and nationhood more than anything else. The film shows no hint of the general reluctance—and even resentment—that many young Nigerians feel about the compulsory year of service under the NYSC. Instead, she bemoans the shallowness of relationships with men her own age and, by contrast, sees in Makinde a man bound by moral principles. Ejura learns, for instance, that he remains emotionally committed to his deceased wife in order to honor her memory. But to grieve without healing can distract one from living life full, and hence Ejura's youthful companionship helps him to heal and learn to live again.

As Adejunmobi astutely argues, New Nollywood seems to extract its characters from the moral economy that animates much of Old Nollywood's narratives. That moral economy conjures death, especially the killing of loved ones or family members, as the price paid for what the protagonist hopes will be a better life. But New Nollywood jettisons death and sees only life and better ways of living it. We never learn the cause of death for Makinde's wife because it is a blameless death, one that implicates nothing about Makinde beyond his capacity to live with grief. But this does not mean that characters are inserted into a storyworld free of moral considerations. On the contrary, they find themselves in a storyworld where freedom and individualized responsibility are the principal moral concern, which *The Meeting* illustrates in a crucial romantic rendezvous at the center of the film's narrative. Ejura turns to Makinde for advice about how to rebuff her boyfriend's demands for sex and make him understand that she wants to postpone sex until marriage. She then stresses that personal choice, and specifically *not* religious observance or concern for virginity, motivates her wish to abstain. Makinde enjoins her to take the decision herself and not be pressured by others. She has "a wonderful policy," he remarks, before the conversation turns to his own policies and principles. How will Makinde meet the minister? "I am not bribing my way in, as I see some others doing. We need to stop doing that in this country. Can you imagine if we all stopped bribing public servants?" To which Ejura responds, as if completing his thought, "We would all earn things by merit? That will be the day." After a pause for reflection, she adds, "You see, you're principled, just like me." The sequence reaches for a larger ethical statement about the reward one earns, in love and at work, that figures in the elaboration of a larger ethical imaginary. Romance and professionalism become categories in service of the negotiation and expression of intimate personal convictions about oneself and one's place in society.

Furthermore, in each case, individual adherence to principled conduct is what matters. Although the individual is central to it, neoliberal governmentality does not simply describe the production of individuated political subjects. It situates the individual's self-making within the broader project of producing social order according to a particular vision of the good society. The better world that New Nollywood envisions emerges when, as Ejura states, "we all earn things by merit." What precisely that will mean for Ejura's decision about sex will be different from what it means for Makinde's dilemma at work, but both will have enacted what it means to be "principled." And the principled practices Makinde and Ejura adopt to succeed would posit the norm by which good work and the good life come to be recognized. Although the narrative never reduces the romantic pair to allegorical figures, the notion of a national well-being resides always somewhere within the frame. Each character's ability to maximize their individual capacities leads to personal accomplishment—as well as a step closer to the good society. Success is not a symptom of Nigeria rising; instead, society is lifted by the swell of accumulated individual efforts. Of course, this is not the uplift of a concerted public project as much as a figural outcome of the amassed efforts of individual citizens working for the betterment of the self, the family, the workplace, and subsequently society itself.

It is worth recalling that, according to Deleyto,[58] the generic conventions of the romantic comedy accommodate fantasies of the transformation of self and society through the transformation of the fictional space itself into a more permissive storyworld wherein the impossible becomes plausible. Screenwriter Tunde Babalola's real accomplishment is in constructing a story in which the very well-being of society seems to hang on the symbolism of a single meeting. Take, for instance, the moment Makinde finally corners the minister. The waiting room bands together to detain Clara while he slips into the main office, down a stairwell, and out a back door to throw himself—business proposal in hand—before the minister's departing vehicle. Bodyguards spill fully armed from the SUV to arrest the businessman, as he introduces himself to the minister, explaining, "I have an appointment to see you." The minister retorts that he should then wait for his appointment. The exchange that follows merits quoting from at length:

> MAKINDE: With all due respect, my original appointment was for Monday. I've been waiting for *five days* now, just to see you.
> MINISTER: Young man, do you realize you could have been shot for this rubbish stunt you pulled?
> MAKINDE: I know some people who should have been *killed* for their ugly, disgraceful conduct this week. [alluding to Clara]
> CLARA: My friend, watch your tongue. You are addressing a minister.
> MAKINDE: A minister who was appointed to serve me, and serve this nation, not just a segment of it.
> MINISTER: Hey, my friend, whatever your name is. If I was to see everybody who randomly walked into my office, you know I would probably not get any job done.
> MAKINDE: But I had an appointment! That should mean something to you. You were in the private sector before you were appointed a minister. You know how it works! What happened to you?!

Clara is presented as the object of satire, but the minister's role is performed in earnest. Setting aside the humor, the exchange is staged like the fulfillment of a fantasy nurtured by many layers of frustration. At the core of the fantasy is, perhaps, the rejection of the lived experience of political powerlessness, as the scene voices an obvious critique of government neglect of duty. But there is a deeper significance embedded in Makinde's assertion that having an appointment "should mean something." What does a meeting mean? As I suggest above, the dramatic culmination of something as mundane as an appointment hinges on the sense that the fortunes of the individual, the company, and the nation hang in the balance.

For what it is worth, I would remark that this scene resembles almost nothing of the way business is done in Nollywood, which is to say in the informal private sector. Conducting business in Nollywood—or getting most anything done in the film industry, it seems at times—demands a great deal of wrangling with others, sorting out ad hoc alliances, improvising arrangements to urgently remove an obstacle, and constantly hastening to fix in place any number of contingencies. It requires politics, albeit of an interpersonal kind. Makinde's complaint voices a rejection of the need to continually reinvent the means of getting work done. It is a plea for some tacit understanding or agreement as to how business is conducted, a formalization of the conduct of conduct. As Makinde exclaims, addressing the minister, "You were in the private sector before you were appointed a minister. You know how it works!" This is to say that embedded within this fantasy is also a longing for work that is reliable and frictionless, a livelihood on which one can plan ahead and build a future.

As if there was ever any doubt, Makinde gets his meeting, secures his contracts, saves the company, attends his daughter's graduation, and delivers a happy ending. What is more important is his willful misinterpretation in this scene of the protocols of power that prevail in the government ministry and the evocation of professionalism as a political rhetoric in and of itself. Much of the literature on neoliberal governmentality in so-called advanced liberal democracies presumes a context in which the state has devolved its authority and responsibility over the welfare of citizens to individuals and the private sector.[59] However, in Nigeria, the state has long "governed from a distance," albeit in a different sense, and it is evident to many Nigerians that the welfare of the citizenry is not the primary political objective of the government. Where then is sovereignty located? For its part, New Nollywood offers audiences a glimpse of a Nigeria unencumbered by family obligations, spiritual struggle, interethnic distrust, political powerlessness, social immobility, economic instability, or material scarcity. One of the most troubling things about the New Nollywood aspirational imaginary is that its protagonists work to transform themselves into the favored subjects of global capitalism who enjoy citizenship-like privileges that the state has little role in defining or upholding. At the same time, it inextricably tethers individual self-making to a wider collective world-making and suggests that to become such a subject, to subject oneself to the governmentality of contemporary capitalism, is the path by which life gets better for society at large. In the end of *The Meeting*, the company prevails as the government retreats from the public—ensconced, like the minister himself, in a sphere of official retreat—while life lived in the margins remains too dreadful for the film to contemplate.

CONCLUSION

Recent romantic comedies envision the self-betterment of a romantic pair and the concentric ripples of upliftment that radiate outward from the workplace to touch upon the individual, work, family, and nation. My argument is not that this represents some grand deception or that the aspiration for better jobs is always already corrupted. Instead, I assert that the self is constructed, rather than "discovered," in the practices taken up in everyday lives, including in conduct at work. What follows from this recognition should be a critical reflection that asks which forms of dependency—on creative collaborators, corporate distributors, business partners, romantic partners, family members, or society at large—are constraining and which are enabling.[60] This is where on- and off-screen labor can be productively placed in comparison. Intriguingly, the promise that on-screen work holds for New Nollywood characters stands in contrast to the precarious possibilities available to screen media professionals off-screen. As I discuss above, their creative labor entails much more uncertainty and fewer guarantees of mobility than is represented on-screen. These constraints are real for individual producers, but a broader view of developments in the industry also suggests that something like the management of Nigerian film culture vis-à-vis the normative expectations of corporate distributors is underway.

Elsewhere in this book, I make the argument against urban normativity on the basis that Lagos cannot survive under those norms. Like many other cities of the Global South sustained by the self-generated organization and activities of its people, Lagos offers a platform for so many precisely because the norms of planners and government have little purchase on the granular practices of everyday life. This openness helps residents to endure and allows the city itself to absorb innumerable activities and intelligences that do not necessarily speak to one another, or bend toward the same aim, or share the same vantage point, and in this way, Lagos remains a place that works. This chapter again confronts the problem that normativity poses, albeit within quite a different framework. New Nollywood romantic comedies offer an index of the growing currency of particular notions and norms of self-conduct associated with the principles of self-governance at the core of neoliberalism. Ironically, these films imagine the city overcoming the material and moral problems that neoliberalism helped to create.

In Judith Butler's theory of subjectivation, power subordinates in the process of the formation of the subject but also enables the agency of the subject that is formed. Therefore, although the process of subjectivation is inherently ambivalent, it leaves the individual with the agency to pursue a course unintended by power.[61] From the perspective of my critique, the ideal response to middle-class subjectivation would be the activation of an agency to become someone that is *unintended* by the power of neoliberal governmentality. (To the extent this critique applies to the gentrification of the city itself, it would mean becoming some place unintended.) This begins with reflection on the way intimate experiences and personal aspirations inscribe such norms within the psyche. In a stronger form, activation would entail the rejection of neoliberal governmentality, the corporate capture of popular aspirations, the emergence of new subjectivities endowed with special privileges, and normative notions of what the good life in Lagos ought to be and what it takes to be a good enough citizen of the city.

If Lagos becomes better by becoming a modern metropolis, as the films discussed above propose, and if its citizens aspire to adopt the lifestyles and privileges enjoyed by the urban middle class elsewhere, this still leaves foreclosed the futures of the majority of Lagosians who live beyond the purview of neoliberal biopolitics. It is important to note that every biopolitics has its complementary necropolitics, which together circumscribe the worlds worth living in and worth letting rot. The romantic comedies discussed above illustrate Elizabeth Povinelli's profound observation that "power over life and death, power to cripple and rot certain worlds while over-investing others with wealth and hope—is produced, reproduced, and distributed when we seem to be doing nothing more than kissing our lovers goodbye as we leave for the day."[62] The aspirational narratives of New Nollywood films invest a great deal of hope in life getting better for the city and the nation, but this is achieved first by erecting a divide. Those who can will opt out of the duress of city life: walls reach higher, security measures are redoubled, tinted windows get darker, antagonism toward the poor grows deeper, and the material signs of class distinction grow more pronounced. Meanwhile, boundless aspiration verges on cruel optimism for those Lagosians who struggle tremendously to see even modest goals through to fruition.[63] Therefore, the prevailing norms, values, and practices of the global urban middle class should be questioned, challenged, and even refused. Such a refusal should begin first and foremost with the notion that special entitlements, citizenship-like privileges, or greater status belong to a class of Lagosians by virtue of the supposed contribution they make to society, whether that be through the nature of their work, the observance of more "enlightened" lifestyles, or the commitment to a narrow notion of how the good life ought to be.

CHAPTER 6

Dark and Gritty / Slick and Glossy

In the opening sequence of Daniel Oriahi's *Taxi Driver: Oko Ashewo* (2015), engines roar as two vehicles tear through downtown Lagos Island at full throttle in the darkness of night. Tires squeal and bass emanates from the sound system of the cars. The sequence delivers velocity and motion. Its fast and furious chase leads down Broad Street, making a hard right just before Freedom Park, formerly a British prison. Neglected colonial administrative buildings rush by at breakneck speed, their deep history compressed into a fraction of a second. Nonetheless, *Taxi Driver*, shot predominantly at night on the streets between Church Missionary Society and Obalende, knows its way around Lagos. The chase comes to a close with a crunching collision, the title credits appear, and the film cuts to a more familiar Lagos street scene: the inside of a rickety *danfo* bus stuck in thick morning traffic. One passenger preaches a fatuous message of prosperity from the back row, while others close their eyes against the fatigue of the commute, the conductor counts grimy naira notes, and the driver weaves around muddy potholes. In fact, the film spends the majority of its time in the streets of downtown Lagos, and this graphic city setting is a large part of the appeal of Oriahi's film, which was distributed in Nigerian cinemas by FilmOne and online by Netflix, where the global video streaming service lists the film under the genre label "Dark and Gritty." When a subscriber clicks the link to other "gritty" films, the website lists titles from around the world that deal with drugs, gun violence, organized crime, and dramatized efforts to police them.

Oriahi's *Taxi Driver* is among a number of New Nollywood films released to cinemas, subscription satellite television, and video streaming platforms that adopt a dystopic urban imaginary stylized after other "noir" cities of dominant global cinema. In this chapter, I am concerned principally with

Taxi Driver, Walter Taylur's *Gbomo Gbomo Express* (2015) and *Catch.er* (2017), Judith Audu and Uduak-Obong Patrick's *Just Not Married* (2016), Dare Olaitan's *Ojukokoro* (Greed) (2016), and *Juju Stories* (2021). These films are linked not only by their depiction of clever criminals but also by their cultivation of a cynical disposition from which transgression appears stylish and violence is rendered "cool." Almost all of them turn on a scheme to dupe others of a large sum of money and are punctuated by backstabbing partners in crime, tables turning by chance, edgy armed standoffs, and a surprising number of bodies in car trunks.

Given the dark portrait of Lagos these films present, one might be inclined to read the genre cycle as a reiteration of the role Lagos has historically played as the embodiment of popular anxieties concerning insecurity, material inequality, and social breakdown. And yet, in recent years, conditions within the city have markedly improved over those of the deepest point of urban crisis in the 1990s, when Lagos was, indeed, paralyzed by a generalized condition of insecurity and dysfunction.[1] Some of Nollywood's early classics dealt narratively and thematically with dilemmas of everyday life during that especially dark time in Lagos. Producers imbued their films with urgency by addressing events that had a degree of immediacy for audiences, sometimes even sourcing stories from newspaper headlines or popular rumors, and in light of this, critical approaches to Nollywood have coalesced around the idea that the films offer insight into experiences of everyday life. A number of essays on early video films interrogate the correspondences between Nollywood and Lagos and illustrate that the films both arise from the social milieu of the city and reflect the city in their narratives and images.[2] This was an important claim in the legitimation of the field, and considered from the present standpoint, it is notable how frequently Lagos was called upon to illustrate this correlation. With particular detail, Jonathan Haynes makes the case, in both material and textual terms, that the city and the industry are mutually constitutive. "The films are," Haynes writes, "a means for Nigerians to come to terms—visually, dramatically, emotionally, morally, socially, politically and spiritually—with the city and everything it embodies."[3] What makes this approach compelling and distinguishes it from previous work on African cinema is, again, this notion of a telling correlation between an emergent film industry, the films it produces, and the city of Lagos. Today, mainstream Nollywood continues to trade in immediacy because stories of proximate experience resonate with audiences for whom the meaning and appeal of the narrative are immediately recognizable. The details of life in Lagos are still evident in the dark films released by contemporary New Nollywood producers, but these new films also know Lagos on a different set of terms.

Genre constitutes one way in which Nollywood organizes its urban imaginary. Nollywood films, for example, adopt a social horizon in keeping with the type of conflicts their genre seeks to dramatize. Cultural epics, some comedies, and village films demand a rural setting, needless to say, and by contrast, a city is the most plausible setting for most campus films, some comedies, and "runs" films. More important, however, is the way genre inflects Nollywood's representation of the village, the city or whatever space it prompts audiences to imagine. As Haynes argues, "This is what genres are: a way of looking at the world, so the same world looks different when cast in another set of terms."[4] Hence, particular generic inflections can render Lagos in a way that conjures up and contends with particular collective anxieties, while another genre's patterns of representing the city may evoke entirely different connotations. In this sense, the worlding that genre performs can allow a film to bring into focus the viewer's understanding of a political, social, or moral problem and, if possible, to postulate solutions or propose what must be done to absorb or come to terms with the conditions in questions.[5] In other words, genre performs what could be called a social function for audiences who return—perhaps again and again—to buy and view yet another family drama, occult film, or vigilante film. From this perspective, genre is important not because it describes a body of films but because it does work—social, political, moral, and psychic work—for a community of viewers, and this observation circles back to the notion of a relationship between cinema and the city. In recent years, both Lagos and Nollywood have witnessed unprecedented changes that challenge the basis for our understanding of this city-cinema relationship.

The entanglement of the screen media industry with a wider array of social and economic changes taking place within Lagos merits some reflection here. In recent years, with the return of relative stability, the neighborhoods generally referred to as "the Island," including Ikoyi, Victoria Island, and Lekki, have attracted the majority of the human, creative, and financial capital flowing into Lagos. As a result, "pleasure concentrates on the Island," as Dele Meiji Fatunla writes, going on to characterize Lagos as the playground of West Africa.[6] The new pleasures of prosperity found on the Island include typical forms of leisure, such as shopping and fine dining, as well as new venues for arts and culture. When FilmHouse sought to construct the first IMAX cinema in Nigeria, Lekki was the natural choice given that the professionals who take their families to such venues will not bother to battle the paralyzing traffic along the one expressway leading in and out of the neighborhood. Similarly, the "concept store" Alara went up along Akin Olugbade Street in Victoria Island in 2015 and has since been dubbed the "Barneys of Nigeria." Alara was designed by Adjaye Associates, the architectural firm of David Adjaye, whose website explains that the company anticipates "the Alara store will promote emerging talent while establishing a creative hub and an essential new destination for Lagos."[7] The notion of a creative hub is a recurring theme of these recent changes. In 2018, I temporarily stayed in the guest quarters of the coworking space called 16/16 (pronounced sixteen by sixteen) along Kofo Abayomi Street in Victoria Island. Such coworking spaces have emerged as the environment of choice for entrepreneurial young "creatives" in major cities around the world, a workplace designed precisely to blur the line between work and play. The owners of 16/16 had recently opened a second coworking space called hFactor near Obalende, to my surprise, where young Lagosians—many "repats" who lived abroad in New York or London before returning to Nigeria—congregated for rooftop parties that lasted into the early morning hours. Both 16/16 and hFactor doubled as gallery spaces for artists to host pop-up exhibitions, which should indicate the overlapping social spheres that make up the community of Lagosians involved in the Island's renaissance. The art "ecosystem" of Lagos is another space where these social and economic transformations manifest.[8] This includes the growth of the art world, with professional galleries such as Rele, Omenka, or Art Twenty One catering to local collectors, as well as the proliferation of international art events based in the city, including Art-X, Lagos Photo, and the fledgling Lagos Biennial, and it also pertains to the turn toward conceptual, abstract, and performance art by artists working within the city.[9] This chapter's conclusion will explore the narrow overlap of these art institutions with the screen media industry.

I agree with Haynes, who understands these transformations as part and parcel of the broader impact of neoliberalism in Nigeria in the new millennium.[10] Another integral factor is surely the return migration of the Nigerian diaspora.[11] Ultimately, the demographic, economic, and social flows driving the change outlined above have spilled over into the film industry in complex ways. To understand the evolving enmeshment of city and industry, one must begin in Lekki, a once swampy peninsula that was reclaimed by tremendous amounts of garbage and sand filling in order to create a swath of highly valuable real estate, a blank slate in an exceptionally overcrowded city, where luxury hotels, restaurants, shopping malls, business centers, and residential estates quickly took root. One implication has been a dramatic tectonic shift in the spatialization of the film industry, as my movements during research suggested to me. Marketers preferred to meet in the Alaba marketplace or Surulere, while the industry's first-generation producers preferred Ikeja or their offices in Surulere, whereas the new generation of producers and corporate distributors inevitably invited me to meet at a restaurant or bar on the Island or at their offices in Lekki, specifically. Some filmmakers who live and work in Lekki never venture over to the mainland. As one producer remarked at my invitation to beers at National Stadium, "I have not been to the mainland in months."

Three historic bridges connect the mainland and the Island, but the city's newest and only high suspension bridge is the Lekki Bridge, which spans a small portion of the lagoon to connect the business hub of Lekki to the former colonial district of Ikoyi, where old money now resides. After completion of the Lekki Bridge, its brightly illuminated high suspension cables seemed to utterly mesmerize New Nollywood cinematographers in search of an inspiring urban establishing shot for narratives set in Lagos. By contrast, Ema Edosio chose the mainland neighborhood of Ojuelegba, with its notoriously frenetic human and motorized traffic at the crossroads of Ikorodu and Lawanson, to shoot her first independently produced feature, having worked over the years on several commissioned projects for EbonyLifeTV. *Kasala!* was the result, a comedy about four neighborhood youths, a busted car, a hot-tempered auto mechanic, and the hustle for money. The film received well-deserved accolades upon its release, as well as special acclaim for having captured an "authentic" urban aesthetic.[12] The specific point of praise is a telling one, bearing in mind that the film's production location in Ojuelegba was within walking distance from Surulere, the home of "Old" Nollywood's producers and guilds. In a sense, this encapsulates the spatial and social divide between the different sectors of the film industry at present. The migration to the Island of so much symbolic and actual capital has drawn with it many young Nollywood producers and new corporate distributor-financiers and, in the process, divided the film industry between Surulere and Lekki, the two centers of gravity, "Old" Nollywood and New Nollywood.

New Nollywood producers appear keen to demonstrate an awareness of how cinema elsewhere in the world looks, sounds, paces itself, creates characters, and resolves its narrative conflict. New Nollywood's repertoire of film styles has expanded to include international film cycles and genres such as romantic comedies, psychological thrillers, and police procedurals, among others. This raises important questions about the nature of correspondences between cinema and the city, such as whether New Nollywood genre films tell us anything about social, cultural, or historical circumstances in Lagos or the place the city occupies in the popular imagination, for instance. The fact that there is a unique relationship between cinema and the city is often taken for granted, even though the nature of the correspondence is understood in a variety of divergent ways. When it comes to New Nollywood, film genre does not necessarily arise in response to a particular social, cultural, or historical context but rather to a cinematic context of stylistic references, allusions, and borrowings. But the industry-wide changes these films make legible *is* the lesson about Lagos these films impart, albeit in an industrial rather than a strictly textual sense. This chapter examines the different kinds of work that genre performs in mainstream and New Nollywood films and proposes a number of ways to critically interpret genre's various registers. From this perspective, recent upmarket films with a dark and gritty aesthetic speak to the evolution of Lagos as a media capital and raise questions about the influence of production and distribution in genre evolution. When viewed as a production practice, genre performs different work for producers and audiences, signaling a producer's participation in global cinephilia, for example, while affording audiences new forms of pleasure and affective socialization.[13] This cinematic context, nonetheless, illuminates a new thread in the entanglement of the film industry, the city, and new global networks of cultural production. In the final section, I argue that some filmmakers, through a distanciated mobilization of video film tropes, remain in intertextual dialogue with the mainstream industry from which they stand apart.

DARK AND GRITTY

Taxi Driver's opening car chase gives way to the story proper. After his estranged father's death, Adigun (Femi Jacobs) journeys to Lagos to collect the man's taxi and, with the help of his father's friend Taiwo (Odunlade Adekola), strives to build a new life in Lagos. He arrives empty-pocketed and must learn the hard lessons that money troubles have to teach, the hustle for money being a central trope of Nollywood. The landlord is a tyrant, the neighbor is combative, and his only regular customer, a sharp-tongued Pidginphone prostitute named Delia (Ijeoma Grace Agu), ridicules his ignorance of the city. These relationships illustrate the individual experience of emotional and moral disjointedness that stems from the precariousness of social bonds among Lagosians and introduces a key thematic preoccupation with social alienation that classic film noir typically probes for dramatic effect.[14]

Years living apart left a rift between father and son, but Adigun now finds himself driving the father's taxi, toasting his friends, and even living in his rented room in what becomes a search for both a place in a hostile city and clues about his father's life and death. Adigun gradually learns of Taiwo's and his father's involvement with the Lagos underground and the shadowy boss Baba Mistura (Toyin Oshinaike), but not soon enough to save himself from becoming implicated as a driver for Mistura's heavies and hitmen. Arguably, the narrative trope of a neighborhood in the grips of a shadowy, underground network of criminal bosses resonates with what Fay and Nieland identify as film noir's broad preoccupation with the figure of the individual embroiled in a wider world of "abstract, intangible social networks and systems" and the psychological instability and distress this engenders.[15] In their study of the global circulation of film noir, Fay and Nieland identify the most persistent features of the genre, including its deep preoccupation with displacement in the face of an inhospitable modernity and the unmooring of the individual's moral and psychological bearings.

The work of a taximan offers a natural vehicle for Oriahi's film to explore similar themes while remaining focalized from below, from the vantage point of the people of the city themselves. The movement through urban space is matched with the movement in search of answers about his estranged father, which leads him deeper into the Lagos underworld, not to mention the movement away from a trusted friend and closer to Delia and his neighbor, the strangers he comes to depend upon for his safety and self-discovery. After Delia is attacked by a client that Taiwo and Mistura arranged, she turns to Adigun for sanctuary, at which point the film's romantic subplot begins to take clear shape. Here danger creates the necessity for trust and vulnerability.

The film's narrative comes to a head when Baba Mistura threatens Delia's life in order to pressure Adigun to surrender a briefcase containing a magically endowed charm from which the boss seems to draw his power. During a standoff in Adigun's tight one-room apartment, Mistura lays out the moral dilemma the taximan must confront. Nothing happens in Lagos that his underworld did not initiate, he explains. "We make Lagos what it is. Without us Lagos would be boring. It's bad people like us, with a little good, that guard the system." Therefore, abide by the "balance" of life in Lagos—compromised and unjust as it may be—or jeopardize one's life in pursuit of the naïve ideal of a city free of violence, extortion, power struggles, and the corrupting influ-

Figure 16. The taxi inherited from the father in *Taxi Driver: Oko Ashewo*

ence of money. At this point, Taiwo bursts in, murders his boss Mistura in a betrayal that underscores the deeply cynical ethos of the scene, and turns the gun on Adigun and Delia. As the two protagonists face death, Adigun's neighbor heroically intercedes, slays the villains in a chaotic struggle, and frees the protagonists, which also rescues the film from resigning itself to this cynical moral vision. The final sequence of the film depicts Adigun and Delia in his father's taxi merging onto the Lagos-Ibadan Expressway to put the rotten world of Lagos behind them and start afresh in a new city.

The film raises questions about who one can trust in the city and whether to ever drop one's posture of constant vigilance, but I would contend that how the film resolves these questions offers an index of the film's own urban imaginary as well as that of the Lagos-based film industry today. According to Oriahi, his original screenplay did not call for this happy ending, which was instead devised and recommended by Don Omope, the supervising producer sent by FilmOne after they signed onto the project as financier and distributor (personal communication, July 10, 2017), the logic being that happy endings sell movie tickets. There is something uncanny about *Taxi Driver*, which looks like a genre film we might have seen before, in many cities or many film industries, and yet the film is undeniably set in Lagos. Shot predominantly at night, when the streets of downtown Lagos Island lie eerily empty, the film mixes cinephilic intertextuality with a grounded sense of the old city. The soundscape includes humming generators, the call to prayer imposing itself over the dialogue, and the mix of Yoruba and Pidgin English, while the setting includes a number of iconic locations—such as Broad Street and

Figure 17. Neighbors conversing in downtown Lagos Island in *Taxi Driver: Oko Ashewo*

Freedom Park—that render the space visually recognizable. The result is a plausible working-class storyworld and a fresh look at Lagos.

Like the other films considered in this chapter, Oriahi's *Taxi Driver* draws upon what I will refer to broadly as "dark" genre conventions, including stylistic features of classic, neo-, and global noir. My attachment to the category of "noir" is loose because situating these films within the genealogy of global film noir is not the aim of this chapter. Instead, I want to ask what the use of skewed chronologies, decentered narrative organization, self-reflexive modes of narration, and dystopic visual iconography do in Nollywood films, as opposed to what they represent. I contend, to begin with, that this mobilization of genre permits a film to stand out in an oversaturated market where a filmmaker must have some strategy in place to differentiate a film from the deluge of new titles. However, even as cinephilic intertextuality distinguishes some New Nollywood films from the genres and cycles that have long sustained mainstream Nollywood, as I argue further below, others draw directly from video films to create unexpected assemblages of texts, perspectives, and visions the city.

CINEPHILIA AS PRACTICE OF DISTINCTION

The structural changes underway in Nollywood should prompt us to reevaluate how genre mediates the correlations we might observe between a text and context and to explore additional registers in which to interpret genre. As Lagos-based producers explore new ways to depart from mainstream practices to distinguish their works in an overcrowded film industry, some consciously adopt long-standing genre conventions—especially from American film and television—as tokens of what some in the industry regard as an elevated cinematic standard. In this case, New Nollywood genres perform a different kind of work for producers and audiences than mainstream Nollywood genres. To echo David Desser's proposition in his oft-cited essay on global noir,[16] whether New Nollywood genres grow out of a particular social, cultural, or historical context is debatable, but that they grow out of a cinematic context of references, allusions, and borrowings is undeniable. It follows that it is perhaps more important to attend to what they reveal about practices within the film industry itself rather than the portrait of Lagos they present within the frame. However, I argue this new cinematic context *is* the historical context to which New Nollywood genres offer access by way of a second-order observation. After all, the emergence of Lagos as a regional media capital *is* what is happening in the city today, or is at least one in an array of changes, and we can observe this in the shift in New Nollywood's genre practices.

Of course, Lagos has served as a regional media capital since the formation of the mainstream video film industry, which must be underscored, but the production technologies, media professionals, and finance that media capitals bring into concentration are changing. As described in chapter 5, a significant portion of the concentration of corporate capital has become fixed in Lagos in the form of investment in infrastructure, film equipment, production budgets, postproduction facilities, and cinema screens. While all the films mentioned in this chapter are independent productions—not films commissioned by a distributor—the filmmakers, with the exception of Dare Olaitan, have worked with one of the new corporate outfits on previous or subsequent films, with such collaborations often enabling or resulting from successful independent productions, as discussed in the previous chapter. Furthermore, Haynes asserts that these "international distribution companies have hitherto done almost all their business in the diaspora and are therefore oriented toward diasporan tastes and interests."[17] Although this has not supplanted video film production in the city, the screen media industry is increasingly fragmented, and as Lagos continues its evolution as a regional media capital, it becomes possible to recognize these transformations inscribed in formal conventions like film genre. Simply put, I argue that this cycle of dark films is not "about" crime, insecurity, or a shadowy underside of Lagos but instead portrays the "old" objects of bad conscience, such as greed, corruption, violence, and betrayal, as the signs of a new cinematic style and sensibility. In them, Lagos becomes the object of attraction rather than the embodiment of anxiety, and in this respect, New Nollywood's dark and gritty films represent examples of the socialization of alternative affective engagements with city life. Therefore, reading for genre in these films tells us more about the segment of the industry that produces them, including the distribution channels currently reshaping Nollywood's audience, the production practices for which producers are rewarded, and the tastes and media literacy the audience can be presumed to have.

For instance, Walter Taylur's heist film, *Gbomo Gbomo Express*, opens with a vignette. An upscale restaurant customer's mobile phone is filched by the waitress, who conscripts the cook in a prank call to the customer's husband, demanding that he surrender a sum of money if he wants his wife returned alive. The husband complies, and the waitress returns the phone to the unwitting customer as a voiceover narrator intones that "a time will come when people will say, 'I remember the good old days when money was really money.' See, nowadays, money is becoming more of an idea than a physical thing. And most of us really haven't noticed the switch." The scene frames the film as a savvy examination of an abstract notion of money's place within society, particularly as action and voiceover combine to strike a postmodern posture in which high-minded philosophizing and underhanded scamming collide. The waitress, Blessing (Kiki Omeli), and the cook, Francis (Gideon Okeke), are members of a gang of kidnappers, and, we learn as the narrative unfolds, the narrator's voice belongs to Austin (Ramsey Nouah), a music record label executive who becomes their hostage in an elaborate scheme that comes to embroil Cassandra (Osas Ighodaro Ajibade), the restaurant customer's friend, who also becomes a hostage.

In one pivotal moment, the film's Pidginphone kidnappers negotiate by telephone with the hard-nosed businesswoman and billionaire Alexis Osita-Park (Shafy Bello) over the ransom to be paid for her daughter Cassandra. Unalarmed by her daughter's dilemma, the wealthy woman bargains down the ransom as she sits surrounded by gleaming crystalware and luxury furniture. Close-up shots detail her designer clothing, jewelry, and iPhone with brand logo prominently displayed. On the other end of the line, the kidnappers pace anxiously through the rubbish strewn about their hideout, an abandoned house in the mainland Lagos neighborhood of Ebute Metta. The camera shows light sockets stripped of bulbs and wiring, crumbling concrete windowsills, moldy walls covered with graffiti, and a car tire on the dusty floor beside the hostages, who sit bound and gagged between oil drums, broken shipping pallets, and a stack of drawers without a dresser. We are made to appreciate the building's decrepitude.

As a result of the trends described above, including the localization of production for content intended for global distribution, Lagos has become the primary setting for corporate and New Nollywood films, both the slick and glossy as well as the dark and gritty. As discussed in chapter 4, many New Nollywood films are designed to organize spectators' senses around the experience of connectivity, mobility, and contemporaneity with global consumer culture. Some glamorous genres, like a recent cycle of romantic comedies, depict Lagos as a global city characterized by lifestyle brands, luxury items, consumer technologies, travel, and other trappings of participation in global consumer culture. By and large, the city that emerges in films like *Wedding Party* (2016), *When Love Happens* (2014), or *Flower Girl* (2013) corresponds with the image that Lagos's moneyed class holds of itself. By contrast, the dark films discussed in this chapter fixate on a dystopic imaginary of the city. In both cases, the adaptation of international film genres itself embodies the participation in global popular culture that many of the films depict diegetically.

Desser calls this type of intertextuality "cinephilia" and contends that the pleasure of stylistic cross-referencing is part of what propels the global circulation of film genres like the global noir.

> The impulse toward cinephilia—that is, the ability and necessity of acknowledging the intertextual chain of references, borrowings, and reworkings—may be at the heart of global noir. For it involves filmmakers and film audiences in a circuit of acknowledgments—the ability of filmmakers to make references and their confidence in the audience's recognition of them.[18]

For instance, *Taxi Driver: Oko Ashewo* illustrates some of the film's parallels with the conventions of film noir, but it bears underscoring that the trope of a taxi driver navigating a despoiled urban landscape represents an homage to Martin Scorcese's film of the same title. In one of our first conversations, Oriahi alluded to his admiration for the American filmmaker's work. Still, among the films in question, Taylur's *Gbomo Gbomo Express* and Olaitan's *Ojukokoro* are the two most concertedly engaged in this type of cinephilic intertextuality, as both employ skewed chronologies, multiple narration along decentered storylines, and self-reflexive treatment of themes of coincidence, chance, and arbitrary encounters, all qualities Desser associates with global noir.[19] *Gbomo Gbomo Express* sets out as a simple story of kidnappers and hostages, but when efforts to secure the ransom from Austin's business partner, Rotimi, fails because the company turns out to be insolvent and when the kidnappers discover that Cassandra, their second, mistaken hostage, is the daughter of a billionaire, the narrative splinters into a caper that pits four character groups against one another. Each group represents a narrative thread, and the film does its best to tangle them up.

Rotimi, the business partner, believing the kidnappers work for Nino, a musician on the record label with whom he is plotting to cheat Austin out of his share of the business, presses Nino to relent and call off the kidnapping. The kidnappers, believing that Rotimi is concealing the company's assets, threaten to kill Austin, at which point Cassandra reveals the fact of her family's tremendous fortune, turning her coincidental kidnapping into a boon for the three inept kidnappers, who set upon the mother with their ransom demands. Alexis takes the upper hand in the ransom negotiations, rejects their demand for "fifty million," and counteroffers "thirty million" and amnesty for the one who will betray and surrender the other two to police. Beset by suspicion of one another, the gang nearly reaches its breaking point before realizing Alexis has been negotiating with them in American dollars, not naira. They promptly accept the figure and prepare to return the hostages, but the most dim-witted of the kidnapers, Filo, does not comprehend the immaterial nature of a wire transfer and brings a crew of gunmen to collect the money for himself. Filo learns there is no physical money involved but only the shifting of figures on balance sheets in a bank in Malaysia, and the ensuing shoot-out leaves dead all three kidnappers. Cassandra and Austin go free, but in a narrative turn that is intended to steal the show, we discover in the final sequence of the film that the foregoing events unfolded precisely as Austin had planned—that Cassandra's kidnapping was no coincidence but rather was orchestrated by Austin to appear so to all involved but himself. The film cuts to footage seen earlier in the narrative of a shadowy figure, who we had presumed to be one of the kidnappers, huddled over an intricate map of names, numbers, news reports, and arrows suggesting the domino-like flowchart of events that would transpire for Austin to walk away with US$30 million in his Malaysian bank account and no one the wiser. Presented in graphic detail, violence here serves no larger moral order, as it would in mainstream Nollywood's "aesthetic of outrage," which depicts spectacular transgressions in order to vivify notions of public morality.[20] On the contrary, the film derives pleasure from imagining transgression without subsequent containment and by untethering outrage from morality, which creates an affective inclination toward shock itself.

Like many heist films that feature a plan gone wrong, double-crossing partners in crime, and intersecting plotlines that hinge upon and highlight the element of chance, *Gbomo Gbomo Express* presents its narrative as a puzzle. The viewer's pleasure lies in anticipating how the film will solve the puzzle it creates for itself. In other words, narration is a game and viewers are invited to play along. This admixture of farce and heist film calls to mind Guy Ritchie's *Lock, Stock and Two Smoking Barrels* (1998) and *Snatch* (2000), and the resonances go right down to the soundtrack's inclination for drum and bass, a UK-style electronic music genre. At one point, Gideon Okeke appears to draw two fingers across his eyes while dancing á la John Travolta and Uma Thurman in *Pulp Fiction* (1994). The film's cinematography and editing techniques provide visual allusions intended to further heighten the sense of stylistic and thematic play, including smash cuts, wipes, split screens, and whip pans, techniques that call attention to themselves as markers of style. Similarly, Taylur places his camera inside open containers, such as plastic bags, cigarette packs, and a toilet tank, which characters then open and peer into, a shot that recalls one especially infamous bathroom scene from Danny Boyle's *Trainspotting* (1996). Cinematography of this sort lends an aura of "cool" to the representation of urban violence and is part of the cultivation of cinephilia and the accompanying affective disposition that finds pleasure in the stylized presentation of transgression. I argue, in contrast to Desser's notion of cinephilia, that the communication of allusions to specific films may not matter here as much as the ability of these filmmakers to capture and reproduce this particular affect, which itself "feels" like other films the viewer may have enjoyed.

The same can be said of the visual pleasure that this type of cinematography and editing affords. Beyond the visual consumption afforded by more glamorous New Nollywood films, their representation of Lagos as a wealthy African city affords its own kind of pleasure for some audiences. This includes viewers I speak to in Jamaica, where I live, who rarely see Africa depicted as prosperous in dominant global media. Along the same lines, dark and gritty Nollywood films may portray a dystopic vision of Lagos, but this aesthetic framing itself conjures up a cinematic urban imaginary that audiences may recognize and thereby situates Lagos alongside other global noir cityscapes. Interspersed throughout *Gbomo Gbomo Express*, for example, are aerial shots of the Lagos cityscape, including the swooping concrete of major expressway interchanges and rows of large high-rise housing complexes. In the past, one rarely saw exterior shots of the Lagos cityscape, given the congestion and danger of shooting on the street, but rather compound gates as a car arrives and the domestic sitting room where the narrative was hashed out in dialogue. Affordable drone-mounted cameras have solved this problem and reintroduced Lagos streets and skyline to the repertoire of Nollywood cinematography. As the final credits of *Gbomo Gbomo Express* boast, "shot entirely on location in Lagos, Nigeria with an all Nigerian cast and crew," a caveat Taylur also attaches to the end credits of his follow-up police procedural, *Catch.er*. The closing credits literally remind viewers that the film was "Made in Nollywood," lest there be any confusion. New Nollywood's other dark films similarly remake the cityscape of Lagos as one appropriate to a film industry on its way to achieving a global recognition, and whether bright and gleaming or dark and brooding, the point is that we witness Lagos represented more cinematographically, for lack of a better term.

In this context, however, cinephilia is arguably as much about pleasure as it is about work, including the measures a producer takes to signify expert appreciation for cinematic style and professional production practices, as mentioned in chapter 5. In this respect, cinephilia represents a "practice of distinction," a term Tejaswini Ganti adopts to designate the efforts by some film producers in Hindi cinema to characterize their work as distinct from the prevailing norms of the industry.[21] As Ganti goes on to explain, distinction connotes difference as well as status and hierarchy, and practices of distinction, therefore, undergird the producer's assertion of the value of their work as compared to a field of other films construed as indistinguishable from one another. The formalization of distribution and marketing has also informed the way producers talk about their films. For instance, it is today possible to ask a producer about his or her film's "comp" titles, a term that media marketing teams use to surmise a film's target market and potential sales trends based on a comparison to similar titles. Corporate distributors and cinema operators want to hear about a film's "comp" in hopes of replicating the release strategy of similar successful films. Genre is bound up in these comparisons, which is why I suggest that our approach to New Nollywood films may require us to interpret genre as an index of industrial circumstances, which we can examine, in turn, as indicative of historical changes taking place in Lagos. In this sense, genre analysis provides second-order observations, rather than direct observations, of tangible social and historical conditions in Lagos today.

INTERTEXTUALITY AND THE LAGOS ART WORLD

While some New Nollywood films interweave references to cinema in other places and times, we might pause to consider how mainstream video films have themselves become referents in unexpected intertextual networks. To do so spotlights the malleability of aesthetic value as certain themes and tropes migrate across spheres of cultural production that discursively define themselves as distinct from one another, such as mainstream Nollywood, New Nollywood, and the "Lagos art world."[22] Nollywood's intersection with global art exhibitions dates back to Platform4 of Documenta11, an event hosted by curator Okwui Enwezor and based in Lagos that examined life in four African cities and produced a publication that includes Onookome Okome's oft-cited essay "Writing the Anxious City," which argues that occult films such as *Rituals* (1997) express popular misgivings about Lagos. Nollywood has since figured centrally in numerous artists' works. However, in many encounters between art and Nollywood, the elements that tend to shake loose include the supernatural or occult themes and aesthetics of mainstream video films. Artists take up the occult in various ways, from the controversial exoticism of Pieter Hugo's photography, for example, to the more substantial engagement of Zina Saro-Wiwa's exhibition "Sharon Stone in Abuja," which itself recycles the title of a famous video film. Composed of installation (*Parlour* [2010] and *Mourning Class* [2010]) and video art (*Phyllis* [2010]), the exhibition deals not only with the occult in video film but also with Nollywood's perpetuation of sociocultural values, emotive performances, and on- and off-screen repertoire of domestic spaces.[23] Where the video *Phyllis* borrows supernatural themes from Nollywood, which it treats as an index of wider cultural and religious patterns in contemporary Nigeria, it does so self-consciously and with the aim of social critique. The video envisions, for instance, a woman whose neon plastic wigs induce a state of spirit possession when worn and thereby interrogates the construction of female subjectivity. In this specific sense, *Phyllis* fits within a pattern whereby supernatural tropes are mobilized by an artist to articulate commentary and critique, perhaps because rumors and stories of occult practices have been understood in scholarship as an idiom expressing *popular* anxieties over abstract—global—phenomenon or as vernacular expressions of critique of millennial capitalism in particular.

In light of this, I would pivot attention to a collective of young filmmakers whose works are situated at the intersection of the art world, and artworks like Saro-Wiwa's *Phyllis*, and the commercial film industry with its audiences of cinemagoers and streaming video on demand subscribers. In 2016, Abba

Makama, Mike Gouken Omonua, and C. J. "Fiery" Obasi formed the Surreal16 Collective in hopes of disrupting the entrenched aesthetic boundaries of Nigerian screen media. As Makama explains in an interview with France 24, the collective envisions itself as a space for filmmakers wishing to express their "singular vision" and thus an alternative to straight-to-video and New Nollywood, which he characterizes as narrowly focused on commercial success, oriented around an established star system, and fundamentally genre driven.[24] Their first film, *Visions*, an anthology of three short films, screened at the 2017 African International Film Festival, where, in a panel discussion, the group delivered a manifesto of sixteen tongue-in-cheek guidelines that convey their aesthetic disaffection with mainstream and New Nollywood: "No wedding films," "Avoid melodrama," "No sequels," and "No establishing shots of Lekki Bridge," among others.

The S16 filmmakers take advantage, through public comments, production practices, and distribution strategy, of what Rosalind Galt and Karl Schoonover describe as art cinema's inherent instability as a category of global culture.[25] In interviews, the collective members cite an eclectic range of influences, from Robert Bresson to Dogme 95 and New Taiwanese Cinema, and are no strangers to the international film festival circuit. Mike Omonua's short films *Born* (2016) and *Brood* (2018) were official selections at the 2018 Rotterdam International Film Festival, and Abba Makama's *Green White Green* (2016) and *The Lost Okoroshi* (2019) premiered at the Toronto International Film Festival, while the collective's latest anthology film, *Juju Stories* (2021), won the Independent Critics Jury prize for Best Film at the 2022 Locarno Film Festival. Moreover, in December 2021, the collective hosted its own S16 Film Festival in the renovated Federal Printing Press building on Broad Street in downtown Lagos, curating their works alongside a selection of other shorts and feature films. The first night's headliner was *Juju Stories*, preceded by several shorts that included Frances Bodomo's *Afronauts* (2014) and Jimi Agboola's *Head* (2016), which situates the narrative feature alongside video works that are equally at home in art exhibitions. For instance, Agboola's single-channel video is represented by Rele Gallery in Lagos. Under the moniker Dodorowski, Makama has exhibited his own artwork at Whitespace on Raymond Njoku Street in the 2020 show "Dodorowski's Artefacts from our Future Past" and the 2019 show "Knock-Offs," which included a painting that subsequently appears in *Juju Stories*. The premise of Makama's "Knock-Offs" paintings is inherently intertextual, with references to David Bowie, Apichatpong Werasethakul, Grace Jones, and former Lagos state governor

Bola Tinubu, among others. All the above illustrates how the assertion of clear authorial identities enables Makama, Omonua and Obasi both to distance their work from Nollywood as popular cinema and to tap into the "auteurist impulse" of global art cinema's legitimating institutions, where authorship often informs the rationale for inclusion of as yet unrecognized filmmakers.[26]

In *Sight and Sound* magazine, Makama addresses criticism that the collective omits acknowledgment of prior Nigerian filmmakers, demanding in retort, "How many Nigerians have seen an Ola Balogun film? Or a Hubert Ogunde film? Where are the films that are going to inspire us? They're not even available."[27] There is something to this point. Young Nigerian cinephiles practice what Thomas Elsaesser has dubbed "second-generation cinephilia," a passion for cinema formed through access to DVDs and the internet and coalesced around communities of shared affective experience that transcend the specific space of the arthouse and second-run cinemas and the material attachment to celluloid film that enthralled an earlier generation of American and European cinephiles.[28] However, video technologies and online distribution are, by the same token, precisely what allows Nollywood to flourish, which undercuts the notion that a lack of access renders Nigerian film culture uninspiring. In fact, the collective may be more influenced—even if unwittingly—by video films than they profess. Indeed, the most intriguing aspect of *Juju Stories* is its mutual indebtedness to world cinema and mainstream video films, which creates an intertextual assemblage that sutures together the distinct aesthetic spheres.

An anthology in three chapters, *Juju Stories* begins with "Love Potion," the melancholic love story of two young Lagosians, Mercy and Leo. She works in advertising, *not* the creative side as she hastens to note, but is passionate about writing and longs to become a novelist. Discouraged, she finds support in her housemate, whose cat we learn is perpetually missing, an allusion to novelist Haruki Murakami's *Kafka on the Shore*. Leo works in real estate, is interested in business and video games, and is engaged to be married. Stylistically subtle, the film's understated tone and fluid narrative perspective glide in and out of Mercy's and Leo's confessional voiceover narrations, revealing the nuances of a romantic attraction that springs from deep interior experiences of longing. We are transported, for instance, as Mercy fantasizes of a future with Leo in which he is strong, affectionate, generous, and a loving father to their children who will protect and comfort her. In this dream he reads and gives thoughtful notes on her novel manuscript. She includes her housemate's missing cat because it reminds her of a Murakami novel, she explains, to which he concurs, "Dis your manuscript, e get dat—how I take tok am—dat *Norwegian Wood* feel" (Your manuscript has that—how would I say—that *Norwegian Wood* feel), because the Leo she imagines loves Murakami too. The Pidgin dialogue is delivered naturalistically because we are fully immersed in Mercy's lovesick daydream. But the viewer learns, as the narrative bleeds from Mercy's dream into Leo's voiceover, that in reality, Leo is losing interest and has resolved to end things with Mercy and recommit to his fiancée. Sensing this, Mercy takes a drastic measure, creating a love potion and with it spiking his tea. Suddenly, her dreams become his dreams, and the narrative slips into the stream of his consciousness, where he envisions the life of love and fulfillment they would share. These scenes are delivered with a stark sincerity that sits at odds with the supernatural premise of the love potion, and yet there is no dissonance or discontinuity. The film appropriates "juju" as simply another trope through which to imagine the almost magical force of romantic love, which can grip one suddenly only to vanish inexplicably. And, indeed, things begin to spoil. A melancholic atmosphere descends on the film as we witness Leo call off the engagement, his heartbroken fiancée move out, and Mercy arrive to replace her. The montage continues in Mike Omonua's understated style, with Mercy offering Leo a Murakami novel that he avoids reading, Leo neglecting her to play video games, and both recognizing their fundamental incompatibility. As Mercy explains, she loved the Leo of her fantasies but feels nothing for the man before her now, so she returns to the apartment where the story began and to her housemate with the missing cat, while Leo, still bewitched, struggles to grieve.

The anthology's second chapter, titled "YAM," opens in a posh home as a refined-looking couple use fork and knife to nibble pounded yam. The man remarks that the stew is remarkable, to which the woman responds, "The guy is an artist. Edet is an artist," referring to the cook they employ. In the background hangs artwork that appears as if someone reproduced the subject matter of Edvard Munch's "The Scream" in the style of Basquiat. The man turns to his newspaper, skims the headline, and reads aloud with skepticism, "Reports of people turning to yams after picking cash from sidewalks?" After a pause, the woman responds, "Do we even have sidewalks in this country?" They sigh, "Ah, this country." The satirical vignette sets the tone for the subsequent story's treatment of the urban legend in the news report. The film cuts to its ironic protagonist, an area boy named YAM, on the dusty street of a Lagos mainland neighborhood, who appears in turns intimidating and pathetic. He hails neighbors in a loud, gregarious mix of Yoruba and Pidgin, shakes down neighbors for petty cash, and wrestles embarrassingly with prostitutes for his share of their earnings. That is, until he discovers and collects a thick fold of naira notes on the sidewalk. Rather than metamorphize into a yam, he walks to the bar to celebrate as the soundtrack, in postmodern pastiche, places "Winter" from Antonio Vivaldi's *The Four Seasons* over the street scene and Johann Strauss's waltz "The Blue Danube" over a beer parlor filled with smoke and empty bottles. YAM spends all the money, passes out, and collapses out of frame.

At this point the narrative again switches focalization. A poor vulcanizer enters the bar and discovers on the concrete floor a yam tuber draped in YAM's silver chains. He carries it home, cooks it, and adds to it a noxious herbal concoction meant to terminate his girlfriend's pregnancy. The vulcanizer's money worries are dire, and he simply cannot support a child. Confronted with the gravity of attempting to abort the child, and the likelihood he will incur the wrath of God, the man retorts, "Do I fear God? Which God? The one that makes me suffer like this?" His girlfriend rejects the yam, but he consumes his portion, only to wake that night with YAM's voice in his head calling to be released from confinement. Believing the voice to be that of the unborn child, the unhinged man grabs a knife and pursues his terrified girlfriend out of the compound, down the street, and into the night. The narrative then cuts back to the bourgeois couple at the breakfast table, who discuss the day's top headline: record rates of mental illness among the poor in Lagos. "This country," they sigh.

The third chapter, titled "Suffer the Witch," resembles the campus film genre of mainstream Nollywood in some ways. At its center is a love triangle between three university students, roommates Chinwe and Joy, who compete for attention from Ikenna, the most handsome student on campus. He makes advances toward Chinwe, but the attraction sours when Joy reveals that, out of jealousy, she had sex with Ikenna. She professes love for her best friend and asks Chinwe for forgiveness. But Ikenna warns Chinwe not to trust her roommate, insisting that she is a witch. He narrates the sexual encounter with Joy and explains the acts she performed that left him emasculated and convinced of her supernatural power. That night, Ikenna is chased by an unmarked van that ultimately overtakes him without incident. In his paranoia, he stops to catch his breath, glances across the road, and sees himself or rather his bloody corpse ejected from his overturned vehicle. Dead. Members of Ikenna's campus cult, two muscled but well-mannered men, resolve to put an end to Joy's witchcraft, invoking the biblical admonition "Thou shalt not suffer a witch to live." The two men are never again seen on campus. Meanwhile, Joy becomes more possessive. Focalized through Chinwe's perspective, the viewer is brought along as her suspicion and fear of Joy grow and as Joy's affection for her friend appears increasingly monstrous. In the final scene, in an empty classroom bathed ominously in neon green and red lights, Joy conspiratorially remarks, "Nobody will ever come between us, Chinwe. Nobody. I love you, darling. And we are going to be best friends, forever." Framed in a close-up shot, she kisses Chinwe on the lips and exclaims, "Let's go get ice cream." The camera cuts to a close-up of feet levitating effortlessly and then a view of the two women floating hand in hand out of the classroom toward a divine white light. This image brings the anthology to a close.

In "Suffer the Witch," the transvaluation of an occult trope, its appropriation as a transgressive affirmation of same-sex desire, nevertheless presumes knowledge of the occult's role in video films as a textual feature with wider social implications. I would argue that *Juju Stories* understands occult representations on the same terms with which they are discussed in film scholarship, as the narrative and visual vocabulary of video films in dialogue with the apprehensions and desires of popular audiences. That is, an intellectual distanciation marks the representation of the supernatural. Furthermore, such distanciation renders occult tropes pliable and allows love potions, cautionary tales of human transformation, or witchcraft accusations to be situated within other networks of meaning, alongside Murakami or Exodus, and thereby deployed toward other purposes. The Surreal16 filmmakers repurpose them into tools of provocation and social commentary, but in doing so find themselves in dialogue with the video films and popular imaginary from which the collective otherwise seeks to distinguish itself.

I have employed the term "intertextuality" as Dresser has, to denote a film's network of references and allusions to other texts, but this is ultimately a narrow, instrumentalist conception of intertextuality. Famously, for Julia Kristeva, all writing is intertextual because it entails an absorption of and reply to prior social texts, meaning it both interpolates history and society into the text and inserts the text into that history.[29] Following the same line, Stefano Harney and Fred Moten conclude that intertextuality names the text as social space itself, which one enters to mix with other people through writing, reading, or filmmaking.[30] Gradually, this conceptualization of intertextuality begins to resonate with the relational turn in urban theory, and it becomes possible to find enregistered here an unexpected correlation between the city and its screen media. We find that Nollywood both generates and absorbs tremendous amounts of what AbdouMaliq Simone calls "the 'fugitive materials' that increasingly find their way into all cities," which include "traditions, codes, linguistic bits, jettisoned and patchwork economies, pirated technologies, bits and pieces of symbols floating around detached from the original places they may have come from." Such fragments are fugitive inasmuch as they have been "long dissociated from their original uses" and seem almost to "'wash up' on the shores of the city."[31] Indeed, New Nollywood might gather its global film references and genre conventions from international currents but it also, almost inevitably, mixes them with other materials that wash up from the mainland side of the lagoon. Nevertheless, to combine this array of elements fugitively dissociates them from their original use and meaning, which seems true for both the genre, narrative, and visual elements sourced globally and the occult and supernatural tropes drawn from mainstream video film's popular imagination, the consequences of which I further reflect upon in the conclusion.

Conclusion

Although this book is dedicated to understanding Lagos through Nollywood, it has resisted the impulse to ontologize the city, to pin down its essential features or offer a transparent account of what the city *is*. As I remark at the outset, the defining feature of Lagos is the profound extent to which life there is continually redefined. The notion of open endurance gives a name to this processual interplay of contingency and persistence and the affective posture that this continual hustle of everyday life seems to demand. In a sense, this book's flexible conceptualization of city life represents a similarly opportunistic tactic meant to permit new interpretations of Nollywood that uncover unexpected and sometimes oblique ways in which screen media produced in or about the city enregister elements of life in Lagos. Nevertheless, the sequence of chapters, which roughly follow chronological order, presents the risk that the book unwittingly folds its findings into the logic of a developmentalist narrative that views the screen media industry as moving along a single trajectory toward "global standards." By way of conclusion, I would like to unsettle the arc of this storyline, which is little more than a disciplinary construct and a normative temporality to which Lagos and Nollywood, in many ways, do not conform. I have attempted throughout this book to adopt as part of my critical method the ambivalence found in the films themselves. To be clear, ambivalence here does not denote a paralyzing indecision between opposed viewpoints or an ossified stasis of mixed feelings. Instead, I argue that Nollywood continually stirs up discourse on Lagos and thereby animates numerous ways of thinking and feeling about the city. In this respect, ambivalence implies the speculative, sometimes opportunistic orientation that residents of Lagos adopt toward an array of possible future events that require elasticity to navigate, affect, or harness to open an avenue to the good life or simply a better ground upon which to endure. It names one response to the failed guarantees of developmentalist temporality.

I find this approach generative in view of the gaps that today divide the screen media industry, for instance, along the lines of informal alternative networks and formal dominant networks of production and distribution,[1] material and immaterial modes of distribution,[2] or even fast and slow film cultures,[3] although the distinction between "Old" and New Nollywood is surely the most widely discussed. I have used the term "mainstream Nollywood" to avoid the suggestion that value accrues inevitably with time, which oversimplifies the screen media scholarship that traces these complex shifts brilliantly in material and structural terms. It is likely that Nollywood will continue to evolve in multiple directions, characterized by different production practices, distribution channels, formal aesthetic patterns, and material emplacements within Lagos. As I contend, and as this book has worked to demonstrate, these distinctions prove most instructive when placed in a comparative relation rather than held apart as unrelated phenomena. Attention to the gaps between underlying structures only enriches the comparative interpretation of these texts and brings into view the ongoing discourse about Lagos that absorbs and stimulates an array of divergent perspectives.

In a final illustration of this point, I would return to the National Arts Theatre, that material trace in the heart of Lagos that serves as a reminder of the celluloid cinema that prefigured Nollywood. In 2018, I visited the theater to speak with a projectionist who had worked there during Festac '77 and had offered to share his personal experiences of the event. As I departed, several tattered film posters pasted along a concrete wall beyond the entrance gate caught my eye, in particular, the announcement printed on one, "Now Showing @ National Art Theatre."

The practice of screening new releases at the theater remains popular in the Yoruba video film industry, typically on public holidays when otherwise busy residents have time and those with a tight budget have an excuse to spend. Audiences can be large, as entire families come out to relax together. These posters advertised *Mod'orisa: The Epic* (2018) and *Agbaje Omo Onile* (2018), two Yoruba-language productions screened to celebrate ìtunnú awẹ̀, or the end of Ramadan, which promised me an opportunity to experience a screening at the theater, in one of the cinema halls where Festac '77 attendees had viewed Ousmane Sembene's *Xala* (1974) and Nigerian audiences had enjoyed the premiere of Moses Olaiya Adejumo's *Orun Mooru* (1982). Lamentably, however, I had arrived too late to attend any of the three nights listed and could only wonder how the screening had unfolded.

Several years later, I was reminded of the posters, at which point it seemed

Figure 18. Film posters outside the National Arts Theatre entrance

plausible, given the structural changes in the industry, that these films had been broadcast on Africa Magic Yoruba or even released online through iROKOtv or iBAKATV. Indeed, a quick search uncovered both video films on YouTube, uploaded to the Yorubahood channel, which has nearly a million subscribers, hundreds of millions of views, and no fees or paywall. The channel is hosted by ArabaTV Entertainment, a shared venture established by Alhaji Kazeem Afolayan, the head of Epsalum Movie Productions, one of the largest and longest-standing Yoruba video marketers and the legal distributor of the video films in question. Thus, rather than view the productions in a shared experience at the National Arts Theatre, I streamed them from my apartment in Kingston, Jamaica, sharing in the experience in a distinctly different sense.

The video film connects several threads of this book. As an example of the mainstream video films that continue to flow from the general intellect of Yoruba film culture, *Agbaje Omo Onile*—meaning "the wealthy son of the soil"—merits a brief summary. The film is set in a community where growth and prosperity have created a demand for land, and while not overtly set in

Lagos, the situation evokes any number of communities immediately surrounding the ever-expanding city. The villainous main character, Agbajé (Odunlade Adekola), has grown extremely wealthy through numerous land sales in which he poses as the landowner to defraud unsuspecting buyers. (In reality, such fraud happens frequently enough that homeowners often inscribe "Beware 419!" or "This House Is Not for Sale" on their property.) The film begins as those who built houses, businesses, schools, and churches on the land are threatened with eviction after the fraudulent sales are uncovered. As one victim exclaims, "We bought land from you, and you gave us documentation, hoping to one day have our places of rest. Suddenly, someone else shows up claiming he owns the land, not you. How is that done in a country with law and order?" But Agbajé cruelly rebuffs them, and the narrative incrementally raises the moral stakes of its premise, as Agbajé moves from scamming powerless individuals to arresting a pastor in order to confiscate his church's land and eventually challenges the *baalè*—or customary town headmaster, here played by Kareem Adepoju—who traditionally has the sole authority to allocate community land. But Agbajé insists, "It is public land, and I am a son of the soil." No consequences befall him because, we learn, a powerful herbalist has granted Agbajé spiritual fortification through a ritual in which he kidnaps and kills an innocent young woman. The ritual's protection springs from an enchanted gourd that will lose its power if ever allowed to touch the earth. Having concealed the gourd, Agbajé believes himself invincible.

However, he is visited by *Ilè*, the spirit embodiment of the land, and commanded to release the innocent woman he already sacrificed. She warns him that, if he wants ground to be buried in, he must not sacrifice her. With characteristic hubris, Agbajé replies that upon death, he will be so powerful that he will refuse burial in the earth. However, when Agbajé has the *baalè* imprisoned, the community rises against him, and during the commotion, Agbajé accidentally topples the enchanted gourd, which falls to the ground and abolishes his power. He dies immediately. When the community attempts to bury Agbajé's body, the grave floods with bubbling waters preventing the burial, so they dig and inter him in a second grave, but his body reappears in the mortuary stained with traces of soil. Ultimately, they must cremate his body in a morally solemn scene in which *Ilè* reappears to deliver a lesson against overreaching greed and human ambition for power.

Within the framework of distinctions currently at hand in scholarship on Nollywood, we might say that *Agbaje Omo Onile* represents an informal alternative production distributed materially through straight-to-disc sales that facilitated a film culture of fast production, circulation, and consumption. It represents a mainstream video film and can be read as an expression of the popular imaginary of ordinary producers and audiences. The narrative structure, characters, setting, and themes, as well as the mode of address in scenes of moral instruction, all represent enduring features of the Yoruba popular theater. Its screening at the National Arts Theatre connects it to a long history of shared public reception and demonstrates its clear material emplacement within Lagos for a specific audience celebrating a particular event, the end of Ramadan. It bears underscoring that these dimensions of Yoruba film culture endure despite the tremendous change witnessed elsewhere in the screen media industry.

Furthermore, *Agbaje Omo Onile* demonstrates that popular themes never die. Many viewers surely note the parallels with Tunde Kelani's *Ti Oluwa Nile* (1993), an early video film also preoccupied, famously, with the communal, cultural, and sacred value of land and the moral critique of corruption and acquisitiveness. In fact, in both video films, the renowned Yoruba dramatist Kareem Adepoju performs the role of *baalè*, connecting the two productions through what Lani Akande calls a "character of recurrence."[4] Other similarities with early video film narratives turn on the performative enactment of social entanglements. In one combinational scenario, the *baalè*'s advisers debate whether to call upon the town's wealthy children in the city for resources to host an annual festival. We are not beggars, one adviser insists, and will not turn to outsiders for help, while another rejoins that relatives in the city are not outsiders, that good upbringing begins at home, and that having been raised at home—in the town—they will surely support the festival. This illustrates, albeit from the standpoint of the hometown, the extent to which city life entails continual concern for relationships between family, friends, and wider networks of social connections.

As I noted, *Agbaje Omo Onile* was financed and distributed by Epsalum Movie Productions, a major marketer of Yoruba productions that, when I visited in 2013, had offices at Idumota Market, the central hub in the material network of this indigenous-language sector. It is remarkable to note that today the video market at Idumota has virtually disappeared, having been uprooted and transplanted in 2018 to Arena Market in Oshodi. The Yoruba sector's new video market shows considerable improvement over the claustrophobic quarters of the old market in the heart of downtown Lagos. Perhaps most importantly, however, the new location situates the video vendors even closer to the *danfo* bus routes that interlink the largest cities throughout the predominantly Yoruba Southwest, these being the grounds of circulation for physical video films.

The pivotal intervention of early scholarship on Nollywood was, arguably, to conceptualize video film as popular culture and, through engagement with the work of Biodun Jeyifo, Christopher Waterman, Johannes Fabian, Karin Barber, and others, to reimagine how we approach African cinema. Within this critical paradigm, cultural positionality, the social relations of production and consumption, and the situatedness of texts within place and history were the elements that opened a text to fuller interpretation. As such a text, *Agbaje Omo Onile* attracts my critical attention precisely because it would seem beyond the reach of the logistical management that is slowly capturing terrain elsewhere in the screen media industry. Nevertheless, the video film was only available to me because it has been uploaded to YouTube, and this fact underscores the extent to which "logistics is in hot pursuit of the general intellect in its most concrete form, that is its potential form, its informality, when any time and any space and any thing could happen, could be the next form, the new abstraction."[5] Streaming services and satellite television networks that acquire and distribute Nollywood on closed channels represent one way in which Nollywood's cultural creativity has been harnessed. But I would argue that the migration of straight-to-disc productions to YouTube better exemplifies the logistical pursuit of Nigerian film culture's general intellect. In fact, the platform today almost resembles a virtual video market, an online Alaba or Onitsha.

This pursuit of Nollywood's cultural creativity, of the generativity without reserve of Nigerian everyday life, can be construed as a form of enclosure, but I would add—ambivalently—that this does not entail "capture," pure and simple. Recall that enclosures within Lagos are designed to keep at bay the surrounding pressures of contingency and provisionality that always threaten to destabilize what an individual hopes to build, and thereby enclosures provide the ground upon which something productive and generative can be created. Ironically, without enclosed modes of distribution, without some alternative to its original model of straight-to-disc sales, one might wonder whether Nollywood would collapse, as some lamented it might a decade ago, before the structural changes we now describe as formalization or corporatization took hold. From the perspective of the popular arts paradigm, this poses a deeply counterintuitive proposition. But as the narrative described above illustrates, to build a house in Lagos, one first buys the land but then immediately builds an enclosure to ensure that *omo onílè*—or anyone with designs to undercut one's prosperity—does not return to sell the land to the next buyer.

Thinking speculatively along these lines, it is debatable whether New Nollywood will remain as distinct from mainstream video films as it once seemed. The influence of the video film star system speaks to the broad appeal these productions still enjoy, which some New Nollywood productions seem to recognize. For instance, Odunlade Adekola, who plays the lead in *Agbaje Omo Onile*, also performs a substantial role in Daniel Oriahi's *Taxi Driver: Oko Ashewo* (2016), a film that I portray in chapter 6 as breaking new ground stylistically. The New Nollywood production's inclusion of Adekola and Afeez Oyetoro surely aims to harness their intense popularity among Yoruba video film audiences. For much of his career, Tunde Kelani has made similarly strategic casting decisions, but now even Kunle Afolayan, whose name is closely associated with New Nollywood, regularly casts famous Yoruba video film actors. In fact, at the time of this writing, Afolayan has entered postproduction on the cultural epic film *Anikulapo*, which features an ensemble of venerated performers who represent what remains of the Yoruba traveling theater. Perhaps this indicates nothing more than the ongoing development of new cycles of films, but that itself is an enduring element of the industry.

Of course, some young filmmakers like the Surreal16 Collective openly reject all of the above. However, intriguingly, *Juju Stories* (2021) shares much more in common with *Agbaje Omo Onile* than it initially appears. The video film's central agents of conflict include the herbalist who can endow characters with occult power, a Christian pastor, and the customary Yoruba authority of the *baalè*. Finally, retribution comes in the form of the female spiritual embodiment of the land, who stands in chthonic consonance with Yoruba cosmology. (Perhaps uncoincidentally, while the video film was screened to celebrate Eid al-Fitr, it features no references to Islam whatsoever.) Arguably, the Surreal16 animate their stories with the same agents of conflict—the occult, Christian orthodoxy, and notions of traditional cultural identity— even if regarded with an intellectual distanciation. Like the video film, *Juju Stories* rebukes the corrosive effects of individual wealth and power on the broader community, albeit through satire and irony rather than aesthetics of outrage and exhortation. Furthermore, both productions conclude in alignment with female figures—whether *Ilè* the chthonic spirit or Joy the campus witch—whose associations with the supernatural symbolize their corrective, ethical force in the world. As further example, take the motif of the *omo onílè*, who greedily confiscates the community's shared lands and exploits those seeking a place to stay put and build a life. The same trope provides Nomusa Makhubu a critical lens through which to conceptualize the idea of "home" in Zina Saro-Wiwa's engagement with Nollywood in her video art and installations. "The notion of a home being sold off through a con echoes the discourse surrounding the flight of the country's oil resources, from which the majority of the citizens do not benefit."[6] As I have argued, these tropes are intertextually powerful beyond the commercial industry precisely because video films remain recognized as expressions of the popular imagination, and rightly so. The force of their distanciated deployment in the cultural spheres of art galleries and film festivals is contingent upon their continued sincere deployment in mainstream video films.

To conclude, I would borrow the notion within urban studies that residents learn a city through dwelling there and that the knowledge generated does not pin down the city—as some object of study or space of developmental intervention—but rather illuminates the rich affordances of the surroundings, the innumerable collaborations possible, and the mutable ways residents can live together. This book does not point to any one thing about the city, one anxiety or one element of the urban imaginary. Ultimately, all corners of the screen media industry continue to release films about Lagos, such that no dominant view of the city, no single way of dwelling with it, prevails over the ongoing discourse itself, and the ambivalence that defers final judgment or pronouncement enables this process of learning the city to unfold indefinitely.

NOTES

INTRODUCTION

1. Babson Ajibade, "From Lagos to Douala: The Video Film and Its Spaces of Seeing," *Postcolonial Text* 3, no. 2 (2007): 1–14; Moradewun Adejunmobi, "African Film's Televisual Turn," *Cinema Journal* 54, no. 2 (2015): 120–25.

2. Why cinema and the city? The amount of scholarship addressing this question in the case of American and European cities and cinemas is substantial. It centers on the notion of a special relationship between the city and cinema. As the argument typically goes, the birth of cinema coincided with that of the modern metropolis. As such, the city influenced the way cinema developed and was experienced, a formative influence that reveals itself in what Mark Shiel refers to as the "telling correlation between the mobility and visual and aural sensations of the city and the mobility and visual and aural sensations of the cinema" (1). In this sense, cinema emerged from urban experience and, in Ackbar Abbas's words, subsequently "incorporated such experience into a new aesthetic principle" (144). For those examining Western city cinema, this correlation has proven to be a generative hermeneutic. It forms the basis for the notion that motion pictures enabled audiences to come to terms with the reorganization of human sense perception in the modern metropolis. Others privilege the spatiality of cinema and cities. From this perspective, film offers representational space for imaginative engagement with cities, or following Anthony Vidler, a "laboratory, so to speak, for the exploration of the built world" (98). In some instances, as with avant-garde cinema's experimentation, film was a tool of critical reflection on urban life, while cinema in the mode of commercial mass media facilitated a collective unconscious bargaining with the psychic and sensory demands of cities. Mark Shiel, "Cinema and the City in History and Theory," in *Cinema and the City: Film and Urban Societies in a Global Context*, ed. Mark Shiel and Tony Fitzmaurice (Malden, MA: Blackwell, 2001); Ackbar Abbas, "Cinema, the City, and the Cinematic," in *Global Cities: Cinema, Architecture, and Urbanism in a Digital Age*, ed. Linda Krause and Patrice Petro (New Brunswick, NJ: Rutgers University Press, 2003); Anthony Vidler, *Warped Space: Art, Architecture, and Anxiety in Modern Culture* (Cambridge: Massachusetts Institution of Technology Press, 2000). See also Anne Friedberg,

Window Shopping: Cinema and the Postmodern (Berkeley: University of California Press, 1993); Ben Singer, *Melodrama and Modernity: Early Sensational Cinema and Its Context* (New York: Columbia University Press, 2001); Janet Ward, *Weimar Surfaces: Urban Visual Culture in 1920s Germany* (Berkeley: University of California Press, 2001);; Miriam Bratu Hansen, *Cinema and Experience: Siegfried Kracauer, Walter Benjamin, and Theodor W. Adorno* (Berkeley: University of California Press, 2011).

3. Charlotte Brunsdon, "The Attractions of the Cinematic City," *Screen* 53, no. 3 (2012): 209; Charlotte Brunsdon, "Towards a History of Empty Spaces," in *The City and the Moving Image: Urban Projections*, ed. Richard Koeck and Les Roberts, (London: Palgrave Macmillan, 2010), 93.

4. Dominique Malaquais, "Douala/Johannesburg/New York: Cityscapes Imagined," in *Cities in Contemporary Africa*, ed. Martin J. Murray and Garth A. Myers (London: Palgrave Macmillan, 2006), 31–32.

5. Jacques Rancière, *Dissensus: On Politics and Aesthetics*, trans. Steven Corcoran (New York: Continuum, 2010), 141–42.

6. AbdouMaliq Simone, *For the City Yet to Come: Changing African Life in Four Cities* (Durham, NC: Duke University Press, 2004), 12.

7. Lindiwe Dovey, "African Film and Video: Pleasure, Politics, Performance," *Journal of African Cultural Studies* 22, no. 1 (2010): 1.

8. Matthew Gandy, "Planning, Anti-planning and the Infrastructure Crisis Facing Metropolitan Lagos," *Urban Studies* 43, no. 2 (2006): 371–96.

9. Babatunde Ahonsi, "Popular Shaping of Metropolitan Forms and Processes in Nigeria: Glimpses and Interpretations from an Informed Lagosian," in *Under Siege: Four African Cities*, ed. Okwui Enwezor (Ostfildern-Ruit: Hatje Cantz, 2003), 129.

10. David Aradeon, "Oshodi: Replanner's Options for a Subcity," *Glendora Review* 2, no. 1 (1997): 51–58.

11. Daniel Agbiboa, "'God's Time Is Best': The Fascination with Unknown Time in Urban Transport in Lagos," in *The Fascination with Unknown Time*, ed. Sibylle Baumbach, Lena Henningsen, and Klaus Oschema (London: Palgrave Macmillan, 2017), 178.

12. Tejumola Olaniyan, *Arrest the Music!: Fela and His Rebel Art and Politics* (Lagos: Kraft Books, 2009 [2004]), 131.

13. Kunle Akinsemoyin and Alan Vaughan-Richards, *Building Lagos* (Jersey, UK: Pengrail, 1977); Lanre Davies, "Gentrification in Lagos, 1929–1990," *Urban History* 45, no. 4 (2018): 712–32.

14. Ayodeji Olukoju, *Infrastructure Development and Urban Facilities in Lagos, 1861–2000* (Ibadan: French Institute for Research in Africa [IFRA], 2003); Matthew Gandy, "Learning from Lagos," *New Left Review* 33 (2005): 36–52.

15. Akin Mabogunje, "An Introspection into the Urban Modernity of Lagos," in *Lagos: A City at Work*, ed. Ololade Bamidele (Lagos: Glendora Books, 2001), 268–351.

16. Eghosa Osaghae, *The Crippled Giant: Nigeria since Independence* (Bloomington: Indiana University Press, 1998); Giles Omezi, "Nigerian Modernity and the City: Lagos 1960–1980," in *The Arts of Citizenship in African Cities: Infrastructures and Spaces of*

Belonging, ed. Mamadou Diouf and Rosalind Fredericks (London: Palgrave Macmillan, 2014), 277–95.

17. Rem Koolhaas et al., *Mutations* (New York: Actar, 2001), 674.

18. A growing body of scholarship on African cities calls for abandonment of modernist urban tropes derived from the Global North and instead invite what Jennifer Robinson and Ananya Roy term "new imaginations of the urban" attuned to the ramifications of Africa's rapid urbanization. As Robinson argues elsewhere, the dominance within urban studies of global-city discourse has introduced an optic of "map-makers" which classifies, charts, and ranks cities by their infrastructure, legal regimes, political relations, and transnational economic activity. Obscured by these accounts are the cultural and artistic activities that inflect the experience of city life, or in Sarah Nuttall and Achille Mbembe's words, "how it is exhibited, displayed, and represented, its colorfulness, its aura, its aesthetics." Jennifer Robinson and Ananya Roy, "Debate on Global Urbanisms and the Nature of Urban Theory," *International Journal of Urban and Regional Research* 40, no. 1 (2016): 181; Jennifer Robinson, *Ordinary Cities: Between Modernity and Development* (New York: Routledge, 2006): 103; Sarah Nuttall and Achille Mbembe, eds., *Johannesburg: The Elusive Metropolis* (Durham, NC: Duke University Press, 2008): 17. See also Ato Quayson, *Oxford Street, Accra: City Life and the Itineraries of Transnationalism* (Durham, NC: Duke University Press, 2014).

19. Sarah Nuttall and Achille Mbembe, "A Blasé Attitude: A Response to Michael Watts," *Public Culture* 17, no. 1 (2005): 193–201. For Nuttall and Mbembe, the primary qualities of "citiness" include "excess, simultaneity, speed, appearance, rapid alternations, relentless change, and indeed ceaseless mutability and discontinuous eventfulness: transience" (2005, 199).

20. Malaquais, "Douala/Johannesburg/New York," 32.

21. Elizabeth Povinelli, *Economies of Abandonment: Social Belonging and Endurance in Late Liberalism* (Durham, NC: Duke University Press, 2011), 102 (original emphasis).

22. Urban theorist AbdouMaliq Simone poses this question repeatedly—nearly verbatim—throughout his writing on cities in the global South.

23. The phrase "open endurance" is meant to capture the "double-edge experience" of everyday urbanism that, according to Simone, "sets in motion a specific way of seeing, of envisioning the environment that will inform how people, things, places, and infrastructure will be used." (Simone, *For the City Yet to Come*, 5).

24. Of course, one might object that cities everywhere exhibit the same accommodation of ongoing social, political, and economic transformations and that urban residents around the world negotiate these shifts. This is true enough! My argument does not propose some shared quality of African urbanism that sets it apart from other cities, but rather argues that in some African cities the intensity with which these features of city life are expressed make them more pronounced, observable, and open to reflection. Others might object that I make too much of too little, that I place focus on relatively unremarkable details of city life and lose sight of more substantial trends or concrete forms that better exemplify Lagos and this historical juncture. But when the basic terms

of ordinary life must be invented anew daily, the individual and collective experience of change as a quality of the everyday becomes both more palpable and pertinent.

25. Filip de Boeck and Marie-Francoise Plissart, *Kinshasa: Tales of the Invisible City* (Ghent-Amsterdam: Ludion, 2005); Sasha Newell, *Modernity Bluff: Crime, Consumption, and Citizenship in Côte d'Ivoire* (Chicago: University of Chicago Press, 2012).

26. Simone, *For the City Yet to Come*, 2015. As Simone points out, "There is an apparent 'promiscuity' of participation in the city. City life, especially at the economic margins, propels an incessant opportunism to make use of all kinds of knowledge, relationships, and positions in multiple social networks in order to access some kind of opportunity to consolidate one's position" (215).

27. Povinelli, *Economies of Abandonment*, 130.

28. Brian Larkin, *Signal and Noise: Media, Infrastructure, and Urban Culture in Nigeria* (Durham, NC: Duke University Press, 2008); AbdouMaliq Simone, *City Life from Jakarta to Dakar: Movements at the Crossroads* (New York: Routledge, 2010).

29. AbdouMaliq Simone, *Improvised Lives: Rhythms of Endurance in an Urban South* (Medford, MA: Polity Press, 2019), 4. Simone's full remarks are worth quoting from at length here. "*No matter how improvised, lives need to be held, supported.* They need a somewhere in which to take place, and places need to be assessed in terms of what they are able to hold. But to hold easily mutates into a form of capture, and if urban life comes to depend upon improvisation, *the holding cannot take the form of a strictly notated score*" (emphasis added, 4).

30. Oka Obono, "A Lagos Thing: Rules and Realities in the Nigerian Megacity," *Georgetown Journal of International Affairs* 8, no. 2 (2007): 31–37.

31. James Ferguson, *Expectations of Modernity: Myths and Meanings of Urban Life on the Zambian Copperbelt* (Berkeley: University of California Press, 1999); Simone, *For the City Yet to Come*, 215.

32. Aradeon, "Oshodi," 60. Aradeon, the prominent Nigerian architect, best expresses this facet of Lagos when he observes that "the anonymity we enjoy in the big city allows us this freedom to violate norms of behavior in a heterogeneous community. In the village or the autochthonous city, several factors compel our conformity to norms: our individual as well as our family's visibility; the sanctity of traditional cultural places and spaces suffused with its religious taboos, as well as sanctions for its violation" (60).

33. As Povinelli notes, "Internal to the concept of endurance (and exhaustion) is the problem of substance: its strength, hardiness, callousness; its continuity through space; its ability to suffer and yet persist. . . . Moreover, endurance encloses itself around the durative—the temporality of continuance, a denotation of continuous action without any reference to its beginning or end" (Povinelli, *Economies of Abandonment*, 32).

34. Lauren Berlant, *Cruel Optimism* (Durham, NC: Duke University Press, 2011).

35. Simone, *Improvised Lives*, 15–16 (emphasis added).

36. Nuttall and Mbembe, "Blasé Attitude," 194.

37. Karin Barber, "Radical Conservatism in Yoruba Popular Plays," *Bayreuth African Studies Series* 7 (1986): 27.

38. Moradewun Adejunmobi, "Streaming Quality, Streaming Cinema," in *A Companion to African Cinema*, edited by Kenneth W. Harrow and Carmela Garritano (Hoboken, NJ: John Wiley and Sons, 2018), 219–43.

39. Larkin, *Signal and Noise*, 178.

40. Manthia Diawara, *African Cinema: Politics and Culture* (Bloomington: Indiana University Press, 1992); Nwachukwu Frank Ukadike, *Black African Cinema* (Berkeley: University of California Press, 1994).

41. Sheila Petty, "Cities, Subjects, Sites: Sub-Saharan Cinema and the Reorganization of Knowledge," *Afterimage* 19 (1991): 10–11, 18.

42. Francoise Pfaff, "African Cities as Cinematic Texts," in *Focus on African Films*, ed. Francoise Pfaff (Bloomington: Indiana University Press, 2004), 89–106.

43 Scholarship on Nollywood first emerged with several important edited volumes that delineated the contours of the industry and films, including Jonathan Haynes and Onookome Okome's "Evolving Popular Media: Nigerian Video Films" in *Nigerian Video Films ed. Jonathan Haynes* (Athens: Ohio University Press, 2000), Pierre Barrot's edited volume *Nollywood: The Video Phenomenon in Nigeria*, trans. Lynn Taylor (Bloomington, IN: Indiana University Press, 2008 [2005]), and a special issue of *Postcolonial Text* (2007) edited by Onookome Okome. Research next branched into debates comparing popular video film and canonical celluloid cinema, as collected in Saul and Austen's *Viewing African Cinema in the Twenty-First Century* (2010) and a special issue of *Journal of African Cultural Studies* (2010), edited by Lindiwe Dovey; investigations of Nollywood's transnational dimensions, as presented in Mathias Krings and Onookome Okome's *Global Nollywood: The Transnational Dimensions of an African Video Film Industry* (2013); and meditations on methodology in a special issue of *Journal of African Cinemas* (2012) edited by Jonathan Haynes. Surveys gave way to honed research topics, as represented by Carmela Garritano's *African Video Movies and Global Desires: A Ghanaian History* (2013), Noah Tsika's *Nollywood Stars: Media and Migration in West Africa and the Diaspora* (2015), Jade Miller's *Nollywood Central* (2016), and Jonathan Haynes's *Nollywood: The Creation of Nigerian Film Genres* (2016). Within this body of literature there is no book-length study of the relationship between Nollywood and Lagos, with the exception of Miller's study of the industry's political economy, which employs a method that omits textual analysis of the films themselves. However, the formation of Nollywood as a subject of scholarship was advanced by several essays that deal directly with the relationship between Lagos and Nollywood, including Akin Adesokan, "Loud in Lagos: Nollywood Videos," *Wasafiri* 19 (2004): 45–49; Jonathan Haynes, "Nollywood in Lagos, Lagos in Nollywood Films," *Africa Today* 54, no. 2 (2007): 130–50; Obododimma Oha 2001"The Visual Rhetoric of the Ambivalent City in Nigerian Video Films," in *Cinema and the City*, ed. Mark Shiel and Tony Fitzmaurice (Oxford: Blackwell, 2001): 195-205; Onookome Okome, "Loud in Lagos," *Glendora: African Quarterly of the Arts* 2, no. 1 (1997): 75–83; Onookome Okome, "Writing the Anxious City: Images of Lagos in Nigerian Home Video Films," *Black Renaissance / Renaissance Noire* 5, no. 2 (2003): 65–75. More recent writing on the subject includes Akin Adesokan, "Anticipating Nollywood:

Lagos circa 1996," *Social Dynamics* 37, no. 1 (2011): 96–110; Jon Haynes, "Neoliberalism, Nollywood and Lagos," in *Global Cinematic Cityscapes: New Landscapes of Film and Media*, ed. Johan Andersson and Lawrence Webb (New York: Wallflower Press, 2015): 59–75; Onookome Okome, "Nollywood, Lagos and the *Good-Time* Woman," *Research in African Literatures* 43, no. 4 (2012): 166–86.

44. Jonathan Haynes, "Nollywood in Lagos, Lagos in Nollywoo Films," 133.

45. Larkin, *Signal and Noise*, 178–94. In Brian Larkin's argument, Nollywood's "aesthetic of outrage" entails the presentation of transgression in a fashion that prompts condemnation and the subsequent consolidation of shared cultural values. Akin Adesokan, by contrast, describes an aesthetic of exhortation grounded in "the strong West African tradition of aesthetic populism that sees politics (or any thematics) as a subcategory of morality" (82). Within this spectatorial paradigm, a film works to exhort the viewer to emulate moral principles for which the figures of the narrative act as conduits. Akin Adesokan, *Postcolonial Artists and Global Aesthetics* (Bloomington: Indiana University Press, 2011).

46. Carmela Garritano, *African Video Movies and Global Desires: A Ghanaian History* (Athens: Ohio University Press, 2013), 11.

47. Doreen Massey, "Making Connections," interview by Karen Lury, *Screen* 40, no. 3 (1999): 233.

48. Larkin, *Signal and Noise*, 251–52. Also see Ash Amin and Nigel Thrift, *Seeing Like a City* (Malden, MA: Polity Press, 2017).

49. Manuel Castells, *The Rise of the Network Society* (Cambridge, MA: Blackwell Publishers, 1996); Ravi Sundaram, *Pirate Modernity: Delhi's Media Urbanism* (New York: Routledge, 2010); Ramon Lobato, *Shadow Economies of Cinema: Mapping Informal Film Distribution* (London: Palgrave on behalf of British Film Institute, 2012); Patrick Jagoda, *Network Aesthetics* (Chicago: University of Chicago Press, 2015); Jade Miller, *Nollywood Central* (New York: Bloomsbury for British Film Institute, 2016).

50. Michael Curtin, "Media Capital: Towards the Study of Spatial Flows," *International Journal of Cultural Studies* 6, no. 2 (2003): 201–28; Michael Curtin, "Comparing Media Capitals: Hong Kong and Mumbai," *Global Media and Communication* 6, no. 3 (2010): 263–70.

51. John McCall, "The Capital Gap: Nollywood and the Limits of Informal Trade," *Journal of African Cinemas* 4, no. 1 (2012): 9–23.

52. See Garritano, *Global Desires*; Miller, *Nollywood Central*; Alessandro Jedlowski, "African Media and the Corporate Takeover: Video Film Circulation in the Age of Neoliberal Transformations," *African Affairs* 116, no. 465 (2016): 671–91; Jonathan Haynes, *Nollywood: The Creation of Nigerian Film Genres* (Chicago: University of Chicago Press, 2016).

53. Nollywood video films are, arguably, the most successful of Africa's evolving forms of popular culture today. These films are produced to meet, stylistically and thematically, generic categories that are repeated until exhausted. The genres that appeal to audiences change with time, but video producers find numerous variations on the occult

thriller, the palace romance, or the campus drama before the genre is deemed unmarketable. The economics of Nollywood have changed significantly, with more investment by formal capital and increasing participation of transnational media houses. However, it is as true today as ever that video films are most successfully circulated through informal distribution to an immensely broad audience. Seeking a sense of the popular in Nigerian videos has meant, for most film critics, reading for anxieties about the place of women in society, desires focused upon ultramodern commodities in real conditions of scarcity, faith in the efficaciousness of religion in everyday life, and adaptations of cosmopolitan styles of modernity, among other experiences of West African life.

54. Manthia Diawara, "Toward a Regional Imaginary in Africa," in *The Cultures of Globalization*, ed. Fredric Jameson and Masao Miyoshi (Durham, NC: Duke University Press, 1998).

55. Haynes, "Nollywood in Lagos," 138.

56. Moradewun Adejunmobi, "Nigerian Video Film as Minor Transnational Practice," *Postcolonial Text* 3, no. 2 (2007): 1–16. Nollywood's style, content, and circulation, as Adejunmobi asserts, "owe a lot to the culture of the West African market place, to a historic practice of buying, selling, and investing, both locally and regionally" (7). Quayson discusses the distinction between the mall and the marketplace as indicative of the divergent cultural logics that operate in each space (Quayson, *Oxford Street*, 28).

57. Miller, *Nollywood Central*, 52.

58. AbdouMaliq Simone, "People as Infrastructure," in *Johannesburg: The Elusive Metropolis*, ed. Sarah Nuttall and Achille Mbembe (Durham, NC: Duke University Press, 2008), 69.

59. Alexander Bud, "The End of Nollywood's Guilded Age? Marketers, the State and the Struggle for Distribution," *Critical African Studies* 6, no. 1 (2014): 91–121.

60. Moradewun Adejunmobi, "Nollywood, Globalization, and Regional Media Corporations in Africa," *Popular Communication* 9, no. 2 (2011): 67–78; Haynes, "Keeping Up: The Corporatization of Nollywood's Economy and Paradigms for Studying African Screen Media," *Africa Today* 64, no. 4 (2018): 2–29.

61. Jedlowski, "Corporate Takeover," 687.

62. Professional galleries such as Rele, Omenka, or Art Twenty One cater to local collectors, while there is also a growing number of international art events based in Lagos, including Art-X, Lagos Photo, and the fledgling Lagos Biennial. Beyond the proliferation of the art ecosystem, also notable is the aesthetic turn toward conceptual, abstract, and performance art. See Jess Castellote and Tobenna Okwuosa, "Lagos Art World: The Emergence of an Artistic Hub on the Global Art Periphery," *African Studies Review* 62, no. 1 (2019): 1–27.

63. Povinelli, *Economies of Abandonment*, 5.

64. Simone asserts that "enclosure reflects the belief in a delirious detachment, where those who exercise rights over territory can withdraw from having to negotiate with the multitude of others who exercise their own particular claims to livelihood and imagination across an urban region." Simone goes on to remark that "increasing numbers of

residents have bought into the possibilities of enclosure as a normative practice, as a modality of living indicative to their worth and eligibility to be part of the city" (Simone, *Improvised Lives*, 127).

65. Stefano Harney, "Creative Industries Debate," *Cultural Studies* 24, no. 3 (2010): 432.

66. Stefano Harney and Fred Moten, *The Undercommons: Fugitive Planning and Black Study* (New York: Minor Compositions, 2013), 90.

67. Maurizio Lazzarato, "Immaterial Labor," in *Radical Thought in Italy: A Potential Politics*, ed. Paolo Virno and Michael Hardt (Minneapolis: University of Minnesota Press, 1996), 133.

68. Matthew Hockenberry, Nicole Starosielski, and Susan Zieger, *Assembly Codes: The Logistics of Media* (Durham, NC: Duke University Press, 2021), 13.

69. Stefano Harney's full quote reads: "To manage in the creative industries is to enter into this contemporary statecraft, where the stakes are far greater than whether an artist can be supervised. The social factory comes to subsume civil society and transform the struggles over neo-liberal governmentality outlined in Foucault's late lectures. The creative industries raise an even more sinister alarm. Civil society in all its morals, tastes, attention and opinions becomes the site not only of control but of direct expropriation, all the more sinister because it does not collapse into categories of the economy but expropriates from the distance of governance" (Harney, "Creative Industries Debate," 443).

CHAPTER 1

1. See also, Onookome Okome and Jonathan Haynes, *Cinema and Social Change in West Africa* (Jos: Nigerian Film Corporation, 1995); Frank Nwachukwu Ukadike, *Black African Cinema* (Berkeley: University of California Press, 1994); Hyginus Ekwuazi, *Film in Nigeria* (Ibadan: Moonlight Publishers for the Nigerian Film Corporation, 1987); Francoise Balogun, *Cinema in Nigeria* (Enugu: Delta Publications, 1987).

2. Wale Oyedele, "Aspects of the Yoruba Popular Films," *Journal of Cultural Studies* 2, no. 1 (2000): 340–49. Wale Oyedele categorizes the latter genre as *ere igbalode*, a phrase that connotes contemporary subject matter, especially that which is regarded as modern and fashionable, as opposed to the theater's repertoire of mythological storytelling.

3. Producer Francis Oladele, with his production company Calpenny Films, was a pioneer of indigenous cinema, having produced *Kongi's Harvest* alongside African American director Ossie Davies and with cooperation from Wole Soyinka, whose stage play provided the film's source text. The following year, Oladele's Calpenny Films released the nation's second feature film, *Bullfrog in the Sun* (1971), an adaptation of Chinua Achebe's *Things Fall Apart* and *No Longer at Ease*. Other filmmakers like Sanya Dosunmu and Jab Adu entered the field, but the most productive companies were Ola Balogun's Afrocult Foundation and Eddie Ugbomah's Edifosa Film Enterprises. Ugbomah debuted *The Rise and Fall of Dr. Oyenusi* in 1977 and continued to release a film nearly every year until

1984. Balogun has numerous original productions to his credit, including as the director of several films produced by Yoruba traveling theater companies.

4. Ekwuazi, *Film in Nigeria*, 15–16.

5. Jonathan Haynes, "Nigerian Cinema: Structural Adjustments," *Research in African Literatures* 26, no. 3 (1995): 97–119.

6. As Toyin Falola and Matthew Heaton note, the Nigerian government largely leased the rights to mineral extraction to foreign petroleum companies—principally Royal Dutch Shell—which means the oil boom was measured in terms of petroleum licensing receipts. In 1970 such revenues totaled a modest 166 million naira. By 1974, the Nigerian state received 3.7 billion naira in revenue from the petroleum sector, which represented 82 percent of all government revenues for that year. Falola and Heaton, *A History of Nigeria* (Cambridge: Cambridge University Press, 2008), 182.

7. Falola and Heaton, *History of Nigeria*, 183.

8. As Matthew Gandy remarks, "The new ruling class and their generally Western-educated architects, engineers and planners favoured prestige projects that could attest to their vision of African modernity; Lagos soon boasted one of the continent's first skyscrapers." Matthew Gandy, "Learning from Lagos," *New Left Review* 33 (2005): 44. See also Matthew Gandy, "Planning, Anti-planning and the Infrastructure Crisis Facing Metropolitan Lagos," *Urban Studies* 43, no. 2 (2006): 371–96.

9. Gilles Omezi, "Nigerian Modernity and the City: Lagos 1960–1980," in *The Arts of Citizenship in African Cities: Infrastructures and Spaces of Belonging*, ed. Mamadou Diouf and Rosalind Fredericks (London: Palgrave Macmillan, 2014), 277–95. For a description of the All Africa Games capital projects, see especially 284–89.

10. As Omezi explains, "The city was beginning to be layered with a skein of cultural production infrastructure as part of the national modernization project" and Festac '77 was central in this process. Omezi, "Nigerian Modernity," 289.

11. For some postcolonial nations, modernist urban planning represented a benchmark of contemporaneity with the West. Newly independent nations turned to "modernist architecture as a universal utopian form" to be adopted as architectural and infrastructural "literalizations" of their participation in global urban modernity (Ananya Roy and Aihwa Ong, eds., *Worlding Cities: Asian Experiments and the Art of Being Global* [Malden, MA: Blackwell, 2011], 8). However, in spite of its modernist overlay, Lagos in the 1970s lacked much of the infrastructure thought essential to a city of its size, including reliable provision of electricity, potable water, and waste removal, to say nothing of a sewer system. The city's population, recently swelled by migrants fleeing civil war in the East, became concentrated in sprawling, underserviced working-class neighborhoods (Gandy "Planning, Anti-planning and the Infrastructure Crisis," 381). Such spaces existed under the looming threat of government slum clearance operations. In fact, several working-class neighborhoods were razed in preparation for the expressways and prestige projects held up by the state as benchmarks of urban modernization.

12. Sarah Nuttall and Achille Mbembe, eds., *Johannesburg: The Elusive Metropolis* (Durham, NC: Duke University Press, 2008), 22.

13. Biodun Jeyifo, *The Yoruba Popular Travelling Theatre of Nigeria* (Lagos: Federal Ministry of Social Development, Youth, Sports and Culture, 1984), 70.

14. As Jeyifo writes, "For virtually all the troupes of the Travelling Theatre movement, economic survival and artistic impact demand year-round road tours along these itineraries and circuits. The special condition of Nigerian roads (especially the secondary, so-called 'Trunk B' roads) makes the professional lives of members of the troupes a high-risk, exacting experience." Jeyifo, *Popular Travelling Theatre*, 73.

15. Patricia Yaeger, "Introduction: Dreaming of Infrastructure," *PMLA* 122, no. 1 (2007): 17.

16. Ayodeji Olukoju, *Infrastructure Development and Urban Facilities in Lagos, 1861–2000* (Ibadan: French Institute for Research in Africa [IFRA], 2003).

17. Omezi, "Nigerian Modernity," 285.

18. Omezi, "Nigerian Modernity," 285.

19. Olukoju, *Urban Facilities in Lagos*.

20. Ola Balogun's *Money Power* (1982), a feature about a young reporter's campaign against corruption in the city, opens with the journalist (played by Shina Peters) interviewing ferry passengers commuting across the lagoon about the city's transportation crisis. The scenario justifies the camera's sweeping panoramic of the skyscrapers along the Lagos waterfront. The film's concluding sequence revisits the lagoon, as the victorious reporter and his paramour are paraded down to the waterfront and lower into a dugout canoe, which glides out into the lagoon while Shina Peters sings in an upbeat tune about the virtues of being charitable. The final shot of the film frames the lovers in a standing embrace with the tremendous swooping concrete flyovers of Third Mainland Bridge not far away in background. By contrast, Eddie Ugbomah's *Death of a Black President* follows military men to secretive meetings in the ultramodern lounges and outside below the grand edifice of the National Theater. The film's portrayal of Murtala Muhammad's assassination by these men was shot on location in the Lagos street where, in fact, the head of state was ambushed and gunned down, the precise point in the road holding a special significance in the mind of the filmmaker (personal communication, May 29, 2013).

21. Brian Larkin, "The Politics and Poetics of Infrastructure," *Annual Review of Anthropology* 42 (2013): 335–36.

22. Birgit Meyer, *Sensational Movies: Video, Vision, and Christianity in Ghana* (Berkeley: University of California Press, 2015).

23. Larkin, "Politics and Poetics," 333.

24. Larkin, "Politics and Poetics," 337.

25. Lindsey Green-Simms, *Postcolonial Automobility: Car Culture in West Africa* (Minneapolis: University of Minnesota Press, 2017).

26. For Barber, those fundamental social shifts included "the long-term and far-reaching transformations unleashed by cash-crop farming, urbanization, wage labor, the breakup of the old lineage-based residential compounds, Western education, and conversion to world religions." Barber, *Generation of Plays*, 5.

27. Barber, *Generation of Plays*, 4.
28. Barber, *Generation of Plays*, 4, 46.
29. Barber, *Generation of Plays*, 4.
30. Yaeger, "Dreaming of Infrastructure," 17.
31. Larkin, "Politics and Poetics."
32. Larkin, "Politics and Poetics," 336–37.
33. Larkin, "Politics and Poetics," 337.
34. A. U. Iwara and E. Mveng, eds., *Colloquium Proceedings on Black Civilization and Education, Lagos, 17th–31st January, 1977* (Lagos: Federal Military Government of Nigeria, 1977). In his account of Festac '77 as a discursive event, Andrew Apter argues that the state emphasized the passage into a new African capitalism and hoped the cultural spectacle would neutralize both the civil war's residual ethnic resentments and the class contradictions that arose from rapid transformations under an oil boom economy. Andrew Apter, "The Pan-African Nation: Oil-Money and the Spectacle of Culture in Nigeria," *Public Culture* 8 (1996): 441–66.
35. Marylin Nance, "Marylin Nance: Remembering Festac," interview by Fanny Robels, *Nka: Journal of Contemporary African Art* 42/43 (2018): 164–68.
36. Omezi, "Nigerian Modernity," 292.
37. Apter, "Pan-African Nation," 444.
38. Apter notes that Festac '77 organizers acknowledged this correspondence, first jokingly referring to the theater as General Gowon's "cap," although the metaphor was also inherited by Gowon's successor, General Obasanjo, the grand patron of Festac. Apter, "Pan-African Nation," 445.
39. Uche Enem. "National Theatre Profile," *Nigeria Magazine* 128/129 (1979): 35–53. During Festac '77, the theater hosted an array of Black arts and culture, including dance, sculpture, folk arts, photography, and film all under one roof.
40. Chuma Adichie, "Review of Filmshows in the National Theatre for 1982," *Cultural News Bulletin: A Quarterly of the Federal Department of Culture* 3, no. 1 (January–March 1983): 11, 15.
41. In a public announcement, independent filmmaker and spokesman for the Nigerian Film Producers Association Sanya Dosunmu petitioned that Nigeria not be represented by the state-sponsored film production unit alone but by independent producers, as well. As one *Daily Times* article states, "He said his association believed that healthy competition should be encouraged to get good film production instead of the unrealistic dependence of Nigerian authorities on civil servants or Ministry of Information productions only for the festival" (*Daily Times* July 2, 1975).
42. Notable titles include Sembene Ousmane's *Xala* (1974), Daniel Kamwa's *Pousse-Pousse* (1976), and Sam Greenlee's *The Spook Who Sat Behind the Door* (Ivan Dixon, 1973), one in a disproportionately large number of American films screened. By contrast, on the opening night of the festival, Nigeria had but two documentary films to offer audiences: *2000 Years of Nigerian Arts* (dir. unknown, n.d.) and *T.B. Can Be Cured* (dir. unknown, n.d.). Fortunately, the following evening featured *Shehu Umar* (Adamu

Halilu, 1976), the only fiction film ever produced by the state's production company, the Federal Film Unit (FFU), and Nigeria's official submission to the festival's film exhibition (Afolabi Adesanya, *Nigerian Film/TV Index*, [Lagos: A-Productions Nigeria, 1991], 12). No fiction films by independent Nigerian filmmakers appear on Festac's monthlong schedule, although the FFU's productions were screened repeatedly.

43. Some of these built spaces adopted modernist planning principles, such as the gridded streets of Festac Town, while others directly reproduced the design plans of specific European buildings, such as the international terminal of Murtala Muhammad Airport, modeled after Amsterdam's Schiphol Airport.

44. Larkin, "Politics and Poetics," 334.

45. Adichie, "Review of Filmshows," 15.

46. Ekwuazi, *Film in Nigeria*, 122.

47. This perception was compounded by the various bureaucratic and financial constraints placed on local filmmakers who sought to exhibit at the National Arts Theatre. Filmmakers paid handsomely to premiere there, splitting as much as 35 percent of the gate with the management and paying another 30 percent in taxes (Haynes "Nigerian Cinema: Structural Adjustments," 175–76, n. 4). Furthermore, Francoise Balogun explains that the "National Theatre has got the best and the largest halls, the gate intake is usually higher than in any other hall. Unfortunately, it is very difficult to obtain access to the Theatre and the use of the National Theatre is thus a privilege that can only be obtained after long negotiations rather than a right" (Balogun, *Cinema in Nigeria*, 42).

48. In fact, Hyginus Ekwuazi discovered no Nigerian film anywhere within the stock of the NFDC and two smaller independent distributors (Ekwuazi, *Film in Nigeria*, 124). Consequently, the likes of Balogun, Ugbomah, Ogunde, and Afolayan had to rent the facilities at the National Arts Theatre and privately screen their films. Ugbomah claims he had coerced Ashiwaju to screen his films without paying the rental fee, and Balogun said that with his films the share of the ticket sales going to the theater precluded their need to charge a rental fee. Interestingly, the NFC absorbed the NFDC but never managed to establish nationwide distribution of Nigerian films. Still, Adesanya points out, the NFDC and the NFC did provide "soft loans" in amounts no larger than 100,000 naira to some filmmakers. Afolabi Adesanya, *Reel Views: A Collection of Essays and Reviews on the Nigerian and African Film Industry* (Jos: Nigerian Film Corporation, 2012), 58–59, 79.

49. Jahman Anikulapo, "The Death Metaphor," in *African Cities Reader III*, ed. Edgar Pieterse (Cape Town: Chimurenga Magazine and African Cities Centre, 2015).

50. Anikulapo, "Death Metaphor."

51. Anikulapo, "Death Metaphor."

52. Tunde Lakoju, "Popular (Traveling) Theatre in Nigeria: The Example of Moses Olaiya Adejumo (alias Baba Sala)," *Nigeria Magazine* 149 (1984): 35–46. According to Lakoju, Olaiya's entertainment career began when he founded the musical group the "Rhythm Dandies" in 1960. He increasingly turned to theater, incorporating performances in which band members served as actors, including soon-to-be jùjú celebrity

King Sunny Ade, which might account for his cameo performance in *Orun Mooru* as band leader at Baba Sala's feast.

53. Lakoju, "Example of Moses Olaiyan Adejumo," 45.
54. Lakoju, "Example of Moses Olaiyan Adejumo," 37.
55. Barber, "Petro-Naira," 97.
56. Lakoju, "Example of Moses Olaiyan Adejumo," 42.
57. Jean Comaroff and John L. Comaroff, eds., *Modernity and Its Malcontents: Ritual and Power in Postcolonial Africa* (Chicago: University of Chicago Press, 1993), xviii.
58. Comaroff and Comaroff, *Modernity and Its Malcontents*, xx.
59. Comaroff and Comaroff, *Modernity and Its Malcontents*, xxvi.
60. Barber, "Petro-Naira," 93.
61. Jean Comaroff and John L. Comaroff, "Millennial Capitalism: First Thoughts on a Second Coming." *Public Culture* 12, no. 2 (2000): 291–343.
62. Barber, "Petro-Naira," 93.
63. Haynes, "Structural Adjustments," 108.
64. Haynes, "Structural Adjustments," 108.
65. Carmela Garritano, *African Video Movies and Global Desires: A Ghanaian History* (Athens: Ohio University Press, 2013).
66. Niyi Osundare, "The King of Laughter," *West Africa Magazine*, July 1982, 1821.
67. Osundare, "King of Laughter," 1821.

CHAPTER 2

1. Ato Quayson, *Oxford Street, Accra: City Life and the Itineraries of Transnationalism* (Durham, NC: Duke University Press, 2014).
2. Wole Ogundele, "From Folk Opera to Soap Opera: Improvisations and Transformations in Yoruba Popular Theater," in *Nigerian Video Films*, ed. Jonathan Haynes (Athens: Ohio University Press, 2000), 110.
3. Jonathan Haynes, "Nollywood in Lagos, Lagos in Nollywood Films," *Africa Today* 54, no. 2 (2007): 142.
4. The representation of city space in Nollywood appears puzzling only from a certain perspective, namely, one that anticipates a cinematic mode of representation in keeping with orthodox—often American and European modernist—traditions and canons of city cinema. For a summary of features of modernist "city discourse," see Charlotte Brunsdon, "The Attractions of the Cinematic City," *Screen* 53, no. 5 (2012): 209–27.
5. Charlotte Brunsdon, *Television Cities: London, Paris, Baltimore* (Durham, NC: Duke University Press, 2018), 1.
6. Esi Dogbe, "Elusive Modernity: Portraits of the City in Popular Ghanaian Video," in *Leisure in Urban Africa*, ed. Paul Tiyambe Zeleza and Cassandra Rachel Veney (Trenton, NJ: Africa World Press, 2003), 233.
7. Jonathan Haynes, *Nollywood: The Creation of Nigerian Film Genres* (Chicago: Chicago University Press, 2016), 9.

8. Akin Adesokan, "Practicing 'Democracy' in Nigerian Films," *African Affairs* 108, no. 433 (2009): 599–619.

9. Segun Olusola, "Film-TV and the Arts: The African Experience," in *Mass Communication in Nigeria: A Book of Reading*, ed. Onuora E. Nwuneli (Enugu: Fourth Dimension Publishers, 1985), 137–76.

10. Ogundele, "Folk Opera to Soap Opera."

11. See also Karin Barber, *Generation of Plays: Yorùbá Popular Life in Theater* (Bloomington: Indiana University Press, 2003), 95.

12. Matthew H. Brown, "The Enchanted History of Nigerian State Television," in *State and Culture in Postcolonial Africa*, ed. Tejumola Olaniyan (Bloomington: Indiana University Press, 2016), 102.

13. Oluyinka Esan, *Nigerian Television: Fifty Years of Television in Africa* (Princeton: AMV Publishing, 2009), 41–42.

14. Ogundele, "Folk Opera to Soap Opera," 94.

15. Esan, *Nigerian Television*, 93.

16. Esan, *Nigerian Television*, 58, 70.

17. F. O. Ugboajah, quoted in Esan, *Nigerian Television*, 100.

18. Esan, *Nigerian Television*, 89.

19. Esan, *Nigerian Television*, 90.

20. Esan, *Nigerian Television*, 74.

21. Haynes, *Nigerian Film Genres*, and O. O. Oreh, "*Masquerade* and Other Plays on Nigerian Television," in *Mass Communication, Culture, and Society in West Africa*, ed. F. O. Ugboajah (New York: Hans Zell, 1985), 108–12.

22. Haynes, *Nigerian Film Genres*, 10.

23. The program sells at the video market in Idumota, along with other NTA programs. The vendor I purchased it from insisted the action takes place in Ibadan, noting that the characters speak Yoruba. At another shop where I tested the disc quality, the vendor recalled that the program was set in the East, probably Onitsha, in his view.

24. As Nkem Owoh explained to me in conversation: "We normally recorded at the state studio but we transmitted on NTA. It was Anambra television. It was recorded on state but went out on national television. Their studio was fantastic, so we shoot in their studio, pay them, and then it was transmitted on Channel 8" (personal communication, July 24, 2018).

25. Brunsdon, *Television Cities*, 26.

26. Brunsdon, *Television Cities*, 35.

27. Brunsdon, *Television Cities*, 1.

28. James Holston and Arjun Appadurai, "Cities and Citizenship," *Public Culture* 8 (1996): 187–204.

29. As quoted in James Brooke, "Enugu Journal: Thirty Million Nigerians Are Laughing at Themselves," *New York Times*, July 24, 1987.

30. Despite the program's best efforts to disabuse its viewers of such a Pollyannaish outlook, the vision of Lagos as a monied city survived into early and mainstream video

films and today definitively marks New Nollywood's Lagos imaginary, even as other cities, particularly Abuja, have successfully claimed their share of urban exuberance, conspicuous consumption, and upward mobility.

31. Karen Lury and Doreen Massey, "Making Connections," *Screen* 40, no. 3 (1999): 233.

32. Tejumola Olaniyan recounts how Sani Abacha's regime sought to "imagineer" a portrait of Lagos undisrupted by any chaos and unblemished by any squalor. As Olaniyan writes, "[Abacha's] propaganda machine produced a video, *Nigeria: World Citizen*, to burnish his image and the image of Nigeria he had dragged into the mud. The clips of Lagos that appeared in it were all high-angle shots of towering skyscrapers." Tejumola Olaniyan, *Arrest the Music!: Fela and His Rebel Art and Politics* (Bloomington: Indiana University Press, 2004), 146–47.

33. Brunsdon, *Television Cities*, 6.

34. Brunsdon, *Television Cities*, 40.

35. Henri Lefebvre, *The Production of Space*, trans. Donald Nicholson-Smith (Cambridge, MA: Blackwell, 1991 [1974]), 42.

36. Dogbe, "Elusive Modernity," 235, 230.

37. Moradewun Adejunmobi, "African Film's Televisual Turn," *Cinema Journal* 54, no. 2 (2015): 122–23.

38. Adejunmobi, "African Film's Televisual Turn," 120–22.

39. Rufus T. Akinleye, "Contesting for Space in an Urban Centre: The Omo Onile Syndrome in Lagos," in *African Cities: Competing Claims on Urban Space*, ed. Francesca Locatelli and Paul Nugent (Leiden: Brill, 2009), 109–34.

40. Laurent Fourchard, "Bureaucrats and Indigenes: Producing and Bypassing Certificates of Origin in Nigeria," *Africa* 85, no. 1 (2015): 37–58.

41. "Having an exclusively indigene staff in local government and state administrations is widely regarded as normal by officials and politicians," with the telling exception of Lagos. "In Lagos State, jobs are not reserved for Lagos indigenes, as has been shown by repeated protests by Lagos State indigene associations" (Fourchard, "Bureaucrats and Indigenes," 41–42).

42. As Stephanie Newell notes, regarding animosity toward non-Lagosian Yoruba expressed by Lagos indigenes during one interview conducted by John Uwa of the University of Lagos: "Clearly, these men's experiences of the pressures for survival in the overcrowded city overrode any collective identity as Yoruba-speaking Nigerians, causing those for whom Lagos was their birthplace to insist on ancient forms of legitimacy based on an antagonistic notion of civic purity." Stephanie Newell, *Histories of Dirt: Media and Urban Life in Colonial and Postcolonial Lagos* (Durham, NC: Duke University Press, 2019), 98.

43. Brooke, "Thirty Million Nigerians."

44. As Stephanie Newell notes, in regards to interviews with Lagos residents conducted by Olutoyosi Tokun, John Uwa, Jane Nebe, and Patrick Oloko of the University of Lagos: "The putative 'other'—whether the microphone, the interviewer, or the prox-

imate urban stranger—acts as a forceful mediating presence in contexts where urban civility involves the careful awareness of the presence of neighbors and their protection from overhearing offensive or inflammatory speech." Newell, *Histories of Dirt*, 95.

45. Newell, *Histories of Dirt*, 114.
46. Newell, *Histories of Dirt*, 112.
47. Newell, *Histories of Dirt*, 112.
48. Jane Feuer, "Narrative Form in American Network Television," in *High Theory, Low Culture: Analysing Popular Television and Film*, ed. Colin McCabe (Manchester: Manchester University Press, 1986), 614.
49. Feuer, "Narrative Form in American Network Television," 615.
50. Newell, *Histories of Dirt*, 97.
51. Akinyele, "Contesting for Space," 112.
52. Newell, *Histories of Dirt*, 98.
53. Haynes, *Nigerian Film Genres*, 223.
54. Akinleye, "Contesting for Space," 109.
55. Haynes, *Nigerian Film Genres*, 223.
56. Obododimma Oha, "The Visual Rhetoric of the Ambivalent City in Nigerian Video Films," in *Cinema and the City*, ed. Mark Shiel and Tony Fitzmaurice (Oxford: Blackwell, 2001), 199.
57. Haynes, *Nigerian Film Genres*, 220–22.
58. Lefebvre, *Production of Space*.
59. Filip de Boeck, "Kinshasa and Its (Im)material Infrastructure," in *Cities of the Global South Reader*, ed. Faranak Miraftab and Neema Kudva (New York: Routledge, 2015 [2005]), 191.

CHAPTER 3

1. Eghosa Osaghae, *The Crippled Giant: Nigeria since Independence* (Bloomington: Indiana University Press, 1998), 207. Nigeria's economic role as a petroleum producer left the country particularly susceptible to rapid fluctuations of one commodity's value. After a plummet in oil prices in 1981, Nigerian oil production dropped by two-thirds, triggering dramatic cuts in revenue. In 1986, the government of Ibrahim Babangida entered into a comprehensive structural adjustment program (SAP), which permitted the country to reschedule its loans only after adopting austerity measures.
2. Osaghae, *Crippled Giant*, 205.
3. Osaghae, *Crippled Giant*, 205.
4. Various student and labor unions and civil liberty organizations, unwilling to wait patiently, mobilized protests and strikes to voice their opposition to the state's bid to delay transition. In response, according to Ihonvbere, the postcolonial state "continued to make the immediate future as uncertain as possible by introducing new rules, reinterpreting existing legislation, and manipulating the transition institutions" (198).

Julius Ihonvbere, "Are Things Falling Apart? The Military Crisis of Democratisation in Nigeria," *Journal of Modern African Studies* 34, no. 2 (1996): 193–225.

5. When elections finally came to pass in June 1993, the Interim National Government set up to oversee the transition annulled the voting results, despite public outcry, and ultimately provided Sani Abacha and his military accomplices with reason to seize power. As Ruth Marshall writes, "Throughout the 1990s the fundamental dynamics underlying this exercise of power did not change, but only grew increasingly predatory and violent. The 'transition without end' of the Babangida regime, continued through the 'Big Scam' of the annulled 1993 elections and the seizure of power by the military dictator Sani Abacha, reinforced the sense in which Nigerian government had become a permanent state of exception." Ruth Marshall, *Political Spiritualities: The Pentecostal Revolution in Nigeria* (Chicago: University of Chicago Press, 2009), 102.

6. Julius Ihonvbere and Timothy Shaw, *Illusions of Power: Nigeria in Transition* (Trenton, NJ: Africa World Press, 1998), 147. The state often sought to co-opt oppositional figures and organizations by offering them posts or responsibilities within the regime. This effectively extended the network of those implicated in corruption and "provided new and unequalled opportunities for people with little or no education, expertise or experience to climb the social and political ladder and become prominent and affluent overnight." Ihonvbere and Shaw, *Illusions of Power*, 153.

7. Ruth Marshall argues that the term "corruption" itself became "overloaded with an excess of symbolic force, implying not a deviation from a certain model, but rather the death and decomposition of social worlds in their absences of a promise of renewal." Marshall, *Political Spiritualities*, 106.

8. Laurent Berlant, *Cruel Optimism* (Durham, NC: Duke University Press, 2011), 2. Following Berlant, I understand "the good life" as a simultaneously normative and deictic attainment, meaning its general contours are shaped by social convention, but individual realization of the good life entails particularity, attachment to *this or that* scenario of life.

9. Simone, *For the City Yet to Come*, 4.

10. Jonathan Haynes, "Nollywood in Lagos, Lagos in Nollywood Films," *Africa Today* 54, no. 2 (2007): 130–50.

11. Moradewun Adejunmobi, "Video Film Technology and Serial Narratives in West Africa," in *Africa through the Eye of the Video Camera*, edited by Foluke Ogunleye (Matsapha, Swaziland: Academic Publishers, 2003), 51–68; Alessandro Jedlowski, "Small Screen Cinema: Informality and Remediation in Nollywood," *Television and New Media* 13, no. 5 (2012): 431–46; Onoookome Okome, "Nollywood, Lagos and the *Good-Time* Woman," *Research in African Literatures* 43, no. 4 (2012): 166–86; Jonathan Haynes, *Nollywood: The Creation of Nigerian Film Genres* (Chicago: University of Chicago Press, 2016).

12. Christine Geraghty, *Women and Soap Opera: A Study of Prime Time Soaps* (Cambridge, UK: Polity Press, 1991), 11, 15.

13. Christine Gledhill, "Speculations on the Relationship between Soap Opera and Melodrama," *Quarterly Review of Film and Video* 14, no. 1–2 (1992): 115.

14. Moradewun Adejunmobi, "African Film's Televisual Turn," *Cinema Journal* 54, no. 2 (2015): 122–23.

15. Akin Adesokan, *Postcolonial Artists and Global Aesthetics* (Bloomington: Indiana University Press, 2011); Brian Larkin, *Signal and Noise: Media, Infrastructure, and Urban Culture in Nigeria* (Durham, NC: Duke University Press, 2008), 178–94.

16. Haynes and Okome, "Evolving Popular Media: Nigerian Video Films," in *Nigerian Video Films*, ed. Jonathan Haynes (Athens: Ohio University Press, 2000), 59.

17. Lani Akande, "Nollywood Cinema's Character of Recurrence," *Journal of African Cultural Studies* 33, no. 4 (2021): 458.

18. Haynes, *Nollywood*, 25.

19. Okome, "Nollywood, Lagos and the *Good-Time* Woman," 182, 183.

20. Connor Ryan, "Nollywood and the Limits of Informality," Interview with Tunde Kelani, Bond Emeruwa, and Emem Isong, *Black Camera: An International Film Journal* 5, no. 2 (2014): 168–85; Haynes, *Nollywood*.

21. Ash Amin and Nigel Thrift, *Seeing Like a City* (Malden, MA: Polity, 2017), 16.

22. Amin and Thrift, *Seeing Like a City* 17, 10.

23. Doreen Massey, *For Space* (London: Sage, 2005), 149–62.

24. In particular, see Sarah Nuttall and Achille Mbembe, "A Blasé Attitude: A Response to Michael Watts," *Public Culture* 17, no. 1 (2005): 193–202; Ananya Roy, "The 21st-Century Metropolis: New Geographies of Theory," *Regional Studies* 43, no. 6 (2009); Ignacio Farías and Thomas Bender, *Urban Assemblages: How Actor-Network Theory Changes Urban Studies* (London: Routledge, 2009); Colin McFarlane, *Learning the City: Knowledge and Translocal Assemblage* (Malden, MA: Wiley-Blackwell, 2011); Amin and Thrift, *Seeing Like a City*.

25. Given the social friction of heterogenous cities, Ofeimun argues for "the necessity to find a common morality that can hold people together." Naturally enough, the poet envisions Lagos as a poem to illustrate his point and asserts that, like a poem that sutures countless elements into "the concentrated time of a metaphor," what is distinctive about Lagos—"the citiness of a city," he says—"lies in the absorption of its many parts" into a shared form that, like a poet's metaphor, "necessarily changes the individuality of images that it hitches together." Odia Ofeimun, "Imagination and the City," *Glendora Review: African Quarterly on the Arts* 3, no. 2 (1998): 12.

26. Oka Obono, "A Lagos Thing: Rules and Realities in the Nigerian Megacity," *Georgetown Journal of International Affairs* 8, no. 2 (2007): 34.

27. Laurent Fourchard, "Bureaucrats and Indigenes: Producing and Bypassing Certificates of Origin in Nigeria," *Africa* 85, no. 1 (2015): 53.

28. Simone, *For the City Yet to Come*, 137.

29. AbdouMaliq Simone, *City Life from Jakarta to Dakar: Movements at the Crossroads* (New York: Routledge, 2010), 21.

30. Sasha Newell, *Modernity Bluff: Crime, Consumption, and Citizenship in Côte d'Ivoire* (Chicago: University of Chicago Press, 2012), 67.

31. Newell, *Modernity Bluff*, 68.

32. Filip de Boeck, "'Divining' the City: Rhythm, Amalgamation and Knotting as Forms of 'Urbanity,'" *Social Dynamics: A Journal of African Studies* 41, no. 1 (2015): 56.

33. De Boeck, "'Divining' the City," 53.

34. Babatunde Ahonsi, "Popular Shaping of Metropolitan Forms and Processes in Nigeria: Glimpses and Interpretations from an Informed Lagosian," in *Under Siege: Four African Cities*, ed. Okwui Enwezor (Ostfildern-Ruit: Hatje Cantz, 2003), 150. Ahonsi discusses the history of Lagos as shaped by two forces. "First are the specific historical, geographical, and political forces that have driven the rapid emergence of Lagos as one of Africa's largest cities. Second is the role of the mass of people that have interacted with and responded to these sweeping conditions in modifying and mediating their consequences for the livability, productivity, serviceability, and manageability of Lagos" (129).

35. AbdouMaliq Simone, "People as Infrastructure," in *Johannesburg: The Elusive Metropolis*, ed. Sarah Nuttall and Achille Mbembe (Durham, NC: Duke University Press, 2008), 69.

36. Jonathan Haynes, *Nollywood: The Creation of Nigerian Film Genres* (Chicago: University of Chicago Press, 2016); Jade Miller, *Nollywood Central, Nollywood Central* (New York: Bloomsbury for British Film Institute, 2016).

37. Caroline Levine, *Forms: Whole, Rhythm, Hierarchy, Network* (Princeton: Princeton University Press, 2015), 113.

38. Here, *intra*-action connotes "ontological inseparability" and stands in contrast to interaction, which relies on a metaphysics of bounded, propertied, individual entities. Interaction implies separate individual elements. Barad's agential realism does not allow that individual elements exist prior to intra-action. Karen Barad, *Meeting the Universe Halfway: Quantum Physics and the Entanglement of Matter and Meaning* (Durham, NC: Duke University Press, 2007), 184.

39. Larkin, *Signal and Noise*.

40. In particular, see David Bordwell, *Poetics of Cinema* (New York: Routledge, 2007), 189–245; Patrick Jagoda, *Network Aesthetics* (Chicago: University of Chicago Press, 2016), 8.

41. Amin and Thrift, *Seeing Like a City*, 17.

42. Barad, *Meeting the Universe Halfway*, 139, original emphasis.

43. Barad, *Meeting the Universe Halfway*, 136–37.

44. See Judith Butler, *The Psychic Life of Power: Theories in Subjection* (Stanford: Stanford University Press, 1997), 10–18. Butler argues that although "a power *exerted on* a subject, subjection is nevertheless a power *assumed by* the subject, an assumption that constitutes the instrument of that subject's becoming," and continues, explaining that "power not only *acts on* a subject but, in a transitive sense, *enacts* the subject into being. As a condition, power precedes the subject. Power loses its appearance of prior-

ity, however, when it is wielded by the subject, a situation that gives rise to the reverse perspective that power is the effect of the subject, and that power is what subjects effect" (original emphasis; 11, 13).

45. Barad, *Meeting the Universe Halfway*, 135. Barad is quick to caution, however, that intra-action is both "nonarbitrary" and "non-determining," suggesting performative enactment does not occur arbitrarily but rather within certain material conditions that remain subject to change.

46. Sarah Nuttall, *Entanglement: Literary and Cultural Reflections on Post-Apartheid* (Johannesburg: Wits University Press, 2009), 1.

47. Filip de Boeck and Marie-Francoise Plissart. *Kinshasa: Tales of the Invisible City* (Ghent-Amsterdam: Ludion, 2005), 233.

48. As Filip de Boeck compellingly proposes, "In spite of the fact that an analysis of the different physical sites through which the city exists and invents itself helps us to better understand the specific ways in which the materiality of the infrastructure generates particular sets of relations in the city, I would submit that in the end, in a city like Kinshasa, *it is not, or not primarily, the material infrastructure or the built form that makes the city a city*." Filip de Boeck and Marie-Francoise Plissart, *Kinshasa: Tales of the Invisible City*, 233–35 (emphasis added).

49. Adesokan, "Anticipating Nollywood," 104.

50. Adesokan, "Anticipating Nollywood," 103.

51. Simone, *City Life*, 26.

52. Daniel Agbiboa, "Informal Urban Governance and Predatory Politics in Africa: The Role of Motor-Park Touts in Lagos," *African Affairs* 117, no. 466 (2018): 62–82.

53. Quayson, *Oxford Street, Accra*, 210, 202.

54. Peter Brooks, "Melodrama, Body, Revolution," in *Melodrama: Stage, Picture, Screen*, ed. Jacky Brattan, Kim Cook, and Christine Gledhill (London: British Film Institute, 1994), 17.

55. Haynes, *Nollywood*.

56. Haynes, *Nollywood*, 103–4.

57. In fact, Haynes identifies homelessness as a "key motif of the SAP era" (*Nollywood*, 99), and notes several classic video films (*Dead End*, *Rattlesnake*, *Onome*, and *Owo Blow*) that feature "sequences of searching the streets of Lagos for lost children." Similarly, in Nnebue's *Died Wretched*, the good brother Chris's suffering culminates in his family's eviction, their meager belongings stacked along the street as neighbors bear witness. In Tunde Kelani's *Ayo Ni Mo Fe*, the eponymous Ayo experiences a prolonged period of homelessness after losing his office job, and when odd jobs on the street leave him still starving, he joins a gang of area boys.

58. As James Ferguson observes elsewhere, "The truly isolated and alienated are those who really are, by virtue of utter destitution, outside of the 'cash nexus'; for the rest, having cash is precisely what enables the myriad mutualities that sustain (what Elizabeth Povinelli [2006] might call) the 'thick life' of the southern African poor." James Ferguson, *Give a Man a Fish: Reflections on the New Politics of Distribution* (Durham, NC: Duke University Press, 2015), 136.

59. Le Pape, quoted in Newell, *Modernity Bluff*, 90.
60. Levine, *Forms*, 6.
61. Simone, *For the City Yet to Come*, 137.
62. Newell, *Modernity Bluff*.
63. Ferguson, *Give a Man a Fish*, 128.
64. In his work, Newell defines the moral economy among young men in Abidjan as "a system in which people often exchange for the purpose of maintaining and accumulating social relations, rather than merely for the purpose of maximizing their profits" (*Modernity Bluff*, 67.) However, he adds that within such an economy exists a "continual tension" between accumulation and redistribution of resources, which is modulated by the social force of moral obligations. Furthermore, moral obligation does not need to be anchored by a specific moral entity like the family, as other personal ties based on dependency and fidelity can lend adequate gravity to a relationship.
65. Moradewun Adejunmobi, "Standup Comedy and the Ethics of Popular Performance in Nigeria," in *Popular Culture in Africa: The Episteme of the Everyday*, ed. Stephanie Newell and Onookome Okome (New York: Routledge, 2014), 181 (emphasis added).
66. Barad, *Meeting the Universe Halfway*, 184.
67. Barad, *Meeting the Universe Halfway*, 208. As Barad explains, "The notion of intra-action is a key element of my agential realist framework. The neologism 'intra-action' *signifies the mutual constitution of entangled agencies*. That is, in contrast to the usual 'interaction,' which assumes that there are separate individual agencies that precede their interaction, the notion of intra-action recognizes that distinct agencies do not precede, but rather emerge through, their intra-action" (emphasis added, 33).
68. Povinelli, *Empire of Love: Toward a Theory of Intimacy, Genealogy, and Carnality* (Durham, NC: Duke University Press, 2006), 3. In her work on intimacy, a term we might construe as denoting close, intense social connection, Povinelli asserts that its modulation under different regimes of power depends upon "which forms of intimate dependency count as freedom and which count as undue social constraint, which forms of intimacy involve moral judgement rather than mere choice, [and] which forms of intimate sociality distribute life and material goods and evoke moral certainty, if not moral sanctimoniousness" (3).
69. Massey, *For Space*, 151.
70. Abubakar Momoh, "Youth Culture and Area Boys in Lagos," in *Identity Transformation and Identity Politics under Structural Adjustment in Nigeria*, ed. Attahiru Jega (Uppsala: Nordic Africa Institute, 2000), 186–88.
71. Adesokan, "Anticipating Nollywood," 103.
72. Wendy Griswold, *Bearing Witness: Readers, Writers, and the Novel in Nigeria* (Princeton: Princeton University Press, 2000).
73. Peter Ekeh, "Colonialism and the Two Publics in Africa: A Theoretical Statement," *Comparative Studies in Society and History* 17, no. 1 (1975): 106. See also Daniel Jordan Smith, *Culture of Corruption: Everyday Deception and Popular Discontent in Nigeria* (Princeton: Princeton University Press, 2007), 95.

74. Levine, *Forms*, 113.
75. Agbiboa, "Informal Urban Governance." As Daniel Agbiboa writes, "Intermediaries come under various epithets, such as 'fixers,' 'brokers,' 'middlemen,' 'auxilliaries,' and 'go-betweens,' 'captains,' and 'bosses.' Intermediaries also surface in many studies of how youth carve out meaningful temporalities and spaces of manoeuvre. . . . Intermediaries portray themselves as those who 'make things happen' and they demand a 'commission' for their role" (66–67).
76. Ekeh, "Two Publics in Africa," 108.
77. Adesokan, "Anticipating Nollywood," 104.
78. Ekeh, "Two Publics in Africa," 107.
79. Adesokan, "Anticipating Nollywood," 104.
80. Haynes, *Nigerian Film Genres*, 21.
81. Haynes, *Nigerian Film Genres*, 27.
82. Haynes, *Nigerian Film Genres*, 41.
83. Povinelli, *Economies of Abandonment*, 43.
84. For further discussion of rural-urban migration in Nigeria, see Josef Gugler, "Life in a Dual System: Eastern Nigerians in Town, 1961," *Cahiers d'Etudes Africaines* 11, no. 43 (1964): 400–412; Josef Gugler, "Life in a Dual System Revisited: Urban-Rural Ties in Enugu, Nigeria, 1961–87," *World Development* 19, no. 5 (1991): 399–409.
85. Brooks, *Melodramatic Imagination*, 24–55.
86. Adesokan, "Anticipating Nollywood," 105.
87. Adesokan, "Anticipating Nollywood," 105.
88. Okome, "Nollywood, Lagos and the *Good-Time* Woman," 177.
89. Larkin, *Signal and Noise*.
90. Larkin, *Signal and Noise*, 186.
91. Peter Brooks, *The Melodramatic Imagination: Balzac, Henry James, Melodrama, and the Mode of Excess* (New Haven, CT: Yale University Press, 1976), 40.
92. Gledhill, "Soap Opera and Melodrama," 116.

CHAPTER 4

1. Carmela Garritano, "Nollywood: An Archive of African Worldliness," *Black Camera: An International Film Journal* 5, no. 2 (2014): 47.
2. According to one film distributor's box office figures, the highest grossing Nollywood film remains Anyaene's *Ijé: The Journey* (2010), which made over 52 million naira (US$325,000) after appearing in just six theaters around the country. For perspective, that figure is double the earnings of most Hollywood films of the same year, like *The Chronicles of Narnia*, *The Twilight Saga*, and *Sex and the City*.
3. Moradewun Adejunmobi, "Streaming Quality, Streaming Cinema," in *A Companion to African Cinema*, edited by Kenneth W. Harrow and Carmela Garritano (Hoboken, NJ: John Wiley and Sons, 2018), 219–43.
4. During the initial home video boom, the trickle of new feature-length films,

about four per week in 1995, became a torrent of at least twenty per week in 2001 (Ferdinand O. Abua, ed., *Film & Video Directory in Nigeria*, vol. 1 [Abuja: National Film and Video Censors Board, 2002]). Productivity steadily grew, and by 2007 the video marketers were cramming thirty-one new feature-length movies onto already crowded shelves every week (P. P. Bala, *Annual Performance Report of the Film Verification Unit*. National Film and Video Censors Board [Abuja: Federal Republic of Nigeria, Ministry of Information and Culture, 2007]). Though records of the Nigerian National Film and Video Censors Board (NFVCB) show the number of films *approved* for release decreasing slightly to about one thousand films a year between 2008 and 2012, those figures mask the influx of films *submitted* for review, which did not decrease. Meanwhile, some producers simply circumvented official review altogether. If we go by numbers generated by the marketers themselves, nearly half the films produced go unrecorded by the NFVCB. At Idumota Market in Lagos, the heart of finance and distribution for Yoruba-language films, the marketers association organizing and regulating the sale of video films has imposed limits on vendors, effectively holding the number of new releases to thirty every two weeks and going so far as to suspend all new releases for a full month. According to the marketers association's own records, even under these self-imposed restrictions, the Yoruba-language producers released twice as many films in 2012 than the 389 recorded by the NFVCB.

5. Jade Miller, *Nollywood Central* (London: Palgrave on behalf of the British Film Institute, 2016).

6. Alexander Bud, "The End of Nollywood's Guilded Age? Marketers, the State and the Struggle for Distribution," *Critical African Studies* 6, no. 1 (2014): 91–121.

7. Carmela Garritano, *African Video Movies and Global Desires: A Ghanaian History* (Athens: Ohio University Press, 2013), 172–73.

8. The Royal Arts Academy is a production company founded by Emem Isong in 2010. Today Royal Arts comprises three branches: a film school, a production unit, and a distribution arm. This production company is vertically integrated and thus has more creative control and more direct oversight of the financing, production, and distribution of its films than many other companies. The studio retains a writing team of four, some of whom also produce the films they write. It owns a full battery of film equipment, including cameras, lenses, tracks and dollies, and lighting and sound recording equipment. Editing and postproduction are done in-house by both contracted and freelance editors, circumventing the Editor's Guild, to whom most producers turn for postproduction facilities and services.

9. Connor Ryan, "Nollywood and the Limits of Informality," Interview with Tunde Kelani, Bond Emeruwa, and Emem Isong, *Black Camera: An International Film Journal* 5, no. 2 (2014): 177.

10. Simon During, "Popular Culture on a Global Scale: A Challenge for Cultural Studies?" *Critical Inquiry* 23, no. 4 (1997): 808–33.

11. Jonathan Haynes, "Keeping Up: The Corporatization of Nollywood's Economy and Paradigms for Studying African Screen Media," *Africa Today* 64, no. 4 (2018): 2–29.

12. Lani Akande, "Nollywood Cinema's Character of Recurrence," *Journal of African Cultural Studies* 33, no. 4 (2021): 456–70.

13. There is considerable evidence of genre mixing, as this portion of the narrative follows the conventions of a moral revelation, where evil befalls the girls as a consequence of their dealings with immoral elements, a typical Nollywood trope. This narrative impulse to imagine the containment of female sexuality and power in the form of material acquisitiveness runs throughout *Jenifa* and *The Return of Jenifa*, but this gendered moral discourse feels insufficient to actually effect that containment for the spectator for whom the moments of laughter outweigh the instances of moral shock that are inserted in order to offer closure.

14. Miller, *Nollywood Central*, 42–46.

15. Olatunji Balogun is a prominent figure in the Yoruba video film marketers association, which serves as the generally recognized governing body for the finance and distribution operations based in Idumota Market (as described in my introduction).

16. Silverbird Group was first founded by Ben Murray-Bruce as an entertainment and event promotions company called Silverbird Productions. Beginning in the late 1980s, its cornerstone event was the Miss Africa World Beauty Pageant, a regional competition for which Silverbird acquired the rights from the Miss World Beauty Pageant. As Patrick Lee of the Silverbird Board of Trustees related to me, the idea to build a multiplex cinema arose when visiting foreign dignitaries for the beauty pageant protested the lack of Lagos nightlife (personal communication, March 13, 2013).

17. During Nigeria's oil boom, when cinema halls enjoyed a peak attendance due to boosted domestic consumption and strengthened purchasing power, Lagos alone hosted twenty-eight licensed cinemas and a rumored forty "pirate" cinemas (Hyginus Ekwuazi, *Film in Nigeria* [Ibadan: Moonlight Publishers for the Nigerian Film Corporation, 1987]). The American Motion Picture Exportation Corporation of Africa (AMPECA) supplied these cinemas with Hollywood B-films from MGM, Columbia, United Artists, and 20th Century Fox. Chinese and Indian films arrived through illicit import networks linking Bombay and Hong Kong films to Nigerian cinemas through pirate distributors in Dubai, Cairo, Abu Dahbi, and Singapore, in part because the cinema halls were often owned by Indian and Lebanese Nigerians with personal relationships (N. K. Murthy, personal communication, July 16, 2013; see also Brian Larkin, *Signal and Noise: Media, Infrastructure, and Urban Culture in Nigeria* [Durham, NC: Duke University Press, 2008]). By the end of the 1990s these cinemas had closed due to growing economic and social instability.

18. Añulika Agina, "Cinema-going in Lagos: Three Locations, One Film, One Weekend," *Journal of African Cultural Studies* 32, no. 2 (2020): 131-45.

19. Ramon Lobato, *Shadow Economies of Cinema: Mapping Informal Film Distribution* (London: Palgrave Macmillan for the British Film Institute, 2012).

20. Amit Rai, *Untimely Bollywood: Globalization and India's New Media Assemblage* (Durham, NC: Duke University Press, 2009), 159.

21. Garritano, *Global Desires*, 176.

22. Achille Mbembe, "Aesthetics of Superfluity," in *Johannesburg: The Elusive Metropolis*, ed. Sarah Nuttall and Achille Mbembe (Durham, NC: Duke University Press, 2008), 60.

23. Rai, *Untimely Bollywood*, 140.

24. Keyan Tomaselli and Arnold Shepperson, "Transformation and South African Cinema in the 1990s," in *Critical Approaches to African Cinema Discourse*, ed. Nwachukwu Frank Ukadike (Lanham, MD: Lexington Books, 2014), 107–34. The "pirate cinemas" that Ekwuazi describes have been substituted by video parlors and football viewing centers that have Nollywood movie channels in their satellite television subscription. Though sports viewing centers must be licensed in Lagos and are prohibited from televising anything but sports, most neighborhoods in the city have several viewing centers that screen with impunity whatever content appeals to patrons. Possessing only the most basic infrastructure—perhaps benches "arranged facing the viewing area while curtains block out light and, unfortunately, air from the outside"—these spaces of exhibition provide the cheapest access to films to perhaps the largest audience (Babson Ajibade "From Lagos to Douala: The Video Film and Its Spaces of Seeing," *Postcolonial Text* 3, no. 2 [2007]: 5).

25. Onookome Okome, "Nollywood: Spectatorship, Audience, and the Sites of Consumption," *Postcolonial Text* 3, no. 2 (2007): 1–21.

26. Anulika Agina, "Cinema-going in Lagos: Three Locations, One Film, One Weekend," 139.

27. Documents from Blu Pictures Distribution show that of the nine Nollywood films that appeared in theaters in 2010, only two, *Figurine* and *Ijé*, earned over 10 million naira. In 2011 only three films earned above the same benchmark, while the other nineteen local films that appeared in theaters rarely broke 3 million naira in ticket sales.

28. Lobato, *Shadow Economies of Cinema*, 4.

29. Miller, *Nollywood Central*.

30. Tejaswini Ganti, "Fuzzy Number: The Productive Nature of Ambiguity in the Hindi Film Industry," *Comparative Studies of South Asia, Africa and the Middle East* 35, no. 3 (2015): 452.

31. Ganti, "Fuzzy Number," 453.

32. Alessandro Jedlowski, "African Media and the Corporate Takeover: Video Film Circulation in the Age of Neoliberal Transformations," *African Affairs* 116, no. 465 (2016): 671–91.

33. James Ferguson, *Global Shadows: Africa in the Neoliberal World Order* (Durham, NC: Duke University Press, 2006), 38.

34. Okome, "Nollywood: Spectatorship," 11. See also Ajibade, "From Lagos to Douala: The Video Film and Its Spaces of Seeing."

35. Alessandro Jedlowski, "Nigerian Videos in the Global Arena: The Postcolonial Exotic Revisited," *Global South* 7, no. 1 (2013): 157–78.

36. I learned of the growing availability of sound stages after a visit to the offices of Femi Odugbemi, formerly the executive producer of *Tinsel*, a popular soap opera on Nigerian satellite television. The program is shot at a sound stage in Ikeja, Lagos.

37. Noah Tsika, "From Yorùbá to YouTube: Studying Nollywood's Star System," *Black Camera: An International Film Journal* 5, no. 2 (2014): 101.

38. Anastup Basu, *Bollywood in the Age of New Media: The Geo-televisual Aesthetic* (Edinburgh: Edinburgh University Press, 2010), 99.

39. Basu, *Bollywood in the Age of New Media*, 80.

40. Brian Larkin, "The Grounds of Circulation: Rethinking African Film and Media," *Politique Africaine* 153 (2019): 123, 124.

CHAPTER 5

1. Nigel Thrift, *Non-Representational Theory: Space, Politics, Affect* (New York: Routledge, 2008).

2. Karin Barber, "Popular Arts in Africa," *African Studies Review* 30, no. 3 (1987): 1–78.

3. See Moradewun Adejunmobi, "Nollywood, Globalization, and Regional Media Corporations in Africa," *International Journal of Media and Culture* 9, no. 2 (2011): 67–78; Alexander Bud, "The End of Nollywood's Guilded Age? Marketers, the State and the Struggle for Distribution," *Critical African Studies* 6, no. 1 (2014): 91–121; Alessandro Jedlowski, "African Media and the Corporate Takeover: Video Film Circulation in the Age of Neoliberal Transformations," *African Affairs* 116, no. 465 (2016): 671–91; Jade Miller, *Nollywood Central* (London: Palgrave on behalf of the British Film Institute, 2016).

4. Jedlowski, "Corporate Takeover," 673. Even as the films travel increasingly in immaterial modes of circulation—not discs but digital content—television and video streaming platforms themselves are underpinned—and constrained—by specific material conditions. Jade Miller (*Nollywood Central, chapter 5*) insightfully illustrates this point in her discussion of the obstacles that impede iROKO's attempts to do business physically within Nigeria.

5. Jedlowski, "Corporate Takeover," 687.

6. Maurizio Lazzarato, "Immaterial Labor," in *Radical Thought in Italy: A Potential Politics*, ed. Paolo Virno and Michael Hardt (Minneapolis: University of Minnesota Press, 1996), 133.

7. Matthew Hockenberry, Nicole Starosielski, and Susan Zieger, *Assembly Codes: The Logistics of Media* (Durham, NC: Duke University Press, 2021), 13–14.

8. Stefano Harney, "Creative Industries Debate," *Cultural Studies* 24, no. 3 (May 2010): 432.

9. Moradewun Adejunmobi, "Streaming Quality, Streaming Cinema," in *A Companion to African Cinema*, edited by Kenneth W. Harrow and Carmela Garritano (Hoboken, NJ: John Wiley and Sons, 2018), 219–43.

10. Michael Curtin, and Kevin Sanson, eds., *Voices of Labor: Creativity, Craft, and Conflict in Global Hollywood* (Berkeley: University of California Press, 2017). As Curtin and Sanson observe, "The line separating autonomy from precarity proved to be a tenuous one as contingent and irregular employment patters started to define the general working conditions in many industries around the world" (10).

11. Kathi Weeks, *The Problem with Work: Feminism, Marxism, Antiwork Politics, and Postwork Imaginaries* (Durham, NC: Duke University Press, 2011).

12. Judith Butler, *The Psychic Life of Power: Theories in Subjection* (Stanford: University of California Press, 1997). In Butler's theory of subjectivation, power subordinates in the process of the formation of the subject but also enables the agency of the subject that is formed.

13. Elizabeth Povinelli, *Empire of Love: Toward a Theory of Intimacy, Genealogy, and Carnality* (Durham, NC: Duke University Press, 2006).

14. Dianna Taylor, "Practices of the Self," in *Michel Foucault: Key Concepts*, ed. Dianna Taylor (Durham, NC: Acumen Press, 2011), 173–86. Neoliberal governmentality refers broadly to the control of the conduct of oneself and others (176). It describes a mode of subjectivation produced through activities an individual performs, what Taylor terms "practices of the self," rather than the position they occupy within society (173). Such practices are shaped by institutions—schools, courts, hospitals, prisons, and workplaces—just as they are shaped by the prevailing norms and values of society and, in this respect, represent a form of constraint. Institutions do not constrain by forcing the norms of society upon the will of the individual. Instead, power manifests in that which makes the individual amenable to voluntarily assuming the responsibility of self-governance, such that each individual actively participates in their own self-formation. This is not a tautological proposition but rather a recognition of the fact that "the self delimits itself and decides on the material for its self-making, but the delimitation that the self performs takes place through norms which are, indisputably, already in place" (Butler qtd. in Taylor, "Practices of the Self," 180). Furthermore, we never completely extricate ourselves from the power of these institutions and values, nor is such an extrication necessary for us to exercise freedom. In Dianna Taylor's words, "The fact that subjects are simultaneously enabled and constrained by the same norms and practices may complicate but does not destroy possibilities for either freedom or subjectivity" (181).

15. My claim resonates with the sense that distribution itself is increasingly integral to any understanding of media globalization but also complicates the thesis that more and more of the world receives its screen media through shadow economies of distribution. For more, see Ramon Lobato, *Shadow Economies of Cinema: Mapping Informal Film Distribution* (London: Palgrave Macmillan for the British Film Institute, 2012).

16. Ann Overbergh, "Kenya's Riverwood: Market Structure, Power Relations, and Future Outlooks," *Journal of African Cinemas* 7, no. 2 (2015): 106.

17. Alessandro Jedlowski, "African Media and the Corporate Takeover: Video Film Circulation in the Age of Neoliberal Transformations," *African Affairs* 116, no. 465 (2016): 671–91.

18. Jonathan Haynes, "Keeping Up: The Corporatization of Nollywood's Economy and Paradigms for Studying African Screen Media," *Africa Today* 64, no. 4 (2018): 2–29.

19. Jade Miller, *Nollywood Central* (New York: Bloomsbury for the British Film Institute, 2016).

20. Haynes, "Keeping Up," 11.

21. Miller, *Nollywood Central*.

22. Michael Curtin and Kevin Sanson, eds., *Precarious Creativity: Global Media, Local Labor* (Berkeley: University of California Press, 2016). As Curtin and Sanson write: "Today's increasingly mobile and globally dispersed mode of production thrives (indeed, depends) on interregional competition, driving down pay rates, benefits, and job satisfaction for media workers around the world. Producers say corporate financial imperatives compel them to contain costs, especially labor costs. Consequently, workdays are growing longer, productivity pressures are more intense, and creative autonomy is diminishing" (2).

23. Curtin and Sanson contend that the new fexible mode of film production "insulates corporate decision makers from creative practice, privileging content that is relentlessly market-tested at all stages or production, resulting in a creative process that begins and ends with competitive positioning." Curtin and Sanson, *Precarious Creativity*, 6.

24. Curtin and Sanson, *Voices of Labor*, 7.

25. In particular, Curtin and Sanson argue that the global respatialization of creative labor "thrives (indeed, depends) on interregional competition, driving down pay rates, benefits, and job satisfaction for media workers around the world. Producers say corporate financial imperatives compel them to contain costs, especially labor costs. Consequently, workdays are growing longer, productivity pressures are more intense, and creative autonomy is diminishing." Curtin and Sanson, *Precarious Creativity*, 2.

26. Miller, *Nollywood Central*, 49–57. Miller importantly points out that marketers hold fast to these practices of informality because it allows them to control information and knowledge, protect their working relationships, and thereby retain their advantage.

27. Moradewun Adejunmobi, "Nollywood, Globalization, and Regional Media Corporations in Africa," *Popular Communication* 9, no. 2 (2011): 67–78; Haynes, "Keeping Up."

28. Michael Curtin, "Comparing Media Capitals: Hong Kong and Mumbai," *Global Media and Communication* 6, no. 3 (2010): 263–70. Los Angeles, New York, London, Hong Kong, Mumbai, Beirut, and Mexico City represent such media capitals. In Curtin's view, "their influence is dependent upon their ability to monitor and discern the imaginary worlds of their audiences and to gather and operationalize resources within their cultural domain" (265).

29. Curtin also argues that media capitals maintain regional dominance insofar as media companies based in such cities advance "a resolute fixation on the tastes and desires of audiences." Curtin, "Comparing Media Capitals," 265.

30. The comments in this section are grounded in interviews I conducted between July and August 2018 with four producers whose films were acquired by iROKOtv. I have omitted their names to avoid jeopardizing the working relationships these individuals still have with iROKOtv.

31. Curtin and Sanson, *Voices of Labor*, 7.

32. Weeks, *Problem with Work*, 8.

33. Miller, *Nollywood Central*, 154.
34. Miller, *Nollywood Central*, 154.
35. Curtin and Sanson, *Voices of Labor*.
36. Tejaswini Ganti, "Sentiments of Disdain and Practices of Distinction: Boundary-Work, Subjectivity, and Value in the Hindi Film Industry," *Anthropological Quarterly* 85, no. 1 (2012): 5–43. Ganti borrows the term from sociologist Thomas Gieryn, who conceptualized boundary work as "a 'stylistic resource' and a 'rhetorical style' that accompanies the ideology of professionalization and its attempts to establish criteria for expertise, authority, and legitimacy. For example, boundary-work demarcates competitors as outsiders, deeming them unfit through the use of labels such as 'pseudo,' 'deviant,' or 'amateur'" (8).
37. Created to honor the late Amaka Igwe, undoubtedly one of Nollywood's most influential producers (male or female), the documentary situates Igwe as a profound agent in the industry's early formation. It asserts that Igwe's example inspired a younger generation of female filmmakers who have come of age and now represent some of the most powerful names in Nollywood.
38. Butler, *Psychic Life of Power*.
39. Kathi Weeks, "Life Within and Against Work: Affective Labor, Feminist Critique, and Post-Fordist Politics," *Ephemera: Theory and Politics in Organization* 7, no. 1 (January 2007): 233–49.
40. "One approach would be to ground the critical standpoint on subjectivity not in a claim about the true or essential self, but in a potential self. . . . The self at work could thus be judged in relation to a self that one might wish to become and both work and non-work time could be assessed in relation to the possibility of becoming different." Weeks, "Within and Against Work," 248.
41. Celestino Deleyto, *The Secret Life of Romantic Comedy* (Manchester: Manchester University Press, 2011), 36.
42. For the most part, these are by-the-book romantic comedies. Some producers with whom I spoke cited American rom-coms as their principal influences. The director of *Flower Girl*, Michelle Bello, described her careful study of American classics, such as *My Fair Lady* (1964) and *Pretty Woman* (1990), as part of the preparation for her film's treatment (personal communication).
43. Michael Hardt, "Affective Labor," *boundary 2* 26, no. 2 (1999): 94.
44. Weeks, *The Problem with Work*.
45. Weeks, *The Problem with Work*, 72.
46. Barbara Cruikshank, "Revolutions Within: Self-Government and Self-Esteem," in *Foucault and PoliticalReason: Liberalism, Neo-liberalism, and Rationalities of Government*, edited by Andrew Berry, Thomas Osborne, and Nikolas Rose (Chicago: University of Chicago Press, 1996), 233.
47. Moradewun Adejunmobi, "Neoliberal Rationalities in Old and New Nollywood," *African Studies Review* 58, no. 3 (2015): 31–53. Adejunmobi sketches Old Nollywood and New Nollywood as distinct articulations of neoliberal subjectivity in contemporary

Africa. Early Nollywood films often represent the acquisition of wealth through some violation of the community's moral code. By contrast, New Nollywood films are governed by their focus on "the commonplace economies of self-governance and autonomous subjectivity" (40). Adejunmobi argues that this combination of characters imbued with a drive toward personal fulfillment and a social field of relatively unconstrained individual choice represents New Nollywood's adoption of particular principles of neoliberalism.

48. Weeks, *Problem with Work*, 74.

49. Carmela Garritano, *African Video Movies and Global Desires: A Ghanaian History* (Athens: Ohio University Press, 2013).

50. Weeks, *Problem with Work*, 74.

51. Laurie Ouellette and James Hay, "Makeover Television, Governmentality, and the Good Citizen," *Continuum* 22, no. 4 (2008): 471–84.

52. Kathi Weeks calls this the "postindustrial work ethic," which finds its "transcendental rationale" in the appeal to "a more individual justification and promise of an even more immediate gratification—namely, fulfilling and meaningful work." Weeks, *Problem with Work*, 46.

53. Rachel Spronk, "Media and the Therapeutic Ethos of Romantic Love in Middle-Class Nairobi," *Love in Africa*, ed. Jennifer Cole and Lynn M. Thomas (Chicago: Chicago University Press, 2009): 188–89.

54. In her anthropological investigation of love among young professionals in Nairobi, Rachel Spronk observed at the turn of the millennium—following the liberalization of Kenyan media markets and during the period of her field research—the introduction of "a therapeutic ethos" into discussions of love. "Rather than accepting didactic and moralizing advice from others, the therapeutic ethos insists that the solution to romantic problems lies in self-knowledge and reflexivity." Spronk, "Romantic Love in Middle-Class Nairobi," 183.

55. Jonathan Haynes, *Nollywood: The Creation of Nigerian Film Genres* (Chicago: Chicago University Press, 2016).

56. It is important here to note that iROKOtv and Multichoice organize their content according to language, which is a proxy of ethnicity. Furthermore, the indigenous-language content and channels filled with mainstream Nollywood films are reportedly more popular than the upmarket corporate Nollywood films. Haynes, "Keeping Up," 16–17.

57. Onookome Okome, "Nollywood: Spectatorship, Audience, and Sites of Consumption," *Postcolonial Text* 3, no. 2 (2007): 1–21.

58. Deleyto, *The Secret Life of Romantic Comedy*, 36.

59. Nikolas Rose, "Governing 'Advanced' Liberal Democracies," in *Foucault and Political Reason: Liberalism, Neo-liberalism, and Rationalities of Government*, ed. Andrew Berry, Thomas Osborne, and Nikolas Rose (Chicago: University of Chicago Press, 1996), 37–64.

60. Povinelli, *Empire of Love*.

61. As Judith Butler explains, "Agency exceeds the power by which it is enabled. One might say that the purposes of power are not always the purposes of agency. To the extent that the latter diverge from the former, agency is the assumption of a purpose *unintended* by power, one that could not have been derived logically or historically, that operates in a relation of contingency and reversal to the power that makes it possible, to which it nevertheless belongs." Butler, *Psychic Life of Power*, 15.

62. Povinelli, *Empire of Love*, 10.

63. Lauren Berlant, *Cruel Optimism* (Durham, NC: Duke University Press, 2011).

CHAPTER 6

1. Pep Subirós, "Lagos: Surviving Hell," in *Africas: the Artist and the City: A Journey Exhibition*, (Barcelona: Centre de Cultura Contemporània de Barcelona: 2001), 34-45; Tunde Agbola, *The Architecture of Fear: Urban Design and Construction Response to Urban Violence in Lagos, Nigeria*. (Ibadan: Institut Francais de Recherche en Afrique, 1997).

2. In particular, see Onookome Okome, "Loud in Lagos," *Glendora: African Quarterly of the Arts* 2, no. 1 (1997): 75–83; Obododimma Oha, "The Visual Rhetoric of the Ambivalent City in Nigerian Video Films," in *Cinema and the City: Film and Urban Societies in a Global Context*, ed. Mark Shiel and Tony Fitzmaurice (Oxford: Blackwell, 2001), 195–205; Onookome Okome, "Writing the Anxious City: Images of Lagos in Nigerian Home Video Films," *Black Renaissance / Renaissance Noire* 5, no. 2 (2003): 65–75; Akin Adesokan, "Loud in Lagos: Nollywood Videos," *Wasafiri* 19 (2004): 45–49; Jonathan Haynes, "Nollywood in Lagos, Lagos in Nollywood Films," *Africa Today*, 54, no. 2 (2007): 130–50.

3. Haynes, "Nollywood in Lagos," 133.

4. Jonathan Haynes, *Nollywood: The Creation of Nigerian Film Genres* (Chicago: Chicago University Press, 2016), 229.

5. Haynes, *Nigerian Film Genres*, 173–74.

6. Dele Meiji Fatunla, "Cityscapes: Lagos, West Africa's Playground," *New African Magazine*, accessed January 7, 2021, March 15, 2017, https://newafricanmagazine.com/15143.

7. See "Alara Concept Store," *Adjaye Associates*, accessed January 6, 2021, https://www.adjaye.com/work/alara.

8. Siddhartha Mitter, "Lagos, City of Hustle, Builds an Art 'Ecosystem.'" *New York Times*, February 8, 2019, accessed June 6, 2019, https://www.nytimes.com/2019/02/08/arts/design/lagos-nigeria-art-x-art.html.

9. Jess Castellote and Tobenna Okwuosa, "Lagos Art World: The Emergence of an Artistic Hub on the Global Art Periphery," *African Studies Review* 63, no. 1 (2020): 170–96. I would add that the visual artist Wura Ogunji, in an effort to promote more experimentation in Nigerian art, converted a leased flat in the YMCA building into an exhibition space called The Treehouse, where she hosts artists who wish to present experimentations or works in progress to friends and other local artists.

10. Jonathan Haynes, "Neoliberalism, Nollywood and Lagos," in *Global Cinematic Cities: New Landscapes of Film and Media*, ed. Johan Andersson and Lawrence Webb (New York: Wallflower Press / Columbia University Press, 2016), 59–75.

11. Haynes, "Keeping Up: The Corporatization of Nollywood's Economy and Paradigms for Studying African Screen Media," *Africa Today* 64, no. 4 (2018): 11.

12. Sophie Bouillon, "Social Realism and a 'New Voice' in Nigerian Cinema," *Agence France-Presse*, July 8, 2018, accessed January 6, 2021, http://www.jamaicaobserver.com/sunday-finance/social-realism-and-a-new-voice-in-nigerian-cinema_137550.

13. I borrow this term from Ignacio Sanchez Prado's study of Mexican romantic comedies in the 1990s, which departed from the prior affective conventions of melodrama within Mexican cinema, music, and theater. Ignacio Sanchez Prado, *Screening Neoliberalism: Transforming Mexican Cinema, 1988–2012* (Nashville: Vanderbilt University Press, 2014), 45. For the purposes of this chapter, I would add that this period of Mexican cinema also produced neo-noirs like Alejandro Gonzalez Inarritu's *Amores Perros* (2000).

14. Jennifer Fay and Justus Nieland, *Film Noir: Hard-boiled Modernity and the Cultures of Globalization* (New York: Routledge, 2010).

15. Fay and Nieland, *Film Noir*, 6.

16. David Dresser, "Global Noir: Genre Film in the Age of Transnationalism," in *Film Genre Reader IV*, ed. Barry Keith Grant (Austin: University of Texas Press, 2012), 628–48.

17. Haynes, "Keeping Up," 7.

18. Desser, "Global Noir," 528.

19. Desser, "Global Noir," 528.

20. Brian Larkin, *Signal and Noise: Media, Infrastructure, and Urban Culture in Nigeria* (Durham, NC: Duke University Press, 2008).

21. Tejaswini Ganti, "Sentiments of Disdain and Practices of Distinction: Boundary-Work, Subjectivity and Value in the Hindi Film Industry," *Anthropological Quarterly* 85, no. 1 (2012): 8.

22. Castellote and Okwuosa, "Lagos Art World."

23. Nomusa Makhubu, "'This House Is Not for Sale': Nollywood's Spatial Politics and Concepts of 'Home' in Zina Saro-Wiwa's Art," *African Arts* 49, no. 4 (2016): 58–69.

24. "'Surreal 16' Set Vision for New Wave of Nigerian Film," *France 24 English*, accessed May 12, 2022, https://youtu.be/EB_wYuSjenk.

25. Rosalind Galt and Karl Schoonover, "The Impurity of Art Cinema" in *Global Art Cinema: New Theories and Histories*, edited by Rosalind Galt and Karl Schoonover (Oxford: Oxford University Press, 2010), 3–-20.

26. Galt and Schoonover, "The Impurity," 8.

27. Tega Okiti, "Surreal16: The Filmmaking Collective Trying to Forge a New Identity for Nigerian Cinema," *Sight and Sound*, September 8, 2018, https://www2.bfi.org.uk/news-opinion/sight-sound-magazine/interviews/surreal16-collective-nigerian-arthouse-cinema-nollywood.

28. Thomas Elsaesser, "Cinephilia or the Uses of Disenchantment," in *Cinephilia: Movies, Love and Memory*, edited by Marijke de Valck and Malte Hagener (Amsterdam: Amsterdam University Press, 2005), 36.

29. Julia Kristeva, "Word, Dialogue and Novel," in *The Julia Kristeva Reader*, edited by Toril Moi (New York: Columbia University Press, 1986).

30. Stefano Harney and Fred Moten, *The Undercommons: Fugitive Planning and Black Study* (New York: Minor Compositions, 2013), 108.

31. AbdouMaliq Simone, *City Life from Jakarta to Dakar: Movements at the Crossroads*. New York: Routledge, 2010, 303.

CONCLUSION

1. Jade Miller, *Nollywood Central* (New York: Bloomsbury for British Film Institute, 2016).

2. Alessandro Jedlowski, "African Media and the Corporate Takeover: Video Film Circulation in the Age of Neoliberal Transformations," *African Affairs* 116, no. 465 (2016): 671–91.

3. Moradewun Adejunmobi, "Streaming Quality, Streaming Cinema," in *A Companion to African Cinema*, edited by Kenneth W. Harrow and Carmela Garritano (Hoboken, NJ: John Wiley and Sons, 2018), 219–43.

4. Lani Akande, "Nollywood Cinema's Character of Recurrence," *Journal of African Cultural Studies* 33, no. 4 (2021: 458.

5. Stefano Harney and Fred Moten, *The Undercommons: Fugitive Planning and Black Study* (New York: Minor Compositions, 2013), 88.

6. Nomusa Makhubu, "'This House Is Not for Sale': Nollywood's Spatial Politics and Concepts of 'Home' in Zina Saro-Wiwa's Art," *African Arts* 49, no. 4 (2016), 58.

FILMOGRAPHY

Agbaje Omo Onile. 2018. Dir. Adebayo Tijani. Yoruba. Digital video. Nigeria. Epsalum Movie Productions.
Aiye. 1979. Dir. Ola Balogun. Yoruba. Celluloid. Nigeria. Ogunde Films.
Alan Poza. 2013. Dir. Charles Novia. English. Digital video. Nigeria. November Productions.
Amaka's Kin: The Women of Nollywood. 2016. Dir. Tope Oshin. English. Digital video. Sunbow Productions.
Anchor Baby. 2010. Dir. Lonzo Nzekwe. English. Digital video. Canada and Nigeria. Alpha Galore Films.
Ayanmo/Destiny. 1988. Dir. Freddie Goode with Hubert Ogunde. Yoruba. Celluloid. Nigeria Ogunde Films.
Basi and Company. Series. 1986–90. Dir. Uzorma Onungwa. Created by Ken Saro-Wiwa. English. Television broadcast and VHS. Nigeria. Saros International.
Blood Money 1 and 2. 1997. Dir. Chico Ejiro. English. VHS. Nigeria. OJ Productions.
Born. 2016. Dir. Michael Omonua. English and Pidgin. Digital video. Nigeria. Cine9ja.
Brood. 2018. Dir. Michael Omonua. Pidgin. Digital video. Nigeria. Cine9ja.
Catch.er. 2017. Dir. Walter Taylaur. Pidgin and English. Digital video. Nigeria. Waltbanger 101 Productions.
The CEO. 2016. Dir. Kunle Afolayan. English. Digital video. Nigeria. Golden Effects.
Checkmate. Series. 1991–94. Dir. Bolaji Dawodu. Created by Amaka Igwe. English. Television broadcast and VCD. Nigeria. Moving Movies/Crystal Gold.
Circle of Doom. 1993. Dir. Chris Obi-Rapu. Igbo. VHS. Nigeria. Videosonic.
Confusion Na Wa. 2013. Dir. Kenneth Gyang. Pidgin. Digital video. Nigeria. Kpatakpata Cinema.
Contract. 2012. Dir. Shirley Frimpong-Manso. English. Digital video. Ghana and Nigeria. Sparrow Productions.
Died Wretched, Buried in a N3.2 Million Casket. 1998. Dir. Kenneth Nnebue. English. VHS. Nigeria: NEK Video Links.
Doctor Bello. 2012. Dir. Tony Abulu. English and Yoruba. Digital video. USA and Nigeria. Black Ivory Communications.

Domitilla: The Story of a Prostitute 1. 1996. Dir. Zeb Ejiro. English and Pidgin. VHS. Nigeria: Zeb Ejiro Productions/Daar Communications.

The Figurine / Araromire. 2010. Dir. Kunle Afolayan. English. Digital video. Nigeria. Golden Effects.

Flower Girl. 2012. Dir. Michelle Bello. English. Digital video. Nigeria. Blu Star Entertainment.

Forever. 1994. Dir. Amaka Igwe. English. VHS. Nigeria. Moving Movies/Crystal Gold.

Fuji House of Commotion. Series. 2001–13. Dir. Amaka Igwe. English, Pidgin, and Yoruba. Television broadcast and VCD. Nigeria. Amaka Igwe Studios/Crystal Gold.

Gbomo Gbomo Express. 2015. Dir. Walter Taylaur. Pidgin and English. Digital video. Nigeria. Waltbanger 101 Productions.

Glamour Girls. 1994. Dir. Chika Onukwafor. English. VHS. Nigeria. NEK Video Links.

Green White Green: And All of the Beautiful Colours in My Mosaic of Madness. 2016. Dir. Abba Makama. English and Pidgin. Digital video. Nigeria: Osiris Creatives.

Hostages. 1997. Dir. Tade Ogidan. English. VHS. English. Nigeria. OGD Pictures.

Husband Shopping. 2015. Dir. Pascal Amanfo. English. Digital video. Ghana. Pascal Amanfo Expression, 50th Film Academy.

Ijé: The Journey. 2010. Dir. Chineze Anyaene. English. Celluloid. USA and Nigeria. Xandria Productions.

Ikuku/Hurricane 1 and 2. 1995. Dir. Nkem Owoh and Zeb Ejiro. Igbo. VHS. Nigeria. Nonks/Andy Best.

Inale. 2010. Dir. Jeta Amata. English. Digital video. Nigeria. BIK Entertainment, Jeta Amata Concepts.

Jack and Jill. 2014. Dir. Pascal Amanfo. English. Digital video. Ghana and Nigeria. Pascal Amanfo Expression.

Jaiyesimi. 1980. Dir. Freddie Goode with Hubert Ogunde. Yoruba. Celluloid. Nigeria. Ogunde Films.

Jenifa 1–2. 2008. Dir. Dir. Muhydeen S. Ayinde. Yoruba. Digital video. Nigeria. Olasco Films.

Jenifa's Diary. Series. 2015–present. Dir. Abdulrasheed Bello. Created by Funke Akindele. English. Digital video. Nigeria. Scene One Productions.

Juju Stories. 2021. Dir. Abba Makama, Michael Omonua, and C. J. "Fiery" Obasi. Pidgin and English. Fiery Film Company, Osiris Creatives, Cine9ja, iFind Pictures, 20 Pounds Production.

Just Not Married. 2016. Dir. Uduak-Obong Patrick. English. Digital video. Nigeria. Judith Audu Productions, Blackcreek Pictures, Asurf Films.

Kasala!. 2018. Dir. Ema Edosio. English and Pidgin. Digital video. Nigeria. Bliss Productions.

Kiss and Tell. 2011. Dir. Desmond Elliot. English. Digital video. Nigeria. Royal Arts Academy Productions.

Kongi's Harvest. 1970. Dir. Ossie Davis. English. Celluloid. Nigeria and USA. Francis Oladele/Calpenny.

Lagos Na Wah!!: Pidgin Comedy 1–3. 1994. Dir. Kehinde Soaga. Pidgin. VHS. Nigeria. Topway Productions.
Lionheart. 2018. Dir. Genevieve Nnaji. English and Igbo. Digital video. Nigeria. Entertainment Network.
Living in Bondage 1. 1992. Dir. Chris Obi-Rapu. Igbo. VHS. NEK Video Links.
Living in Bondage 2. 1993. Dir. Chika Onukwafor. VHS. NEK Video Links.
The Lost Okoroshi. 2019. Dir. Abba Makama. English. Digital video. Nigeria. Osiris Creatives.
Love Brewed in the African Pot. 1981. Dir. Kwaw Ansah. English. Celluloid. Ghana. Film Africa.
Maami. 2011. Dir. Tunde Kelani. Yoruba and English. Digital video. Nigeria. Mainframe Productions.
Mandingo. 1975. Dir. Richard Fleischer. English. Celluloid. USA. Paramount Pictures.
The Meeting. 2012. Dir. Mildred Owko and Rita Dominic. English, Pidgin, Igbo, Hausa, and Yoruba. Digital video. Nigeria. Mord Pictures Production and Audrey Silva Company.
The Mirror Boy. 2011. Dir. Obi Emelonye. English. Digital video. UK and Gambia. OH Films.
Mod'orisa: The Epic. 2018. Dir. Adebayo Tijani. Yoruba. Digital video. Nigeria. Kaas & Dees Entertainment.
Mókálìk. 2019. Dir. Kunle Afolayan. Yoruba. Digital video. Nigeria. Golden Effects.
New Masquerade. Series. 1983–ca. 2001. Dir. Charles Ugwu. Created by James Iroha. English and Pidgin. Television broadcast and VCD. Nigeria. Nigerian Television Authority.
Nollywood Hustlers 1–4. 2009. Dir. Emem Isong. English. Nigeria. Royal Arts Academy Productions.
October 1st. 2014. Dir. Kunle Afolayan. Yoruba and English. Digital Video. Nigeria. Golden Effects.
Ojukokoro/Greed. 2016. Dir. Dare Olaitan. English, Yoruba, and Bini. Digital video. Nigeria. Singularity Media, House Gabriel Studios.
Okon Lagos. 2012. Dir. Uduak Isong Oguamanam. Ibibio. Digital video. Nigeria.
Onome 1. 1996. Dir. Chico Ejiro and Opa Williams. English. VHS. Nigeria: Consolidated Fortunes.
Orun Mooru / Heaven Is Hot. 1982. Dir. Ola Balogun with Moses Adejumo Olaiya. Yoruba. Celluloid and VCD. Nigeria. Alawada Movies.
Owo Blow 1–3. 1996, 1997. Dir. Tade Ogidan. Yoruba. VHS. Nigeria. First Call.
Owo L'Agba / Money Power. 1982. Dir. Ola Balogun. Yoruba. Celluloid. Nigeria. Afrocult Foundation.
Phone Swap. 2012. Dir. Kunle Afolayan. English, Pigdin, Yoruba, and Igbo. Digital video. Nigeria. Golden Effects.
Phyllis. 2010. Dir. Zina Saro-Wiwa. English. Digital video. Nigeria: Zina Saro-Wiwa.
Rattlesnake 1 and 2. 1995, 1996. Dir. Amaka Igwe. VHS. Nigeria. Moving Movies/Crystal Gold.

The Return of Jenifa 1 and 2. 2011. Dir. Muhydeen S. Ayinde. Yoruba. Digital video. Nigeria. Olasco Films, Scene One Productions.

Rituals. 1997. Dir. Andy Amanechi. English. VHS. Nigeria. NEK Video Links.

Scores to Settle. 1998. Dir. Chico Ejiro. English. VHS. Nigeria. Grand Touch Pictures.

Silent Night. 1996. Dir. Chico Ejiro. English. VHS. Nigeria. Grand Touch Pictures.

Single and Married. 2012. Dir. Pascal Amanfo. English. Digital video. Ghana and Nigeria. Pascal Amanfo Expression, YN Production, Media GH.

Streets of Calabar. 2012. Dir. Charles Aniagolu and Frank Adekunle Macaulay. English and Pidgin. Digital video. UK and Nigeria. Spirit Creations.

Tango with Me. 2010. Dir. Mahmood Ali-Balogun. English. Celluloid. Nigeria. Mahmood Ali-Balogun.

Taxi Driver. 1983. Dir. Adeyemi Afolayan. Yoruba. Celluloid. Nigeria. Ade Love Films.

Taxi Driver: Oko Ashewo. 2015. Dir. Daniel Emeke Oriahi. Yoruba. Nigeria. Digital video. Nigeria. House5 Production, Orbit Imagery, FilmOne Production.

Terror. 2001. Dir. Teco Benson. English. Digital video. Nigeria. RemmyJes Production.

3 Is Company. 2015. Dir. Ernst Obi. English. Digital video. Nigeria. MMI Productions.

Vigilante. 1988. Dir. Adedeji Adesanya. English. Celluloid and VHS. Nigeria. A-Productions.

Village Headmaster. Series. 1968–74. Dir. Sanya Dosunmu. Created by Segun Olusola. English. Television broadcast and VCD. Nigera. Nigerian Television Authority.

Violated: A Tale of Secrets. 1996. Dir. Amaka Igwe. English and Pidgin. Nigeria. Moving Movies/Crystal Gold.

Visions. 2017. Dir. Abba Makama, Michael Omonua, and C. J. "Fiery" Obasi. English and Pidgin. Nigeria. Digital video. Fiery Film Company, Osiris Creatives, Cine9ja.

Wedding Party. 2016. Dir. Kemi Adetiba. English, Yoruba, and Igbo. Digital video. Nigeria. EbonyLife Films.

Weekend Getaway. 2012. Dir. Emem Isong. English. Digital video. Nigeria. Royal Arts Academy.

When Love Happens. 2014. Dir. Seyi Babatope. English. Digital video. Nigeria. Future Gate Pictures, PHB Films.

BIBLIOGRAPHY

Abbas, Ackbar. "Cinema, the City, and the Cinematic." In *Global Cities: Cinema, Architecture, and Urbanism in a Digital Age*, edited by Linda Krause and Patrice Petro, 142–56. New Brunswick, NJ: Rutgers University Press, 2003.

Abua, Ferdinand O., ed. *Film & Video Directory in Nigeria*. Vol. 1. Abuja: National Film and Video Censors Board, 2002.

Abua, Ferdinand O., ed. *Film & Video Directory in Nigeria*. Vol. 2. Abuja: National Film and Video Censors Board, 2004.

Adedeji, J. A. "Theatre Forms: The Nigerian Dilemma." *Nigeria Magazine* 128 (1979): 26–34.

Adejunmobi, Moradewun. "African Film's Televisual Turn." *Cinema Journal* 54, no. 2 (2015): 120–25.

Adejunmobi, Moradewun. "Charting Nollywood's Appeal Locally and Globally." *African Literature Today* 28 (2010): 106–21.

Adejunmobi, Moradewun. "Neoliberal Rationalities in Old and New Nollywood." *African Studies Review* 58, no. 3 (2015): 31–53.

Adejunmobi, Moradewun. "Nigerian Video Film as Minor Transnational Practice." *Postcolonial Text* 3, no. 2 (2007): 1–16. Accessed June 20, 2015. http://journals.sfu.ca/pocol/index.php/pct/article/view/548/405

Adejunmobi, Moradewun. "Nollywood, Globalization, and Regional Media Corporations in Africa." *Popular Communication* 9, no. 2 (2011): 67–78.

Adejunmobi, Moradewun. "Standup Comedy and the Ethics of Popular Performance in Nigeria." In *Popular Culture in Africa: The Episteme of the Everyday*, edited by Stephanie Newell and Onookome Okome, 175–94. New York: Routledge, 2014.

Adejunmobi, Moradewun. "Streaming Quality, Streaming Cinema." In *A Companion to African Cinema*, edited by Kenneth W. Harrow and Carmela Garritano, 219–43. Hoboken: John Wiley and Sons, 2018.

Adejunmobi, Moradewun. "Video Film Technology and Serial Narratives in West Africa." In *Africa through the Eye of the Video Camera*, edited by Foluke Ogunleye, 51–68. Matsapha, Swaziland: Academic Publishers, 2003.

Adesanya, Afolabi. *Nigerian Film/TV Index*. Lagos: A-Productions Nigeria, 1991.
Adesanya, Afolabi. *Reel Views: A Collection of Essays and Reviews on the Nigerian and African Film Industry*. Jos: Nigerian Film Corporation, 2012.
Adesokan, Akin. "Anticipating Nollywood: Lagos circa 1996." *Social Dynamics* 37, no. 1 (2011): 96–110.
Adesokan, Akin. "Loud in Lagos: Nollywood Videos." *Wasafiri* 19 (2004): 45–49.
Adesokan, Akin. *Postcolonial Artists and Global Aesthetics*. Bloomington: Indiana University Press. 2011.
Adesokan, Akin. "Practicing 'Democracy' in Nigerian Films." *African Affairs* 108, no. 433 (2009): 599–619.
Adichie, Chuma. "Review of Filmshows in the National Theatre for 1982." *Cultural News Bulletin: A Quarterly of the Federal Department of Culture* 3, no. 1 (1983): 11, 15.
Agbiboa, Daniel. "'God's Time Is Best:' The Fascination with Unknown Time in Urban Transport in Lagos." In *The Fascination with Unknown Time*, edited by Sibylle Baumbach, Lena Henningsen, and Klaus Oschema, 167–87. London: Palgrave Macmillan, 2017.
Agbiboa, Daniel. "Informal Urban Governance and Predatory Politics in Africa: The Role of Motor-Park Touts in Lagos." *African Affairs* 117, no. 466 (2018): 62–82.
Agbola, Tunde. *The Architecture of Fear: Urban Design and Construction Response to Urban Violence in Lagos, Nigeria*. Ibadan: Institut Francais de Recherche en Afrique. 1997.
Agina, Añulika. "Cinema-going in Lagos: Three Locations, One Film, One Weekend." *Journal of African Cultural Studies* 32, no. 2 (2020): 131–45.
Ahonsi, Babatunde. "Popular Shaping of Metropolitan Forms and Processes in Nigeria: Glimpses and Interpretations from an Informed Lagosian." In *Under Siege: Four African Cities*, edited by Okwui Enwezor, 129–52. Ostfildern-Ruit: Hatje Cantz, 2003.
Ajibade, Babson. "From Lagos to Douala: The Video Film and Its Spaces of Seeing." *Postcolonial Text* 3, no. 2 (2007): 1–14.
Akande, Lani. "Nollywood Cinema's Character of Recurrence." *Journal of African Cultural Studies* 33, no. 4 (2021): 456–70.
Akinleye, Rufus T. "Contesting for Space in an Urban Centre: The Omo Onile Syndrome in Lagos." In *African Cities: Competing Claims on Urban Space*, edited by Francesca Locatelli and Paul Nugent, 109–34. Leiden: Brill, 2009.
Akinsemoyin, Kunle, and Alan Vaughan-Richards. *Building Lagos*. Jersey, UK: Pengrail, 1977.
Amin, Ash, and Nigel Thrift. *Seeing Like a City*. Malden, MA: Polity Press, 2017.
Anikulapo, Jahman. "The Death Metaphor." In *African Cities Reader III*, edited by Edgar Pieterse. Cape Town: Chimurenga Magazine and African Cities Centre, 2015. Accessed January 8, 2020. https://www.africancentreforcities.net/african-cities-reader-iii-out-now/
Apter, Andrew. "The Pan-African Nation: Oil-Money and the Spectacle of Culture in Nigeria." *Public Culture* 8 (1996): 441–66.

Aradeon, David. "Oshodi: Replanner's Options for a Subcity." *Glendora Review* 2, no. 1 (1997): 51–58.
Bala, P. P. *Annual Performance Report of the Film Verification Unit*. National Film and Video Censors Board. Abuja: Federal Republic of Nigeria, Ministry of Information and Culture, 2007.
Balogun, Francoise. *Cinema in Nigeria*. Enugu: Delta Publications, 1987.
Barad, Karen. *Meeting the Universe Halfway: Quantum Physics and the Entanglement of Matter and Meaning*. Durham, NC: Duke University Press, 2007.
Barber, Karin. *Generation of Plays: Yorùbá Popular Life in Theater*. Bloomington: Indiana University Press, 2003.
Barber, Karin. "Popular Arts in Africa." *African Studies Review* 30, no. 3 (1987): 1–78.
Barber, Karin. "Popular Reactions to Petro-Naira." In *Readings in African Popular Culture*, edited by Karin Barber, 91–99. Bloomington: Indiana University Press, 1997 (1982).
Barber, Karin. "Radical Conservatism in Yoruba Popular Plays." *Bayreuth African Studies Series* 7 (1986): 5–32.
Barrot, Pierre, ed. *Nollywood: The Video Film Phenomenon*. Bloomington, IN: Indiana University Press, 2008 (2005).
Basu, Anastup. *Bollywood in the Age of New Media: The Geo-televisual Aesthetic*. Edinburgh: Edinburgh University Press, 2010.
Bentsi-Enchill, Nii. "Money, Power and Cinema." *West Africa Magazine* August 1982, 2093–94.
Berlant, Lauren. *Cruel Optimism*. Durham, NC: Duke University Press, 2011.
Bordwell, David. *Poetics of Cinema*. New York: Routledge, 2007.
Brooke, James. "Enugu Journal: Thirty Million Nigerians Are Laughing at Themselves." *New York Times*, July 24, 1987.
Brooks, Peter. "Melodrama, Body, Revolution." In *Melodrama: Stage, Picture, Screen*, edited by Jacky Brattan, Kim Cook, and Christine Gledhill, 11–24. London: British Film Institute, 1994.
Brooks, Peter. *The Melodramatic Imagination: Balzac, Henry James, Melodrama, and the Mode of Excess*. New Haven, CT: Yale University Press, 1976.
Brown, Matthew H. "The Enchanted History of Nigerian State Television." In *State and Culture in Postcolonial Africa*, edited by Tejumola Olaniyan, 94–110. Bloomington: Indiana University Press, 2016.
Brunsdon, Charlotte. "The Attractions of the Cinematic City." *Screen* 53, no. 3 (2012): 209–27.
Brunsdon, Charlotte. *Television Cities: London, Paris, Baltimore*. Durham, NC: Duke University Press, 2018.
Brunsdon, Charlotte. "Towards a History of Empty Spaces." In *The City and the Moving Image: Urban Projections*, edited by Richard Koeck and Les Roberts, 91–103. London: Palgrave Macmillan, 2010.

Bud, Alexander. "The End of Nollywood's Guilded Age? Marketers, the State and the Struggle for Distribution." *Critical African Studies* 6, no. 1 (2014): 91–121.
Butler, Judith. *The Psychic Life of Power: Theories in Subjection*. Stanford: University of California Press, 1997.
Castellote, Jess, and Tobenna Okwuosa. "Lagos Art World: The Emergence of an Artistic Hub on the Global Art Periphery." *African Studies Review* 62, no. 1 (2019): 1–27.
Castells, Manuel. *The Rise of the Network Society*. Cambridge, MA: Blackwell, 1996.
Comaroff, Jean, and John L. Comaroff. "Millennial Capitalism: First Thoughts on a Second Coming." *Public Culture* 12, no. 2 (2000): 291–343.
Comaroff, Jean, and John L. Comaroff, eds. *Modernity and Its Malcontents: Ritual and Power in Postcolonial Africa*. Chicago: University of Chicago Press, 1993.
Cruikshank, Barbara. "Revolutions Within: Self-Government and Self-Esteem." In *Foucault and Political Reason: Liberalism, Neo-liberalism, and Rationalities of Government*, edited by Andrew Berry, Thomas Osborne, and Nikolas Rose, 231–52. Chicago: University of Chicago Press, 1996.
Curtin, Michael. "Comparing Media Capitals: Hong Kong and Mumbai." *Global Media and Communication* 6, no. 3 (2010): 263–70.
Curtin, Michael. "Media Capital: Towards the Study of Spatial Flows." *International Journal of Cultural Studies* 6, no. 2 (2003): 201–28.
Curtin, Michael, and Kevin Sanson, eds. *Voices of Labor: Creativity, Craft, and Conflict in Global Hollywood*. Berkeley: University of California Press, 2017.
Curtin, Michael, and Kevin Sanson, eds. *Precarious Creativity: Global Media, Local Labor*. Berkeley: University of California Press, 2016.
Davies, Lanre. "Gentrification in Lagos, 1929–1990." *Urban History* 45, no. 4 (2018): 712–32.
Deleyto, Celestino. *The Secret Life of Romantic Comedy*. Manchester: Manchester University Press, 2011.
Diawara, Manthia. *African Cinema: Politics and Culture*. Bloomington: Indian University Press, 1992.
Diawara, Manthia. "Toward a Regional Imaginary in Africa." In *The Cultures of Globalization*, edited by Fredric Jameson and Masao Miyoshi, 103–24. Durham, NC: Duke University Press, 1998.
De Boeck, Filip. "'Divining' the City: Rhythm, Amalgamation and Knotting as Forms of 'Urbanity.'" *Social Dynamics: A Journal of African Studies* 41, no. 1 (2015): 56.
De Boeck, Filip. "Kinshasa and Its (Im)material Infrastructure." In *Cities of the Global South Reader*, edited by Faranak Miraftab and Neema Kudva, 188–91. New York: Routledge, 2015 (2005).
De Boeck, Filip, and Marie-Francoise Plissart. *Kinshasa: Tales of the Invisible City*. Ghent-Amsterdam: Ludion, 2005.
Dogbe, Esi. "Elusive Modernity: Portraits of the City in Popular Ghanaian Video." In *Leisure in Urban Africa*, edited by Paul Tiyambe Zeleza and Cassandra Rachel Veney, 227–47. Trenton, NJ: Africa World Press, 2003.

Dovey, Lindiwe. "African Film and Video: Pleasure, Politics, Performance." *Journal of African Cultural Studies* 22, no. (2010): 1–6.

Dresser, David. "Global Noir: Genre Film in the Age of Transnationalism." In *Film Genre Reader IV*, edited by Barry Keith Grant, 628–48. Austin: University of Texas Press, 2012.

During, Simon. "Popular Culture on a Global Scale: A Challenge to Cultural Studies?" *Critical Inquiry* 23, no. 4 (1997): 808–33.

Ekeh, Peter. "Colonialism and the Two Publics in Africa: A Theoretical Statement." *Comparative Studies in Society and History* 17, no. 1 (1975): 91–112.

Ekwuazi, Hyginus. *Film in Nigeria*. Ibadan: Moonlight Publishers for the Nigerian Film Corporation, 1987.

Elsaesser, Thomas. "Cinephilia or the Uses of Disenchantment." In *Cinephilia, Movies, Love and Memory*, edited by Marijke de Valck and Malte Hagener, 27–43. Amsterdam: Amsterdam University Press, 2005.

Enem, Uche. "National Theatre Profile." *Nigeria Magazine*, 128/129 (1979): 35–53.

Esan, Oluyinka. *Nigerian Television: Fifty Years of Television in Africa*. Princeton: AMV Publishing, 2009.

Ezepue, Ezinne, M. "The New Nollywood: Professionalization or Gentrification of Cultural Industry." *SAGE Open* 9 (2020): 1–10. https://doi.org/10.1177/2158244020940994

Falola, Toyin, and Matthew Heaton. *A History of Nigeria*. Cambridge: Cambridge University Press, 2008.

Farías, Ignacio, and Thomas Bender, eds. *Urban Assemblages: How Actor-Network Theory Changes Urban Studies*. London: Routledge, 2009.

Fatunla, Tayo. "Cityscapes: Lagos, West Africa's Playground." *New African Magazine*, March 15, 2017. Accessed January 8, 2020. https://newafricanmagazine.com/15143/

Fay, Jennifer, and Justus Nieland. *Film Noir: Hard-Boiled Modernity and the Cultures of Globalization*. New York: Routledge, 2010.

Ferguson, James. *Expectations of Modernity: Myths and Meanings of Urban Life on the Zambian Copperbelt*. Berkeley: University of California Press, 1999.

Ferguson, James. *Give a Man a Fish: Reflections on the New Politics of Distribution*. Durham, NC: Duke University Press, 2015.

Ferguson, James. *Global Shadows: Africa in the Neoliberal World Order*. Durham, NC: Duke University Press, 2006.

Festac '77. London: African Journal and the International Festival Committee, 1977.

Feuer, Jane. "Narrative Form in American Network Television." In *High Theory, Low Culture: Analysing Popular Television and Film*, edited by Colin McCabe, 610–19. Manchester: Manchester University Press, 1986.

Fourchard, Laurent. "Bureaucrats and Indigenes: Producing and Bypassing Certificates of Origin in Nigeria." *Africa* 85, no. 1 (2015): 37–58.

Friedberg, Anne. *Window Shopping: Cinema and the Postmodern*. Berkeley: University of California Press, 1993.

Galt, Rosalind and Karl Schoonover, eds. *Global Art Cinema: New Theories and Histories*. Oxford: Oxford University Press, 2010.
Gandy, Matthew. "Learning from Lagos." *New Left Review* 33 (2005): 36–52.
Gandy, Matthew. "Planning, Anti-Planning and the Infrastructure Crisis Facing Metropolitan Lagos." *Urban Studies* 43, no. 2 (2006): 371–96.
Ganti, Tejaswini. "Sentiments of Disdain and Practices of Distinction: Boundary-Work, Subjectivity, and Value in the Hindi Film Industry." *Anthropological Quarterly* 85, no. 1 (2012): 5–43.
Ganti, Tejaswini. "Fuzzy Numbers: The Productive Nature of Ambiguity in the Hindi Film Industry." *Comparative Studies of South Asia, Africa and the Middle East* 35, no 3 (2015): 451-465.
Garritano, Carmela. *African Video Movies and Global Desires: A Ghanaian History*. Athens: Ohio University Press, 2013.
Garritano, Carmela. "Nollywood: An Archive of African Worldliness." *Black Camera: An International Film Journal* 5, no. 2 (2014): 44–52.
Geraghty, Christine. *Women and Soap Opera: A Study of Prime Time Soaps*. Cambridge, UK: Polity Press, 1991.
Geschiere, Peter, ed. *The Modernity of Witchcraft: Politics and the Occult in Postcolonial Africa*. Charlottesville: University of Virginia Press, 1997.
Gledhill, Christine. "Speculations on the Relationship between Soap Opera and Melodrama." *Quarterly Review of Film and Video* 14, no. 1–2 (1992): 103–24.
Glissant, Edouard. *Poetics of Relation*. Translated by Betsy Wing. Ann Arbor: University of Michigan Press, 1997.
Green-Simms, Lindsay. "Occult Melodrama: Spectral Affect and West African Video-Film." *Camera Obscura* 27, no. 2 (2012): 25–59.
Green-Simms, Lindsay. *Postcolonial Automobility: Car Culture in West Africa*. Minneapolis: University of Minnesota Press, 2017.
Griswold, Wendy. *Bearing Witness: Readers, Writers, and the Novel in Nigeria*. Princeton: Princeton University Press, 2000.
Gugler, Josef. "Life in a Dual System: Eastern Nigerians in Town, 1961." *Cahiers d'Etudes Africaines* 11, no. 43 (1964): 400–412.
Gugler, Josef. "Life in a Dual System Revisited: Urban-Rural Ties in Enugu, Nigeria, 1961-87." *World Development* 19, no. 5 (1991): 399–409.
Hansen, Miriam Bratu. *Cinema and Experience: Siegfried Kracauer, Walter Benjamin, and Theodor W. Adorno*. Berkeley: University of California Press, 2011.
Hardt, Michael. "Affective Labor." *boundary 2* 26, no. 2 (1999): 89–100.
Harney, Stefano. "Creative Industries Debate." *Cultural Studies* 24, no. 3 (2010): 431–44.
Harney, Stefano, and Fred Moten. *The Undercommons: Fugitive Planning and Black Study*. New York: Minor Compositions, 2013.
Haynes, Jonathan, and Onookome Okome. "Evolving Popular Media: Nigerian Video Films." In *Nigerian Video Films*, ed. Jonathan Haynes, 51–88. Athens: Ohio University Press, 2000.

Haynes, Jonathan. "Keeping Up: The Corporatization of Nollywood's Economy and Paradigms for Studying African Screen Media." *Africa Today* 64, no. 4 (2018): 2–29.
Haynes, Jonathan. "Neoliberalism, Nollywood and Lagos." In *Global Cinematic Cityscapes: New Landscapes of Film and Media*, edited by Johan Andersson and Lawrence Webb, 59–75. New York: Wallflower Press, 2015.
Haynes, Jonathan. "Nigerian Cinema: Structural Adjustments." In *Cinema and Change in West Africa*, edited by Onookome Okome and Jonathan Haynes, 2–41. Jos: Nigerian Film Corporation, 1995.
Haynes, Jonathan, ed. *Nigerian Video Films*. Athens: Ohio University Press, 2000.
Haynes, Jonathan. "Nollywood in Lagos, Lagos in Nollywood Films." *Africa Today* 54, no. 2 (2007): 130–50.
Haynes, Jonathan. *Nollywood: The Creation of Nigerian Film Genres*. Chicago: University of Chicago Press, 2016.
Hockenberry, Matthew, Nicole Starosielski, and Susan Zieger, eds. *Assembly Codes: The Logistics of Media*. Durham, NC: Duke University Press, 2021.
Holston, James, and Arjun Appadurai. "Cities and Citizenship." *Public Culture* 8 (1996): 187–204.
Ihonvbere, Julius. "Are Things Falling Apart? The Military Crisis of Democratisation in Nigeria." *Journal of Modern African Studies* 34, no. 2 (1996): 193–225.
Ihonvbere, Julius, and Timothy Shaw. *Illusions of Power: Nigeria in Transition*. Trenton, NJ: Africa World Press, 1998.
Iwara, A.U., and E. Mveng, eds. *Colloquium Proceedings on Black Civilization and Education, Lagos, 17th–31st January, 1977*. Lagos: Federal Military Government of Nigeria, 1977.
Jagoda, Patrick. *Network Aesthetics*. Chicago: University of Chicago Press, 2016.
Jedlowski, Alessandro. "African Media and the Corporate Takeover: Video Film Circulation in the Age of Neoliberal Transformations." *African Affairs* 116, no. 465 (2016): 671–91.
Jedlowski, Alessandro. "Nigerian Videos in the Global Arena: The Postcolonial Exotic Revisited." *Global South* 7, no. 1 (2013): 157–78.
Jedlowski, Alessandro. "Small Screen Cinema: Informality and Remediation in Nollywood." *Television and New Media* 13, no. 5 (2012): 431–46.
Jeyifo, Biodun. *The Yoruba Popular Travelling Theatre of Nigeria*. Lagos: Federal Ministry of Social Development, Youth, Sports and Culture, 1984.
Koolhaas, Rem, et al. *Mutations*. New York: Actar, 2001.
Krings, Matthais, and Onookome Okome, eds. *Global Nollywood: The Transnational Dimensions of an African Video Film Industry*. Bloomington: Indiana University Press, 2013.
Kristeva, Julia. "Word, Dialogue and Novel." In *The Julia Kristeva Reader*, edited by Toril Moi. New York: Columbia University Press, 1986.
Lakoju, Tunde. "Popular (Traveling) Theatre in Nigeria: The Example of Moses Olaiya Adejumo (alias Baba Sala)." *Nigeria Magazine* 149 (1984): 35–46.

Larkin, Brian. "The Grounds of Circulation: Rethinking African Film and Media." *Politique Africaine* 153 (2019): 105–26.

Larkin, Brian. "Hausa Dramas and the Rise of Video Culture in Nigeria." In *Nigerian Video Film*, edited by Jonathan Haynes, 227–28. Athens: Ohio University Press, 2000.

Larkin, Brian. "The Politics and Poetics of Infrastructure." *Annual Review of Anthropology* 42 (2013): 327–43.

Larkin, Brian. *Signal and Noise: Media, Infrastructure, and Urban Culture in Nigeria*. Durham, NC: Duke University Press, 2008.

Lazzarato, Maurizio. "Immaterial Labor." Generation Online. 2003. Accessed January 8, 2020. http://www.generation-online.org/c/fcimmateriallabour3.htm

Lefebvre, Henri. *The Production of Space*. Translated by Donald Nicholson-Smith. Cambridge, MA: Blackwell, 1991 (1974).

Levine, Caroline. *Forms: Whole, Rhythm, Hierarchy, Network*. Princeton: Princeton University Press, 2015.

Lobato, Ramon. *Shadow Economies of Cinema: Mapping Informal Film Distribution*. London: Plagrave Macmillan for British Film Institute, 2012.

Mabogunje, Akin. "An Introspection into the Urban Modernity of Lagos." In *Lagos: A City at Work*, edited by Ololade Bamidele, 268–351. Lagos: Glendora Books, 2001.

Makhubu, Nomusa. "'This House Is Not for Sale': Nollywood's Spatial Politics and Concepts of 'Home' in Zina Saro-Wiwa's Art." *African Arts* 49, no. 4 (2016): 58–69.

Malaquais, Dominique. "Douala/Johannesburg/New York: Cityscapes Imagined." In *Cities in Contemporary Africa*, edited by Martin J. Murray and Garth A. Myers, 53–70. London: Palgrave Macmillan, 2006.

Marshall, Ruth. *Political Spiritualities: The Pentecostal Revolution in Nigeria*. Chicago: University of Chicago Press, 2009.

Massey, Doreen. *For Space*. London: Sage, 2005.

Mazumdar, Ranjani. *Bombay Cinema: An Archive of the City*. Minneapolis: University of Minnesota Press, 2008.

Mbembe, Achille. "Aesthetics of Superfluity." In *Johannesburg: The Elusive Metropolis*, edited by Sarah Nuttall and Achille Mbembe, 37–67. Durham, NC: Duke University Press, 2008.

Mbembe, Achille. *On the Postcolony*. Berkeley: University of California Pres, 2001.

McCall, John. "The Capital Gap: Nollywood and the Limits of Informal Trade." *Journal of African Cinemas* 4, no. 1 (2012): 9–23.

McFarlane, Colin. *Learning the City: Knowledge and Translocal Assemblage*. Hoboken, NJ: John Wiley and Sons, 2011.

Meyer, Birgit. "'Praise the Lord': Popular Cinema and Pentecostalite Style in Ghana's New Public Sphere." *American Ethnologist* 31, no. 1 (2004): 92–110.

Meyer, Birgit. *Sensational Movies: Video, Vision, and Christianity in Ghana*. Berkeley: University of California Press, 2015.

Miller, Jade. *Nollywood Central*. New York: Bloomsbury for British Film Institute, 2016.

Mitter, Siddhartha. "Lagos, City of Hustle, Builds an Art 'Ecosystem.'" *New York Times*, February 8, 2019. Accessed January 8, 2020. https://www.nytimes.com/2019/02/08/arts/design/lagos-nigeria-art-x-art.html

Momoh, Abubakar. "Youth Culture and Area Boys in Lagos." In *Identity Transformation and Identity Politics under Structural Adjustment in Nigeria*, edited by Attahiru Jega, 186–88. Uppsala: Nordic Africa Institute, 2000.

Newell, Sasha. *Modernity Bluff: Crime, Consumption, and Citizenship in Côte d'Ivoire.* Chicago: University of Chicago Press, 2012.

Newell, Stephanie. *Histories of Dirt: Media and Urban Life in Colonial and Postcolonial Lagos.* Durham, NC: Duke University Press, 2019.

Nuttall, Sarah. *Entanglement: Literary and Cultural Reflections on Post-Apartheid.* Johannesburg: Wits University Press, 2009.

Nuttall, Sarah, and Achille Mbembe. "A Blasé Attitude: A Response to Michael Watts." *Public Culture* 17, no. 1 (2005): 193–201.

Nuttall, Sarah, and Achille Mbembe, eds. *Johannesburg: The Elusive Metropolis.* Durham, NC: Duke University Press, 2008.

Obono, Oka. "A Lagos Thing: Rules and Realities in the Nigerian Megacity." *Georgetown Journal of International Affairs* 8, no. 2 (2007): 31–37.

Ofeimun, Odia. "Imagination and the City." *Glendora Review: African Quarterly on the Arts* 3, no. 2 (1998): 12–15, 137–41.

Ogundele, Wole. "From Folk Opera to Soap Opera: Improvisations and Transformations in Yoruba Popular Theater." In *Nigerian Video Films*, ed. Jonathan Haynes, 89–130. Athens: Ohio University Press. 2000.

Ogunleye, Foluke, ed. *Africa through the Eye of the Video Camera.* Matsapha, Swaziland: Academic Publishers, 2003.

Oha, Obododimma. "The Visual Rhetoric of the Ambivalent City in Nigerian Video Films." In *Cinema and the City*, edited by Mark Shiel and Tony Fitzmaurice, 195–205. Oxford: Blackwell, 2001.

Okiti, Tega. "Surreal16: The Filmmaking Collective Trying to Forge a New Identity for Nigerian Cinema." *Sight and Sound*, September 8, 2018. https://www2.bfi.org.uk/news-opinion/sight-sound-magazine/interviews/surreal16-collective-nigerian-art-house-cinema-nollywood

Okome, Onoookome. "Nollywood: Spectatorship, Audience, and Sites of Consumption." *Postcolonial Text* 3, no. 2 (2007): 1–21.

Okome, Onoookome. "Nollywood, Lagos and the *Good-Time* Woman." *Research in African Literatures* 43, no. 4 (2012): 166–86.

Okome, Onoookome. "Writing the Anxious City: Images of Lagos in Nigerian Home Video Films." *Black Renaissance / Renaissance Noire* 5, no. 2 (2003): 65–75.

Okome, Onookome, and Jonathan Haynes, eds. *Cinema and Change in West Africa.* Jos: Nigerian Film Corporation, 1995.

Olaniyan, Tejumola. *Arrest the Music!: Fela and His Rebel Art and Politics.* Lagos: Kraft Books, 2009 (2004).

Olukoju, Ayodeji. *Infrastructure Development and Urban Facilities in Lagos, 1861–2000*. Ibadan: French Institute for Research in Africa (IFRA), 2003.

Olusola, Segun. "Film-TV and the Arts: The African Experience." In *Mass Communication in Nigeria: A Book of Reading [sic]*, edited by Onuora E. Nwuneli, 137–76. Enugu: Fourth Dimension Publishers, 1985.

Omezi, Giles. "Nigerian Modernity and the City: Lagos 1960–1980." In *The Arts of Citizenship in African Cities: Infrastructures and Spaces of Belonging*, edited by Mamadou Diouf and Rosalind Fredericks, 277–95. London: Palgrave Macmillan, 2014.

Opubor, Alfred E., and Onuora E. Nwuneli, eds. *The Development and Growth of the Film Industry in Nigeria*. Lagos: Third Press International, 1979.

Oreh, O. O. "*Masquerade* and Other Plays on Nigerian Television." In *Mass Communication, Culture, and Society in West Africa*, ed. F. O. Ugboajah, 108–12. New York: Hans Zell, 1985.

Osaghae, Eghosa. *The Crippled Giant: Nigeria since Independence*. Bloomington: Indiana University Press, 1998.

Osundare, Niyi. "A Grand Escape into Metaphysics." *West Africa Magazine*, May 1980, 827.

Osundare, Niyi. "The King of Laughter." *West Africa Magazine*, July 1982, 1821.

Ouellette, Laurie, and James Hay. "Makeover Television, Governmentality, and the Good Citizen." *Continuum* 22, no. 4 (2008): 471–84.

Overbergh, Ann. "Kenya's Riverwood: Market Structure, Power Relations, and Future Outlooks." *Journal of African Cinemas* 7, no. 2 (2015): 97–115.

Oyedele, Wale. "Aspects of the Yoruba Popular Films." *Journal of Cultural Studies* 2, no. 1 (2000): 340–49.

Petty, Sheila. "Cities, Subjects, Sites: Sub-Saharan Cinema and the Reorganization of Knowledge." *Afterimage* 19 (1991): 10–11, 18.

Pfaff, Francoise. "African Cities as Cinematic Texts." In *Focus on African Films*, edited by Francoise Pfaff, 89–106. Bloomington: Indiana University Press, 2004.

Povinelli, Elizabeth. *Economies of Abandonment: Social Belonging and Endurance in Late Liberalism*. Durham, NC: Duke University Press, 2011.

Povinelli, Elizabeth. *Empire of Love: Toward a Theory of Intimacy, Genealogy, and Carnality*. Durham, NC: Duke University Press, 2006.

Prado, Ignacio Sanchez. *Screening Neoliberalism: Transforming Mexican Cinema, 1988–2012*. Nashville: Vanderbilt University Press, 2014.

Quayson, Ato. *Oxford Street, Accra: City Life and the Itineraries of Transnationalism*. Durham, NC: Duke University Press, 2014.

Rai, Amit. *Untimely Bollywood: Globalization and India's New Media Assemblage*. Durham, NC: Duke University Press, 2009.

Rancière, Jacques. *Dissensus: On Politics and Aesthetics*. Translated by Steven Corcoran. New York: Continuum, 2010.

Robinson, Jennifer. *Ordinary Cities: Between Modernity and Development*. New York: Routledge, 2006.

Robinson, Jennifer, and Ananya Roy. "Debate on Global Urbanisms and the Nature of Urban Theory." *International Journal of Urban and Regional Research* 40, no. 1 (2016): 181–86.

Rose, Nikolas. "Governing 'Advanced' Liberal Democracies." In *Foucault and Political Reason: Liberalism, Neo-liberalism, and Rationalities of Government*, edited by Andrew Berry, Thomas Osborne, and Nikolas Rose, 37–64. Chicago: University of Chicago Press, 1996.

Roy, Ananya. "The 21st-Century Metropolis: New Geographies of Theory." *Regional Studies* 43, no. 6 (2009): 819–30.

Roy, Ananya, and Aihwa Ong, eds. *Worlding Cities: Asian Experiments and the Art of Being Global*. Malden, MA: Blackwell, 2011.

Ryan, Connor. "Nollywood and the Limits of Informality." Interview with Tunde Kelani, Bond Emeruwa, and Emem Isong. *Black Camera: An International Film Journal* 5, no. 2 (2014): 168–85.

Saul, Mahir, and Ralph A. Austen, eds. *Viewing African Cinema in the Twenty-First Century: Art Films and the Nollywood Video Revolution*. Athens: University Ohio Press, 2010.

Shiel, Mark, and Tony Fitzmaurice, eds. *Cinema and the City: Film and Urban Societies in a Global Context*. Malden, MA: Blackwell, 2001.

Simone, AbdouMaliq. *City Life from Jakarta to Dakar: Movements at the Crossroads*. New York: Routledge, 2010.

Simone, AbdouMaliq. *For the City Yet to Come: Changing African Life in Four Cities*. Durham, NC: Duke University Press, 2004.

Simone, AbdouMaliq. *Improvised Lives: Rhythms of Endurance in an Urban South*. Medford, MA: Polity Press, 2019.

Simone, AbdouMaliq. "People as Infrastructure." In *Johannesburg: The Elusive Metropolis*, edited by Sarah Nuttall and Achille Mbembe, 68–90. Durham, NC: Duke University Press, 2008.

Simone, AbdouMaliq. "Urban Social Fields in Africa." *Social Text* 56 (1998): 71–89.

Smith, Daniel Jordan. *A Culture of Corruption: Everyday Deception and Popular Discontent in Nigeria*. Princeton: Princeton University Press, 2007.

Spronk, Rachel. "Media and the Therapeutic Ethos of Romantic Love in Middle-Class Nairobi." In *Love in Africa*, edited by Jennifer Cole and Lynn M. Thomas, 181–203. Chicago: Chicago University Press, 2009.

Subirós, Pep. "Lagos: Surviving Hell." In *Africas: the Artist and the City: A Journey Exhibition*, 34-45. (Barcelona: Centre de Cultura Contemporània de Barcelona: 2001).

Sundaram, Ravi. *Pirate Modernity: Delhi's Media Urbanism*. New York: Routledge, 2010.

"'Surreal 16' Set Vision for New Wave of Nigerian Film." *France 24 English*, May 12, 2022. Accessed May 14, 2022. https://youtu.be/EB_wYuSjenk

Taylor, Dianna. "Practices of the Self." In *Michel Foucault: Key Concepts*, edited by Dianna Taylor, 173–86. Durham, NC: Acumen Press, 2011.

Tcheuyap, Alexie. *Postnational African Cinemas*. New York: Manchester University Press, 2011.

Thrift, Nigel. *Non-Representational Theory: Space, Politics, Affect*. New York: Routledge, 2008.

Tomaselli, Keyan G., and Arnold Shepperson. "Transformation and South African Cinema in the 1990s." In *Critical Approaches to African Cinema Discourse*, edited by Nwachukwu Frank Ukadike, 107–34. Lanham, MD: Lexington Books, 2014.

Tsika, Noah. "From Yoruba to YouTube: Studying Nollywood's Star System." *Black Camera: An International Film Journal* 5, no. 2 (2014): 95–115.

Tsika, Noah. *Nollywood Stars: Media and Migration in West Africa and the Diaspora*. Bloomington: Indiana University Press, 2015.

Ukadike, Nwachukwu Frank. *Black African Cinema*. Berkeley: University of California Press, 1994.

Ward, Janet. *Weimar Surfaces: Urban Visual Culture in 1920s Germany*. Berkeley: University of California Press, 2001.

Weeks, Kathi. "Life within and against Work: Affective Labor, Feminist Critique, and Post-Fordist Politics." *Ephemera* 7, no. 1 (2007): 233–49.

Weeks, Kathi. *The Problem with Work: Feminism, Marxism, Antiwork Politics, and Postwork Imaginaries*. Durham, NC: Duke University Press, 2011.

Yaeger, Patricia. "Introduction: Dreaming of Infrastructure." *PMLA* 122, no. 1 (2007): 9–26.

INDEX

abandonment, 24, 106–8, 117
Abeokuta (Nigeria), 144–45
Abuja (Nigeria), 72, 170, 175
Adekola, Odulade, 1,129, 187, 207, 210
Adejunmobi, Moradewun, 109; distribution, 125, 149; New Nollywood, 167, 176, 241n47
Adesanya, Afolabi, 43, 46, 63, 224n48
Adesokan, Akin, 63, 101, 119; aesthetics of exhortation, 17, 92
affect, 17, 25, 124, 147, 204; and family, 106, 112, 115; spatialized, 36, 75–76, 133
affective socialization, 79, 187, 192, 195, 199
Afolayan, Adeyemi ("Ade Love"), 34, 45, 51
Afolayan, Kunle, 51, 137, 143–45, 210; production practices, 140–42
Agbaje Omo Onile (Adebayo Tijani), 205, 208–10
Agbiboa, Daniel, 234n75
Agina, Añulika, 135
Ajibade, Babson, 237n24
Akande, Lani, 92, 128, 208
Akindele, Funke ("Jenifa"), 1, 128–30, 163
Akinleye, Rufus, 83
Alaba (Lagos), 20, 123, 186, 209
ambivalence, 12–15, 27, 211; toward infrastructure, 36, 45; as methodology, 146, 204; and morality, 87; and social connections, 102, 107, 180–81; spectatorial, 56, 119; of visible city, 31, 34–36. See

also contingency; provisionality
Amin, Ash, 94, 97
Anikulapo, Jahman, 48
anonymity, 108–9, 216n22
Aradeon, David, 24, 216n32
archive, 57–60
area boys, 111, 118–19, 200
Asaba (Nigeria), 61
audiences, 13–14, 18; data collection on, 155–56; diaspora, 124, 152; of early Nigerian films, 29, 37, 46, 59; enclosure of, 25, 148–49, 209; local, 126–27, 129, 202, 208; multiplex cinema, 134–35; television, 64–65

Balogun, Ola, 29, 50, 55, 63, 199, 222n20; Festac '77, 44–46
Barad, Karen, 97–98, 110, 117, 120, 231n38, 232n45, 233n67
Barber, Karin, 12, 37, 50–51, 54–55, 209
Basu, Anastup, 143, 145
Basi and Company (Ken Saro-Wiwa), 22; ethnicity, 77–79; television sitcom, 71–74, 82; visible city, 66–68, 70, 76
Berlant, Lauren, 229n8
Blu Pictures Distribution, 135
body/bodies, 103, 168, 207; and rituals, 53; spectatorial 36, 41–42, 132, 134; in urban space, 99
boundary work, 161–62, 170, 241n36
Brown, Matthew, 64

Brunsdon, Charlotte, 3, 62, 67, 70–71
built environments, 29, 48, 91, 94; envisioned, 34–36, 62, 99
Butler, Judith, 98, 180

capture, 181, 209, 216n29
Carter Bridge, 32, 74
character of recurrence, 92–93, 128, 208
Church Missionary Society (Lagos), 34, 182
cinema theaters, 58, 142, 153, 157, 182, 205; ambient experience in, 42, 48, 132–34, 139; formalization of film industry, 23, 123–25, 136–37, 148, 191; multiplexes, 24, 131–35; urban space, 18, 21, 59–60, 184, 206. *See also* New Nollywood
cinematic city, 4, 62
cinephilia, 187, 193, 195–96, 199
circulation: as dimension of city life, 18, 94 109, 138; of films 18, 20, 148–49; of money, 31, 55, 113. *See also* networks
city situations, 70–71, 77
classes. *See* social classes
combinational narration, 93–94, 103, 116–17, 119–20
comedy, 83, 129
consumerism, 124, 133–34, 168, 193
contingency, 6, 9–10, 204. *See also* ambivalence; provisionality
corporatization. *See* formalization
creative labor, 24, 148–50, 158–60, 180
crime, 88, 102, 112–13, 118–19; in New Nollywood, 182–83, 191–92, 195
Curtin, Michael, 153, 154

dark films, 183–84, 187, 190; and affective socialization, 192; and global noir, 194–95; noir stylization of, 182, 190
De Boeck, Filip, 87, 96, 99
diaspora, 142–43, 152, 185, 191
Diawara, Manthia, 20
Died Wretched (Kenneth Nnebue): 22, 106, 117; social network, 89–91
distinction, practices of, 161, 170, 196
distribution, 18–19, 23, 125, 205, 234n4; and cinema theaters, 131, 134–37; formalization of, 148, 152–53; informal economy of, 20–21, 136, 152
Dogbe, Esi, 62, 76
Domitilla (Zeb Ejiro), 16, 93, 119
Dovey, Lindiwe, 4

Eastern Nigeria Television Network (ENTV), 64, 66
EbonyLifeTV, 148, 163; production practices, 154, 156, 161, 162
Ebute Metta (Lagos), 192
Edosio, Ema, 161–62, 186
Ekeh, Peter, 112–13, 114
Eko Bridge, 32, 35, 70
Èkó ò ní bàjé, 5
Ekwuasi, Hyginus, 224n48, 237n24
enclosure, 4; within film industry, 26, 146–47, 154, 158, 209–210; and individual freedom, 176, 180–81; narrative closure as, 82, 90, 174, 179; as response to social obligations, 24–25; urban spaces of, 132–34, 184–85. *See also* formalization; logistical management
enregister, 17, 71, 91, 202, 204
entanglement, 4; of city and film industry, 12, 22, 158, 184, 187; of city and village, 115–17; of family bonds, 107, 208; Karen Barad's notion of, 97–99; moral economy's enactment of, 25, 109–10, 117, 120; with neighbors, 73, 101–2; of social connection, 89, 94–96, 102–3, 122. *See also* mutuality; networks
ENTV (Eastern Nigeria Television Network), 64, 66
Enugu (Nigeria), 64–66, 72, 83
Esan, Oluyinka, 64
ethnic groups, 6, 87, 159, 242n56; in *Basi and Company*, 77–79; and civic consciousness, 79; and entanglement, 101, 110; in *Fuji House of Commotion*, 80–81; in *Lagos Na Wah!!*, 83–84; in *New Masquerade*, 65–66; in New Nollywood, 170, 172–75, 179; Yoruba ethnicity v. Lagos indigeneity, 82–83
exhibitionism, 17, 56, 129–30, 168

families: as constraint v. support, 16, 89, 107, 165–66; as cross-section of wider community, 65, 79–81; as figure of good life, 41, 113; linked to the village, 90, 114–16, 144–45; in New Nollywood, 172–74. See also moral economy
Ferguson, James, 109, 138
Festac '77 (Second World Festival of Black and African Arts and Culture), 29–30, 205; infrastructure, 43–45, 221n10, 224n43; celluloid Nigerian cinema, 223nn41–42
Filmhouse Cinemas, 131, 134, 148, 184. See also Film One Distribution
film noir. See dark films
FilmOne Distribution, 23, 148, 154; production practices, 156, 161, 189. See also Filmhouse Cinemas
flexible accumulation, 148–49, 153, 155, 158
Flower Girl (Michelle Bello), 168
formalization, 13, 196, 209; and cinema theatres, 125–26, 136–37; corporatization, 23, 147–49, 163; of distribution, 152–53, 155; and enclosure, 25–26, 154, 180–81; and gender, 150; and sponsorships, 142–43
Fourchard, Laurent, 227n41
freedom, 9, 110, 133, 165–66, 176
Fuji House of Commotion (Amaka Igwe), 74, 80–82

Gandy, Matthew, 221n8
Ganti, Tejaswini, 136, 161, 196
Garritano, Carmela, 17, 56, 124, 126, 132, 168
Gbomo Gbomo Express (Walter Taylaur), 26, 192, 194–95; visible city, 192–93, 195–96
gender, 93, 151, 158, 162–63
generic space, 75–76, 87
Genesis Deluxe Cinemas, 131
genre: in celluloid Nigerian films, 28; and combinational narration, 93; mainstream v. New Nollywood, 183–84, 187

Ghanaian films, 17, 46, 56, 165, 168; urban spaces in, 76, 132
globalization, 10, 27, 138, 153
good life, 10–11, 89, 98, 113, 177, 181, 229n8
governmentality, 26, 179, 181, 239n14
Green-Simms, Lindsey, 36

Harney, Stefano, 149, 202
Hausa, 77, 79, 176
Haynes, Jonathan, 14, 20, 55–56, 191; genre, 107, 115, 184–85; *Living in Bondage*, 93, 115–16; television, 62–63; visible city, 61, 91
homelessness, 70, 108–10, 119, 232n57
homosexuality, 201–2

Ibadan (Nigeria), 64, 77
Idumota (Lagos), 18–20, 57, 59, 129, 208
Igbo: ethnic group, 81, 90, 106, 173; language, 115, 174
Igwe, Amaka, 67, 74, 80, 105, 105, 241
Iganmu (Lagos), 30, 43
Ikeja (Lagos), 1–2, 33, 186
Ikoyi (Lagos), 24, 31, 184, 186
improvisation, 12, 179
informal economy: corporate dependence on, 148, 153–54; of distribution, 20–21, 136, 152; and gender, 150, 161, 163; and general intellect, 26, 209; and production practices, 156–58
infrastructure: in African cities, 23, 33, 232n48; breakdown of, 48; NAT as, 42, 45; people as, 21–22, 26, 96, 102; synonymous with visible city, 35, 61, 78, 91; transportation, 32–33, 36, 99
insecurity, 16, 91, 183, 191
intertextuality, 189–90, 193, 202
intimacy, 233n68; and romantic love, 171–72; and vulnerability, 105, 116, 119
iROKOtv, 23, 26, 206; formalization of film industry, 148, 149, 152–54; and *Jenifa* franchise, 128, 130; language, 242n56; production practices, 155–57, 160–61, 240n30; women in film industry, 162. See also ROK Studios

itineraries, 13, 20, 95
Isong, Emem, 162, 235n8; production practices, 126–27

Jankara (Lagos), 7
Jedlowski, Alessandro, 139; distribution, 137, 148
Jenifa, 127–30
Jeyifo, Biodun, 32, 209
Juju Stories (Abba Makama, Michael Omonua, and C. J. Obasi), 26, 198–202, 210

Kasala! (Ema Edosio), 144, 162, 186
Kelani, Tunde, 63, 136, 144, 210
Koolhaas, Rem, 7

labor. *See* work
Lagos Na Wah!! (Kehinde Soaga), 83–86
Larkin, Brian, 97, 145, aesthetics of outrage, 17, 92, 121; infrastructure, 35–36, 42
Lefebvre, Henri, 76, 86
Lekki (Lagos), 24, 157, 184–86
Lekki Bridge, 186, 198
Levine, Caroline, 96, 109
Living in Bondage (Chris Obi-Rapu), 22; combinational narration 93; occult ritual in, 54, 108; village in, 115–16
logistical management, 25–26, 148–49, 209
love: in celluloid Nigerian films, 38, 54; in mainstream Nollywood, 107, 116, 176; in New Nollywood, 151, 172–73, 199–200, 202; therapeutic ethos toward, 171, 242n54

Maami (Tunde Kelani), 136, 144–45
Mainland (Lagos), 24, 32, 186, 203
mainstream Nollywood, 127, 129–30, 137, 138–39, 153, 162, 187, 197, 205
Makama, Abba, 144, 197, 198–99
Makhubu, Nomusa, 197, 211
marketers, 21, 125, 128–29, 162–63, 206
marketplace: 18–21, 57–59, 186, 219n56; and mainstream Nollywood, 124–26, 127, 208
marriage, 39, 41, 86, 90, 114–15; in New Nollywood, 164, 171–73
Massey, Doreen, 17, 73, 94, 110
Mbembe, Achille, 31, 133
Meeting, The (Mildred Okwo), 25, 140, 175–79
media capital, 18, 27, 154, 187, 191
melodrama, 16, 103, 113, 119, 121, 198
migration: transnational, 24, 185; urban-rural, 10, 72, 82–83, 234n84
Miller, Jade, 21, 125, 129, 153, 159
Mókálik (Kunle Afolayan), 143–44
moral economy, 10, 109–10, 113, 176, 233n64
morality, 121, 218n45; in celluloid Nigerian films, 33–34, 37–38; legibility of, 92, 215–16; untethered from outrage, 194–95
Moten, Fred, 202
Multichoice (broadcast company), 143; and Africa Magic channels, 206, 242n56; formalization of film industry, 148, 154
multiculturalism, 77–78, 80–81, 173
Mushin (Lagos), 33
mutuality, 79–80, 82, 89, 98. *See also* entanglement

NAT. *See* National Arts Theatre
National Arts Theatre (NAT), 29–30, 125, 130; celluloid Nigerian films exhibited at, 43, 45–46, 59, 205, 224n47; distribution, 46–47, 205, 224n48; Festac '77, 43–45; as infrastructure, 41–42, 47–48; Yoruba video films exhibited at, 205–8
National Film and Video Censors Board (NFVCB), 125, 134, 234n4
neighbors, 73–75, 79–80, 90, 101–5, 189–90
neoliberalism, 24, 150–51, 175, 177, 179–81
Netflix, 23, 26, 182
networks, 18–22, 54–55, 94–98, 117–18. *See also* entanglement

Newell, Sasha, 95–96, 109, 233n64
Newell, Stephanie, 79, 83
New Nollywood, 25, 123–24, 205; and moral economy, 176; optimism of, 179; production values of, 143–45; role of genre in, 166, 187, 191
NFDC (Nigerian Film Distribution Company), 46–47
NFVCB (National Film and Video Censors Board), 125, 134, 234n4
Nigerian Film Distribution Company (NFDC), 46–47
Nigerian Television Authority (NTA), 63–66, 226n23
Nigerian Television Service (NTS), 64
Nnebue, Kenneth, 89, 232n57
NTA (Nigerian Television Authority), 63–66, 226n23
NTS (Nigerian Television Service), 64
Nuttall, Sarah, 31, 98

Obalende (Lagos), 182, 185
occult, 39, 52–54, 93, 115, 210; in New Nollywood, 197, 202–3
Ofeimun, Odia, 95, 230n25
Ogidan, Tade, 94, 99, 110
Ogunde, Hubert: 63, 199, 224n48; National Arts Theatre, 45, 47
Ogundele, Wole, 61, 63, 64
Oha, Obododimma, 85
oil boom, 30–32, 52–54
Okome, Onookome, 92–93, 119, 135, 197
Okpala, Chika, 65
Olaiya Adejumo, Moses ("Baba Sala"), 49–50, 224n52
Olaniyan, Tejumola, 227n32
Old Nollywood. *See* mainstream Nollywood
Olukoju, Ayodeji, 33
Olusola, Segun, 63, 65
Omezi, Giles, 33, 36
Onitsha (Nigeria), 20, 61
open endurance, 9–12, 24, 110, 204
Oriahi, Daniel, 182, 189–90

Orun Mooru (Ola Balogun and Moses Olaiya Adejumo), 29, 50; National Arts Theatre, 46
Oshin, Tope, 162
Oshodi (Lagos), 5, 20, 208
Osundare, Niyi, 56, 57
Owo Blow (Tade Ogidan), 16; crime, 103, 112–13, 118; family, 101, 112, 114–15, 119; homelessness, 108, 111; visible city 99–100; work, 102, 114
Owoh, Nkem, 72, 78–79, 106, 226n24
Ozone Cinema, 131, 133

pedagogical mode of address, 17, 35, 37–38, 59, 129
peripeteia, 120
periphery, 24, 179
Phone Swap (Kunle Afolayan), 25, 166, 170–71, 174; production, 140, 142, 144
Phyllis (Zina Saro-Wiwa), 197, 211
Pidgin, 77–78, 84, 189, 200
piracy, 58–59, 123, 126, 137, 152
popular culture: methodology, 14, 147, 208–9; global, 128, 143, 193
Povinelli, Elizabeth, 8, 110, 181, 233n68
precariousness: as dimension of city life, 11–12, 89, 187; within film industry, 26, 149, 163
production values, 124, 128, 143–46
professionalism, 141, 167–68, 170, 179
prostitution, 16, 93, 187
provisionality, 8–9, 11, 102, 146, 209. *See also* ambivalence; contingency

Quayson, Ato, 8, 61, 103, 219n56

Radio Television Kaduna (RTK), 64
Rattlesnake (Amaka Igwe), 16, 105–6, 116
Return of Jenifa, The, 129
ROK Studios, 149, 156–57. *See also* iROKOtv
romantic comedy, 151, 164–65; and cliché, 166; permissiveness of, 165, 168, 177
Royal Arts Academy, 162–63, 235n8
RTK (Radio Television Kaduna), 64

Sanson, Kevin, 153
Saro-Wiwa, Ken, 66, 71–72, 78
Saro-Wiwa, Zina, 197, 211
scenarios of estrangement, 104–6, 108–9
Scores to Settle (Chico Ejiro), 107
Simone, AbdouMaliq, 4, 21, 102, 203; open endurance, 10–11, 215n23; social connection, 89, 95
Silverbird Group: 130, 236n16; film distribution, 131, 135; Galleria cinema, 132–34
situation comedy (TV sitcom), 73, 77
soap opera, 92, 121
social classes, 39, 113; downward mobility, 16, 89–90, 100; elitism, 72, 81, 133; narrative perspective of, 36–37, 38, 143–44, 192–93; and normativity, 163–64, 181; and onscreen settings, 62, 144, 190
social connection, 22, 89, 108, 110, 233n68
spatialization of film industry, 18, 24; cinemas, 131; mainstream Nollywood, 159–60, 186; New Nollywood, 184–86, 203; production v. distribution, 153–54, 157, 191
spatial representation, 35, 73–75, 99; challenging primacy of vision, 61–2, 87, 94; in Western city cinema, 213n2; through dialogue, 68–70; and Lefebvre, 76; in New Nollywood, 190, 195–96
sponsorships. *See* formalization
strangers, 79, 84–85, 91, 108
streaming, online, 148–49; and cinemas, 124–25; enclosure within film industry, 152, 209; production practices, 155–58
structural adjustment program (SAP), 7, 88, 108
subjectivation, 98, 163, 180–81, 239n12
Surulere (Lagos), 30, 32, 125, 159–60, 186

Taxi Driver (Adeyemi Afolayan): 15, 29; exhibition 56; infrastructure, 34–36; pedagogical address, 37–41, 59
Taxi Driver: Oko Ashewo (Daniel Oriahi): 26, 187–89, 193; visible city, 182–83, 190
televisual space, 73–74, 87

Third Mainland Bridge, 7, 24
Thrift, Nigel, 94, 97, 147
traffic, 20, 24, 33; screen depictions of, 35–36, 99–100, 174
transportation, public (danfo), 85, 99, 102–3, 182, 209
trust, 95, 109–10, 129, 159
Tsika, Noah, 142

Ugboma, Eddie, 220n3, 222n20; Festac '77, 44–45
University of Lagos, 79, 128
urban normativity, 3, 9, 181; as constraint, 25, 180, 204; and optimism, 151, 163–64
urban residents, 5–6, 91
urban specificity, 17, 215n24

Victoria Island (Lagos), 24, 31, 138, 184–85
video film, 218n53
vigilantism, 63, 112, 184
village: as foil of city, 114–17; in New Nollywood, 144–45, 164, 172–73, 174; village/city comedies, 82–86, 93; in *Village Headmaster*, 64–66
violence, 108, 112, 182–83, 192, 194–95
visible city, 227n32; in celluloid Nigerian films, 35–36; in mainstream Nollywood, 61–62, 86–87, 91, 99–100; in New Nollywood, 182–83, 190, 192–93, 195–96; and television, 66–67, 76
vulnerability: 9, 12, 188; and anonymity, 108; and intimacy, 105, 116, 119

Wedding Party, The (Kemi Adetiba), 25, 164–65, 172–73
wealth: and big men, 38, 112, 128; of elites, 36, 51, 114, 164, 192; in mainstream v. New Nollywood, 241n47; morality of, 38–39, 40, 89–90, 113, 208; oil, 30–32; sources of, 54–55, 57, 114, 116, 207
Weekend Getaway (Emem Isong), 168, 171
Weeks, Kathi, 158, 167–68
Western Nigeria Television Service (WNTV), 63, 64

When Love Happens (Seyi Babatope), 172, 193
WNTV (Western Nigeria Television Service), 63, 64
work: of media professionals in Lagos, 149–50; and morality, 16, 50–51, 101–2, 151; neoliberal ethic of 150, 163; subjectification function of, 158–59, 163. *See also* creative labor

Yaba (Lagos), 131
Yoruba: ethnic group, 6, 77–79, 83, 114–15; branch of film industry, 19–20, 59, 126, 128–30, 153, 205–6, 208; language, 5, 33, 51, 56, 143, 174, 189
Yoruba traveling theater (popular theater), 12, 28–29, 32–33, 37–38, 59
YouTube, 127, 141; and enclosure, 209; and piracy 152, 206